CAMBRIDGE STUDIES IN EARLY MODERN HISTORY

Editors

J. H. ELLIOTT   H. G. KOENIGSBERGER

GUNPOWDER AND GALLEYS

CHANGING TECHNOLOGY AND MEDITERRANEAN WARFARE AT SEA IN THE SIXTEENTH CENTURY

CAMBRIDGE STUDIES IN EARLY MODERN HISTORY

Edited by Professor J. H. Elliott, The Institute for Advanced Study, Princeton, and Professor H. G. Koenigsberger, King's College, University of London

The idea of an 'Early Modern' period of European history from the fifteenth to the late eighteenth century is now widely accepted among historians. The purpose of the Cambridge Studies in Early Modern History is to publish monographs and studies which will illuminate the character of the period as a whole, and in particular focus attention on a dominant theme within it, the interplay of continuity and change as they are represented by the continuity of medieval ideas, political and social organization, and by the impact of new ideas, new methods and new demands on the traditional structures.

GUNPOWDER AND GALLEYS

CHANGING TECHNOLOGY AND MEDITERRANEAN WARFARE AT SEA IN THE SIXTEENTH CENTURY

JOHN FRANCIS GUILMARTIN JR

CAMBRIDGE UNIVERSITY PRESS

Cambridge

London   New York   New Rochelle
Melbourne   Sydney

Published by the Press Syndicate of the University of Cambridge
The Pitt Building, Trumpington Street, Cambridge CB2 1RP
32 East 57th Street, New York, NY 10022, USA
296 Beaconsfield Parade, Middle Park, Melbourne 3206, Australia

Library of Congress catalogue card number: 73-83109

ISBN 0 521 20272 8

First published 1974
Reprinted 1980

First printed in Great Britain by
Alden & Mowbray Ltd
at the Alden Press, Oxford
Reprinted by Weatherby Woolnough
Wellingborough, Northants

CONTENTS

Contents

ILLUSTRATIONS

The jacket illustration shows a woodcut of the battle of Zonchio, *c.* 1500 in the British Museum. It is reproduced by permission of the Museo Storico Navale, Venice.

Figures

Illustrations

Maps

PREFACE

The historian generally deals with his subject chronologically, topically, or chronologically with topical appendices. None of these methods is entirely suited to a work dealing with armed conflict at sea in the sixteenth-century Mediterranean. Here, the basic problem is a structural one: how did the Mediterranean system of armed conflict at sea operate? This suggests a topical organization, yet a purely topical organization would be unsatisfactory since the operation of the Mediterranean system of armed conflict at sea changed markedly during the course of the sixteenth century. While the major subsidiary problems – the tactical characteristics of the war galley and the capabilities of sixteenth-century artillery – suggest a topical organization as well, they also changed markedly with time. Simple recognition of the changes which took place in these areas is not sufficient; the manner in which the changes occurred is the crux of the problem.

Finally there is the necessity of dealing with the history of Mediterranean warfare at sea in the orthodox manner, naval history in the usual sense of the word. Any attempt to describe the functioning of the Mediterranean system of armed conflict at sea must, as a beginning, place the great galley fights of the sixteenth century – Prevesa, Djerba, and Lepanto – in their historical context. This could best be done through a chronological organization, in direct contradiction to the other requirements of the subject.

The solution was to base the organization around six topical chapters and to intersperse these between seven chronological segments, each one dealing with a historically significant or technically illustrative campaign, engagement or battle. Read in sequence, these chronological segments form a rough history of Mediterranean naval warfare during the sixteenth century.

More important, there is a certain interplay between the chronological segments and the topical chapters: the chronological segments almost invariably illustrate or give an example of a major point made in the preceding topical chapter. They occasionally introduce a problem which is dealt with in the following topical chapter.

To a degree this interplay between topical chapters and chronological segments was contrived. But to a large extent it simply happened. The most basic problems, those which had to be dealt with first in our topical sequence, generally demonstrated their importance most prominently early in the chronological sequence. This interplay – which lay unsuspected until the final stages of research and organization – justifies in itself the organizational scheme which we have selected.

J. F. G.

ACKNOWLEDGEMENTS

It is customary to attach to a work such as this a virtually interminable list of those to whom the author feels indebted. I shall make no exception to this custom, and with good reason. Because of the nature of the subject the usual phrase, 'without whose help the completion of this work would have been impossible', is, in many cases, literally true.

First of all, I must express my appreciation to Professor H. G. Koenigsberger and Professor J. H. Elliott, editors of the Cambridge series of monographs in Early Modern History, for their kind assistance. Their editorial suggestions were of material aid in helping me to reduce the amount of technical material with which the reader must contend, while at the same time retaining and expanding the essential points of my argument.

I am particularly indebted to Professor Theodore K. Rabb of Princeton University, my advisor for the doctoral dissertation from which the following work sprang. His aid in helping me to establish a conceptual framework within which to develop my thesis was irreplaceable. If I have met with any success in the organization and presentation of the ideas growing out of my research, much of the credit belongs to him.

I am indebted to the Superintendent and the Dean of Faculty, United States Air Force Academy, and their respective staffs, for having sponsored me under the Air Force Institute of Technology for the three years of study at Princeton University during which the bulk of the research and analysis represented by this book was accomplished.

I am indebted to Professor Norman T. Itzkowitz, Department of Oriental Studies, Princeton University, for his encouragement and guidance during the earliest stages of what might easily have seemed an impossible project. Many of the ideas presented here concerning the interrelationship between cultural factors and the development of military technology first took shape in his seminars in Ottoman history. I am indebted to Professor Geoffrey Lewis, also of the Department of Oriental Studies at Princeton, for his encouragement and specific recommendations.

Professor Andrew C. Hess of Temple University provided many useful suggestions and continuing encouragement. His deep knowledge of Ottoman naval history, willingly shared, saved me from many mistakes and led me directly to the solution of several problems. Professor Joel Shinder of Fredonia State College, New York, a fellow graduate student at Princeton and an Ottoman naval historian, shared not only the knowledge gained in attacking many similar problems, but his excellent Russian vodka as well.

I am particularly grateful to the personnel of the Museo Naval, Madrid, for their willing cooperation and for having provided me with the most appropriate and pleasant working conditions imaginable. Capitán de Corbeta Don Roberto Barreiro Meiro and Doña Ana Maria de Vigon, librarian *par excellence*, were instrumental in bringing to my attention the source material which formed the hard core of the study which follows. They are the recipients of my warmest appreciation.

For the portions of this study relating to cannon design, I am deeply in debt to Professor Robert F. Mark, Department of Civil Engineering, Princeton University, and to his incomparable machinist, Mr Joe Thompson.

Mr Carlo Ramelli, Assistant Director of the Museo Storico Navale, Venice, with the encouragement and support of his Director, Count Rubin de Cervin, went to considerable trouble for the sake of my studies. Without his understanding of the shorthand notation used by his Venetian forebears I would still be floundering in the dark with regards to the diet of Venetian galley crews. Admiral Ramos Periera, Portuguese Navy, Director of the Museu de Marinha, Lisbon, was instrumental in bringing to my attention certain critical facets of the history of Portuguese expansion overseas. I am deeply appreciative of the cooperation which he and his staff gave to my project. A similar debt of gratitude goes to Colonel Gonzalo Garcia Garcia, Subdirector, Museo del Ejercito, Madrid, and to the members of his staff. The fellowship and trust which they showed a fellow officer on a difficult assignment will not be forgotten. The directors of all three of these museums kindly – and in contradiction to all informed predictions – permitted me certain liberties with the cannon in their custody. For this, I can only offer the work which follows as partial payment.

For the portions of the book relating to internal ballistics – and it was here in a sense that the study began – I am indebted to the personnel of the H. P. White Ballistics Laboratory, Bel Aire, Maryland. My dealings with Mr William Dickinson, Director, and Mr L. S. Martin, Assistant Director, were intellectually extremely stimulating. It is unusual to encounter the great depth of theoretical knowledge commanded by these two men in combination with such a formidable practical expertise. My

Acknowledgements

experimental work with them, undertaken under a special grant of $300 from the Department of History, Princeton University, was extremely informative and even more enjoyable. Mrs Dickinson's incomparable hospitality – and her knowledge of external ballistics – are also warmly appreciated. I only regret that we were unable to test the pyrotechnic properties of black powder compounded with clerical urine. Maybe next time.

I am indebted as well to Mr Robert Lieske and Mr Joseph Kochenderfer, Firing Tables Branch, United States Army Ballistics Research Laboratory, Aberdeen Proving Ground, Maryland, for having applied their computer programs and knowledge of external ballistics to Luis Collado's sixteenth-century range data. I am indebted to Mr Herman Gay and his personnel in the Internal Ballistics Laboratory at the Aberdeen Proving Ground, particularly Mr Arthur Thrailkill and Mr Bert Grollman, for having given me the first nudge in the right direction toward solving a number of basic technical problems which led ultimately to my revised view of sixteenth-century gunnery and ballistics. I am indebted to Mr Harold George and to Mr Samuel Sietelman of the United States Army Frankford Laboratory, Philadelphia, Pennsylvania. Mr George gave me invaluable assistance in penetrating the thicket of non-ferrous metallurgical theory while Mr Seitelman and his co-workers in the Quality Assurance Directorate gave freely of their time and effort in analyzing specimens of cannon metal. Their findings were confirmed and amplified by Captains David Olson and Joseph Delfino of the Department of Chemistry, United States Air Force Academy, Colorado. It is my hope that the fine analytical work so generously contributed by these men can eventually be expanded into a full-scale study of sixteenth-century cannon design and founding techniques.

I am particularly indebted to Captain Douglas Tocado, United States Air Force, a fellow historian and formerly a fellow instructor, for having combed, with ruthless integrity, the superfluous verbiage from both the dissertation which preceded the book and from the book itself. Our long sessions together were as enjoyable as they were productive. I am indebted to Wing Commander R. A. Mason, Royal Air Force, for certain information on Maltese topography and to Professor Michael Finefrock of California State College, Long Beach, for having given me access to his fine collection of early published works on Ottoman history. I am indebted to Captain Jack Cole, to Captain Bob Colwell, to Captain Russell Vick and his good wife Lore and to my own wife Judy for having been good drinking companions, thus giving me the emotional stability to see the thing through.

Acknowledgements

Finally, as a professional soldier and a helicopter pilot, I am keenly aware of my debt to those who carried on while I studied. As I write these words two fellow helicopter pilots, masters of the art of extracting downed aircrew members under fire, are very much in mind: Captains Thomas A. Kenny and Carl W. Oliver, USAF, killed in the line of duty in October of 1969. Perhaps most of all, I am indebted to Lieutenant Colonel David H. Zook, Jr., USAF, missing in action from November 1967, a sound historian, a superb teacher, a good officer and a friend. Without his encouragement and personal example it is most unlikely that I would ever have undertaken the professional study of history.

J. F. G.

INTRODUCTION

Between the end of the fifteenth century and the first decade of the seventeenth the Mediterranean world underwent a commercial and economic revolution. From being a largely self-contained economic unit and the commercial and cultural center of Europe, the Mediterranean became an increasingly less important part of an expanding Western European economic community. The nature of this commercial and economic change was outlined by Fernand Braudel[1] as early as 1949. He and others have subsequently filled in many of the outlines. But these changes had a military and technical dimension which Braudel only hinted at. Only recently with the publication of Francisco-Felipe Olesa Muñido's *La Organización Naval de los Estados Mediterraneos y en Especial de España Durante los Siglos XVI y XVII*,[2] has a start been made in that direction.

In 1500 the war galley, operating from secure fortified ports, ruled the Mediterranean. Cargos moved by sea in one of two ways: a few select cargos of precious stuff – fine fabrics and above all spices – moved over long distances in heavily manned and carefully armed ships which were almost invariably government or community owned. Bulk goods – cheap fabrics, wheat and salt fish – tended to move over short distances in small, individually owned boats which were at the mercy of any armed ship which could overhaul them.

By 1600 the scene had changed drastically. The great fleets of war galleys were in decline and their ports were beginning to decay. The old Mediterranean luxury routes had first been partially blocked by the Portuguese, then bypassed by the Dutch. The growing Mediterranean bulk trades were increasingly dominated by lightly manned and heavily armed merchantmen from the north. These Englishmen and Hollanders had blunted the teeth of predatory galiots on more than one occasion and had demonstrated their ability to take care of themselves so convincingly that many seized the opportunity offered by their superior armament to capture and loot less well armed Mediterranean craft. A few surrendered

[1] *La Méditerranée et le Monde Méditerranéen à l'Époque de Philippe II* (Paris, 1949).
[2] Madrid, 1968.

I

to greed entirely and turned pirate in earnest, operating out of Tunis and Algiers from the 1580s.

The most important manifestations of this change were economic. But behind them lay a military and technical revolution fully as dramatic as the economic and commercial one described by Braudel. The two cannot be dealt with independently. Sixteenth-century patterns of trade were inextricably linked to the patterns of armed conflict at sea, more closely than in later periods and particularly so in the Mediterranean.

We will deal with the nature of this relationship at some length since the traditional historiography of armed conflict at sea has been based upon a number of implicit assumptions which do not apply to the sixteenth-century Mediterranean. Almost without realizing it, modern historians of maritime affairs have used as their analytical framework the series of relationships which existed in the eighteenth century between maritime trade, naval forces, and the nations supporting them.

These relationships contrast sharply with those which applied in the sixteenth-century Mediterranean. In the eighteenth century, a handful of powerful navies, contesting the command of the sea in brief periods of intensive violence, fought to keep the sea lanes open for their own merchant ships and to deny them to those of their enemies. They were able to do this because of the ability of eighteenth-century warships to cruise without touching land for extended periods of time. This ability enabled the eighteenth-century navy which had defeated its opponent in battle to blockade his ports, thus cutting off his maritime trade altogether. The rising importance of maritime trade and the increased opportunity of interfering with it militarily combined with the growth of colonial empires (empires which both produced and depended upon trade) to impart an overriding economic importance to naval forces. This was an emphasis which, except perhaps in the case of Venice and in a very different way, was entirely new.

The resultant series of relationships was described and brilliantly expounded by the American naval theorist Alfred Thayer Mahan late in the nineteenth century. Not least because the relationships which he described continued to apply into the ages of oil and airpower, Mahan's theory of seapower has dominated naval historiography ever since. But all too many historians have forgotten that Mahan himself was careful to qualify the applicability of his theories to the Mediterranean. He was even more careful to question their applicability to galley fleets. His reluctance to extend his generalizations was well founded.

Until the sixteenth century, because of the scarcity of effective heavy ordnance and the unperfected state of sailing ship design, the only effective

2

warships were the war galley and its smaller derivatives. The war galley, because of its intrinsic limitations of mobility and endurance, did not command the monopoly of armed violence at sea which the sailing warship later did. The war galley monopolized only *offensive* violence, an important limitation. Large and heavily manned sailing ships could be built whose essentially passive defensive capabilities were more than a match for the galley's powers of attack under ordinary circumstances. These ships, though expensive to man and operate, were able to trade with relative impunity in the face of oar-driven commerce raiders. The galley was therefore incapable of exercising command of the sea in the Mahanian sense. Specifically, the galley fleet was unable to maintain a close and continuous blockade. Because of this inability the climactic battle between opposing national fleets for command of the sea – the decisiveness of which was the core of Mahan's theory of seapower – was largely irrelevant to the sixteenth-century Mediterranean. It should be evident from this alone that an analysis of conflict at sea in the sixteenth-century Mediterranean which begins with Mahan's assumptions will produce serious distortions.

We must therefore throw out our preconceived ideas about the relationship between naval strength and mercantile success – not least because a clear-cut distinction between merchant ships and warships did not exist in the sixteenth century. Neither did the clear-cut distinction between war and peace – to which we are accustomed – exist in the sixteenth century. We must therefore throw out our preconceived ideas about the proper role of naval forces in wartime and start instead with the geographic and climatic peculiarities which gave rise both to the war galley and to the Mediterranean 'system' of commerce and conflict as it existed at the beginning of the sixteenth century.

This approach offers the important advantage of providing a relatively fixed starting point for analysis. We can hardly evaluate change without an established benchmark against which to measure it. It also brings us very quickly to the basic instrument of Mediterranean armed conflict at sea – the war galley. This is appropriate. The Mediterranean 'system' and the war galley were so closely linked as to be inseparable. As one prospered, so did the other. Then, as the galley's role in warfare became more circumscribed, the commercial power of the Mediterranean nations declined accordingly. Even if the mechanism connecting the two is not immediately apparent, the high degree of correlation between the military importance of the war galley and the commercial importance of the nations which used it as an instrument of policy is enough to justify further investigation.

3

It is necessary to declare at the start that the significance of the galley did not hinge solely on tactical or technical considerations. The elaborate bureaucratic, governmental and fiscal infrastructure of the Mediterranean system was very largely based upon the requirements, capabilities and limitations of the galley and galley fleets. The intrinsic characteristics of the galley and its logistic and social demands upon the state established the limits of Mediterranean maritime strategy.

It is therefore clear that any attempt to connect the decline of the Mediterranean world to technical military developments must concentrate heavily upon the role of the galley. This necessary emphasis will be turned to advantage in the following study by using the changing role of the war galley as a central theme. After having established a proper conceptual framework, we will begin with an analysis of the intrinsic characteristics of oared fighting vessels – which are by no means well understood – and their military, social and economic repercussions. Focusing on the impact of changing technology, we will then examine the pattern of change in Mediterranean warfare at sea and attempt to isolate and analyze its major causes.

In conjunction with our central connecting theme – the galley – we will pursue a closely interrelated and equally important one – the impact of gunpowder, particularly in the form of artillery, on the Mediterranean system of warfare at sea. If there was any single technological development which caused the decline of the Mediterranean world and brought about the rise of northern commercial dominance it was the development and spread of the use of effective heavy cannon.

The crucial importance of artillery to the age of exploration and to the expansion of the sphere of North Atlantic commercial dominance has long been recognized. Carlo Cipolla's excellent monograph, *Guns, Sails and Empires*,[1] makes the point well. But the tactical and technical mechanisms involved, particularly as they applied within the Mediterranean world, have never been adequately examined. In particular, the impact of artillery on the Mediterranean world before its commercial penetration by the nations of the North Atlantic has hardly been examined at all. The hard core of the following study is therefore an extended analysis of the changing relationship between gunpowder weapons, cannon in particular, and the war galley.

It would be excessively ambitious in a work of moderate length to attempt to trace the contribution of military technology to the entire process of Mediterranean decline. We shall therefore limit ourselves to

---

[1] Subtitled *Technological Innovation and the Early Phases of European Expansion 1400–1700* (New York, 1966).

the initial stages of this process, that is to the period from the general adoption of heavy artillery aboard galleys to the War of Cyprus. This choice offers two fundamental advantages: it eliminates from consideration the enormous technical, military, and commercial questions raised by the massive influx of armed English and Dutch merchant ships into the Mediterranean from the 1580s and it covers almost completely the mature life of the Mediterranean system of armed conflict at sea. Through this self-imposed limitation we are able to undertake a much deeper examination of the technical military aspects of the operation of the 'uncorrupted' Mediterranean 'system'. This in turn enables us – indeed forces us – to undertake an analysis of the impact of gunpowder weapons, particularly artillery, upon that system during the sixteenth century.

We are faced with two primary tasks: to describe and analyze the conduct of Mediterranean warfare at sea and to trace its ebb and flow during the sixteenth century. The emphasis will be on the former task with the latter resolving itself into an analysis of the tactical and strategic significance of the major campaigns and battles of Mediterranean fleets during the sixteenth century.

The obstacles in the way of such an approach are considerable. This is particularly true for the investigator who begins within the Anglo-American tradition of naval history. The basic concepts and traditions of the English and American experience are at wide variance with the conditions which prevailed in the sixteenth-century Mediterranean. Even the nautical vocabulary of the English language militates against an understanding of galley warfare and Mediterranean conditions. The deliberate and necessary omission of the term 'naval warfare' from the preceding pages is an illustration of just how basic this conceptual difficulty is.

As outlined above, this approach seems to ignore almost completely the cultural, intellectual and social developments which contributed to the decline of the Mediterranean world. In fact it does not. If the following study has one generally applicable historiographical point it is this: technological factors cannot be analyzed outside their social, cultural, and economic context without inducing serious distortions. This conviction is implicit to our entire approach.

The study which follows can be viewed as an analysis of the changing balance betweeen human energy – the use of animate propulsive power to drive a galley, swing a sword, or draw a bow – and the use of artificially derived chemical energy – gunpowder. As we pursue our investigation of this change it will become increasingly apparent that the crucial turning points hinged more often upon cultural, social or economic factors than upon narrowly technical ones. Changing technology made a critical contribution to the decline of the Mediterranean system of armed conflict at sea. It was an important factor in the decline of the Mediterranean world. But the technology involved did not develop – and cannot be analyzed – in a vacuum.

Jiddah, 1517

It is almost an article of faith among western naval historians that the war galley was outclassed from the first by the broadside sailing warship. This conclusion is arrived at by a straightforward process of logic: the broadside sailing warship ultimately superseded the galley; therefore it must have been a superior weapons system all along. Since the primary function of the warship is to fight other warships – or so western naval historians have assumed – the broadside sailing warship must have out-fought and outclassed the galley on a one-for-one technical basis.

There is an underlying fallacy in this line of reasoning. The galley and the broadside sailing warship did not compete in isolation on a one-for-one basis. They competed as constituent parts of two fully developed systems of maritime conflict. The roles played by the two within their respective systems of conflict were quite different. A direct technical comparison of the two is therefore inherently misleading.

There is, in addition to the above conceptual fallacy, a basic factual error behind this line of reasoning – the assumption that the sailing warship always won. When these two types of warships and the systems which they represented first came into conflict early in the sixteenth century, the result was a defensive victory for the galley. For the very good reason that it was a defensive victory of a system which lost in the end, the battle in question has remained virtually unknown. The Atlantic system of maritime conflict ultimately triumphed over its older rivals; so we therefore tend to view all of naval history through North Atlantic eyes. Thus western historians have almost entirely lost sight of an engagement between Ottoman and Portuguese forces which took place in the spring of 1517 off the port of Jiddah, at an elevation of $21\frac{1}{2}°$ north latitude on the east coast of the Red Sea, about 40 miles west of Mecca.

Recent work by A. C. Hess, analyzing the Portuguese–Ottoman conflict of the early 1500s from the Ottoman point of view, has placed the battle of Jiddah in overall historical perspective, laying invaluable groundwork for further study of the struggle between the Mediterranean system of maritime warfare and commerce and that of the North Atlantic.[1] Still,

[1] Andrew C. Hess, 'The Evolution of the Ottoman Seaborne Empire in the Age of the Oceanic

basic technical and tactical questions remain unanswered. Why did the broadside sailing ship in the hands of the Portuguese and their successors fail to sweep all before it at once? How did the presumably obsolete galley manage to survive? A partial answer to these questions can be found in an analysis of the battle of Jiddah.

When the Portuguese moved to establish a trans-oceanic empire in the waning years of the fifteenth century, they went well armed. Technically, intellectually and in their understanding of what lay between them and their goals they were amazingly well prepared. But there were certain limitations on the type of power which they chose to exercise, limitations of which they were at first unavoidably ignorant and which they could find only through trial and error.

Their successes have blinded us to their failures. In retrospect, their seizure of bases along the west coast of India in the face of heavy opposition, their circumnavigation of Africa and their subsequent interdiction of the old trade routes through the Red Sea and the Persian Gulf constitutes an amazing story of success for so small a nation. So improbable does their success seem that it has diverted our attention from their initial goals. It seems absurd to us now that Portugal, acting alone, with its scanty manpower and meager resources, would have attempted to bring the entire eastern commerce of the Mediterranean nations to a grinding halt by a thrust at the very heart of Muslim power. Such grandiose motivation does not seem to belong to the modern era; but then there was always a touch of the crusade in Portuguese impulses. Technically advanced as they were, the religious motivations of the age were strongly with them. Perhaps in part for this reason, the Portuguese were initially quite insensible to the limitations imposed upon them by their scanty resources and the intrinsic limitations of trans-oceanic naval power alike. But it could hardly have been otherwise: they were the first to try.

Alfonso Alberquerque's capture of Ormuz in 1507 for a time all but closed the old spice route through the Persian Gulf to Basra and Aleppo; but the southern route through the Red Sea proved more difficult to block. This was largely because of the absence of bases near the mouth of the Red Sea from which a tight blockade could be mounted – the island of Socotra off the tip of Arabia proved to be waterless and Aden successfully resisted attack. Unable to mount a close blockade, the Portuguese turned to the interdiction of Muslim trade throughout the Arabian Sea.

Their initial effectiveness in blocking the Red Sea route from relatively

Discoveries, 1453–1525', *American Historical Review*, LXXV, No. 7 (December, 1970), 1892 ff. This article contains the only printed reference to Jiddah which I have found in modern historiography.

distant bases is attested to by the decline in the spice trade through Cairo in the first decades of the sixteenth century.[1] It must have seemed to the Portuguese that complete success was within their grasp. All that was needed was a blockading base near the mouth of – or in – the Red Sea.

It is likely, therefore, than when Lopo Soárez de Albergaria departed Lisbon in the spring of 1515 with the King's commission as Captain General and Governor of India at the head of a flotilla of thirteen ships he went with an ambitious strategic plan in mind. He was no doubt motivated in part by knowledge that the Muslim counter-offensive was again gathering momentum in the eastern Mediterranean. Intelligence had been obtained to the effect that Mamluk naval forces were once more staging south into the Red Sea as they had in prelude to Hussein Paşa's unsuccessful expedition of 1508–9.[2] Their point of assembly was to be Jiddah, the port of Mecca.

Lopo Soárez was beyond doubt thoroughly aware of the fate of the initial Muslim counterattack, launched with extensive Venetian and Ragusan assistance and culminating in Pyrrhic victory at Chaul in 1508. Though the threat had seemed for a time severe, it had been initially repelled with local forces alone, then crushed entirely at Diu the following year. The time must therefore have seemed ripe to carry the fight to the foe: to seize a position which would cut off the Red Sea trade altogether. The seizure of Jiddah would not only accomplish this, for Jiddah was the final trans-shipment point for the north-bound coastal trade, but would provide an opportunity to nip the Muslim counter-offensive in the bud before it ever left its staging base. Finally – and this is not something which a Portuguese would have ignored – Jiddah lay less than a dozen Portuguese leagues from Mecca, the spiritual heart of Islam. These ideas were to bring the Portuguese into direct conflict with a type of power quite different from their own, the continental might of the Ottoman Empire.

In the years following Hussein Paşa's defeat at Diu the Mamluk Sultanate had fallen to Sultan Selim I of the house of Osman. But the

---

[1] See F. C. Lane, 'The Mediterranean Spice Trade', *American Historical Review*, XLV, No. 3 (April 1940), 581–90. The picture given by Lane, an authority on the subject, suggests that the Portuguese severely dislocated the Mediterranean spice trade in the first decades of the sixteenth century; but that the trade then began a revival which peaked at about 1560 before being undercut by the Dutch and English. Lane estimates that the total volume of the spice trade increased from about $1\frac{1}{2}$–2 million pounds annually *ca.* 1500 to about 3 million pounds in 1560.

[2] João de Barros, *Da Ásia* (Lisbon, 1563), IIIrd *decada*, Book 1, *capitulo* i, fol. 1–4. I am indebted to the custodians of the William H. Scheide Collection, housed in the Firestone Library, Princeton University, for having permitted me to view this rare edition of de Barros.

economic motivation which had sent Hussein Paşa's force east to repel the Portuguese attack was still present. Under the vigorous unifying impulse of the rising Ottoman power it was, if anything, stronger than before. Indeed, there is evidence that Salman Re'is, the Muslim commander at Jiddah, was an Ottoman who had been 'forwarded' to the Mamluks by the Ottoman Sultan to lead the fight against the Portuguese in the east during a period of open Mamluk–Ottoman hostilities.[1] Be this as it may, the defeat of his Mamluk superiors by the Ottoman Sultan in 1516–17 in no way affected Salman's position as theater commander in the Red Sea. The maritime economy of the Mediterranean world, in which the Ottomans had a large stake even before their conquest of Egypt, rested on the continued integrity of the eastern trade routes which the Portuguese threatened.

The clashes between the Portuguese and their Muslim opponents in the Red Sea, the Persian Gulf, and along the Coromandel Coast were thus more than a simple war over trade. They represented the first innings of a protracted struggle between the Mediterranean world and the nascent naval power of the North Atlantic. They were the first tests in a clash between two systems of maritime conflict, the one fully developed and highly sophisticated, the other as yet crude, raw and just beginning to develop its techniques and recognize its potential. Jiddah, therefore, had a technical importance beyond its outcome.

In retrospect, the issue of Jiddah seems pre-ordained. It was much too close to the Ottoman sources of power; the Portuguese resources of men and material were far too slim and their bases too far away. But to men who were capable of standing off odds of six hundred to one with a mixture of bluff, bravery, and sheer contempt for odds, then attack bareheaded and win, as Alfonso d'Alberquerque's men had done at Ormuz in 1507, nothing seemed impossible. Then, too, they had never before come up against the Mediterranean system of warfare on its home ground.

The size of the force with which Lopo Soárez appeared before Jiddah in 1517 is unclear. A contemporary Arab account speaks of thirty vessels, both sailing ships and galleys.[2] We can be certain that the Portuguese had made every effort to tailor their force to the expected opposition and to the peculiar demands of navigation in the Red Sea. The provision of galleys which Alfonso d'Alberquerque had caused to be built in India

[1] Hess, 'The Evolution of the Ottoman Seaborne Empire', pp. 1909–10.
[2] L. O. Schuman, *Political History of the Yemen at the Beginning of the 16th Century* (Amsterdam, 1961), pp. 31–3. Schuman has translated and reproduced several contemporary Arabic accounts in their entirety. I take his barshas to be sailing warships and his ghurabs to be galleys.

'for being the most useful vessels for navigating in the Red Sea' attests to this.[1]

We have, likewise, little detailed information about the Muslim force under Salman Re'is which met the Portuguese at Jiddah. Contemporary Portuguese sources credit him with a naval force of 'twenty-six sail, between galleys, galiots and sailing ships of high freeboard' including two 'very well equipped' galleys and a total of 3,000 fighting men.[2] This is probably not far from the truth. It would seem fairly evident that Salman Re'is' naval force was inferior to that of the Portuguese. But this was not the whole story, for Salman's position was palpably a defensive one.

The Portuguese account credits him with having among his ordnance three or four basilisks[3] firing balls of thirty palms in circumference.[4] This is a key fact. If we take a palm as about three inches, this indicates a cannon firing a cut stone ball of approximately 1,000 pounds. These were, from our knowledge of sixteenth-century artillery and from the results of the ensuing battle, first-class guns fired by first-class gunners. It is almost certain that the best of Salman Re'is' ordnance and artillerists were of Ottoman origin, sent to the Red Sea even before the Ottoman conquest of Egypt in January of 1517.[5] The Ottomans, unlike the Mamluks, were known for the quality and efficiency of their artillery.

This was to mark a first for the Portuguese. Never before in the east had they come up against artillery of a quality comparable to

---

[1] de Barros, *Da Ásia*, IIIrd *decada*, Book 1, *capitulo* i, fol. 4.

[2] de Barros, IIIrd *decada*, Book 1, *capitulo* iii, fol. 8.

[3] See Henry Kahane and Andreas Tietze, *The Lingua Franca in the Levant* (Urbana, Ill., 1958), entry 81, 'basilisco', p. 100. This word, common to Spanish, Portuguese, Catalan, French, Greek and Ottoman Turkish, apparently designated an unusually large cannon of almost any description in the early 1500s. It could be either a cast-bronze piece, as it invariably was later on, or a composite piece built up of closely spaced wrought-iron hoops and staves. See Vannoccio Biringuccio, *The Pirotecnia*, C. S. Smith and Martha T. Gnudi trans. (New York, 1941), p. 225. To Biringuccio, writing in the 1530s, the basilisk was smaller than a bombard but 'much longer', though presumably of the same wrought-iron construction. This supports our suspicion, explained in note 5 below, that the Muslim basilisks used at Jiddah were of wrought iron though, unlike Biringuccio's, they undoubtedly fired a stone projectile.

[4] de Barros, IIIrd *decada*, Book 1, *capitulo* iiij, fol. 10.

[5] See Fevzi Kurtoğlu, 'Meshur Türk Amirali Selman Reisin Layihasi', *Deniz Mecmuasi*, Cild 47, Sayi 335 (January 1935), for the reproduction of an inventory of Ottoman naval armament at Jiddah in June 1525. This report lists a number of *bachiliska* in addition to smaller pieces. The attached list of specialized personnel includes numbers of blacksmiths. This suggests that the basilisks may have been large wrought-iron muzzle-loading guns like two large and absolutely contemporary cannon (made in 1516) on display in the park near the Deniz Musesi (Naval Museum), Istanbul. The inventory also includes heavy ropes, suggesting that these large cannon were mounted on traversing mounts for coastal defense. This fits precisely with our knowledge of the method used by the Ottomans for traversing the large cannon mounted in the water batteries of the forts along the Bosporus.

their own. It was not, to be sure, all shipboard artillery, but therein hangs the tale.

The fortifications of Jiddah had been begun in support of Hussein Paşa's expedition and were subsequently strengthened by Salman Re'is. No detailed information about them survives, but it is plain from the record of the ensuing battle that they included a wall around the city itself of sufficient strength to make direct infantry assault an unprofitable project. Even more important, they included well placed earthworks garnished with heavy artillery – the basilisks – dominating the difficult S-shaped channel which was the only entry into the port.[1]

This presented Lopo Soárez with what proved to be an insoluble tactical problem. The channel was so narrow and sinuous and the Muslim artillery dominating it so effective that any attempt to force it directly with his sailing ships would plainly have been suicidal.[2] If, on the other hand, he were to engage the earthworks directly with the heavy bow guns of the Portuguese galleys, they would be exposed to flank attack by the Ottoman galleys waiting further up channel.

While the Ottoman naval forces were incapable of engaging the superior Portuguese fleet in open water, they complemented the power of the earthworks perfectly. Operating under cover of their artillery, Salman's best galleys were able to harass the Portuguese fleet effectively with their heavy bow guns – possibly basilisks as well – at long range. A contemporary Arabic account describes his tactics in explicit terms: 'not one of the Franks landed on the coast at Jiddah: on the contrary the Emir Salman sought them out in a *grab* [a galley] or two. When he got within range of them he fired at them with his guns.'[3]

Hampered by their lack of maneuverability in close waters, the Portuguese sailing warships were unable to close with the Muslim galleys. If, on the other hand, the Portuguese galleys were to attempt to attack Salman's galleys, the Muslims could retire under the guns of the earthworks in safety. A series of inconclusive – at least from the Portuguese point of view – engagements on this pattern ensued. Despite an accident which burned away most of the bow of one of the best armed Muslim

---

[1] de Barros, IIIrd *decada*, Book 1, *capitulo* iii, fol. 6. This passage gives a general description of the channel and the fortifications of the city.

[2] *Ibid. capitulo* iiij, fol. 10. The Portuguese account states that the channel could be forced only by 'fast rowing vessels [*navios de remo rasos*] running great risk' because the artillery posted in the earthen fortifications dominated it so completely.

[3] From the Hadrami Chronicles translated by R. B. Serjeant, *The Portuguese off the South Arabian Coast* (Oxford, 1963), p. 50. See de Barros, IIIrd *decada*, Book 1, *capitulo* iiij, fol. 10, who confirms the use of these tactics. As is explained in our discussion of artillery in ch. 4, we can take 'long range' as around 500 yards.

galleys,[1] it became apparent that the Portuguese would not be able to force the channel and get at the walls of the city itself with their shipboard ordnance. Stalemated, the Portuguese briefly considered a desperate amphibious night assault on the earthworks, thought better of it, and withdrew.[2] They were hurried on their way by the oared Muslim fighting craft which followed them down the coast and recaptured a prize near Loheida which the Portuguese had earlier taken.[3]

Lopo Soárez was criticized for his actions; but it is unlikely that he could have done any better or foreseen the tactical combination of seaside fortress and Mediterranean war galley against which his strategic plan crumbled. Given the quantity and quality of available artillery which prevailed early in the sixteenth century, this combination was, on its home ground and in competent hands, virtually unbeatable except by similar and considerably stronger forces. In retrospect, the difficult channel at Jiddah was probably a blessing in disguise for the Portuguese: it clearly rendered a project, which they might otherwise have attempted with serious tactical and strategic losses, totally impossible.

But what were the home grounds of the system of warfare based on the war galley and the seaside fortress? Jiddah, Ormuz, Chaul and Diu provide a partial answer. Lopo Soárez' attack on Jiddah must have seemed less rash tactically and less daring strategically than Alberquerque's attack on Ormuz ten years earlier. But there were important differences. Alberquerque's opponents of 1507 were not backed by the resources and technical expertise of a major continental power. Their artillery was sparse and largely ineffective. The approaches to the harbor of Ormuz were easy. Finally, Ormuz was on an island accessible to Portuguese naval power and remote from major Mamluk and Ottoman bases. Once captured, it could be held.

With Jiddah the reverse was true. It was accessible to Portuguese power neither tactically nor strategically. Even had Lopo Soárez' men captured Jiddah by prodigies of valor they could never have held it for long. It was far too close to Ottoman sources of power and far too accessible to their armies.

---

[1] Serjeant's and Schuman's documents both mention this incident, asserting that a Christian gunner in the Ottoman service 'put something in the powder' causing a gun to burst and setting fire to the bow of Salman's galley. What that 'something' may have been is hard to imagine. More probably the gun simply burst from a hidden flaw or, if it were a wrought-iron piece as is probable, internal corrosion. The fact that Salman executed the gunner for his 'sabotage' illustrates the difficulties traditionally encountered by the technical military specialist in his dealings with technically untrained commanders.

[2] de Barros, IIIrd *decada*, Book I, *capitulo* iiij, fol. 10.

[3] Serjeant, *The Portuguese off the South Arabian Coast*, p. 50.

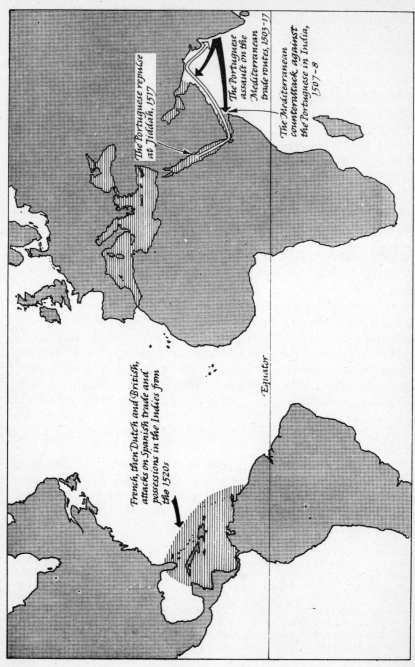

The Portuguese assault on the Mediterranean trade routes, 1503–17

The Portuguese repulse at Jiddah, 1517

The Mediterranean counterattack against the Portuguese in India, 1507–8

French, then Dutch and British, attacks on Spanish trade and possessions in the Indies from the 1520s

Equator

Map 1 The Mediterranean world from the technical military point of view, shown at the point of its greatest extent during the period 1530–60.

Generally, the system of warfare which the Portuguese encountered at Jiddah prevailed wherever the Mediterranean war galley could operate effectively and where it had access to nearby bases. This included, throughout most of the sixteenth century, the Mediterranean, the Black Sea, the Red Sea and most of the Caribbean (see Map 1).

The Mamluks had tested the capabilities of the Mediterranean system away from its bases in 1507–8 and had failed. Ten years later the Portuguese pressed too far into the war galley's home waters with similar results. This established an initial balance, the basis for a geographic boundary between the two competing systems of maritime conflict which held good for over a century. After 1517 this boundary shifted, but only as the technical balance of war at sea shifted slowly against the galley.

Jiddah clearly showed the defensive military strength of the Mediterranean system of warfare at sea. The tactical verdict of Jiddah was not to be reversed for a century. During the period covered by this study, the Mediterranean system of warfare at sea retained its viability in the face of external threat. We can therefore afford to devote ourselves primarily to internal changes within the Mediterranean system of armed conflict at sea.

I

THE MAHANIANS' FALLACY

In 1884 an American naval officer, a veteran of the Civil War better known for his scholarly leanings than for his combat record, was offered an assignment at the Naval War College as lecturer on naval history and tactics.[1] The recipient of this offer, Alfred Thayer Mahan, requested and got a delay en route to his new assignment so that he might prepare himself for his duties. He devoted this period of preparation to a thorough scholarly study of the lessons of the not too distant past with a shrewd eye toward the demands of the future. The results of his labors were epoch making: *The Influence of Sea Power upon History, 1660–1783*, published in Boston in 1890, became the primer of an age of American expansionism.

Not surprisingly, *The Influence of Sea Power upon History* was also warmly received in England. It was, in essence, the distillation of a hundred and twenty years of highly successful English experience. Mahan was not an original thinker of startling brilliance as Clausewitz had been. But he was a thorough analyst and a competent scholar. Much as Jomini had sought the 'system' in Napoleon's victories, Mahan sought the wellsprings of English success. To a large extent he accomplished what he had set out to do. He examined the success of England as a great power from all angles. He was very careful to qualify his conclusions; but he emerged with a number of lessons which he felt were generally applicable. In an age which eagerly embraced them, he was not shy in pressing for their official acceptance. In this, too, he was amazingly successful. Even more surprising, his lessons, all admittedly based upon very particular circumstances, retained their validity into the age of steam and through it into the ages of oil and airpower.

But our concern with Mahan's impact upon the development of naval doctrine – profound as it was – is indirect, for his influence on the historiography of maritime conflict was, if anything, even more powerful. In codifying and giving shape to traditional Anglo-American naval doctrines he established an analytic framework for naval history which has endured

[1] Margaret Tuttle Sprout, 'Mahan, Evangelist of Sea Power', ch. 17 in Edward Meade Earle, *Makers of Modern Strategy* (Princeton, 1943), p. 415.

to the present day. This Mahanian framework is so all-pervasive, and in the case of sixteenth-century Mediterranean naval historiography so misleading, that we must come to grips with it before proceeding further.

It is perhaps presumptuous to condense Mahan's precepts, the core of Anglo-American naval doctrine for three centuries, into a single paragraph. Nevertheless the essence of what he had to say can be stated briefly: commerce raiding, that which the French call the *guerre de course*,[1] is a waste of effort and resources. If a nation's economic interests are to be served and her strategic capacity for defense maintained, then her maritime trade must be preserved at all cost. Conversely, the quickest way to bring an enemy to her knees is through the destruction of her seaborne commerce. The best and only sure way to accomplish this is to destroy the enemy fleet in battle. Having accomplished this, you can sweep her ships from the seas at your leisure and blockade her harbors, thus choking off her trade at the source. Defeat the enemy fleet in battle and all else falls into place. The 'true end' of naval forces, said Mahan, 'is to preponderate over the enemy's navy and so control the sea ... the enemy's war ships and fleets are the true objects to be assailed upon all occasions'.[2] Assigning geographic objectives to a fleet is non-productive at best and dangerously divisive of effort at worst.

Stated baldly, as we have done here, the implicit assumptions behind Mahan's dicta are clear enough. Maritime trade must be vitally important to the nations involved. The technical means of enforcing a blockade must exist. Given these conditions, Mahan's two concepts, sea power and control of the sea, are valid as they stand.

Unfortunately, historians have not been as careful as Mahan in examining the necessary pre-conditions for the application of these concepts. Mahan took pains to point out the fallacy of the usual parallel drawn between the war galley of the sixteenth century and the steam warship of the nineteenth.[3] He was cautious about extending his generalizations into the Mediterranean.[4] But the deceptive simplicity of his allied concepts of seapower and control of the sea – and perhaps the military and cultural

---

[1] The *guerre de course* involves the systematic use of privateering or raiding craft, usually inferior in military power to a regular warship, to destroy enemy commerce.

[2] *The Influence of Sea Power upon History* (Boston, 1890), p. 219.

[3] *Ibid.* p. 3.

[4] Although mainly by omission. Mahan simply did not have a great deal to say about the Mediterranean, but he was quite explicit in drawing his historical lessons specifically from trans-oceanic conflict. 'It is ... in these wider operations, which ... in a maritime contest may cover a large portion of the globe, that the teachings of history have a more evident and permanent value, because the conditions remain more permanent.' *The Influence of Sea Power upon History*, p. 7.

dominance of the nations who so successfully espoused them – has lent them the force of unquestioned dogma.

No effective intellectual counterpoise to the Mahanian scheme ever developed.[1] Where the ideas which Jomini made into a 'system' were put into a broader philosophical context by Clausewitz, Mahan's concepts have remained alone, unchallenged, and essentially unmodified. Western scholars, therefore, tend to analyze naval problems automatically in terms of the system of relationships pointed out by Mahan. Put in another and equally valid way, western scholars tend to view naval history within a conceptual framework based upon the Anglo-American experience, a framework which was codified and rationalized by Mahan. While this approach has been conspicuously successful in some areas – English and American naval planning in the two world wars – it has obscured certain problems badly.[2] One of these is sixteenth-century Mediterranean naval history.

To understand why, we must analyze Mahan's concept of control of the sea within a sixteenth-century context. Whether or not we consider control of the sea a militarily valid concept, we must accept the fact that sixteenth-century naval warfare in the Mediterranean revolved around fleets of galleys, fleets which by their very nature could not 'control the sea'. Limitations in the motive power and sea-keeping capabilities of the war galley made year-round blockades an impossibility. This consideration alone renders control of the sea a concept of dubious value in analyzing sixteenth-century Mediterranean affairs. Yet we are told time and again by historians that the Turkish victory over the combined Spanish

[1] At least as a formal doctrine. The closest was the French *Jeune Ecole* of the late nineteenth century. This doctrine was, in essence, the old French preference for the *guerre de course* adapted to the technical conditions of the age of steam. It was based upon the supposition that modern technology in the guise of the torpedo boat had made the blockade of harbors impossible and thus rendered Mahan's doctrine *hors de combat*. Mahan, to his credit, correctly predicted that the changed technical conditions of war would only make the blockade more distant, not less effective. See Theodore Ropp, 'Continental Doctrines of Sea Power', in Earle, *Makers of Modern Strategy*, ch. 18, pp. 446–56.

[2] Including the understanding of Japanese naval doctrine, an area of considerable interest to American and English naval planners in the early days of World War II. This inability of English and American naval planners to understand Japanese motivation provides powerful confirmation for our general argument. Anglo-American naval intelligence experts were, most of them, men of great technical competence and intellectual ability; but the Japanese operated within a totally different conceptual framework from that to which they were accustomed. Japanese doctrine evolved after the era of the wooden sailing warship from which all of Mahan's precepts sprang. The Japanese, as a result, arrived at a quite different set of ideas as to what the proper objectives of a fleet should be. Because of their pragmatic approach, firmly rooted in Japanese cultural concepts, Japanese naval planners approached their task in a totally non-Mahanian manner (though clothed with just enough Mahanian rhetoric to totally obscure the issue). Consequently, their strategic and tactical decisions and risk-taking rationale remained incomprehensible to Allied planners throughout World War II.

and Venetian fleets at Prevesa in 1538 gave the Ottoman Empire control of the sea until Lepanto.

The all-pervasiveness of Mahanian concepts is such that historians of the sixteenth century have succeeded in avoiding the distortions which they induce only with considerable difficulty. V. J. Parry, for example, states that Prevesa:

> marked a more ominous phase of the conflict for naval supremacy: the Ottomans had met and repulsed the combined strength of the two fleets alone capable of thwarting their ambition to win control of the Mediterranean. From this time forward until Lepanto in 1571 the initiative at sea was to rest largely with the sultan.

Note that while Parry employs the usual Mahanian terminology, he qualifies his statement carefully. He does not say that the sultan gained control of the sea; but that the initiative at sea rested largely with him. This is a significant shade of meaning: by using it, Parry tells us that the Turks did not exercise control of the sea in the Mahanian sense. He, along with a handful of modern historians including J. H. Parry and A. C. Hess, has demonstrated an understanding of why this was so. Note, however, that he begins with the stated assumption that the Ottoman objective was 'to win control of the Mediterranean'.[1] This is pure Mahan. Parry obviously does not mean that the Ottoman goal – even in the long term – was to control the entire land mass of the Mediterranean basin as the Romans had done. His reference is clearly, if indirectly, to control of the sea in the Mahanian sense. But while V. J. Parry is careful to qualify his statements and understands the peculiar conditions of the Mediterranean well, others have been less successful in purging their arguments of inappropriate Mahanian assumptions.

If the concept of control of the sea is of dubious value in furthering our understanding of the sixteenth-century Mediterranean, the second of Mahan's implicit assumptions – that maritime trade is vitally important to nations engaged in naval warfare – is equally suspect. To two of the three great Mediterranean naval powers, Spain and the Ottoman Empire, seaborne commerce was critically important only in a few narrowly delineated areas. Spain's traffic with the Indies was of vital concern to her; but this commerce traversed the Mediterranean only at the extreme western end.[2] If we exclude shipments of precious metals from the Americas, commerce raiding probably netted Spain as much as trade, and

---

[1] V. J. Parry, 'The Ottoman Empire, 1520-66', ch. 17, *The New Cambridge Modern History*, vol. 11, *The Reformation* (Cambridge, 1958), pp. 519-20.

[2] The Andalusian fishing fleet was a partial exception, but the Andalusians brought their catch in from the Atlantic armed and ready to look out for themselves. The extent of Spanish trade with the western hemisphere and its importance to Spain are covered exhaustively in Huguette and Pierre Chaunu's eight-volume study, *Séville et l'Atlantique, 1504-1650* (Paris, 1955-9).

most of her Mediterranean trade was not conducted in her own ships to begin with. The primary Spanish concern with 'seapower' was therefore almost entirely defensive and non-economic in nature: to prevent strategic and tactical cooperation between the Spanish Moriscos and their co-religionists across the straits of Gibraltar.[1]

The Ottomans carefully guarded their control of the Black Sea and excluded the vessels of all other nations from trading there.[2] They went to great lengths to assure the safe arrival in Constantinople of the annual grain convoy from Alexandria;[3] but the Ottoman Empire was primarily a continental power, mainly concerned with the expansion of its control over land areas. The Ottomans had no particular aversion to trade, but since maritime commerce was mostly carried out in the Ottoman Empire by non-Ottomans acting in their own interests, maritime commerce was regarded as a political and economic tool which could be manipulated at will.

Of the three great Mediterranean naval powers only Venice depended upon maritime trade for her existence. Venice was therefore – though this point must be treated with caution – essentially Mahanian in her strategic outlook where Spain and the Ottomans were not. This difference in outlook, solidly grounded in economic factors, was reflected in differing strategic and tactical objectives. The histories of the so-called Sacred Alliances of 1538 and 1570 are filled with bitter Venetian accusations that the Spanish commanders, first Andrea Doria the elder, then Gian Andrea Doria and Don Juan of Austria, deliberately shirked their duty in their repeated failures to close with and destroy the Ottoman fleet.[4]

[1] See Andrew C. Hess, 'The Moriscos: an Ottoman Fifth Column in Sixteenth-Century Spain', *American Historical Review*, LXXIV, No. 1 (October 1968), 1-25, for the only modern and comprehensive treatment of the Morisco problem. Spanish documents expressing concern over the security of coastal regions on account of this restive subject population are legion: see for example a document of 1543 in the *Colección Navarrete*, vol. IV, dto. 7, fol. 74, entitled 'What the Turks have done in the year of '43 on the coast of Spain and in other places...', expressing particular fear over the prospect of Ottoman-Morisco cooperation in Valencia where 'are found ... 600 households of Moriscos who are very distrustful of the old Christians, and they of the Moriscos' and where the Christians had abandoned the coast on the approach of the Ottoman fleet.

[2] See Carl M. Kortepeter, 'Ottoman Imperial Policy and the Economy of the Black Sea Region in the Sixteenth Century', *Journal of the American Oriental Society*, LXXXVI, No. 2.

[3] This was the so-called 'caravan' which brought in the Egyptian wheat, vital to the populace of Constantinople, and the considerable economic surplus of Egypt.

[4] The Venetians were particularly bitter about Andrea Doria's actions in 1538. Their accusations and the circumstances of the battle of Prevesa have led to serious speculation among historians that he was bought off by the Turks and deliberately avoided contact with Barbarossa's fleet. There is an enormous amount of material dealing with the tactical disputes between the Spanish and the Venetians, notably the *Relazioni* of the two Venetian commanders in the *Liga Santa* of 1570-2, Sebastiano Venier and Giacomo Foscarini, reproduced in *opusculo* 3000, Archivo di Stato Veneziano, Venice. Venier's report is contained in the original in *Busta* 75, *Collegio* V (*Secreta*), *Relazioni*.

Spain, to whom trade with the infidel meant little, was eager to pursue the Crusade when it served her territorial and strategic military interests, whether financial gain was in prospect or not. But Venice depended heavily upon trades which were controlled at one point or another by the Turk. The spice trade and the import of wheat from the Ionian islands are prime illustrations of the Venetian dependence on Ottoman goodwill. To Venice, protracted war with the Ottoman Empire meant certain economic ruin which could hardly be balanced by strategic and territorial gains. Much of the acrimony between Venice and Spain was an inevitable reflection of this difference of interests.

The continental powers, less interested in maritime trade and unable to 'control the sea' in any case, were generally unconcerned with the destruction of the enemy fleet as an end in itself. This lack of pre-occupation with one of Mahan's central tenets has proved confusing to historians. Conditioned to expect an inbred desire in successful naval commanders to engage and destroy the enemy and not finding it, they have labeled Mediterranean admirals as dilatory and over-cautious. Much confusion has resulted. Modern naval historians are hard pressed to explain the great respect accorded Andrea Doria by his contemporaries and have almost entirely lost sight of Khaireddin Barbarossa except as an unusually successful 'pirate'. Don Juan of Austria, on the other hand, one of the few Mediterranean naval commanders to destroy his opponent in a general fleet engagement, has gained more prominence than is probably his due. One of the secondary objectives of this study is to examine the achievements of the great Mediterranean naval commanders within a Mediterranean context, an exercise which reveals quite clearly the inappropriateness of Mahanian criteria.

The same Mahanian assumptions concerning desired objectives and cause and effect relationships have clouded the analysis of sixteenth-century Mediterranean naval battles. Conditioned to measure the decisive-ness of a naval battle by the degree of destruction suffered by the defeated fleet, modern historians have encountered great difficulty in explaining the importance of several highly significant engagements, notably Khaired-din Barbarossa's victory over Andrea Doria at Prevesa in 1538, a battle which we will examine at length following this chapter. Prevesa, probably the greatest Ottoman fleet victory of the sixteenth century, was won with so little loss on the Christian side that Sir Charles Oman called it 'a trifling affair' that 'can hardly be called a battle'.[1]

The reverse is true as well. Conditioned to expect great things to come from the near-annihilation of a major power's fleet in battle, historians

[1] C. W. C. Oman, *A History of the Art of War in the Sixteenth Century* (London, 1937), p. 10.

have looked long, hard, and in vain for any great result from Lepanto. V. J. Parry's comments about the results of Lepanto are most instructive in this context: 'Although it broke the initiative that the Ottomans had held at sea since the battle of Prevesa in 1538, Lepanto must be considered as a triumph symbolic in character rather than positive in actual consequences.'[1] Here again, we find sound analysis straining against an inappropriate Mahanian framework. Lepanto did not produce control of the sea for the victor; therefore – in a Mahanian context – it could not have been decisive. This produces a direct conflict with contemporary accounts which almost unanimously agree that Lepanto *was* decisive. Historians have traditionally resolved this conflict by proclaiming Lepanto decisive, but only symbolically so, a judgment which we question further on.

Mention of the battle of Lepanto is an appropriate point at which to cut short our discussion of the Mahanian assumptions concerning the proper employment of fleets in wartime and the cause and effect relationships between naval battles and overall maritime strategy. Our purpose here has been simply to point out that the application of these assumptions to the analysis of sixteenth-century Mediterranean naval battles and commanders is at best misleading.

It is not enough, however, simply to abandon the Mahanian scheme. Secondary technical, economic, and cultural considerations quickly emerge and the issues become far more complex than we have suggested here. As an example, the Venetians wanted to bring about a general fleet engagement in 1538 and in 1570-1 in the worst way (a thoroughly Mahanian impulse), but not for Mahanian reasons. There is perhaps no better example of this complexity than the battle of Lepanto, which we shall analyze at length in the concluding chapters. Suffice it to say here that there is, in fact, reason to believe that Lepanto was decisive, though – once again – not in the Mahanian sense.

The most powerful argument against the use of the Mahanian conceptual framework, however, is not made on technical grounds as we have done above, but on semantic ones. In applying the label 'naval warfare' to all armed conflict at sea, we do subtle things to our frame of reference. In the literal sense, 'naval warfare' encompasses all armed conflict at sea just as 'naval architecture' encompasses all ship design. But the very word 'naval' carries with it a whole train of Mahanian suppositions rooted in the eighteenth-century English experience with seapower. It implies orderly fleets of warships under centralized control

---

[1] 'The Ottoman Empire 1566-1617', ch. 11, *The New Cambridge Modern History*, vol. III, *The Counter Reformation and Price Revolution, 1559-1610* (Cambridge, 1968), p. 252.

in pursuit of purely military objectives. It implies a sharp distinction between periods of intense military conflict and periods of peaceful commerce. It stands in opposition to 'piracy', the use of armed violence at sea for private gain, uncontrolled and unorganized by any higher authority.

These distinctions are no doubt useful in understanding the finer points of war at sea in the eighteenth century; but in a study of the sixteenth-century Mediterranean they simply do not hold. There was no clear distinction in the sixteenth century between piracy and commerce, religious, political, and economic motivation, individual acts and acts as an agent of government. Particularly where religious motivation was a factor, distinctions of this type are difficult to make and of dubious validity once made. Were the Knights of St John of Rhodes and Malta crusaders, or pirates? A good case can be made for either. The same sort of consideration applies to the *ghazi*[1] seafarers of North Africa, eager to swing a sword for Islam in support of their co-religionists in Spain, but anxious to make a paying business of it at the same time. A few examples should make clear the degree to which the modern distinctions are muddled and inappropriate.

The first of these is a Spanish document of 12 December 1551 signed in Messina, the deposition of one Dimas de Gustaldo, the captain of a Spanish *fusta*[2] (a small oared warship) just returned from a cruise in the Aegean.[3] Leaving Messina in October, Gustaldo captured several small boats sailed by 'Turks' and 'Armenians' (probably Greek Christian

---

[1] *The Encyclopedia of Islam*, new edition, B. Lewis, C. Pellat and S. Schacht, eds. (London, 1960), p. 1043, *ghazi*. *Ghazi* is an Arabic word used to designate those who took part in raids (*razzias*) for the faith. It came to be used as a title of respect for those who had been particularly successful in such raids. *Ghazi* differs from its rough western equivalent, 'crusader', in that it has a more permanent connotation. Where the crusader generally took part in a single, though perhaps sustained and arduous, military act of faith, the *ghazi* considered perpetual raids against the infidel to be a way of life.

[2] The subclasses within the general category of galleys were, in order of decreasing size, the galley, the galiot, the *fusta* and the *bergantin*. Although the sizes varied somewhat, this order of categorization held constant in Spanish and Venetian practice. Gustaldo's *fusta* was probably a vessel of 15 rowing banks to a side and two men to an oar. If this were the case, it would have carried 60 oarsmen, probably Muslim slaves for the most part, and as many as 30 or 40 soldiers. This estimate is based upon several sources. The first of these is the manning and armament list of a Spanish galiot, compiled in 1546, in the *Colección Sanz de Barutell* (*Simancas*), *Articulo* 4, vol. I, dto. 138, fol. 421. The galiot with which this document is concerned carried 57 soldiers, two artillerists and a boatswain. It was rowed by nine free oarsmen, 15 royal *forzados* condemend to the galleys, and 53 Muslim slaves. Dto. 36, *Articulo* 5, *Colección Sanz de Barutell* (*Simancas*), is a directive of 1566, signed in Málaga, concerning the 'commission of two galiots to go privateering [*en corso*]'. Since the vessels mentioned are of 17 rowing banks, we would expect Gustaldo's *fusta* to be smaller. The 15-bank estimate satisfies this requirement and tallies exactly with the reconstruction of a Venetian *fusta* in the Museo Storico Navale, Venice, built under the direction of Admiral Fincati in 1881.

[3] *Colección Navarrete*, vol. IV, dto. 6, fol. 80

subjects of the Porte) which his men looted and let go. They then boarded a ship flying the French flag bound from Alexandria with a cargo of wheat. When the crew protested that they were 'subjects of his majesty' the Spaniards shook them down for 'five empty sacks of biscuit' [*sic*] and let them go. They then boarded a Genoese ship – assuredly the property of a Spanish ally – from which they extorted '300 and some ducats' with which 'to buy victuals' for 'his majesty's galleys'.

Entering a small port in the Morea, Gustaldo's men looted a number of small merchant vessels, capturing forty men. They sent the Christians ashore, keeping the Muslims for slaves. Later in the same day, the Spaniards encountered a larger ship which put up an active defense. Boarding and finding it to be Venetian, Gustaldo's men robbed it of 300 ducats and stole the fine clothes off the backs of the Venetian merchants, but left them otherwise unharmed.

Homeward bound, after having run for almost twenty miles with a Venetian squadron of 14 galleys in hot pursuit, Gustaldo sighted and gave chase to a Turkish *fusta*. The Turkish vessel, apparently finding itself outgunned, took to its heels. Unable to outsail the Spaniard, the Turks ran their ship aground and fled ashore, leaving their Christian slaves behind, chained to their rowing benches. Among the slaves set free was a 'Venetian captain of cavalry who had been very badly treated, and to whom we gave good clothes'. After having run for his life from a Venetian squadron for the better part of a day, Gustaldo was still filled with indignation at the treatment which his Venetian co-religionist had received at the hands of the Turks, and all but glows with pride in recounting his worthy act.

Gustaldo next recorded the seizure of 300 ducats (apparently a standard figure, probably the smallest one which his superiors would believe) from a Florentine ship. His account then describes an action which totally defeats any attempt to apply modern categories.

The Spaniards sighted a rich-looking sailing vessel and gave chase. There must have been little wind and a flat sea. Their quarry, unable to outdistance the swift *fusta*, ran aground on a small island, the crew abandoning ship and running for it ashore. Gustaldo's men, arriving on the scene, found to their disgust that the ship was laden with wheat and that the crew had taken all the cash and valuables with them when they ran. They were appraised of this by their would-be victims, who had run no farther than the nearest hilltop from which they shouted down their readiness to negotiate. Unwilling to spend hours ashore running their quarry down (and probably expecting momentary intervention by the local Ottoman garrison), Gustaldo's men struck a bargain. In return for

'500 escudos' (slightly less than 500 ducats) they agreed not to destroy the ship or take it with them. In one way or another the money changed hands and the bargain was consummated to the satisfaction of all concerned. The Spanish got their cash, the 'Turks' got their ship and cargo back. Nobody was unduly put out.

The only loser in the bargain is the analyst who insists on applying modern labels to Gustaldo's men. Were they privateers, a unit of the Spanish navy operating in a commerce raiding role, or thieves pure and simple? It is doubtful that Gustaldo or his superiors were particularly concerned with the matter; nor should we be, except to be aware that such episodes, confusing to twentieth-century sensibilities, were part and parcel of sixteenth-century maritime conflict.

A second suggestive example is the anomalous position of the Genoese naval condottieri in Spanish service as revealed by the details of their contractual relationships with the Spanish crown, preserved in transcriptions of the contracts themselves in the Museo Naval, Madrid. These are of general interest to us in pointing out the utter inapplicability of the usual modern assumptions about the relationship between naval commanders and their governments. They are of specific interest to us in casting light upon the historically critical roles of the foremost of these Genoese condottieri, Andrea Doria and his great-nephew and ultimate heir Gian. The importance of placing these within their proper historical perspective will become evident in our discussion of the battles of Prevesa and Lepanto. Inasmuch as Andrea Doria the elder initiated the pattern of Spanish-Genoese naval cooperation which was characteristic of the last seven decades of the sixteenth century, and in so doing established the precedent for the contracts which we are about to analyze, we shall begin with him.

Andrea Doria (1466–1560), a member of one of Genoa's oldest noble families, began his career as a condottieri in the classic mould and found great success both ashore and at sea – finally at the head of his own squadron of galleys. From this position Doria was able to exercise considerable military and political leverage. Apparently a sincere Genoese patriot, he effectively converted that military leverage into independence for Genoa and financial success for himself.

When Doria's habitual allegiance to France brought a French army under Lautrec to Genoa in 1527 to expel the Imperial garrison, the way was cleared for a coup which Doria must have contemplated for some time. In the summer of 1528, with Lautrec's army far away to the south at the siege of Naples (covered by part of Doria's fleet under his nephew Filippino), Doria put himself up for bid. His offer was accepted with alacrity by Emperor Charles V who was hard up for naval forces at the time and for whom the news of the disaster of Mohacs was still fresh from two years before.

The terms of agreement between Doria and the Emperor, or more accurately the Spanish crown, are instructive. Genoa's independence was guaranteed by force of Imperial arms, but no Imperial garrison was to be allowed in Genoa. So long as she worked within the Spanish orbit – she had already begun to do so out of a sense of economic realism in any case – Genoa was free to pursue her economic destiny. This included a degree of political freedom. The island of Chios, a key Genoese commercial enclave in the Aegean, was never permitted to become involved in the Ottoman–Habsburg dispute; yet it remained under physical Genoese control until it was seized by the Turks in 1566 without resistance, a suggestive circumstance. The Ottomans did not permit the continued existence of such possessions so near their sources of power without receiving something in return. The description of the relationship between Doria's power and Ottoman influence over Chios given by Philip F. Argenti, the recognized authority on the subject, is therefore of some interest: 'Chios, which remained under the sovereignty of the Genoese Republic ... was, therefore, one of the group of states to which the Sublime Porte was hostile. Nevertheless, it was noticeable, as long as Doria the elder was alive, Suleyman made no attempt to conquer the island.' This passage is suggestively indexed by Argenti under the heading, 'Doria, Andrea: fleet of, shelters Chios from the Turks'.[1] Since it is evident from what we know of galley fleets that Doria was unable to shelter Chios in any direct military sense, he must have 'sheltered' it in some other, more devious, manner. It would be interesting indeed to know the extent of Andrea Doria's economic interest in the Chios trade and to learn the nature of the Ottoman–Genoese *modus vivendi* in the Aegean during the period from 1528 to his death. This might provide the key to Doria's often puzzling conduct as commander of the fleet of the Holy League in 1538–40. Of more immediate interest to us, Doria's talents as naval commander and entrepreneur were placed thereafter in the service of Spain. Doria was immediately named Captain General of the Sea[2] (a title assumed by his great-nephew shortly before the elder Doria's death), and his squadron was placed under contract.

[1] *The Occupation of Chios by the Genoese and Their Administration of the Island*, vol. I (Cambridge, 1958), pp. 330-1, 684. For a thorough treatment of Genoa's response to changing economic conditions in this period see Robert S. Lopez, 'Market Expansion: The Case of Genoa', *Journal of Economic History*, XXIV (1964), 445 ff.

[2] The holder of this title was the designated lieutenant of the King of Spain for all operational naval matters within the Mediterranean. It was held in turn by Hugo de Moncada, Andrea

The details of the initial agreement between the elder Doria and Charles V are contained in two Imperial letters, dated respectively 10 August 1528 and 18 March 1530, copies of which are preserved in the Museo Naval, Madrid.[1] The first of these names Doria Captain General of the Sea, while the second outlines the provisions under which Doria had served with fifteen galleys during the two previous years. The Museo Naval also has a copy of the elder Doria's contract of 1539 and Gian Andrea Doria's contracts for 1566 and 1568.[2] Following the contract of 1568, which expired at the end of 1570, there was a one-year extension under the same terms dated 18 May 1571. The coverage of Gian Andrea Doria's contracts is thus complete from 1566 through 1571. We have, in addition, copies of similar but less advantageous contracts for considerably smaller numbers of galleys between the Spanish crown and three other Genoese entrepreneurs: Jorge Grimaldo, Pedro Bautista Lomelin, and Lucian Centurion.[3] These, like Doria's contract of 1568, expired in the winter of 1570–1. They were extended for a year in the spring of 1571 – significantly, four and a half months after Doria's extension. Finally, we have a Spanish document completed during the winter of 1571–2 which gives a detailed analysis of the cost to Spain of Doria's contract during the preceding year.[4] This is reproduced in tabular form as Fig. 2 (below, p. 33).

Doria, Garcia de Toledo, Gian Andrea Doria, and, after a lapse, Filibert of Savoy. See Francisco-Felipe Olesa Muñido, *La Organización Naval de los Estados Mediterraneos y en Especial de España Durante los Siglos XVI y XVII* (Madrid, 1968), pp. 541-50, for a thorough analysis of this office.

[1] *Colección Sanz de Barutell* (*Simancas*), *Artículo* 5, dto. 1, fol. 1-4, entitled 'Copy of the commissions and contract which His Majesty has with Prince Andrea Doria . . .' The first of the two letters must represent the initial formalization of the agreement between Doria and Charles V. Its date places it between the withdrawal of Doria's squadron from the French service before Naples and its appearance before Genoa on 9 September.

[2] All of these are in *Artículo* 5 of the *Colección Sanz de Barutell* (*Simancas*). Doria's commission and contract of 1539, dto. 5, fol. 67-8 was to run for two years and covered twenty galleys. Dto. 20, a Spanish commentary on Doria's 1539 contract, indicates that its provisions were essentially unchanged from those of the agreement of 18 March 1530 except that a larger number of galleys was covered. Gian Andrea Doria's contract of 1566, dto. 35, fol. 141-4, ran for two years from 1 January 1566 and was superseded by the contract of 1568, dto. 37, fol. 149-52. The 1568 contract was for three years and was renewed for a year after its expiration. The renewal, dto. 43, fol. 175, was dated 31 December 1570.

[3] These documents are also in *Artículo* 5 of the *Colección Sanz de Barutell* (*Simancas*). Pedro Bautista Lomelin's contract for four galleys, dated 3 April 1568, is dto. 39, and Jorge Grimaldo's for two galleys, dated 27 May 1568, is dto. 40. All of these contracts were to be effective for three years from 1 January 1568 and all were extended for a year after their expiration. The extensions, all dated 18 May 1571, are documents 41 and 42 respectively.

[4] The Spanish document analyzing Doria's, Centurion's and Lomelin's contracts was, according to internal evidence, completed late in the winter of 1570-1. This is in the *Colección Sanz de Barutell* (*Simancas*), *Artículo* 4, vol. II, dto. 324, fol. 430-1. Copies of Grimaldo's and Centurion's 1568 contracts are also in the *Colección Navarrete*, vol. VIII, dto. 6, fol. 39-46; and dto. 7, fol. 47-54, respectively.

The provisions of these contracts are revealing. Doria's contract of 1528 provided for the payment of 500 ducats per galley per month – a figure common to all the later documents. It is apparent, however, that this figure was artificial. Although payment was made for a twelve-month year on this basis, it was understood that the galleys sailed at the owners' risk except during the normal Mediterranean campaigning season of mid-March to mid-October. The contracts of 1568 specifically provided for a financial penalty if the galleys were risked during the season of winter storms on the owner's authority. If, on the other hand, the galleys were required to go to sea by royal order during the winter months, the owner was to receive a bonus. The size of this bonus, 200 ducats per galley per month for Centurion, Lomelin and Grimaldo, 270 ducats per galley per month for Doria, clearly indicates that the Genoese galleys were not ordinarily expected to sail in the winter.

Thus the figure of 500 ducats per galley per month was not based on actual costs, but was a customary figure based on the rule of thumb which provided a convenient starting point for bargaining. The real meat of these contracts lay in the fringe provisions. These provisions were elaborate, varied from entrepreneur to entrepreneur, and changed considerably with time. Though they are deserving of detailed analysis in themselves, a cursory examination of the basic provisions will serve us here. They fall into several fairly clear-cut categories.

First of all there were those provisions which applied only to the Dorias and seem to have been more or less straightforward monetary compensation for their services. Andrea Doria's contracts of 1528 and 1529 included an annual allowance of 12,000 ducats[1] for the powder and shot expended by the fifteen galleys in his squadron. This provision was absent from Doria's contract of 1539; but Gian Andrea Doria's contracts all provided for a personal salary (there being no powder allowance like that given his great-uncle) which must have served the same purpose. This salary amounted to 5,000 ducats per year in the 1566 contract and 6,000 ducats per year in the 1568 and 1571 contracts.

Next, there were those provisions which – and we make this statement guardedly – seem to have been primarily intended to defray the actual costs of maintaining a galley in commission. Into this category falls an allowance in Gian Andrea Doria's contracts for payment of the salaries of such gentlemen adventurers as sailed with his squadron. This amounted to 1,500 ducats per year in his 1566 contract and 2,000 ducats per year

---

[1] The gold ducat was a basic Castilian unit of currency. During the period covered by this study its value was fixed at 375 *marevedis* of silver of 11 *reales* of silver. The value of the *real* was usually taken as 34 *marevedis* for convenience.

in his 1568 and 1571 contracts, generally realistic values. Also in this category was the permission, granted to Jorge Grimaldo and Lucian Centurion in 1566, to purchase ship's biscuit, the staple of war at sea, free of taxes.[1]

Next, and standing alone, is the provision for an interest payment of 14 per cent per annum on the unpaid balance of all monies owed the entrepreneur by the crown. Probably negotiated separately in the case of the earlier contracts, this provision was explicitly written into all of the contracts from 1566 on with which we are here concerned. The importance of this provision is underlined by the perilous state of Spanish government finances which led to bankruptcies in 1557, 1575, 1595 and to a suspension of payments in 1607.[2] We thus have a situation, anomalous to the modern mind, where the commanders of fleets and ships served as bankers, financing the very operations which they commanded. It is obvious that Doria and his fellow condottieri, knowing that they were unlikely to be paid promptly and in full, must have made the most of the situation, not only financially, but in other ways as well.

Finally, and certainly most important, was the granting to the Genoese naval condottieri of trading concessions which were completely unrelated to any military services rendered. The most striking of these, though probably not the most important economically, was the granting of currency export rights. The relevant clause in Jorge Grimaldo's three-year contract of 1 January 1568 ran:

... for the harm which the said Jorge de Grimaldo claims to sustain in paying the salary of the said galley in those kingdoms, because of the currency exchanges and interests and differences which exist in the moneys of those kingdoms and Italy, we have the mercy to make him recompensation and satisfaction in this: that the said Jorge de Grimaldo, or whomever he shall authorize, shall be allowed to take from these kingdoms in each of the three years 12,500 ducats ... in ducats of gold or *reales* of silver.

The granting of such rights by the Spanish government, despite its intense preoccupation with measures designed to prevent the outward flow of precious metals from Spain, is remarkable indeed.[3] Although the fiction was maintained that the right to export currency from Spanish

---

[1] It seems unlikely that much direct monetary incentive was involved since the non-military market for biscuit – hard, dry and unpalatable – must have been negligible except in times of famine. The importance of biscuit and biscuit prices to Mediterranean warfare at sea, equivalent to the importance of fuel oil in modern naval warfare, is dealt with in the concluding chapters.

[2] See F. C. Spooner, 'The Economy of Europe, 1559–1609', *The New Cambridge Modern History*, vol. III, *The Counter Reformation and Price Revolution, 1559–1610* (Cambridge 1958), p. 15.

[3] See Fernand Braudel, *La Méditerranée*, Spanish edition (Mexico, 1953), pp. 461ff.

Figure 1   Export rights for Sicilian wheat covered in the contracts of certain Genoese with the Spanish crown

	Contract	Number of galleys covered	Total allowable wheat export	*Salmas* per ordinary galley per year[a]	Other provisions
	Andrea Doria, 1528–30	15	10,000 *salmas*	333[b]	Two-year contract
	Andrea Doria, 1539	20	6,000 *salmas*/yr	300[b]	
	Gian Andrea Doria, 1566	12		350	
Three-year contracts	Gian Andrea Doria, 1568	12		350	
	L. Centurion, 1568	4		300	
	P. Lomelin, 1568	4		300	
	J. Grimaldo, 1568	2		300	
One-year contracts	Gian Andrea Doria, 1571	12	'normally' 4,500 *salmas*/yr	350	Wheat to be purchased at the fixed price of 2 ducats per *salma*[c]
	L. Centurion, 1571	Unclear		300	
	P. Lomelin, 1571	5[d]		300	

[a] In the Dorias' contracts the flagship and vice-flagship were normally given a weighted value of 1½ ordinary galleys each, thus in 1566 Gian Andrea Doria was allowed 525 *salmas* for his flagship and in the 1568 contract he was allowed 525 *salmas*/yr. for his flagship and vice-flagship.

[b] This is arrived at by counting the flagship as an ordinary galley since no weighted average is specified in the contract.

[c] See Fig. 2. The Spanish computed the market value of the grain to be 4 *escudos* per *salma*, the *escudo* being the Sicilian equivalent to the Castilian ducat worth about 350 Castilian *marevedis* to the ducat's 375. The fixed 'pegged' price was thus just over half the actual market value.

[d] The number of galleys is not specified in the surviving transcription of the contract, but Lomelin is known to have appeared at Lepanto with five galleys.

dominions was granted solely to defray the costs of maintaining a galley in commission, the amounts involved – in this case 12,500 ducats per year for only two galleys – and the extreme variation from contract to contract makes it clear that this was not the case.[1]

Clearly the most significant trade concession contained in the Genoese contracts, however, was the granting of the right to purchase and export grain, particularly Sicilian grain, free of all taxes and imposts. In view of the recognized value to Spain of the Sicilian wheat harvest and the tax revenue which it produced, this was a remarkable concession.[2] The amount of grain which each entrepreneur was allowed to export, usually pro-rated on the basis of so many *salmas*[3] per galley per year, varied from contract to contract. The figures relevant to the contracts under discussion are shown in Fig. 1.

Note that Gian Andrea Doria was invariably allowed not only a greater total amount of grain than his lesser compatriots, but a larger share per galley as well, a clear reflection of his political pre-eminence and of the value of the grain.

This data is placed in perspective by Fernand Braudel's figures, based on Spanish sources, showing the total amount of Sicilian grain exported during the years in question – about 210,000 *salmas* from the harvest of 1567 and about 90,000 *salmas* from that of 1568.[4] If these totals are approximately correct and if Doria took all of the Sicilian grain that he was allotted, then he would personally have accounted for about 2 per cent of the total legal export in 1568 and just over 5 per cent in 1569. One final point must be mentioned. In 1571 the Spanish, in desperate need of well manned galleys following the fiasco of the campaign of 1570, offered the added incentive of artificially 'pegging' the price of Sicilian grain at just over one half its market value.

[1] *Colección Navarrete*, vol. VII, dtos. 6–7, fol. 39ff, the 1568 contracts of Jorge Grimaldo and Lucian Centurion. Centurion, with four galleys to Grimaldo's two, was allowed to export annually only 1,500 ducats at most (the wording is unclear and only 500 ducats may be involved). Centurion's 1571 extension of his 1568 contract allowed him to export a flat sum of 5,000 ducats, as did Lomelin's, Grimaldo's 1571 contract not being on record. That this may have been a consolation prize of sorts – presumably for not having been given a larger slice of the Sicilian grain harvest, a provision which we discuss next, is suggested by the fact that none of Gian Andrea Doria's contracts contain such a currency export clause.

[2] Braudel, *La Méditerranée*, Spanish edition (Mexico, 1953), pp. 504–5.

[3] The *salma* was a Sicilian unit of bulk used for the measurement of grain. While its approximate value is known with certainty, its precise value, usually given as about 440 pounds, defies definition. See Olesa Muñido, *La Organización Naval*, vol. I, pp. 246–7. If we think of a *salma* as being between a fourth and a fifth of a modern U.S. ton (2,000 pounds) of wheat, we will not be too far wrong.

[4] Braudel, *La Méditerranée* (Paris, 1966), vol. I, p. 541, Fig. 51. No value is given for the harvest of 1570.

The Spanish estimate of what the Genoese contracts cost them is shown by a contemporary document giving an itemized breakdown of Doria's, Centurion's and Lomelin's contracts of 1571. The portion of it relating to Gian Andrea Doria's squadron is reproduced in Fig. 2. It estimates that each of Doria's ordinary galleys cost Spain 9,731⅔ ducats per year. It similarly estimates that Centurion's and Lomelin's contracts (the 5,000 ducat currency export licenses are estimated to have cost Spain 375 ducats each) cost Spain 8,095 ducats per galley per year.

These figures are placed in context by contemporary Spanish data on the annual cost to the crown of one of the galleys of Spain (that is a galley whose captain was a royal appointee and whose payroll was met by a royal paymaster) based in Messina. This estimate, dated 19 December 1571, is a thorough, complete, and apparently realistic one.[1] The Spanish galley considered in this estimate was almost identical to those used by Doria, Centurion, and Lomelin in every important particular. It carried the same number of oarsmen and was, if anything, somewhat better provided with fighting men. The total cost to Spain for maintaining such a galley for a year was 7,921 ducats, some 174 ducats a year less than Centurion's and Lomelin's and a whopping 1,711 ducats a year less than each of Doria's ordinary galleys by the most conservative computation.

All of this is shown in Fig. 2. Even when we subtract the estimated cost to Spain of the Sicilian wheat, Doria's personal salary, and the cost of the 200 loaned *forzados*, we come out with an annual cost of about 8,038 ducats for each ordinary galley, slightly above the cost to Spain of a comparable Spanish galley. Thus it seems certain that Doria and the other Genoese were able to cover their operating costs easily with the direct payments provided for in their contracts and turn a handsome profit on the trade concessions and side benefits.

This entrepreneurial approach to naval warfare does not fit easily into a Mahanian analysis. Recognition of its existence goes far to explain the difficulty encountered by modern historians in explaining the actions of the two Dorias at Prevesa and Lepanto. This difficulty should hardly surprise us. A naval commander serving under contract to a foreign sovereign in command of an expedition which he was in part personally

[1] *Colección Sanz de Barutell (Simancas)*, *Artículo* 4, vol. II, dto. 232, fol. 420-2, an 'Account of what each galley of Spain which sails from Messina has cost His Majesty in this year of 1571'. This account of costs is remarkably complete, follows a standard format, and is entirely consistent with the estimate of the cost to Spain of the Genoese contracts. The author has hedged his bets by assuming at least some operations along the coasts of Spain by averaging in the higher cost of Spanish biscuit, the largest single expense in operating a galley. He used a value of 20 *reales* per hundredweight (there being 11 *reales* in a ducat) for Spanish biscuit and 12 *reales* per hundredweight for biscuit in Italy. This averages out to his value of 16 *reales*.

Figure 2   A Spanish account of the cost to Spain of Gian Andrea Doria's contract for twelve galleys; covering the period 1 January to 31 December 1571[a]

Direct payments to Prince Doria

For the maintenance and upkeep of his flagship and vice-flagship, each armed with 75 fighting men and 174 oarsmen, at the rate of 750 ducats per month
For the maintenance and upkeep of ten ordinary galleys, each armed with 50 fighting men and 174 oarsmen, at the rate of 500 ducats per month
    78,000 ducats (6,000 ducats per ordinary galley per year)

Payment to Prince Doria for money in arrears   6,000 ducats

Prince Doria's salary   6,000 ducats

Given to Prince Doria as salaries for his gentlemen adventurers   2,000 ducats

Sub Total   92,000 ducats

Additional costs to Spain

4,500 *salmas* of Sicilian wheat valued at 4 *escudos/salma*; released to Prince Doria at 2 ducats/*salma*   9,000 ducats

Payment to Prince Doria for 200 *forzados*,[b] loaned to Spain for the above year at 35 ducats per *forzado* per year   7,000 ducats

Sub Total   108,000 ducats

Salaries of Royal officers and Spanish soldiers attached to Prince Doria's Squadron

Royal Accountant (*Contador*)   500 ducats

Royal Inspector and Disburser (*Veedor*)   500 ducats

500 Spanish soldiers at 5 ducats per month apiece for seven months; to cover the salaries of their captains and officers; a total of 2,500 ducats per month   17,500 ducats

Total   126,500 ducats

Counting the said squadron as 13 galleys,[c] the cost per galley comes to 9,731⅔ ducats per year. Counting the said squadron as 12 galleys, the cost per galley comes to 10,541⅔ ducats per year.

---

[a] This document is from a transcription of the original in the *Colección Sanz de Barutell* (*Simancas*), *Artículo* 4, vol. 2, dto. 324, fol. 430–1. The form and wording of the original have been retained wherever possible.
[b] *Forzados* were convicts used as oarsmen.
[c] It was customary to count flagships and vice-flagships (*capitanas* and *patronas*), more heavily manned and armed than ordinary galleys, as a galley and a half.

financing and which was, at the same time, a private commercial venture, could hardly be expected to act according to purely military impulses. Though we have delved deeply into the affairs of the two Dorias because of the central importance of the roles which they played in the great Mediterranean sea fights of the sixteenth century, this sort of conflicting motivation was by no means uniquely Genoese. As a general rule, only a minority of the galleys in Spanish service had their payrolls made directly by a royal paymaster. Most of them were commanded by private owners, both Spanish and Italian, who had placed themselves and their galleys under contract to the crown, just as the Genoese condottieri habitually did. Command relationships, of course, were quite different in Ottoman and Venetian service; but the main point – that military decisions were habitually influenced by non-military factors even at the tactical level – still holds. Economic motivation, in particular, constantly emerged at every level in sixteenth-century Mediterranean naval operations. In 1564, for example, we find Don Garcia de Toledo, Philip II's Captain General of the Sea, admonishing his captains to use moderation in allowing their officers to ship private trading merchandise aboard royal galleys. While thoroughly opposed to the practice on military grounds – decks clogged with merchandise made a poor fighting platform – he was forced to accept it because of the inadequacy of his officer's salaries. He similarly warned against the shipping of illicit, 'unlicensed', exports – almost surely a euphemism for precious metals.[1]

But our conceptual problems are not limited to general considerations of the scope and nature of sixteenth-century Mediterranean maritime conflict. Our Mahanian heritage has placed a number of formidable obstacles in the way of an understanding of certain basic technical and tactical facts of life at sea. Recent experience with naval affairs has accustomed us to brief and intensive periods of naval warfare where the issue is settled, usually quickly, by a limited number of highly specialized warships. These warships are designed and used for battle and nothing else. The combat value of the normal merchant ship is negligible by comparison – hence, once the decisive fleet victory is won, warships can dominate the seas easily. Battles and, in the Mahanian concept, wars are won on the strength of the technical capabilities of the combatants'

---

[1] *Colección Navarrete*, vol. III, dto. 8, fol. 152. The admonitions cited are items numbers 15 and 16 in the above document. The earlier items deal with the usual concerns of maintaining regular provisioning, good discipline, etc. Interestingly enough, the concern of Spanish naval commanders with the use of royal galleys for private trade by their officers and crew shows a definite change with time. Early in the sixteenth century this sort of activity was accepted as a matter of course; by its end, the carrying of private trade goods on the Galleys of Spain was strictly forbidden.

warships. Barring an overwhelming numerical superiority, battles lost or won can usually be attributed to some technical advantage enjoyed by the warships of the victor.

The sort of analysis which this suggests does have its place in the study of maritime conflict in the sixteenth century. Michael Lewis has used it well in his study of the defeat of the Spanish Armada. His conclusion that the Armada was defeated largely because the English ships were better armed and better sailed is the sort of conclusion we would expect and, by and large, it is a correct one. But the direct technical comparison of a limited number of combatant ships produces results which cannot be applied in isolation to a study of sixteenth-century Mediterranean conflict.

The implicit assumption behind the type of analysis which Lewis employs so well is that the ships being analyzed exercised an effective monopoly of armed violence at sea. This assumption is usually valid for a given campaign or battle; but for an analysis of long-term change in the patterns of maritime conflict in the sixteenth century it is demonstrably false.

By the middle of the seventeenth century there was a wide disparity in military potential between the ship of the line and the most heavily armed merchant ships and privateers. This disparity became more marked with time and underlies much of our thinking on naval matters. In the sixteenth century, however, there was no such clear-cut disparity. All ships of any size – and many which were quite small – had some military potential. Carefully armed and heavily manned merchant ships frequently had a greater combat capability than the run-of-the-mill warship, just as many warships carried cargo. There was therefore no clear distinction between the two. If we combine this situation with the absence of control of the sea in the Mahanian sense, the implications become clear. We are not primarily concerned with sharp dramatic battles which cleared the sea of hostile ships, but with the long-term effects of protracted periods of *guerre de course* in which warships came up against merchant ships more often than not and did not always get the better of it. In this sort of situation a direct technical comparison between the warships of opposing nations can be quite misleading. For a start, the role of warships was apt to be quite different from that which we would suppose. In the second place, their long-term effectiveness might well have depended upon secondary factors such as cost or a need for specialized manpower which was difficult to satisfy. Such factors as these would not be likely to emerge from a narrowly technical analysis. Finally, it might well develop that the types of ship with the greatest military potential in absolute terms were not those most critical to the final outcome.

35

We have been conditioned to explain naval victory by some technical advantage of the victor's ships over those of the vanquished. We expect to discover that advantage by means of a narrowly technical comparison of the warships of the two sides. This kind of comparison is essential to a proper understanding of the patterns of maritime conflict in any period. It can tell us a great deal about the short-term rhythms of war at sea – the ebb and flow of conflict on a weekly or daily basis. Why was Barbarossa initially reluctant to become closely engaged at Prevesa? Why did Don Juan attack with such serene confidence at Lepanto? Such questions are largely answerable by means of the above type of technical analysis. But for the long view it is not enough. The difficulties become apparent when we attempt to explain the gradual obsolescence of the galley through a comparative technical analysis of warship types.

The accepted explanation is straightforward – and wrong. The broadside sailing warship won out in the end: therefore it must have been intrinsically superior from the first. Looked at in this way, the perseverance of the war galley in the Mediterranean long after the appearance of the broadside sailing ship is attributable to force of tradition and little else. This point of view and its two necessary supporting assumptions – that the broadside sailing ship's one-to-one tactical advantage over the galley on the open sea was the critical factor and that the Mediterranean nations could have adopted the broadside sailing ship had they so desired – are generally accepted.[1]

The problem is: if the galley was a tactical anachronism, why did it survive so long? The broadside sailing ship made its appearance in strength during the last decades of the sixteenth century, yet when the eighteenth century dawned, every Mediterranean fleet of consequence was composed in part of galleys. If Mediterranean conservatism was solely to blame, it must have been tenacious indeed. The best historians of maritime affairs have long recognized that this survival was not entirely attributable to the force of tradition, but no arguable alternative has presented itself. A generally accepted Mahanian summation is as follows: 'The light galley long remained important in the Mediterranean war fleets because galleys were needed to chase galleys.'[2] But just why galleys were needed to chase galleys – or more precisely why galleys had to be chased at all – has never been spelled out.

Implicit to the accepted point of view is the belief that the galley was

[1] See for example, Carlo Cipolla, *Guns, Sails and Empires*, p. 84, and J. R. Hale, 'Armies, Navies and the Art of War', ch. 16, *New Cambridge Modern History*, vol. II, *The Reformation* (Cambridge, 1958), p. 506.

[2] Frederick C. Lane, 'Venetian Shipping During the Commercial Revolution', *American Historical Review*, xxxviii, No. 2 (1933), 219–39.

doomed from the start by the *idea* of the broadside sailing warship. Broadside armament, however, had been around for a long time before the triumph of the sailing warship, a point which we will amplify in our discussion of early broadside sailing warship tactics following chapter 2. The logical difficulty which this presents is evaded by assuming that the earliest broadside sailing warships used a different and less effective type of armament. The need for this assumption is the basis of the old idea of the dichotomy between the 'man-killing' armament of the older ships and the 'ship-killers' which the English and Dutch ships of the late sixteenth century are supposed to have introduced.[1]

If the earliest sailing ships with broadside armament were unable to sweep the seas of galleys, it must have been because they were armed only with light 'man-killers' with which to repel boarders and were thus unable to sink their opponents as a proper warship should. We are thus back to a narrowly technical explanation. Instead of the broadside sailing ship driving the galley from the seas, we now have the broadside sailing ship plus a 'ship-killing' armament to do the job. But there is a major problem with this hypothesis: there is little evidence to back it up.

The artificiality of this hypothesis is exposed by examining the credentials of the 'ship-killing' gun. Were the 'ship-killing' guns of the sixteenth century really different from what went before? Did they really kill ships? When we examine the armament of the Dutch and English ships of the late sixteenth and early seventeenth centuries, the ships which finally started the war galley on the road to obsolescence, we must return a highly qualified verdict on the first point. The guns aboard these Dutch and English vessels were sound enough; but they were no better than what had gone before and were certainly not of a novel or even markedly different size or design. Their sole mark of distinction by Mediterranean standards was the large number in which they were employed.

This was important – decisively important – over the long run; but even when employed in large numbers these cannon were not truly 'ship-

---

[1] The use of the terms 'man-killers' and 'ship-killers' to describe sixteenth-century naval ordnance is so widespread as to demand little documentation. Michael Lewis, the premier analyst of sixteenth-century naval ordnance, bases his entire scheme of analysis on the dichotomy between the two, although he backs away from the logical implications of their names in his eminently sound conclusions. See, for example, his initial methodological remarks in 'Armada Guns, A Comparative Study of English and Spanish Armaments', *The Mariner's Mirror*, xxviii (January, 1942), 44–8. Non-specialists, however, are not generally so careful. Garrett Mattingly, *The Armada* (Boston, 1962), p. 196, unabashedly refers to the 'revolutionary' changes wrought in shipboard armament by the English in the years preceding the onslaught of the Armada. This 'revolution' consisted of reducing the number of 'man-killing guns' and increasing the number of 'ship-killing guns' aboard the Queen's ships. The difference in their capabilities is not spelled out.

killers' by any standard. They could, it is true, sink a ship upon occasion; but this was almost invariably a lengthy and painful process. When ships were actually destroyed, fire, often as not, provided the *coup de grâce*, just as it had for centuries.

The immoderate length of single-ship contests between broadside sailing warships should drive this point effectively home. So should the fact that these contests seem, on the whole, to have become longer – not shorter – as the quantity and quality of shipboard ordnance increased throughout the seventeenth and eighteenth centuries. The reasons for this are somewhat involved; but the main factor seems to have been advances in ship design. As shipwrights learned to build vessels which stood higher in the water without sacrificing seaworthiness or handling characteristics, the sailing ship became increasingly difficult to board.[1] This left no tactical alternatives to the prolonged cannonade. It is important to note in this context that shipbuilding materials, and hence the vulnerability of ships to cannon fire, remained essentially unchanged. It is even more important to note that the external ballistics of shipborne ordnance – the mass and velocity of the projectiles thrown – remained essentially unchanged from the early sixteenth century into the early nineteenth. Put another way, the range and impact of shipboard cannon changed hardly at all for three centuries. The main point, however, is that the increased numbers of cannon mounted on warships did not serve to reduce the length of single-ship contests; rather it acted in conjunction with the secondary factors mentioned above to increase their length. With boarding no longer a viable alternative – largely due to increased fire-power – all that remained was the slow and tedious process by which one ship bashed another into bloody splinters. This was about all that our 'ship-killers' were capable of.

An example which should be familiar to American students of history and perhaps English ones as well is the protracted contest between the *Bon Homme Richard*, commanded by John Paul Jones, and the *Serapis* in 1779. Here two ships plentifully supplied with 'ship-killing' ordnance lay yardarm to yardarm for three and a half hours and had at it with everything they could muster. At the end *Richard* was leaking faster than the remaining crew was able to pump the bilges dry and the *Serapis* was on fire; but both ships were assuredly afloat. The issue was finally settled when one of Jones' men, probably hanging by his toenails from *Richard's* main yard, lobbed a hand grenade aboard *Serapis* and got the powder

---

[1] Also important in this context was the development of design techniques which permitted the construction of ships' sides with 'tumble home', or an inward slope, thus rendering boarding more difficult still.

magazine with a carom shot. So much for the ship-killing guns of the eighteenth century – or the sixteenth.[1]

In fact the process which finally drove the galley from the seas was not due so much to the invention of any particular ship design or type of gun, but to the gradual increase in the amount of relatively heavy armament carried aboard merchant ships, particularly the merchant ships of the northern nations. Ships were, by the third or fourth decade of the sixteenth century, carrying guns as heavy and powerful as any they would carry until the age of steam. But there were very few heavy cannon of sound construction around. This was mostly a matter of economics. Cannon founders of the early sixteenth century knew how to make cannons which, except for their somewhat greater bulk and less efficient mounts, compared well with those of the eighteenth. But the best bronze cannon were very expensive, both relative to the other requirements of naval power and in absolute terms. There was, moreover, little capital available to finance their construction. The resultant shortage of good, heavy cannon dictated the way in which they were employed.

The sixteenth-century naval planner was not faced with a choice between the broadside sailing warship and the war galley. He was confronted with the problem of how to get the most out of a very limited quantity of good, heavy ordnance. It is not surprising that what good heavy artillery there was generally wound up in the royal siege train, in fortresses or on the bows of galleys. It was felt – with good reason – that it would do the most good there.

A Spanish report on the state of the Ottoman fleet, and in particular

[1] An apparent exception, which will occur immediately to students of English naval history, is Richard Hawkins' fight with the Spanish West Indies Fleet in the harbor of San Juan de Ulloa (Vera Cruz, Mexico) in September of 1568. See Edouard A. Stackpole, *Those in Peril on the Sea* (New York, 1962), pp. 35–44, for a contemporary English account of the engagement. Hawkins' force of two carracks of moderate size, the *Jesus of Lubeck* and the *Minion*, and a small bark, the *Judith*, sank the Spanish flagship and another 'principal' vessel by gunfire in the first half hour of the action. This engagement, however, took place under optimum conditions: in a flat calm and sheltered waters at point-blank range. With a steady platform to shoot from and motionless targets, Hawkins' gunners – probably more skilled than those of later generations – could pick their points of impact on the Spanish hulls and hit them with precision. The same general conditions seem to have applied to the last fight of the *Revenge* some years later. Gunners of the mid-sixteenth century were rare individuals who had mastered a dangerous art on their own initiative and could take full advantage of such conditions. Mid-eighteenth-century gunners, by contrast, were generally mere technicians: ordinary soldiers or seamen trained to perform certain mechanical functions reliably with no emphasis on accuracy or precision. The high skill of Hawkins' gunners and the ideal conditions for gunnery off San Juan de Ulloa account for the effect of the English ordnance. We might also note that the relatively heavy armament of the *Jesus* included several cast-iron cannon and cannon designed to fire stone cannonballs, factors of no small significance for reasons which we will make clear before long.

of Barbarossa's squadron, written in the spring of 1534 bears this out well.[1] The report indicates that: 'all of the galleys of Barbarossa carry cannons for stone cannonballs and have not a single piece which throws iron excepting the galley of Barbarossa which has a *basilisco* [here used as a generic term denoting almost any long cannon of unusual size] in the prow.' We should not expect too high a standard of accuracy to lie behind this. Nonetheless it is clear that the flagship was the best armed galley in the squadron and that the average quality of the main guns aboard the other galleys of Barbarossa's squadron did not overly impress the author of the report (from internal evidence, probably a diplomat resident in Constantinople). Significantly, he adds: 'Likewise he [Barbarossa] has up to thirty-four pieces of bronze which are carried . . . for battery on land and for the breaching of castles.' The report makes it clear that these thirty-four pieces – the author goes out of his way to specify that they are of bronze, implying by indirection that the others were not – were the cream of Barbarossa's artillery and that they were carried as a siege train.

The general pattern is clear, although many of the details are no doubt in error. The best guns available were not even mounted aboard ship, but were reserved for the siege train. After that, the flagship was carefully armed. What was left over went onto the bows of the remaining galleys, with indications that antiquated wrought-iron pieces were being pressed into service to fill the requirement. This is the pattern which we would expect and, by and large, which we find. We will see it clearly aboard Spanish galleys in 1536 in our final segment dealing with the battle of Lepanto.

Also significant is the modest provision of artillery in absolute terms. This is also a pattern which will emerge again and again in our study. Barbarossa's squadron of fifty-two galleys was the pride of the Ottoman fleet and one of the most effective naval units of its day. Yet the total weight of artillery carried by these 52 galleys was probably little more than that of the 56 guns carried by the English warship *Prince Royal*, built in 1610. It was surely less than the weight of metal carried by the English *Sovereign of the Seas* of 100 guns, launched in 1637.[2] These two ships, of course, were the finest and biggest of their day, but they were atypical only in their size, not in the type or provision of armament relative to that size. These two English warships represented in their day, like Barbarossa's squadron in his, the epitome of armed might afloat. But where Barbarossa's squadron stood alone, these two English warships served as flagships for entire fleets of ships which were perhaps smaller and less

[1] *Colección Sanz de Barutell (Simancas)*, *Artículo* 6, dto. 20, fol. 41–2.
[2] See Björn Landström, *The Ship* (New York, 1961), pp. 142, 152.

grand than they, but similarly armed nonetheless. Behind this enormous difference in scale lay an economic revolution, not an isolated idea about the way in which ships should be built or armed.

All of this serves to point us away from a narrowly technical explanation for the decline of the Mediterranean 'system'. This is evident when we examine the reasons for the disappearance of the galley. The usual reason given – the idea of the broadside sailing warship – does not suffice. The narrowly technical argument which attributes the decline of the galley to the appearance of the broadside sailing warship makes sense only if we assume the parallel appearance of the 'ship-killing' gun; yet the concept of the 'ship-killing' gun lacks a sound basis in fact.

It is evident therefore that the decline of the galley and of the Mediterranean system was a much more involved and subtle process than is generally supposed. To examine that process we must go back to the climatic and geographic realities which underlay the structures of the Mediterranean system of armed conflict at sea. First, however, it would be well to form an idea of how Mediterranean warfare at sea was conducted in the period when the galley was dominant.

Prevesa, 1538

Before proceeding with a systematic analysis of the Mediterranean system of warfare at sea a concrete illustration of the way in which it operated at the period of its greatest power and efficiency is in order. This is necessary to give substance to the generalizations made in chapter 1 and to give the reader a feel for the tactical realities of sixteenth-century galley warfare.

For both of these purposes, as well as for orthodox historical reasons, an analysis of the battle of Prevesa is the logical choice. There is general agreement that the series of naval and land engagements fought around the mouth of the Gulf of Prevesa and to the south, along the western flank of the island of Santa Maura (now known as Levkas), between 25 and 28 October 1538 marked a significant turning point in Mediterranean history. But how and why this was so has never been adequately explained. A great deal of confusion surrounds Prevesa in the minds of modern analysts who have consequently been reluctant to come to grips with the historical problems which it poses. Modern historiography has produced only sketchy and incomplete explanations of Prevesa's unquestioned strategic significance. It has not yet produced a coherent tactical analysis of the battle itself.[1]

This is undoubtedly due largely to the utter strangeness of Prevesa to the modern naval historian operating within the orthodox Mahanian framework. Beyond the unfamiliarity of the essentially amphibious tactics of Prevesa, there is the matter of the conduct of the opposing commanders, particularly Andrea Doria. Doria's conduct can be explained in orthodox Mahanian terms only as treason. To the modern naval historian, therefore, Doria has been either entirely guilty or entirely innocent, modern standards of conduct admitting no intermediate shades. It is almost inconceivable to the modern western scholar that the commander of an

[1] The best modern account of Prevesa in English is given, almost as an aside, by Roger B. Merriman, *The Rise of the Spanish Empire*, vol. III, *The Emperor* (New York, 1925), pp. 324ff. Although based almost entirely on a single contemporary Spanish document, Merriman's brief account is intelligently done. Surely the best account of the battle in English, and probably the best extant is from Richard Knolles' late sixteenth-century account in Richard Knolles and Sir Paul Rycaut, *The Turkish History* (London, 1687).

allied fleet would openly engage in secret negotiations with the enemy commander – negotiations to which his allies were not privy – just before a major battle, then lose the battle and yet continue to retain his position of favor with his royal patron. Most modern historians, unable to rationalize Doria's actions within their own moral framework, have leaned toward the explanations offered by his most ardent apologists. Though we cannot offer an authoritative explanation of Doria's conduct before Prevesa – a question which has clouded analysis of the battle itself – we can place the established facts in a more relevant perspective than has been done heretofore. It is necessary to come to grips with this problem before dealing with the battle of Prevesa itself.

Without getting embroiled in the debate surrounding the documentary evidence, a few statements can be made *prima facie*. It seems fairly evident that some sort of secret negotiations were going on between Doria and the Ottoman Kapudan Paşa, Khaireddin Barbarossa, before Prevesa.[1] But, allegations made by apologists for Doria aside, there is no evidence, direct or indirect, that Barbarossa ever considered changing his allegiance. Nor is there any logical reason to suppose that he would have. He is shown by his entire career to have been a dedicated defender of his faith and a staunch opponent of Habsburg power. It is obvious in any case that Charles V had little to offer him. In 1538 Barbarossa had reached the pinnacle of success in the Sultan's service. Subsequent failure and disgrace were, it is true, always possible, but these were possibilities which he had faced with equanimity in the past and was not apt to fear in the future. Khaireddin Barbarossa was a recognized champion of his cause who had received full recognition from his Sultan. He was clearly not a disgruntled malcontent.

There is every reason to suspect, in short, that evidence of Barbarossa's supposed malfeasance emanates directly from cover stories spread by Doria's partisans to justify his negotiations with the infidel. For while Charles V had little to offer Barbarossa, Suleiman I had a great deal to offer Genoa – if not Doria himself.

The question of Doria's involvement can be illuminated by recalling the Genoese dependence on their trade with Chios – deep in the Aegean

---

[1] Merriman, *The Rise of the Spanish Empire*, vol. III, p. 324. Properly known as Hızır Re'is, Barbarossa acquired the *nom de guerre*, originally shared with his elder brother Aruj, from the vivid red facial hair which the two brothers possessed. Aruj was killed in battle by the Spanish after his flight from Tlemcen in 1518 and the nickname, 'Redbeard', was left in sole possession of the younger brother. See Henry Kahane and Andreas Tietze, *The Lingua Franca in the Levant* (Urbana, Illinois, 1958), p. 19. To the *nom de guerre* of Barbarossa was prefixed the title of Khair-ad-din, defender of the faith, usually shortened to Khaireddin by western writers.

and left in Genoese hands at Ottoman sufferance. The extent of his personal economic interest is unknown, but it is difficult to believe that the Prince of Genoa was insensitive to the fate of Chios. There is no evidence that he was other than a sincere Genoese patriot. The economic situation of Genoa, in which the Chios trade in gum mastic, alum, salt and pitch played no small part, was therefore of direct interest to him.[1] Secondly, even if he were not personally involved it is obvious that many of the *Alberghi*[2] (upon whom he was dependent for political support in the maze of family alliances which dominated Genoese politics) had an important stake in the trade.

If Andrea Doria's fleet 'shielded' Chios from the power of the Turk, as Philip Argenti, a recognized expert on the subject, believes,[3] then it was done through concessions of one kind or another arranged through secret negotiations of the sort which took place before Prevesa. Doria's squadron was obviously incapable of shielding Chios in any direct military sense and the island's fortifications were virtually nonexistent.

The Ottomans clearly did not leave Chios unmolested out of good will for Genoa – a member of a coalition openly at war with them. The Genoese corporation which ruled Chios at Ottoman sufferance got a great deal from the island directly, the Ottomans (aside from an annual tribute which was three years in arrears in 1536) nothing; but the same Genoese corporation controlled the bulk of tin imports into the Ottoman Empire, a fact of immense military significance.[4] If the cannon foundries of the *Tophane* were directly dependent upon English tin which they could get only through Genoese entrepreneurs, Genoa clearly had a great deal to offer the Ottoman Empire – or a great deal with which to threaten it. Just what Doria may have offered and obtained in return is a matter of speculation. Certainly there was a large enough gap between the Venetian objectives and those of his patron Charles V to leave considerable room for maneuver in the negotiations over Genoese interests, and there is no

[1] Philip P. Argenti, *The Occupation of Chios by the Genoese and Their Administration of the Island 1346–1566*, vol. I (Cambridge, 1958), pp. 482–90.

[2] The *Alberghi* were family alliances formed beneath the name of one of the original Genoese families with a patent of nobility. See Argenti, *The Occupation of Chios*, pp. 332–3. There were a total of 28 *Alberghi*.

[3] The reference is from Argenti, *The Occupation of Chios*, pp. 326–8, and particularly the entry in the index under 'Doria, Andrea', p. 684.

[4] For the tribute (10,000 Venetian ducats), Argenti, *The Occupation of Chios*, pp. 221, 268, 319, 352. My source for Genoese control of Ottoman tin imports is William H. McNeill, *Venice: The Hinge of Europe, 1081–1797* (Chicago, 1974), ch. 4, pp. 135 ff., on information from Halil Inalcik. I am indebted to Professor McNeill for having allowed me to view his incisive and highly informative manuscript prior to publication.

reason to believe that his discussions with Barbarossa centered on problems other than these – or that they are necessarily evidence of double dealing.

This interpretation stems too from the fact that most of what happened at Prevesa can be explained in straightforward military terms when analyzed within the proper conceptual framework. The only exception is Doria's late appearance in the Adriatic, which admittedly seems to form a strong case against him on the surface. Late appearance, however, seems to have been a common Spanish and Genoese trait – Don Juan of Austria was almost equally late in 1571.

The Holy League of Spain, Venice and the Papal States had been formed in February of 1538; yet Doria's fleet failed to make its appearance at Corfu, the designated rendezvous, until 7 September, almost three months after the Papal contingent had joined the Venetian fleet there. By the time he appeared on the scene it should have been obvious that only through good luck could anything of consequence be accomplished.

Before reaching a conclusion, though, a general chronological review is in order. During the late 1530s gradually worsening relations between Venice and the Ottoman Empire were leading inexorably toward war. Meanwhile, in 1536, Francis I of France delivered one of his periodic attacks on the Spanish positions in northern Italy. Perhaps with the consequent diversion of Habsburg attention in mind, Suleiman I mounted a major expedition in the Adriatic the following year. It was primarily aimed, however, not at the Habsburgs, but at the vital Venetian island fortress of Corfu directly astride the narrow neck of the Adriatic.

We can only guess about Suleiman's ultimate strategic goals. Lutfi Paşa's cavalry raid into Apulia, launched in July 1537 in conjunction with the attack on Corfu, suggests that he may have had in mind a repetition of Mehmed II's attack on Italy in 1480, capped by the capture of Otranto and terminated by the struggle for succession following his untimely death the following year. The capture of Corfu would have paved the way for an invasion of southern Italy. In addition, it would have slipped an economic noose around Venice's neck by placing a block astride her primary commercial artery. Finally, a Muslim fleet based on Corfu would have made naval cooperation between Spain and Venice extremely difficult.

But developments in the art of fortification ruined the Ottoman scheme. Sixteen years earlier Rhodes, considerably closer to the Ottoman logistical bases and without any real hope of relief by sea, had proved a long and expensive conquest. Though they have received little attention for it, Venetian fortress designers, perhaps spurred by the shock of the loss of

Coron and Modon in the Morea to Ottoman cannon in 1500,[1] responded
quickly and well to the rise of effective siege artillery in the first decades of
the sixteenth century. We must suppose, therefore, that the fortifications
which the Ottomans encountered at Corfu in 1537 were quite comparable
in strength to those of Rhodes. Furthermore, they were within easy reach
of Venetian relieving squadrons. After a brief and bloody siege Suleiman
drew off. It was apparent that the direct approach, however desirable
strategically, was not tactically feasible.

The scene was now set for the campaign of 1538. The apparent Ottoman
objective was to drive up the Dalmatian coast, capturing as many important places as possible in order to dominate the Venetian recruiting
grounds for soldiers and oarsmen, thus continuing the slow process of
demographic strangulation which had been going on since the capture of
Negropont in 1479. Suleiman did not take the field in person in 1538,
but entrusted the campaign to his Kapudan Paşa, Khaireddin Barbarossa.

The common danger forced consummation of the so-called Holy
League of Venice, Spain and the Papal States in February of 1538. The
terms of the alliance were quite specific with regard to naval matters –
Andrea Doria was given command of the combined fleet and Corfu was
named as the rendezvous point.

Well before the Christian fleet effected its belated September rendezvous, Barbarossa, joined by Muslim contingents from North Africa, had
brought the Ottoman fleet around the Morea and up the west coast of
Greece. He held short of the outnumbered Venetian squadrons at Corfu.
The better than two to one numerical odds in the Muslims' favor reduced
the Venetians to the purely passive role of watching and waiting. But
Barbarossa also was effectively paralyzed in the strategic sense if not the
tactical.

If he laid siege to a major place he would almost certainly have to commit
a considerable portion of his force ashore, thus leaving his fleet unprepared
to face a sudden attack by the Venetians – let alone the entire allied fleet
if it should join up in the meantime. A sudden and resolute attack by a
quite inferior naval force upon an opponent who had committed most of
his guns (bearing in mind that his best were reserved for sieges), soldiers,
and oarsmen to the prosecution of a siege ashore could be devastating.

[1] See Sydney N. Fisher, *The Foreign Relations of Turkey 1481–1512* (Urbana, Ill., 1948), pp.
75–8. The brevity of these sieges makes it plain that the Venetian fortresses were inadequately
built to withstand the tremendous battering force of the Ottoman siege guns. This impression
is reinforced by a contemporary depiction of Coron reproduced in Vice Admiral William L.
Rodgers, *Naval Warfare Under Oars* (Annapolis, 1939), which shows a typical medieval
fortress with high, vertical curtain walls. Such construction would have been terribly vulnerable to artillery fire.

This was a danger well known to Barbarossa and one which he was not likely to risk. The Venetians were much too close at hand and much too good at the game. An attack on a minor place, holding back enough force to stand off a naval attack in relief, would have wasted men and munitions and was unlikely to yield any gain worth the cost. The art of fortification was too well advanced by 1538 to permit quick, easy gains.

Thus the Ottoman and Venetian fleets very nearly stalemated one another. Barbarossa did derive the major advantage of relative freedom of movement from his numerical superiority prior to the arrival of the Spanish and Papal contingents. While the Venetians were effectively pinned to Corfu, he could move about at will, using the available time to pick his spot for the confrontation which he knew would come soon.

According to the best estimates Barbarossa's fleet consisted of about 90 galleys and 50 galiots.[1] The Venetian squadron at Corfu under Vicenzo Capello had 55 galleys and was joined on 17 June by 27 galleys of the Pope under Marco Grimani.[2] Doria, the designated commander-in-chief, arrived at the head of 49 Genoese and Spanish galleys on 7 September, bringing the Christian total up to about 130 galleys.[3] We should note that all of the Christian total consisted of full-sized war galleys, while many of the warships in Barbarossa's total of 140 oared fighting craft were galiots unfit to stand against galleys in a formal, head-on engagement.

With this reinforcement the Allied fleet, with a clear-cut superiority in

---

[1] Olesa Muñido, *La Organización Naval*, vol. II, p. 1118, says that Barbarossa had '160 ships: 87 galleys among them', evidently echoing the figures given by Chalcondyle, *Histoire Générale des Turcs*, vol. I (Paris, 1662), pp. 559–60. Chalcondyle, however, adds about 30 large galiots 'equal in power to galleys' to the 87 galleys. Haji Kahlifeh, *The History of the Maritime Wars of the Turks*, James Mitchell trans. (London, 1831), p. 62, gives Barbarossa credit for 122 'light galleys'. Merriman, *The Rise of the Spanish Empire*, vol. III, p. 325, n. 1, cites in full a brief contemporary Spanish account of the battle which gives Barbarossa 140 'good galleys'. Knolles and Rycaut, *The Turkish History*, p. 467, state that Barbarossa sailed with 130 galleys. This count, based on Knolles' sixteenth-century Ottoman sources, is important in its general confirmation of our other sources. Knolles, whose *Generall Historie of the Turks* . . . first came out in 1603, wrote almost within living memory of Prevesa. It is probable, taking all of the above into account, that the observed Spanish total of 140 included numbers of North African galiots, some of them nearly as long as a galley but lower in the water, less heavily manned and therefore – Chalcondyle to the contrary – at a serious disadvantage in a head-on frontal clash. This would explain Haji Kahlifeh's lower total. Mitchell almost certainly rendered *kadirga* as 'light galley' while Haji Kahlifeh apparently ignored the *kalite*, galiots, altogether in his total. This would give Barbarossa about 90 galleys, 30 large galiots and 20 ordinary ones.

[2] Haji Kahlifeh, *The History of the Maritime Wars of the Turks*, James Mitchell trans. (London, 1831), p. 62, gives the Venetians 70 galleys, the Pope 30 and the Knights of St John 10, for a total of 110.

[3] Haji Kahlifeh, *Ibid.* p. 62, gives Doria 52 galleys and states that there were 80 Spanish and Portuguese roundships of some size, 10 large Venetian carracks and 300 'other ships'.

fighting strength,[1] was ready to move. They found themselves in much the same strategic bind as that faced by Barbarossa before Doria's arrival. It would have been unwise to use the considerable Christian strength to reduce some important place while an intact Ottoman fleet was ready to pounce on their rear in an unguarded moment. The Turkish fleet had to be defeated, driven off or immobilized before anything could be accomplished on land. Doria, no doubt hard pressed by the Venetians to seek a general fleet action, sortied from Corfu on 21 September, just one day before the Imperial support contingent of round ships arrived carrying 16,000 troops and a considerable quantity of artillery.[2]

The Allies found Barbarossa's fleet, as he no doubt intended that they should, inside the Gulf of Prevesa protected by the guns of the fortress of Prevesa and Muslim batteries on both sides of the entrance[3] (see Map 2). This position gave the Ottomans an enormous advantage.

The curving entrance to the Gulf was narrow – less than 800 yards across at the narrowest point.[4] Even ignoring the effect of artillery fire from the batteries on both sides of the entrance there was obviously insufficient room in the channel for any considerable number of Christian galleys to deploy in line abreast. In order to force the entrance, the Christian galleys would have had to issue from the channel in disorder and in column while the Turkish galleys, with greater elbow room inside the Gulf, could await them in well ordered ranks and overwhelm them one by one.

But the Muslim cannon dominating the entrance prevented the

[1] Even if we ignore the probability that some 50 of Barbarossa's 140 'galleys' were actually galiots the advantage would still have rested with the Christians. The bulk of the Papal, Spanish and Genoese contingents consisted of the heavier western galleys, ideal for the head-on fighting of a formal fleet engagement in line abreast, while the Muslim galleys – let alone the galiots – had lower hulls and fewer fighting men. R. C. Anderson, *Naval Wars in the Levant* (Princeton, 1952), p. 4, states that Doria fought with a numerical advantage of roughly three to two. This seems a fairly accurate estimate to me and agrees well with the tone of Knolles and Rycaut's account, pp. 464–7, which makes Barbarossa's numerical inferiority clear.

[2] Merriman, *The Rise of the Spanish Empire*, vol. III, p. 323, says 2,500 cannon, but this figure undoubtedly includes all shipboard cannon including relatively small swivel pieces.

[3] Knolles and Rycaut, *The Turkish History*, p. 463. Knolles' description of Barbarossa's situation is worth repeating: 'For Barbarossa then lay with the Turk's Fleet in the Bay of Ambracia [Prevesa] where he had on both sides placed divers pieces of Great Ordnance to have sunk them in their coming in.'

[4] This measurement, actually a shade under 800 yards, was taken from the Department of the Navy, Oceanographic Office Chart 3961, Mediterranean, Albania–Greece, Corfu Channel to Nisis Proti (1:250,000). A contemporary but rather rough map of the Gulf of Prevesa by Giovanni B. Camocio in the Museo Storico Navale, Venice, suggests that the channel was somewhat narrower in the sixteenth century and that the narrowest part lay right at the entrance to the Adriatic opposite the castle of Prevesa rather than farther back as it does now.

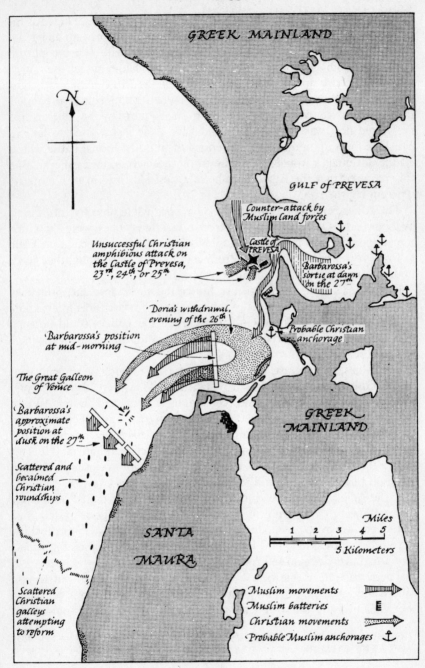

Map 2 The battle of Prevesa, 27 September 1538

Christians from enjoying the same advantage in reverse. The Muslim galleys could issue out of the channel in column and form up along the shore under the guns of the fortress in relative security. They could be prevented from doing this only by a vigorous counterattack put in at considerable risk and with no assurance that the Muslim galleys would not simply pull back into the channel until a better opportunity presented itself. In practice there was little point to such a move by the Allies. Since the Allied fleet was stronger it would have done just as well to let the Muslims form up unmolested and entice them into a formal battle where all the advantages would have gone to the heavier western galleys.[1] But this required that the Allied fleet be in a position to form in line itself. Therein lay the rub.

The Allies could not afford to tackle a worthwhile objective elsewhere as long as the Ottoman fleet was free to interfere. They were therefore forced to maintain a reasonably close blockade of the entrance to the Gulf to Prevesa to prevent the Turks from coming out. In so doing they were under a number of serious disadvantages.

Barbarossa's fleet, with a secure hinterland to its rear and protected from direct attack by the guns of the fortress of Prevesa, was free to pull up against the shore of the Gulf in security. The galleys could be kept fully victualled and watered and the oarsmen rested and many of the men sent ashore.

The Allies, by contrast, had to maintain a close watch on the entrance to the Gulf to guard against surprise attack. They were therefore constantly expending energy and consuming stores and water. While Barbarossa could bide his time and be ready to move at full efficiency at an hour's notice, Doria was forced to accept a continuous drain on his resources. His situation is summed up by the Oriental aphorism, 'He who rides a tiger finds it difficult to dismount.' Having got in close to blockade the Gulf of Prevesa he found it difficult indeed to get away.

If the Allied fleet dropped its guard momentarily or pulled back from the entrance to the Gulf in disorder, Barbarossa's fleet, rested and victualled, was ready to pounce. To cap it all, the Christian anchorages were fully exposed to a hard blow from the north-west, something which Doria had every reason to expect so late in the season.

There was one viable course of action open to Doria: to put troops ashore and force the Muslim positions dominating the channel, replacing the Muslim batteries with Christian ones. This, at least, would have

---

[1] The tactical ramifications of regional variations in galley design are examined fully in ch. 5. Here it is enough to say that the western galleys had a clear-cut advantage in a formal, head-on battle.

stabilized the immediate tactical situation. An initial attempt was made to do just that. According to a nearly contemporary account based on Ottoman sources: 'Doria had with his . . . Gallies begun to besiege Prevesa . . . and landing some of his soldiers, with three great pieces of artillery so battered the Castle of Prevesa, that he was like enough to have taken it, had not the Turks from Aetolia come to relieve it with a strong Power both of Horse and Foot.'[1] This land engagement, perhaps the most critical action of the campaign, has completely escaped the attention of modern historians. With their eyes fixed firmly upon the actions of the opposing fleets at sea in the North Atlantic tradition, they have missed the point that Prevesa was not a naval campaign in the orthodox sense, but an amphibious one.

The appearance of strong local Ottoman land forces placed the Allied commanders in a quandary. The general of the Christian land forces, the Spanish Viceroy of Naples, favored going at the Muslim positions hammer and tongs: 'to assault the Castle of Prevesa; which once taken, and their [i.e. the Christian] ordnance there planted, the Enemie's Fleet might in the Bay, be utterly defeated.'[2] His logic, however, did not prevail. For reasons which are not entirely clear, no further Christian attempt was made to force the Muslim positions. Perhaps the Imperial troop commanders were reluctant to be put ashore so late in the season knowing that the fleet might be driven off by a sudden blow, leaving them stranded in the face of an immense concentration of Muslim force. This was a valid concern and one which Doria seems to have emphasized in the Christian council of war. Perhaps the Muslim land forces were simply too strong. Conceivably the Christian inactivity was the pay-off in some agreement between Doria and Barbarossa. This, however is pure speculation.

There are indications that Barbarossa tried the same kind of thing in reverse, moving a force of infantry across the neck of land separating his anchorage from that of Doria[3] (see Map 2). They do not seem to have been able to establish themselves in the face of the Christian fleet's artillery in sufficient strength to mount a battery capable of driving the Allies from their anchorage. But the demonstration must have made its

---

[1] Knolles and Rycaut, *The Turkish History*, p. 463.

[2] Knolles and Rycaut, *The Turkish History*, p. 463. Also see Merriman, *The Rise of the Spanish Empire*, vol. III, pp. 324–5.

[3] Haji Kahlifeh, *The History of the Maritime Wars of the Turks*, pp. 62–3. Although somewhat distorted in detail, Kahlifeh's account is clear in its general outline and its chronology of events. He goes so far as to imply that the Muslims succeeded in implanting their batteries along the shore opposite the Christian anchorage. E. Bradford, *The Sultan's Admiral* (London, 1969), p. 171, draws the same general conclusions about the Muslim land action from E. Hamilton Currey's *Sea Wolves of the Mediterranean* (London, c. 1903), but states that the artillery of the Christian roundships drove the Muslims back.

point: Muslim infantry could and would disembark from the fleet to assist the troops of the local *sanjak beys* in preventing any similar Christian move.

Viewed from this perspective, it is not necessary to invoke Doria's alleged treason to explain the outcome of Prevesa in the narrowly tactical sense. So long as Barbarossa held his ground and prevented the establishment of hostile batteries ashore, his position was secure. The Allied fleet could maintain its necessary watch over the mouth of the Gulf for only so long. Sooner or later it would have to withdraw for logistic reasons. If it withdrew in anything less than perfect order when the time came – an unlikely contingency in view of the intense distrust between the Venetians and Genoese – Barbarossa would have an opportunity to strike.

In fact, this is precisely what happened. The wonder is that the Christian loss was so light. The strength of a galley fleet ordered for battle stemmed largely from its ability to maintain its line abreast formation. We shall dwell on this at length in our treatment of Djerba and Lepanto. If a galley fleet was able to catch another by surprise in a disordered state the effect was likely to be overwhelming, a generalization amply confirmed by the results of Djerba in 1560.

Doria had arrived off the mouth of the Gulf of Prevesa on 2 September. Barbarossa came out to oppose the Allied fleet about three weeks later, probably on the 25th; but both fleets formed into a solid battle line and the result was a stand-off with virtually no contact.[1] We may take Barbarossa's inconclusive sortie as evidence that, at least in his opinion, the Allied fleet was nearing the end of its logistic tether.

No more than two days later, probably sometime on the afternoon of the 26th, Doria decided to throw in the sponge. Taking advantage of a northerly wind, the Allied fleet slipped its anchors and attempted to get away unseen in the early morning hours of the 27th. The need for a covert night departure – which made effective formation keeping impossible – speaks volumes for the gravity of the tactical situation in which the Allies found themselves. Under the circumstances, Doria's decision was the best possible. His fault lay not in his technique for dismounting, but in having got on the Tiger in the first place.

The wind, however, did not hold. Dawn found the Christian fleet strung out to the south along the flank of Santa Maura with the largest and slowest of the round ships to the rear and most of the galleys so far downwind that they were unable to come to their aid. At this point

---

[1] Haji Kahlifeh, *The History of the Maritime Wars of the Turks*, p. 63. Kahlifeh does not specify this date, but the order of events is clear.

Barbarossa struck. He moved cautiously at first, for he could see only the foremost of the Christian ships. Many of these were well armed – the Great Galleon of Venice under Alessandro Bondulmier was nearest to the Muslims – and for all Barbarossa knew Doria had managed to maintain formation during the night and was lying just beyond the roundships, formed on line in superior strength. If this were the case, and it would be hours before Barbarossa knew for sure, then the out-numbered Muslims, disordered in passing around the straggling Christian round ships, would have been fair game for Doria's heavier and more numerous galleys moving down in a solid line abreast. Barbarossa seized upon this uncertain and dangerous opportunity with great resolution, a fact which speaks eloquently for his great ability as a commander.

We are fortunate in having a nearly contemporary and technically knowledgeable account of the ensuing action by Richard Knolles, a sixteenth-century Englishman who spent a good deal of time in the Ottoman Empire and who drew heavily on Ottoman sources. His description of the battle of Prevesa contains technical details of undoubted authenticity which are found nowhere else and is so perceptive and revealing as to bear repeating in full:

Auria [Doria] keeping on his [southward] course was come to Leucade [Santa Maura], when the Enemie's Fleet was descried out of the top of Bondulmierus Galleon, to be come out of the Bay [the Gulf of Prevesa], and to make towards them, keeping close to the shore; which manner of Course the crafty Turk, misdoubting his own strength, held of purpose, that if he should chance to be overmatched by the Christians, he might turn the Prow of his Gallies upon them and running their Poops aground, so to land his men and great Ordnance, and from Land as he might defend his Fleet; accounting it a less loss (if the worst should chance) to lose the Gallies than the Men.[1]

It would be difficult to find a more revealing passage on sixteenth-century galley warfare. The defensive tactic which Knolles described – beaching the galleys stern first so that their guns would still bear out to sea and their non-fighting men could be taken off – was as basic to six-teenth-century galley warfare as the line ahead was to eighteenth-century naval warfare; yet no subsequent author in English has mentioned it. The relatively slight importance attached to the galleys themselves and the great importance given to the 'great ordnance' and to the men is an emphasis utterly alien to the naval traditions of the North Atlantic. The Mediterranean emphasis is, in fact, almost the exact reverse of the standing byword of the Anglo-American naval tradition, 'Don't give up the ship'. We will have a great deal to say about both of these points in the following chapter.

[1] Knolles and Rycaut, *The Turkish History*, p. 464.

In the event, the Allied fleet was badly spread out and in disorder. This was just as Barbarossa had hoped. Forming his fleet in a loose crescent formation, Barbarossa moved down on the Christian stragglers:

Both the wings of his fleet had, a little before sun set, begun in divers places to encounter with the Christians; some were in vain still assailing Bondulmierus his Great Galleon; others with their great ordnance had so sore beaten two tall ships [carrying Spanish infantry] that they were given up for lost.[1]

Knolles, in the above passage, makes two more points deserving of comment. The first of these is the slowness with which the battle developed. Barbarossa had probably sortied at first light, but was just coming to grips with the Christian fleet at sunset, having taken all day to cover a distance of no more than twenty miles. The galley's appearance of speed is deceptive – human muscle could only drive a vessel so fast and the need to maintain formation slowed fleets of galleys even more. Finally, we should note Knolles' reference to the galleys' 'great ordnance'. More than one modern historian has blindly recited the mistaken view that galleys had only light armament, holding the introduction of effective heavy artillery on shipboard to have been a uniquely northern development – the doctrine of the ship-killing gun in a different guise. These two points will occupy a good bit of our attention in the concluding chapters.

Returning to our narrative, the Allied fleet was very nearly done in completely by a combination of shifting winds, poor tactical and strategic judgment on the Christian side, and the consummate skill and decisiveness of Khaireddin Barbarossa. A contemporary Spanish account puts it succinctly:

[As was] Passing Andrea with his fleet near Santa Maura, which is an island, Barbarossa sortied from the Gulf with his fleet and came out against ours. Andrea was forced to stand by [helplessly] because the wind fell calm and the roundships were unable to move. And Barbarossa took the wind and began to bombard our roundships and they to reply to him. He sent to the bottom one of our ships with 300 Spanish soldiers. He took a galley of the Pope without resistance. He took another of the Venetians. He destroyed another Vizcayan roundship in which were 400 Spanish soldiers.[2]

The modern writer is unable to improve on this somber and straightforward tale of disaster. Only a final shift in the wind about nightfall allowed the Christian survivors to pull clear. The Christian losses were relatively light – a modern author maintains that only seven galleys were lost, discreetly neglecting to mention the roundships which were hardest

[1] Knolles and Rycaut, *The Turkish History*, p. 464.
[2] This is from the document given by Merriman, *The Rise of the Spanish Empire*, vol. III, p. 325. These losses are confirmed by Chalcondyle, *Histoire Générale des Turcs*, vol. I (Paris, 1662), p. 560.

hit[1] – but the Allied fleet had been outmaneuvered and badly cut up. The only bright spot was the successful resistance of the Great Galleon of Venice, a slow sailer which had been one of the first and hardest hit by the Muslim attack. She held out all day against repeated attacks, apparently doing considerable damage among her assailants with her heavy artillery armament.[2]

Whether Doria could have formed his fleet into line and moved north to rescue the stragglers is doubtful. From the moment that the Allied fleet appeared off the mouth of the Gulf of Prevesa it was in trouble.

Barbarossa had gained and held the upper hand through his tactical mastery of galley warfare. If Doria deliberately prejudiced the outcome of the battle, his treachery was not of the crudely obvious sort. His bargain, if he swung one with the Turk at all, was probably simply to arrive late at Corfu. The Turk had convincingly demonstrated his superiority in the mechanics of galley warfare and – just possibly – in secret diplomacy as well. We may rest assured that Barbarossa found the uncertainty which Doria's ambiguous conduct had created as satisfying as we find it frustrating.

Ironically, the Ottoman fleet was subsequently decimated by a sudden storm which drove it up against the Albanian coast with the loss of 70 galleys and galiots though apparently without great loss of life.[3] The Allies who had retreated north into the Adriatic, subsequently captured Castelnuovo near their base of Cattaro on 27 October after a short siege, leaving a garrison of 4,000 Spanish infantry behind.[4] Corfu survived unmolested. But this transitory success should not deceive us. The result of Prevesa had heightened Venetian distrust of Spanish intentions in general and of Andrea Doria in particular. The Holy League was unworkable.

Barbarossa reappeared in the Adriatic the following summer at the head of a fleet of 200 ships and retook Castelnuovo after a siege which lasted from 12 July to 7 August. This focusing of Ottoman power on a place which was held by an Imperial garrison – put there over Venetian objection – may have served as a hint to Venice that the Ottomans were prepared to offer them separate terms. The Venetians, too weak to oppose the Turk independently and with no confidence in their allies, sued for peace independently.

[1] C. W. C. Oman, *A History of the Art of War in the Sixteenth Century* (London, 1937), p. 692.
[2] Oman, *Ibid.* p. 692.
[3] Oman, *Ibid.* p. 693; Haji Kahlifeh, *The History of the Maritime Wars of the Turks*, p. 65. We have no indication of Barbarossa's manpower losses, which, in the light of the next year's events, were probably light.
[4] Merriman, *The Rise of the Spanish Empire*, vol. III, p. 328.

Our investigation of the campaign and battle of Prevesa reinforces our previous suppositions about the Mediterranean system of naval warfare at sea. The fight off Jiddah in 1517 showed the defensive strength of the combination of war galley and shore batteries which formed the tactical heart of that system. Prevesa showed how that defensive strength could be turned into victory over a stronger opponent.

Beyond this, our study of Prevesa provides a concrete illustration of two basic characteristics of Mediterranean warfare at sea. The first of these is essentially political. The motivations and objectives of sixteenth-century Mediterranean naval commanders were not always narrowly military in nature. We cannot evaluate them as if they were.

The second point is more narrowly tactical. Engagements between galley fleets were not ordinarily 'naval battles' in the classic sense. Particularly where large fleets of galleys were involved, Mediterranean sea battles were normally fought near land. The configuration of the nearest shoreline, who occupied it and in what strength – all of these were critical in determining the victor in a galley fight. Mediterranean naval warfare was not purely 'naval', but amphibious in nature. An analysis which ignores the land engagements which were an essential part of most Mediterranean naval campaigns misses at least half the story. Of this there is no better example than Prevesa.

But while our investigation of Prevesa has provided a classic example of the way in which galley fleets operated, it has left unanswered the question why the galley and galley fleets dominated the Mediterranean. Why did the war galley prevail there and not the broadside sailing warship? We will address ourselves to this question in the following chapter.

THE MEDITERRANEAN SYSTEM OF WARFARE AT SEA: GEOGRAPHIC ORIGINS AND OPERATIONAL CHARACTERISTICS

Our investigation of the battles of Jiddah and Prevesa indicates that Mediterranean warfare at sea was not naval warfare in the orthodox sense, but that it was a form of amphibious warfare in which the relationship of the fleet to the shore was at least as important as its relationship to the opposing fleet. This was true both tactically and strategically. We have hinted at the reasons for this.

The galley could not, for logistic reasons, stand out to sea for extended periods of time. Since it could not, because of this limitation, maintain a continuous blockade, the galley fleet was unable to exercise control of the sea in the Mahanian sense. Defeat of the enemy fleet at sea was dangerous to attempt, difficult to bring about, and not necessarily productive if accomplished. In order to obtain decisive results the galley fleet had to capture the enemy fleet's bases. It was limited in its ability to do so by the logistic limitations which we have mentioned and by the seasonal character of Mediterranean galley warfare. All of these factors were closely interrelated.

Tied strategically to its bases by the need for frequent revictualing and to the land by the need to take on water at even more frequent intervals, the galley fleet was tied even more closely to the shoreline by tactical considerations. The effects of this dependence were mitigated – at least in Mediterranean waters – by the galley's amphibious capability. The logistic burden imposed by its large crew and its narrow hull with small internal capacity forced the galley to touch shore frequently, but the oared mobility which they provided allowed it to work close inshore to considerable tactical and strategic advantage.

This suggests a closely forged relationship between the galley fleet, its bases, and the shoreline along which it operated. An extended examination of this relationship will occupy the bulk of this chapter. This is appropriate since it was the nature of this relationship which established the strategic and tactical parameters of Mediterranean warfare at sea.

But before turning to the analysis of the internal workings of the Mediterranean system of warfare at sea – largely free of outside inter-

ference during our period of concern – we must establish the viability of
that system in the face of external challenge. We have made a start in this
direction by describing the results of the first – and for a time the only –
direct clash between the Mediterranean system of armed conflict at sea and
the broadside sailing ship of the North Atlantic. But our examination of
the reasons for the Portuguese defeat before Jiddah in 1517 touched only a
portion of the historical problem. Our initial discussion presupposed that
the system of armed conflict at sea based on the galley was the only viable
one in Mediterranean waters. We will examine the validity of this assumption and in so doing explain why oared fighting ships were developed in
the Mediterranean long before the appearance of specialized warships
elsewhere.

Having thus established a logical foundation, we can address ourselves
to one of the major questions which inspired our thesis: How did the war
galley continue to dominate Mediterranean waters for almost two centuries
after the appearance of effective heavy artillery? The logical starting point
would appear to be an analysis of the geographic and climatic conditions
which fostered the development of the war galley in the Mediterranean;
but the historiography of naval warfare attaches certain disadvantages to
this approach. Almost without exception, naval historians have operated
under the assumption that the broadside sailing warship was the logical
and inevitable consequence of the development of effective heavy artillery.
The non-appearance of the broadside sailing warship in the Mediterranean
is therefore attributed to traditional resistance to changing technology.
It is implicitly assumed that the Mediterranean nations would have been
better off if they had turned to the broadside sailing warship much earlier
than they did.

It is necessary to disprove this assumption before explaining how
Mediterranean conditions fostered the development of the war galley.
We shall therefore begin by showing why the war galley did *not* develop
in the North Atlantic, a question which can be explained in terms of local
geographic and climatic peculiarities. The discussion of geographic factors
leads naturally into a discussion of the conditions which led to the
development of the war galley in the Mediterranean. Finally – for the
question is no longer a relatively simple matter of geography and weather
patterns – we will suggest an explanation of why the broadside sailing
warship did not appear in the Mediterranean until long after the development of effective heavy artillery.

As the sixteenth century dawned mastery of the wind and waves was
far less complete anywhere than it was to be a century later almost everywhere. It was by no means clear that the final solution to the problems of

maritime commerce would be a general, trans-oceanic one. A highly specialized solution based upon local conditions had already been perfected in the relatively benign and undemanding waters of the Mediterranean. This solution gave the Mediterranean nations an impressive lead in organization and continued to be pursued successfully for some time to come. The specialization which made the Mediterranean solution less flexible in other areas gave it added strength on its home grounds and in areas such as the Red Sea and the Caribbean where similar conditions prevailed. The product of some three centuries of evolutionary development, the Mediterranean system of maritime trade and warfare was, by the sixteenth century, perfectly adapted to Mediterranean conditions.

Behind the early development of Mediterranean commerce and methods of warfare lay geographic realities. Northern waters were far more hostile than those of the Mediterranean. The mariners of the north began the sixteenth century far closer to failure in the struggle against the sea for bare survival than their Mediterranean rivals. Most of their energies were still devoted to that struggle, with the result that the organization and level of northern commercial and military activity at sea were still far below the standards of the Mediterranean. Specialized warships were virtually unknown in northern waters. Most of the effort of the northern shipwright went, of necessity, into meeting the demands of the sea. The state of his art and level of his financial support left him little leeway to introduce specialized features to give his ships advantage in battle. The addition of temporary fighting castles to the superstructures of merchant ships was as far as the northern shipwright had gone, except perhaps in Portugal. Until the age of gunpowder, the specialized warship was, for technical as well as for fiscal reasons, an impracticality in northern waters. The challenge of the northern waters eventually produced fleets of warships able to dominate the sea in the Mahanian sense, but in the year 1500 the sea still dominated the ships. Meanwhile, in the comparatively placid waters of the Mediterranean the specialized warship had long been a reality.

Before gunpowder, the only decisive maneuver which could successfully terminate a naval engagement was boarding: the occupation of the enemy's decks with your own troops. In theory there were two other alternatives: fire and ramming below the waterline to sink. But both of these presupposed a desire to destroy the enemy vessel rather than capture it. This in turn supposed a higher level of organization and financial support than was prevalent until well into the modern era. From the fall of the Byzantine Empire as a major power almost until the advent of the industrial revolution governments could not afford to support fleets of warships which were good only for purely destructive purposes and the lure of prize money exercised a powerful and frequently dominant influence on military activity at sea. A specialized vessel built to ram its opponents below the waterline was hardly adept at capturing prizes. This consideration alone would have made it highly unattractive to the six-teenth-century naval commander. It was generally expected, or at least hoped, that naval forces would partially pay for themselves. There also seem to have been valid technical reasons for the abandonment of the true ram sometime during the Dark Ages: the projecting underwater ram undoubtedly made a ship difficult to beach and made no positive contribu-tion to seaworthiness. Deleting the underwater ram resulted in a lighter, stronger prow. R. C. Anderson has advanced the sensible theory that the development of Greek fire and of a means of projecting it for some distance out over the bows allowed Byzantine designers to do away with the true ram since Greek fire effectively fulfilled the underwater ram's sole function – destruction of the enemy ship.[1]

Fire was always a possibility; but fire was the weapon of desperation. The means of spreading it – fire-arrows and hand-thrown faggots – were unreliable, short range, or both. These could be employed with a reason-able expectation of success only against an enemy who was pulled up close alongside. There was therefore an excellent chance of the conflagration spreading to both sides since the dry timber, cordage and pitch of which ships were built made them virtual tinderboxes. This was precisely what occurred at Zonchio in 1499, an early Mediterranean attempt to solve the problems of tactical employment posed by the broadside battery firing warship which we shall examine following this chapter. With the loss of the secret of Greek fire in the sack of Constantinople in 1204, there was no way in which fire could be reliably and safely controlled and directed as a weapon.[2] This problem was not solved in the sixteenth century.

---

[1] *Oared Fighting Ships* (London, 1962), p. 39.

[2] The story of the discovery and disappearance of Greek fire is one of the great riddles of history. There can be no doubt that the Byzantine Greeks possessed a liquid incendiary of unusual effectiveness. The secret of its manufacture was subsequently lost. None of the facile explanations of Greek fire as a dry mixture based on red phosphorus or a liquid one based on naphtha or petroleum stand up under close examination. These explanations come from the confusion of Greek fire with other and quite different substances, principally 'wild fire', a dry incendiary mixture used in the Middle Ages. Greek fire was expelled from pump-like pro-jectors by the action of water, which also ignited it. Once ignited, water poured on it served to intensify its burning. There is no known mixture which possesses these properties. When we consider the extreme complexity of the chemistry of black powder, still not fully under-stood (see Appendix 2), we can understand how the composition of such a substance, undoubtedly far more complicated than gunpowder, could be lost and not subsequently rediscovered. The best technical discourse on the employment of Greek fire, and the only educated speculation about its possible composition, is to be found in William L. Hime, *The Origin of Artillery* (London, 1915).

Fire could be used as a last resort, and often was. But it was used with the knowledge that it was an equal hazard to friend and foe alike except under the most unusual of circumstances. Fireships could occasionally be used with great effect; but these required precisely the right conditions of wind and tide for their employment, and unflinching courage from their crews. They were also expensive and apt to miscarry under the best of conditions. Boarding alone remained.

The almost total predominance of this tactic for more than 300 years left a strong imprint on the way in which war at sea was conducted. This was particularly true in the Mediterranean where the prevailing conditions made boarding a peculiarly viable alternative. The necessity to board and the practicality of doing it gave birth to the galley.[1]

To board, it was not enough simply to overhaul an enemy ship, run up alongside and grapple. The attacker had to place his ship in firm contact with his victim, preferably at some weakly defended point, and hold there long enough for his men to get aboard. He had to get a good many of his fighting men over the enemy railing in the first rush to maximize his chances of overwhelming resistance at the point of contact. Then he had to hold his position for as long as needed to support them with missile fire and reinforcements – or to provide an avenue of retreat if needed – while they fought for control of the enemy decks.

If all of this could be accomplished considerable advantage accrued to the attacker, even if the ships and crews were evenly matched. This was particularly true if the attacking ship were specially designed for boarding and if the attacking party could make its assault from a part of the ship designed to facilitate the assault, usually through the provision of a raised platform. All of this placed a premium on tactical skill. Boarding has often been represented as a crude and 'unscientific' means of combat at sea; but this was true only of combat between sailing ships where boarding was generally a hit or miss affair.

The attacker's need to place a particular part of his ship against a precise location on his opponent's hull and then hold there demanded a degree of close-in maneuverability beyond that which sails could provide. Unless hopelessly outsailed, crippled, or in restricted waters, one sailing vessel could usually avoid with ease a boarding attempt by another for extended periods of time. This was because of the dependence of both attacker and attacked upon a source of power – the wind – which made movement in

[1] The term 'galley' has both a general and a specific meaning. In the sixteenth century the specific meaning applied to an oared ship of at least 21 or 22 rowing banks and at least three oarsmen to a bench. This meaning is normally used by modern writers. But 'galley' also had a general auxiliary meaning. 'Galley' in this sense meant 'warship', usually an oared warship, but sometimes a warship of almost any description.

certain directions difficult or impossible. By choosing his direction wisely, the commander under attack could effectively restrict his opponent's tactically useful choices of maneuver and thus evade his attack. It seems clear, therefore, that the peculiar tactical requirements of boarding could be met only by an oared vessel large enough to carry a boarding party of a size sufficient to overcome the defensive manpower of its victims. Oared vessels, however, were effectively restricted from use in northern waters

The reasons for this were many. First of all, the velocity of the tidal currents at many points along the French, English and Flemish coasts exceeds the maximum sustained speed of the best full-sized galley. A galley could maintain its maximum speed under oars of some seven knots for no more than twenty minutes and the best sustained speed which it could manage was only about three knots or a little more. This sort of performance left little leeway for battling the tides of the English Channel and the North Sea which run as fast as ten or twelve knots in places.[1] This essentially removed the oared vessel's greatest navigational advantage in the age before the perfection of sail, its ability to make port, a necessary advantage for specialized rowing craft as we shall presently see.

To be efficient under oars, a vessel must be relatively low-lying in the water; otherwise the oarsmen will have to use excessively long oars and work against an unfavorable mechanical advantage. It should be long and narrow in order to seat the maximum number of oarsmen in relation to its total displacement and to minimize hydrodynamic drag.[2] These require-ments are in direct conflict with the demands of the North Atlantic for a vessel capable of withstanding prolonged exposure to high winds and heavy seas. The difficulties of the four galleys which accompanied the Invincible Armada of 1588 should drive this point home.[3] Long, narrow hulls of low freeboard and no great depth are not noted for their sea-worthiness.

In addition, the large crews of specialized rowing vessels consumed provisions at a high rate. Since the long, slender hulls of such vessels were anything but spacious, they had to land frequently to take on stores. The requirement for water was even more critical: the supply carried by the

---

[1] See D. W. Waters, *The Rutters of the Sea* (New Haven, 1967), Appendix 1, 'The Tides, Moonlight and Tidal Prediction'.

[2] Adding length to a hull increases displacement and mass arithmetically. Adding breadth, assuming that the same cross-section is retained, increases displacement geometrically. Note the design of modern racing shells.

[3] None of the four galleys which sailed with the Armada from La Coruña on 21 July 1588 made it far enough to engage the English fleet. One strained its seams, parted company on the 26th, and eventually ran aground off Bayonne and broke up. The rest were driven into ports of opportunity in assorted stages of disrepair by a hard blow on the 29th. See Garrett Mattingly, *The Armada* (Boston, 1962), pp. 268-70.

typical sixteenth-century war galley was good for no more than two
weeks at most. Admiral W. L. Rodgers estimated that a galley could carry
no more than 20 days' supply of water. This meant that its cruising radius
was ten days at most. This, of course, varied, depending on how hot the
weather was and how much the oarsmen had to row. Figuring an absolute
minimum daily water requirement of two quarts per man, the typical
Mediterranean galley of the early sixteenth century with 144 oarsmen and
30 to 40 soldiers, sailors and officers would have needed about 90 gallons
of water a day. Thus a twenty-day period would have involved the consumption of at least 1,800 gallons of water, a considerable amount when
we consider the severe limitation on storage space.[1]

But ports and safe anchorages are relatively few and far between in
northern waters. Violent storms, heavy seas and adverse winds can come
up suddenly and without warning in all seasons. Ships sailing in northern
waters had to be prepared to run out to sea for weeks, or even months, to
ride out a hard blow which kept them from making port.

All of these factors combined to virtually preclude the use of specialized
rowing vessels in northern waters. They could be used there if the need
were great enough, but only occasionally or in a highly specialized role
operating close to their bases. The Spanish, under heavy pressure from
French commerce raiders in the Caribbean, successfully took galleys
across the Atlantic on several occasions.[2] Henry VIII of England at one
point experimented with a full-fledged Mediterranean galley.[3] The
French used galleys against English shipping in the Channel with some
occasional success in the wars of the eighteenth century.[4] But by and large,
the game was not worth the candle. The times when a galley could be used
in northern waters were so few as not to justify the expense, particularly
in the earlier period when much less money was available to the state for
military experiments of limited usefulness.

But for a number of reasons, Mediterranean conditions encouraged the
development of specialized rowing vessels. Perhaps most important, the

---

[1] Vice Admiral William L. Rodgers, *Naval Warfare Under Oars* (Annapolis, 1939), p. 232.
[2] Huguette and Pierre Chaunu, *Séville et l'Atlantique*, vol. VII, *Construction Graphique* (Paris,
1957), p. 34, show 9 galleys crossing the Atlantic in 1560-4 and 38 more between 1577 and
1595. These were presumably taken across as sailing vessels with a skeleton crew.
[3] This was the *Galley Subtyle* of 1544 of which an excellent contemporary representation by
Anthony Anthony survives in the British Museum, reproduced in R. C. Anderson, *Oared
Fighting Ships*, pl. 10B.
[4] Several examples of successful attacks on English and Dutch shipping by French galleys
operating out of Dunkirk in the early 1700s are given by Jean Marteilhe, *Galley Slave*
(London, 1957), a slightly condensed translation of Marteilhe's autobiographical account.
Marteilhe makes it plain that operating galleys in these waters was an arduous proposition
at best and at times an unsafe one.

weather of the Mediterranean is predictable to a degree. Mediterranean storms can be as violent as any, but they are generally confined to the winter months between mid-October and mid-March. Before the dawn of recorded history Mediterranean seamen learned that they could avoid most of the danger of shipwreck by not sailing during this period. For the balance of the year Mediterranean weather is generally fine. Dangerous seas are rare, poor visibility is uncommon and even clouded skies are unusual.

The condition of the shore and sea bottom worked to the advantage of the Mediterranean mariner as well. Where the bottom off most northern coasts is gradual, shelving and studded with dangerous rocks and shoals far offshore, the bottom of the Mediterranean drops off quickly to a safe depth almost everywhere. Except along the Barbary coast, safe, deep anchorages and protected ports are common (see Map 3). An extraordinarily high proportion of the shores of the Mediterranean are lined with easy beaches of firm, yellow sand. These could be used as temporary ports during the good portion of the year and frequently were.[1]

In the absence of tides – for the Mediterranean has no appreciable tide – sizeable ships can be pulled up against these beaches during the summer sailing season and safely moored with stern or bow lines, a fact the considerable military significance of which we have already mentioned.[2] The absence of tides simplified the life of the Mediterranean mariner in other ways as well. The entrances to northern ports, particularly the smaller ones, were notoriously tricky due mostly to the shifting tides and to the vicious currents which they induce in many areas.[3] It was not enough for a northern mariner to find his port; he had to calculate the local tidal state to a nicety and time his arrival to coincide with a favorable phase. Simply computing the 'age' of the moon and all the other information necessary to predict the local tides was a considerable feat – let alone coordinating it with the handling of the vessel and timing the whole works with an hourglass.[4]

The Mediterranean navigator was spared all of these complexities and normally did not need detailed and specialized information about each port at which he planned to call. Timing, in particular, was not critical.

---

[1] Spanish documents of the early sixteenth century, in fact, treat ports and beaches almost interchangeably except as locations for wintering. The statement that a particular directive applies to all galleys operating from the ports and beaches (*puertos y playas*) of a particular region is characteristic.

[2] See above, p. 53.

[3] This was particularly true inasmuch as many of the Atlantic ports were at or inside the mouths of rivers with shifting bars and constantly moving channels.

[4] All of this is explained and illustrated by Waters, *The Rutters of the Sea*, Appendix I, 'The Tides, Moonlight and Tidal Prediction'.

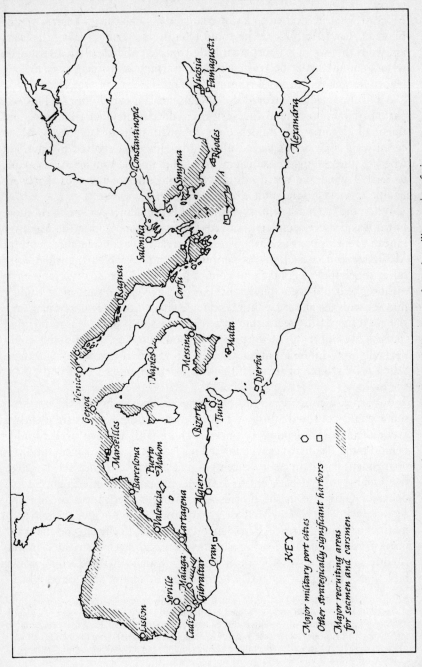

Map 3   The sixteenth-century Mediterranean from the military point of view

Most of what he needed to know could be obtained from a fairly simple pilotage chart. With its aid he could identify his position along the coast and work his way into port with little trouble. The clear Mediterranean waters could usually be trusted to give warning of a rising bottom long before he was in danger of running aground.

All of these factors favored the development of oared vessels. This was particularly important to the very early development of commerce and thus had an important influence on the institutions of later years. Many centuries passed before sails, hulls, and rigging had evolved to the point where a pure sailing vessel could make port unaided under a reasonable variety of wind and sea conditions or stand safely out to sea if it were unable to make a safe landfall.[1]

When the sixteenth century dawned, this problem was close to solution, but it was not yet completely solved. Oars therefore offered the Mediterranean sailor numerous advantages. The relatively considerable depth of Mediterranean coastal waters permitted him to work close inshore with safety, something his northern counterpart could not do. Working close inshore, he could accurately fix his position by visual observation, finding himself with the aid of a nautical pilotage chart if he were unfamiliar with the coastline. If the wind shifted on him in the process – bear in mind that he was probably sailing in the good summer months – he could normally row himself out of trouble. If not, chances were that there was a good stretch of firm sand within reach where he could pull up for the night.

But a pause close inshore to fix his position was a luxury the northern sailor could not often afford. When he made landfall it was frequently a do or die situation coming in on a lee shore with a heavy swell running behind him. The mariner who missed his landfall under such conditions – or misidentified it in poor visibility – seldom had a chance for a second try. Unable to beat back out to sea and with nowhere else to go, he was doomed. Only late in the fourteenth century did advances in hull and rigging, many of them of Mediterranean origin, begin to give the northern mariner a fighting chance. These involved the use of the lateen sail on the mizzen mast to aid in steering and the increased strength yielded by the Mediterranean caravel system of planking which, in turn, led to better hull lines. The great Atlantic contribution to sailing ship development

---

[1] Most of the inventions which made sailing vessels truly maneuverable in a wide variety of wind and weather conditions – clewlines, buntlines, and the lateen mizzen mast – belong to the last three-quarters of the fifteenth century. See the comment by M. Oppenheim, *A History of the Administration of the Royal Navy and Merchant Shipping in Relation to the Navy* (London, 1896), p. 40, to the effect that a sailing ship of 1485 differed less in appearance from one of 1785 than from one of 1425.

was the stern post rudder.[1] The steering oar hung on aboard Mediterranean sailing vessels until the fourteenth century because it could be lifted vertically out of the way and did not interfere with beaching the vessel stern first as a permanently hung stern rudder would have. (Characteristically, the rudders on Mediterranean galleys could be lifted vertically out of their hinges. Though mechanically delicate, this arrangement permitted stern-first beaching, a maneuver whose tactical value we have already commented upon, by allowing the rudder to be quickly unshipped.)

It is small wonder that before these advances made themselves felt, northern mariners tended to stick to a particular area or a given trade route where they knew every sounding and trick of the tides by heart.[2] Until then, they could not afford to stray far afield on the strength of the inadequate and inaccurate information which the crude 'maps' of the time provided, and until then the sailing warship was an impractical proposition.

We have established that the war galley was the only type of vessel capable of producing decisive and favorable military results before the advent of effective gunpowder weapons. Since the range and power of pre-gunpowder weapons were severely limited, a hand-to-hand encounter was needed to produce results. The appearance of cannon did not immediately change this. Cannon began by influencing the way in which the hand-to-hand encounter took place; they did not render it instantly obsolete.

To produce a hand-to-hand encounter at sea under favorable conditions an oared vessel was required. We have established that climatic and geographic conditions effectively restricted such vessels to the Mediterranean. Given the dominance of oared fighting vessels within the Mediterranean, we are then faced with two general problems of a somewhat different nature. The first of these is two-pronged and relatively non-chronological: what were the inherent characteristics of the war galley and how did these determine the nature of maritime conflict in the Mediterranean? The second has a critical chronological component: how

[1] See Björn Landström, *The Ship* (New York, 1961), for a clear and well founded explanation of this process of borrowing and adapting.

[2] See John A. Gade, *The Hanseatic Control of Norwegian Commerce During the Late Middle Ages* (Leiden, 1951), for a discussion of the early development of northern trade routes. The reasons for this localization of trade are thoroughly explained by D. W. Waters, *The Art of Navigation in Elizabethan and Early Stuart Times* (London, 1958). The heavy reliance of the northern mariner on soundings, testing the depth and condition of the bottom with a lead line, was crucial. Nautical charts seem to have been virtually unknown to practical mariners outside the Mediterranean until well into the fifteenth century. See Waters, *The Rutters of the Sea*, pp. 8ff.

did the advent of effective gunpowder weapons, and in particular cannon, affect the role of the war galley?

The second question is crucial. The war galley and its smaller relatives constituted the heart of the Mediterranean system of maritime conflict. By the time cannon appeared on the scene that system was a highly developed one, both technically and structurally. All of its parts were closely interdependent and formed a tightly integrated whole. No essential part of the system could be undermined without eventually bringing the whole edifice down or altering it radically. Any development which degraded the effectiveness of the war galley or changed its role significantly was bound to produce change in other areas affected by the manner in which armed violence was employed at sea. Since that encompassed nearly the whole of maritime commercial activity, we can state with some assurance that our investigation of the viability of oared fighting vessels in technical military terms should provide useful insight into the direction and strength of long-term economic and social trends. This question will also bear on cultural and intellectual questions inasmuch as the development and proliferation across formidable cultural and religious barriers of gunpowder weapons and the technology associated with them was a critical component of the problem as well.

First, however, we must establish the essential characteristics of maritime conflict within the Mediterranean before the advent of gunpowder. These, to a large extent, depended on the inherent capabilities and limitations of oared fighting vessels. It should therefore be possible to gain considerable insight into the one through analysis of the other. Other considerations are important, in some cases crucial; but this is a useful starting point and provides our study with a central strand of organization. With this as a firm base, we can then observe the effects of the introduction of gunpowder weapons in a relatively controlled manner. By this means we can also observe the interplay between larger economic trends, principally the price revolution, and the way in which armed violence was employed at sea.

The logical place to start is with an examination of the intrinsic characteristics of oared fighting vessels. These were determined, to an overwhelming degree, by their system of motive power. Pound for pound and cubic foot for cubic foot, man is a most inefficient source of mechanical energy. An oarsman aboard a sixteenth-century Mediterranean galley produced a peak power output of about one-eighth horsepower.[1] If we combine this figure with the known dimensions of an early sixteenth-

---

[1] Rodgers, *Naval Warfare Under Oars*, pp. 231-2. See our discussion of speed under oars, ch. 5.

century Venetian galley, probably the fastest under oars of all full-sized galleys, we get a vessel of about 170 tons displacement with less than 19 horsepower to drive it – the peak output of about 150 sweating oarsmen.

Man's limitations as a source of propulsive power present few difficulties in small craft, but size was a desirable military characteristic as well as a key determinant of seaworthiness. A number of complications therefore quickly arose.

From a purely military point of view, a large vessel with high freeboard offered compelling advantages. It could carry more fighting men and gave them the important advantage of fighting from a higher platform in combat. But speed was also important in an oared fighting vessel and the whole *raison d'être* of the oared fighting vessel was offensive. To fight its quarry it had to be able to catch it. These two requirements were not compatible. They were not compatible because larger vessels with higher freeboard required longer oars and longer oars entailed a loss of propulsive efficiency. The relationship between oar length and efficiency is a complex one; but the problem is central to our investigation and must be gone into in some detail.

Rowing involves an oscillatory motion: the oar must be halted and reversed twice in each cycle. The greater the mass of the oar, therefore, the greater the amount of energy which must be expended simply to start it and stop it each time, leaving less for the propulsion of the vessel. To a certain extent this problem can be solved by having a number of men pull a large oar together. In this way, the mass of oar per oarsman stays the same or even declines a bit. But there is a limit to the increase in efficiency which this solution can offer. The reason for this is fairly straightforward. As the inboard length of the oar is increased, the length of its sweep -- the distance which it must be pulled – is increased also. This means that the inboard oarsmen must move more of their own body mass farther just to keep up with the oar. The energy which they expend in moving their own bodies is wasted insofar as the propulsion of the ship is concerned. Once again, it is difficult to estimate just where this effect becomes critical, but it seems fairly clear that there are a number of plateaus.

At one end of the scale is the seated stroke. Here the sweep of the oar is short enough for the oarsmen to pull while remaining seated. Next we have the 'rise and fall', a stroke which is long enough to require the oarsmen to rise off their benches during recovery, then throw the whole force of their bodies back against their heels during the stroke, returning to a seated position on their benches just before recovering. This stroke, compared to the seated stroke, undoubtedly produced more power – all the powerful muscles of the oarsmen's thighs and torsos were brought into play – but at the cost of a loss in efficiency and endurance. Medieval galleys and the oared vessels with which we are mainly concerned here used this stroke almost without exception.[1] Finally we reach a point at which the inboard sweep of the oar is so long that the inboard oarsmen must rise to their feet and follow it along the deck to keep pace with it. Once again it is difficult to say when this happens but the point seems to have been reached with a normal sized oar and a full stroke when the sixth man from the thole pin was added.

It is impossible to make precise statements as to which stroke was best and for what reasons. All might be used at once on a large oar. Nevertheless, a number of conclusions are fairly clear. Three men to a bench pulling individual oars seems to have represented some kind of an optimum solution. This arrangement was used on full-sized medieval war galleys (that is on 'ordinary' galleys) almost as far back as there is clear evidence, and continued to be used almost exclusively on full-sized war galleys until the middle of the sixteenth century, when more than three men began to be used per rowing bench by replacing the individual oars with a single large one. This arrangement was at first used only on flagships and *bastardas*, larger than average galleys. When this arrangement began to be used on ordinary galleys it was apparently – a matter which we discuss at length in the concluding chapters – because of a decline in the quality of oarsmen, not because of any intrinsic mechanical advantage.

Higher freeboard meant longer oars and hence a loss of efficiency. This acted to make galleys low, narrow vessels. But limitations on oar length were not the only factor which conspired to make the galley a narrow ship of low freeboard. Rowing is not only an oscillatory motion as far as each oar is concerned; the entire vessel progresses through the water in a rhythmic series of accelerations and decelerations. Each time the oarsmen put their backs into it, they had to accelerate the mass of the entire vessel to restore the velocity lost to hydrodynamic drag during the recovery portion of their previous stroke.

Thus the limitations of human muscle as a source of power which placed an effective limitation on the freeboard and width of galleys by restricting the length of their oars placed an equally stringent and even more direct limitation on their total displacement. Great power was needed to drive a heavy hull, but great power could only be obtained at considerable cost in efficiency and endurance. Some seventeenth-century galeasses

---

[1] This is evident from the arrangement of their oars and benches. See Rodgers, *Naval Warfare Under Oars*, pp. 230–8, for a discussion of the technical aspects of galley design.

used as many as eight men to an oar, but these vessels were notably slow and unwieldy.[1]

Galley design was a three-way compromise between speed under oars, effectiveness as a fighting platform, and safety and efficiency as a sailing vessel. Speed under oars, however, was for tactical reasons the dominant requirement and the severe limitations of human muscle as a source of propulsive energy left little room for compromise. Design features which made the galley more effective in combat or a better sailing craft were of little value if they reduced the speed under oars to the point that it could not run down its prey or escape from a more powerful opponent. The galley, galiot or *bergantin* which was inefficient as a rowing vessel was of little value for anything else. This fact dominated galley design.

As a result, every scrap of available space aboard a galley was occupied by oarsmen and their benches. Such specialized fighting superstructures as were added had to be kept light and were confined to the tapering portions of the prow and stern where oarsmen could not be properly seated. If we neglect raised platforms, light projections extending out from the body of the hull and so on, something on the order of 95 per cent of a galley's deck space was devoted to the oarsmen and their benches.[2] This had a direct and profound effect upon galley tactics.

To give the oarsmen better leverage and to permit the hull to be narrower, the thole pins of Mediterranean galleys were mounted on a longitudinal beam, the *apostis*, set well out from the hull and running parallel to it for most of its length. The *apostis* was mounted on two transverse beams, one at each end of the galley, running across the thwarts. The resultant rectangular arrangement was known as the rowing frame. The sides of a galley were thus not only low in the water and lined with non-fighting men, they were also comparatively weak structurally. All of these factors combined to preclude the use of a galley's sides for military purposes except defensively and in desperate circumstances.

That left the small, tapering areas of deck at the bow and stern. But the stern was effectively ruled out. The posts of the helmsmen, the captain, and most of those concerned with the handling of the ship were there of necessity. The limited signalling equipment, the flagstaff, the pennant halliards and the stern lanterns, were there as well. Though this provision

[1] Even the Ottoman *maonas* of this period, somewhat smaller than western galeasses, had seven men to an oar. This information is from Haji Kahlifeh, *The History of the Maritime Wars of the Turks*, cited by Sir George Hill, *A History of Cyprus*, vol. III (reissue, Cambridge, 1972), p. 896.
[2] This estimate is based on measurements taken from the reconstruction of a Venetian trireme by Admiral Fincati in the Museo Storico Navale, Venice. The figure would probably have been slightly lower on western galleys, but not by much.

of signalling gear seems quite modest to the modern reader, it was not so viewed by contemporaries. The equivalent of flagships in galley fleets were the *galeras de lanterna*, lantern galleys, so called because of their increased number of stern lanterns (usually three) for signalling and as a rallying point at night. These large and often elaborately decorated triple stern lanterns, invariably mounted on an unusually powerfully armed galley, were the cherished symbol of command *par excellence* and rightly so. The stern platform was the galley's brain, its nerve center. Involving it in combat entailed a loss of control.

In addition, the stern – particularly the removable rudder and its hinge pins – tended to be structurally fragile. The stern was a useful post from which to direct the battle. Reinforcements could be held there and dispatched down the *corsia*, the narrow gangway running the length of the galley between the rowing benches, as needed or at the crucial moment. But from the operational point of view, that was about all. The stern was a logical point to attack an enemy galley, not the logical place to voluntarily receive an onslaught. Its sole advantage was that it stood higher in the water than the waist of the ship.

This left the prow – logically enough since the galley was by nature an offensive weapon and offensive weapons attack by moving forward. The boarding party could be mustered there, ready to leap aboard the enemy ship as soon as the power of the oars ran them up against it. A light, raised platform could be erected just behind the prow of a full-sized galley to give men with missile weapons a vantage point from which to deliver covering fire. Finally, the beak of the galley, the 'spur',[1] provided a useful boarding bridge for the attackers. On the galleys of most nations it angled upward slightly and had a reinforced, iron-shod tip. If the spur could be lodged forcefully among the rowing banks of an enemy galley it would ride up and over the *apostis* and give the boarding party an all-important height advantage in launching their assault.

Many misconceptions have arisen concerning the uses of the spur. It is generally viewed as a ram, yet its position well above the water line makes abundantly clear that it was not a ram in the classical sense. The classical parallel for the spur of modern and medieval galleys is clearly the Roman boarding bridge, not the Greek ram. Misunderstanding of this point has distorted the tactical analysis of even the best historians as we will show in our discussion of Lepanto. The spur was sufficiently sturdy to penetrate the light upper planking of a galley or a small sailing ship and lodge there. Its ability to do so aided considerably in accomplishing its main purpose –

---

[1] It was called just that in both Spanish and Venetian. The respective words were *espolón* and *sprone*.

to provide a bridge for a boarding party, not to inflict major structural damage upon an enemy hull.

It should be evident by now that the galley was only capable of attacking an enemy vessel directly off its bow. The same was true in reverse: a galley could resist an attack by another galley only by turning bows on toward it. The power of this tactical dictum was reinforced by the appearance of effective heavy artillery.

The bow was the only place on a galley where heavy guns could be mounted. Even there space was so restricted that there was no room for large cannon to traverse: the galley's main battery could fire only straight forward. Thus the only way to aim a galley's main ordnance was by aiming the galley itself. The effect of this was to enhance the influence of all the factors mentioned above. Like the modern fighter aircraft, the sixteenth-century galley had to turn toward its opponent to deliver an attack or to receive one. Tactically, at least in small engagements, it was an almost purely offensive weapon. In this, as we shall see, it contrasted strongly with the sailing warship.

As a result, engagements between two, three or half a dozen galleys were quick and decisive. A running fight on more or less even terms was impossible. A galley confronted by a more powerful one and with no opportunity to deliver a flank attack had few options. It could accept combat head-on, knowing that it would almost certainly be bowled over by superior armament and manpower. Even if it managed to beat off a superior opponent in this way it could expect heavy casualties. This was hardly a viable alternative if any other were available.

If the weaker galley turned to fly and was subsequently run down from astern, it was as good as done for. This was particularly true following the generalization of heavy bow artillery from the last decades of the fifteenth century on, since the pursuer could open fire with his heavy bow guns at a distance while the pursued had no effective means of reply. But flight was still the only viable defensive alternative for an overmatched galley; it at least offered a chance of getting away clean. If the weaker galley stood to fight it would be crippled at best and captured at worst.

It goes almost without saying that a galley caught by surprise or force of circumstances by another – even one of considerably inferior force – and attacked from the flank or stern was in serious trouble. The tactical advantages conferred by the superior height and specialized construction of the prow were usually decisive. They were even more so when the attacker mounted several pieces of heavy forward-firing ordnance which could clear the way for the boarding party with a simultaneous discharge at the moment of impact. This was the central fact of galley tactics in the sixteenth century. This initial discharge at close range could wreak havoc on the crowded decks and fighting platforms of a galley. As many as forty men aboard a galley are known to have been laid low in this way before the battle came to handstrokes.[1]

We should expect from this that engagements between small numbers of galleys would almost invariably produce very lopsided results: one side being nearly obliterated and the other getting away almost without loss. A general survey of available secondary accounts and the relevant source material which has come to hand bears this out.[2] Fleet engagements in which one side was taken by surprise or in a disorganized state show the same characteristic. Gian Andrea Doria's disaster off Djerba in 1560 is a prime example. Caught at anchor and disorganized by the sudden appearance of the Ottoman fleet under Piali Paşa, the Imperial fleet was scattered with heavy loss. Only the Christians' roundships seem to have made an effective resistance while Muslim losses were trifling.[3]

Contrary to the tendency described above, however, full-dress engagements between competently deployed fleets of galleys tended to be indecisive affairs with little tactical advantage accruing to either side. There were several reasons for this. Once a galley was committed in a boarding fight it was almost impossible to withdraw and re-commit elsewhere. If a galley got the worst of it and somehow managed to clear her decks and get away, it was only with serious gaps in her fighting manpower and probably her *ciurma*[4] as well. Thus not only her fighting power, but also her mobility was impaired. If she won, then most of her fighting men – and a

---

[1] This occurred in 1528 when Filippino Doria loosed his entire bow armament of a *basilisco*, two half cannons, two *sacres* and two *falconetes* into Don Hugo de Moncada's galley (see Appendix 6). The incident is mentioned in a letter from Paolo Giovio to Pope Clement VII, quoted in *I Diarii Marino Sanuto*, vol. XLVI, col. 666–7 (Venice, 1897).

[2] So many examples of such outcomes appear in contemporary sources that specific reference can be made only to a few. Vol. XII of the *Colección Navarrete* is a particularly rich lode for accounts of small galley actions of the early seventeenth century, notably dto. 13, fol. 68–73, an account of an engagement between the Galleys of Sicily and eight Muslim opponents in 1613; dto. 10, fol. 54, an account of a Spanish victory over the Galleys of the Guards of Rhodes and Cyprus in the same year; and dto. 33, fol. 156, an account of an engagement between the Galleys of Malta and a small Ottoman squadron. Particularly noteworthy for its graphic description of the devastating affect of a galley's bow artillery on a fleeing galley's stern as a preliminary to boarding is dto. 42, fol. 188ff., a letter of 1636 describing the capture of two Muslim galleys in the eastern Mediterranean by two of the Galleys of Malta. A quick survey of relevant portions of R. C. Anderson, *Naval Wars in the Levant* (Princeton, 1952), with an eye to the results of small galley actions, leads to the same conclusion.

[3] See the account of Djerba following ch. 4 (pp. 129–30).

[4] The Venetian word for rowing gang, pronounced 'che oor mə', plural *ciurmi*. This term covered the entire rowing gang regardless of status. I have elected to use the Venetian word throughout. There is no English equivalent and the Spanish synonym, *chusma*, shows every evidence of being an Italian loan word like so many other Castillian technical terms relating to galleys.

good part of the *ciurma* too if they were free oarsmen (the situation on most Venetian and many Ottoman galleys until well after Lepanto) – would be aboard their beaten opponent, reluctant to abandon their prize. It took time to organize a proper prize crew, halt the looting and get the rest of the men back aboard and at their posts. Consequently, commitment to battle was irrevocable. In a three or four-galley fight where the odds could be quickly evaluated, a competent commander could see his advantage and attack with confidence. In a large battle where the decision could go either way and where even a victory was sure to entail heavy loss the decision was considerably more difficult to make.

The basic tendency toward indecisiveness in large engagements fought under close control, however, largely the result of a second factor. The galley's close-in maneuvering ability made it possible for large fleets in good weather to maintain a line abreast formation accurately across an unbroken front of sixty galleys or more.[1] A line abreast with bows facing the enemy was a powerful defensive formation. There was nothing to be gained through individual assaults upon it by one or two galleys. Each attacking galley would quickly be overwhelmed by superior odds at the point of contact. Meanwhile, the defenders could feed in reinforcements as needed by means of a reserve force of galleys, galiots, and smaller craft which were free to shuttle behind the unbroken front. These could tie onto the stern of a threatened galley and feed it extra fighting men or, if necessary, tow it out of the line and replace it.

Thus there was usually no point to a partial fleet engagement. These only occurred when one fleet, usually aided by surprise or poor discipline on the part of their opponents, was able to outmaneuver the other and catch a number of galleys out of position and engage them without breaking formation. Barbarossa's victory at Prevesa in 1538 is a good example of this. The fleet commander who found himself caught by such a maneuver had an option: he could cut his losses by sacrificing the galleys which were engaged, hold his defensive formation and extricate his fleet intact; or he could allow the engagement to become general. The second option was rarely taken by sixteenth-century Mediterranean commanders.

The defensive strength of the line abreast was further reinforced by the ability of a galley to row backward.[2] This tactic ordinarily made little sense

---

[1] As was done at Lepanto and Prevesa. Apparently the difficulties of maintaining formation began to mount rapidly when the line was extended beyond 60 galleys and 63 or 64 seems to have been a practical limit. Squadrons which were expected to maneuver seldom had more than 52–3 galleys on line.

[2] Evidence of this maneuver is found in a contemporary miniature of the siege of Rhodes in 1480 in the Bibliothèque Nationale, Paris, reproduced by George G. Feudouzo *et al.*, *Histoire de la Marine* (Paris, 1959), p. 83. Jean Marteilhe, *Galley Slave*, writing over two hundred

in a small engagement. Rowing astern was a slow and awkward business and an agile opponent could get around you and engage your flank. In a large fleet engagement, however, where neither side had a clear-cut advantage, it provided a means of disengaging a fleet without exposing it to attack at a severe disadvantage.

This maneuver had still greater advantages when the fleet using it had an open beach close to their rear. They could back right up to the shore, guns still pointed at the enemy, and moor there. This offered no serious disadvantages to the defenders and gave them a number of substantial advantages. By sacrificing their mobility to a point – they could always shove off and re-engage if a favorable opportunity presented itself – they strengthened the defensive power of their formation considerably. Men could be transferred from ship to ship along the shore and the ships of the reserve, formerly needed for this task, could form in line with the others. The bow artillery of the moored galleys would be, if anything, more effective than when under way. Oarsmen could be disembarked to cut losses if the enemy persisted and chose to attack. And, if friendly land forces were nearby, additional soldiers could be embarked to take their places. This maneuver seems to have been used from the earliest times by galley fleets confronted by superior force.[1] It does much to explain why greatly inferior fleets retained a degree of freedom of action even when their superior opponents were at sea during the campaigning season. This was a constant feature of Mediterranean naval warfare and one which has puzzled modern analysts working within the Mahanian tradition.

Unless bad weather intervened, the inferior fleet could remain where it was, moored to the beach, almost indefinitely. Its more powerful assailant offshore, however, was involved in a continuous expenditure of energy simply to hold its formation and position against the force of the wind and waves. While the galleys backed up to the beach could dispatch their oarsmen ashore for water, those offshore had to rely on what they had on board. This could not go on indefinitely. Sooner or later the superior fleet had to pull off to rest its oarsmen and revictual. At that point the inferior one, rested and in good order, was free to go discreetly about its business. It might even counterattack with the hope of catching a superior foe in disarray.

Seaside fortresses and secure ports offered the galley fleet even stronger protection. If the maneuver described above could be executed beneath

years after the siege of Rhodes, mentions rowing backwards as a means of withdrawing from a fight while keeping the guns on the enemy.
[1] Rodgers, *Naval Warfare Under Oars*, p. 137, cites a contemporary account, *ca.* 1285, describing a squadron of French galleys spending the night 'anchored ... with stern lines to the beach' in a protected bay the night before the battle of Las Hormigas.

the walls of a friendly fortress well provided with artillery, the galley fleet's position was almost unassailable regardless of the odds against it. We have seen this maneuver at Prevesa. It was systematically adopted by the Ottoman fleet in the year following Lepanto with considerable success.

The relationship between fortress and galley was not a one-sided one by any means and requires amplification. A skilfully handled galley squadron could make the difference of life or death to an isolated seaside fortress under siege. When the besieging army had no effective fleet, revictualing and reinforcement of the fortress from the sea could be undertaken at will. In such a case sailing ships served as well as galleys unless the harbor entrance were a particularly difficult one or closely defended by the besiegers. But where the besieging army was supported by a strong galley squadron, the situation was more complicated.

In the first place, the support of a galley fleet was of great value to a besieging army whether naval relief attempts had to be repelled or not. If the fortress under attack were on an island or an exposed peninsula it was indispensable. Heavy siege guns could be transported and landed by galleys with relative ease. By the second or third decade of the sixteenth century the main bow guns of war galleys were themselves heavy enough for siege battery work and were often dismounted and used for that purpose. The galleys of a besieging fleet were not ordinarily kept at sea, but were normally laagered up along the shoreline or anchored in a nearby bay and the oarsmen sent ashore to dig siege parallels or, if they were free men, to swell the ranks of assault parties. The fighting men of the galleys were put ashore to enlarge the besieging army if, in fact, they did not constitute the bulk of it. This constitutes a basic fact of galley warfare. The manpower and armament of a besieging fleet's galleys were convertible. They could be used on land or at sea as the occasion demanded. This was a salient characteristic of war at sea in the sixteenth-century Mediterranean.

If a relief squadron were lurking nearby, ready to make a dash for a beleaguered fortress with men and supplies, the besieger had to hold back sufficient guns and manpower from the siege to arm enough galleys to meet and repel it. By thus denying the besieger the full use of his resources for the prosecution of the siege, a relieving squadron could make a substantial contribution to the defense of a fortress even before it appeared on the horizon.

This was particularly true if the attacking army had to be transported to the site of the siege by sea. In this case the besieging fleet had to play its cards very close to the chest. If the siege were long and hard and all available manpower were committed, a sudden unexpected onslaught by a quite inferior relieving force could spell disaster for the besieger. With his empty or undermanned ships destroyed at the water's edge, he would be trapped between a replenished fortress to his front and a victorious fleet to his rear. It was the possibility of precisely this development which must have prompted Charles V to launch his attack of 1541 on Algiers in October.

In 1535, with a more favorable balance of power at sea, Charles had laid siege to Tunis in July and subdued it by mid-September. But in 1541 he apparently felt – probably correctly – that he had insufficient forces at his disposal to take Algiers and to stand off a relieving naval force as well. He was consequently forced to attack in the autumn and take his chances with the weather, banking on Ottoman reluctance to sortie all the way from Constantinople in the dead of winter. This gambit was surely a deliberate and calculated risk. Charles was a thoroughly competent – even brilliant – planner of expeditions of this sort, as the Tunis expedition of 1535 shows. Andrea Doria went on record as warning him against the dangers of an autumn sailing,[1] but Charles took his chances. The results, as we know, were horrendous. The Ottoman fleet did not confront Charles' army before Algiers, but a terrible storm did, turning the expedition into one of the great shipwrecks of all times.

The problem of relieving a fortress under attack varied, depending on the balance of resources between the contending powers and their geographic situations. The Venetians had a peculiarly difficult problem in light of their slender resources, particularly of manpower, in comparison with those of the Ottomans. While the Ottomans almost invariably had an ample fleet on hand to cover the siege of a Venetian fortress, the Venetians generally had to launch their relief on a shoestring. But the peculiar characteristics of Mediterranean warfare under oars gave even a very small relief force a fighting chance if it were skilfully and resolutely handled. Taking full advantage of the protection offered by nearby forts and beaches, an inferior relieving force would work its way in as close to the besieged fortress as possible, waiting for the right combination of wind and weather. When the chance came, it would make a sudden dash for it with surprise on its side, perhaps after drawing off the besieging fleet with a ruse, and attempt to blast its way into the friendly harbor without becoming closely engaged.

The Venetians showed consummate skill at the slapdash, hit-and-run tactics which this sort of operation required. Their galleys were, as we shall see, specifically designed for them. The relief of Famagusta during the

---

[1] Ignacio Bauer Landauer, *La Marina Española en el Siglo XVI* (Madrid, 1921), p. 25.

winter of 1570–1 by Antonio Quirini was a minor classic of the genre.[1] But the Venetians did not have a patent on the ability to conduct such operations skilfully. The relief of a besieged fortress with an inferior fleet was an essential part of the competent Mediterranean naval commander's repertoire. Andrea Doria, the arch enemy of Venice, showed considerable skill under these circumstances.[2]

Only the Ottomans were saved, by their retention of the initiative and by their geographic position, from having to send out inferior naval relief forces with any great frequency. Most of the places which they held were accessible to relief by land even if, as in the case of Coron in the Morea, maintaining land communications was a difficult and extended business. If the Ottomans' opponents managed to capture an important place, the Ottomans were generally content to wait until the following campaigning season and then mount a major effort to recapture it. This was the course of action which they took following Don Juan of Austria's capture of Tunis in 1573. When the Ottomans did choose to react immediately to a Christian thrust, their response could be an overwhelming one as it was at Djerba in 1560.

The nature of the symbiotic relationship between the seaside fortress and the war galley was not restricted to a mutual dependence based on logistic factors. Because of the characteristics and capabilities of the galley, there was a closely forged tactical relationship between the two as well. This point requires some clarification. In the era of sailing warships there was a good deal of ineffectual cannonading back and forth between ships and forts, but – with the exception of the enormous shells thrown by specialized bomb ketches[3] – it rarely had much effect on either side. This was because of limitations in the maneuverability and source of motive power of sailing warships and their relatively great depth in the water. These conditions generally made it impossible for them to work close enough inshore to do any real damage to a seaside fortress without real danger of running aground. It also kept them so far away that the guns of the fortress could do little harm in return.

[1] See below, p. 213, for a full analysis of Quirini's operation.

[2] Roger B. Merriman, *The Rise of the Spanish Empire*, vol. III, *The Emperor* (New York, 1925), pp. 298–300. Doria had captured Coron with a force of 44 galleys, 17 of them Spanish, and 10,000–12,000 Imperial troops in the early autumn of 1532. The Ottomans laid siege to the place the following May, but Doria got in a relief force on 2 August which brought a reinforcement of 2,500 soldiers plus needed munitions, and supplies, and – most critical – money, for the garrison's pay was in arrears and they were on the verge of mutiny.

[3] The bomb ketch was introduced by the French in 1679. See Landström, *The Ship*, p. 170. These were specialized siege vessels mounting one or two enormous mortars sunk in the hull forward and firing out over the bowsprit. Their explosive shells were as heavy as 230 pounds. These had little impact on fortress walls, but could do considerable damage inside them.

But a galley could, in reasonably calm weather, move right up to the walls of such a fortress and let fly with its main bow gun with some precision. If the fortress were a first-class one and if the galley's captain picked the wrong spot, he could get sunk for his troubles; but if not, he could remain right where he was and repeat the performance indefinitely. This was a major difference from the situation of a sailing ship which had to keep moving to retain sufficient steerageway to maintain control. Furthermore a galley's main bow gun was usually of sufficient power and size to do a reasonable amount of damage to the walls of a fortress at ranges of as much as 200 yards or even more.

For this reason, a galley fleet with no land support whatever could present a genuine threat to an old medieval fortress with thin curtain walls, an improvised field fortification, or to a fortress which was undermanned, undergunned, or short of powder. In a formal siege, galleys could cooperate very effectively with a land army, forcing the defenders to man their walls on the sea side and lending gun power to the task of reducing those portions of the land walls which came down to the shore.

If the fortress harbor were inadequately protected on the inside and if the entrances were not securely closed with a chain or boom, there was always the chance of a surprise assault in that quarter by a party carried in oared vessels. This procedure was frequently attempted as were direct attacks on the sea wall of a fortress if it were low and weak.

But seaside fortresses were not necessarily impotent in their ability to respond to their naval tormentors. Some of the earliest of the large fortress guns, stone-throwing cannon of gargantuan proportions, had real ship-killing potential. The biggest of these guns, firing a granite or marble ball of 600 to 900 pounds or even more, were capable of sinking a galley with a single well-directed shot – a feat which seems to have been accomplished on several occasions. The effectiveness of Sultan Mehmed II's blockade of the Dardanelles with such cannon in 1452–3 bears witness to this. Though only Portuguese and Ottoman guns of this type have survived in numbers, it seems clear that the use of genuine 'ship-killers' in shore batteries was widespread among the Mediterranean nations during the sixteenth century.[1] The Ottomans used them extensively in siege batteries and all Mediterranean military men of any experience would have been familiar with their characteristics.

---

[1] Many such guns of Ottoman and Portuguese manufacture are still in existence. The surviving Turkish specimens are bored for balls of from 600 pounds to over 1,000. The surviving Portuguese pieces (notably Nos. MMR26 and MMR23 in the Museu Militar, Lisbon) are bored for balls weighing from 200 to 250 pounds. The fittings on all of these guns make it clear that they were intended to be slewed around rapidly by the use of heavy ropes for use against moving targets, clear evidence of the use for which they were intended.

But the amphibious character of Mediterranean warfare at sea was not limited to siege operations. If the bow guns of galleys could be used with effect against 'hard' land targets in a siege, they were at least as useful against 'soft' ones in the interminable amphibious raids and skirmishing of the 'little war'. If the defenders were not well dug in, the bow artillery of a galley could give effective cover to a landing party either in the assault or withdrawal phase of a raid. The key point here was that a galley could be maneuvered with precision right up against the shoreline to bring its guns to bear. A check of source materials in the Museo Naval, Madrid, relating to small actions by Spanish galleys and those of the Knights of Malta, reveals numerous examples of such tactics.[1] Nor were they confined to the Spanish. In their raid on Malta in 1552 the Ottomans covered the debarkation of their landing party with their galleys' bow guns. Finding their desired landing spot occupied by Christian troops, the Turks pulled in close to shore 'and the galleys shot off all their arquebusery and artillery, and in this manner skirmished [with the Christian troops on shore] for more than an hour' before putting their landing party ashore in skiffs.[2]

Finally, it should be noted that – fire power aside – oared mobility was of great value in the irregular operations of the 'little war' at sea. English corsairs preying upon Spanish possessions in the West Indies considered it absolutely necessary to take an oared 'pinnace' along with a force of larger and more powerfully armed sailing ships to conduct landing operations under fire and to pursue prizes close inshore.[3] The Spanish, not surprisingly, brought galleys into the Indies to counter the use of such tactics by the English and, above all, by the French. A detailed and knowledgeable contemporary account of Spanish measures taken to protect the West Indies from French buccaneers in the late 1570s, written by one Diego Sanchez de Sotomayor, has survived.[4] Like many other documents going back to Charles V's first anti-piracy directive of 13 June 1522,[5] Sotomayor's account expresses particular concern for the security of the annual plate fleet and the pearl fisheries. While *en route* security for the plate fleet was provided by armed galleons, local anti-piracy forces in

---

[1] For example, an account of a Spanish raid on the Barbary coast in 1614 given in the *Colección Navarrete*, vol. XII, dto. 22, fol. 106, where reembarkation was covered by the galleys' bow guns. See also the account of a similar Spanish raid by Don Álvaro de Bazan in 1565 in the *Colección Navarrete*, vol. IV, dto. 18, fol. 218ff.

[2] This is from a letter written from Malta by one Don Álvaro de Paz, 28 July 1551, in the *Colección Navarrete*, vol. IV., dto. 5, fol. 76ff.

[3] K. R. Andrews, *Elizabethan Privateering* (Cambridge, 1964), pp. 35–6.

[4] *Colección Navarrete*, vol. XXVII, dto. 51, fol. 406–25.

[5] *Ibid.* vol. XXI, dto. 3, fol. 16.

the Caribbean revolved around a galley in Cumaña, two in Cartagena, one in Puerto Rico, one in Santo Domingo, one in Puerto de la Plata, one in Yaguana and one in Cuba, a total of eight. The tactical purpose of the amphibious forces centered around these galleys is succinctly stated in a memorandum of 1595 to the Casa de Contratación in Seville by one Pedro de Ludena.[1] The galleys, in cooperation with smaller craft and local land forces, were to render aid to threatened towns along the coast 'with men, munitions and warning' and to prevent the French from putting men ashore or wintering nearby. Also of interest is a document executed on 12 July 1577 by the Governor of Cartagena, arguing at length that galleys were of more value than armed galleons in anti-piracy operations.[2]

It is well to reflect in this context that the attention of the naval historian has been fixed primarily on the large, formally declared wars of the Mediterranean nations with the emphasis upon the major campaigns and the big battles. Only recently has it begun to shift slightly, principally due to the efforts of economic historians.

The impression of the nature of maritime conflict which this older focus yields can be misleading. The 'little wars' which ran parallel to the more spectacular clashes, and were to some extent spawned by them, could be even more important in their long-range results. To take a few examples: the carrying of the wars of Habsburg and Valois into the West Indies by French privateers overflowed the boundaries of the various peace treaties and created a major drain on Spanish resources.[3] Even more important in the long run, it showed the way to the English and Dutch. Similarly, the attempt by the Portuguese to bar the Persian Gulf and Red Sea to Islamic commerce in the first decades of the sixteenth century had profound consequences. The perpetual war of the Knights of St John on Muslim shipping and coasts (and almost anything else if times were lean) played a central part in the struggle between Habsburg and Ottoman at sea. The contribution of the North African sea *ghazis* to that struggle was, if anything, even more important: virtually every Ottoman naval commander of any consequence was schooled in the perpetual raids and skirmishes of the Barbary coast. Possibly the most revealing example of the crucial importance of these little wars was Venice's struggle to protect her commerce against the depredations of raiders of all persuasions, a struggle

---

[1] *Colección Navarrete*, vol. XXIII, dto. 2, fol. 9.
[2] *Ibid.* vol. XXVII, dto. 49, fol. 193–5.
[3] Vol. XXV of the *Colección Navarrete* is filled with an array of documents on this subject. Their frequency and the urgency of their language leaves little doubt that the Spanish considered piracy a matter of paramount concern. The fishing industry was considered peculiarly vulnerable. See the *Colección Vargas Ponce*, vol. III, dto. 14, fol. 40–1, for a mid-sixteenth-century expression of royal concern on this score.

which was the central fact of her existence for almost 200 years.[1] Finally, it was the entry of large numbers of Dutch and English merchantmen-freebooters – not Dutch and English war fleets – into the Mediterranean in the 1580s and 1590s that sounded the death knell of the Mediterranean system.

The organization, tactics and equipment of Mediterranean naval forces were moulded by the demands of these little wars to a very large extent. The war galley, in particular, was largely the product of these demands. It would be futile to attempt a thorough analysis of Mediterranean naval conflict without considering what they were, a consideration which brings us back to our starting point.

Sixteenth-century Mediterranean naval warfare must be analyzed within a conceptual framework based upon Mediterranean conditions and upon the methods and techniques of warfare to which they gave rise. That conceptual framework must be expanded to include not only the spectacular wars of major campaigns and fleet engagements, but the endless little war of economic attrition as well. It must include not only the techniques and tactics by which military force was applied in Mediterranean waters, but their economic consequences and social demands too.

But before we proceed with the details of galley warfare in chapter 3, a final backward look at the broadside sailing warship is necessary. This is necessary to make two points which strongly support our thesis: that heavy broadside armament was tried experimentally on sailing warships in the Mediterranean long before its general adoption in the North Atlantic, and that the adoption of relatively heavy broadside armament aboard the sailing ships of the North Atlantic did not immediately endow them with a decisive increase in military efficiency.

We will do this through the use of two specific examples: the battle of Zonchio, fought between the Venetians and Turks off the mouth of the Gulf of Lepanto in 1499, and a nameless engagement between a Portuguese squadron and a combined force of French and English freebooters fought off the Guinea coast in 1558. The former is the earliest naval engagement of which a detailed record survives in which we can be certain that heavy broadside-firing armament was employed. It shows clearly that the Mediterranean nations were alive to the possibilities of a broadside armament at an early date and strongly suggests that they abandoned it for valid technical reasons.

---

[1] This is the only one of these 'little wars' to have received much scholarly attention, notably from Alberto Tenenti. Abundant source material exists for a searching and comprehensive study of the Spaniards' side of their struggle against French, English and Dutch freebooters in the West Indies, but as yet no use has been made of it.

Our second example is the earliest detailed tactical record of a confrontation on the high seas between squadrons of well armed and well sailed broadside sailing warships. It is also the earliest known example of the use of the tactical formation upon which the broadside sailing warship's subsequent triumphs were based – the line astern. This suggests an important point of chronology. The late appearance of the line astern compared with that of its Mediterranean equivalent, the line abreast formation used by galley fleets from the earliest times, effectively drives home a major point essential to the viability of our thesis – the tactical impotence of the broadside sailing warship in the first half of the sixteenth century.

William Towerson's fight off the Guinea Coast, 1557

A general impression has been left by naval historians, English naval historians in particular, that the broadside sailing warship did not truly exist until the English discovered it in the second half of the sixteenth century – just in time to meet the Armada. The English, so the story goes, were first in recognizing the value of a 'ship-killing' armament. Sometime (but not long) before Hawkins' fight at San Juan de Ulloa in 1568 certain Englishmen began to experiment with a broadside armament of heavy cannon. Seeing, perhaps from Hawkins' fight, that this radical new idea worked, the English adopted it generally.[1] The term 'revolutionary' has been used unabashedly to describe the idea behind this process of adoption.[2]

Conversely, the naval thinkers and officers of other nations are held to have 'scorned' the value of a powerful broadside armament[3] or to have been ignorant of its potential. The Mediterranean nations in particular are generally held to have 'lagged behind' in recognizing the value of the new idea.[4] In fact the purely intellectual aspects of a problem of evolving technology have mistakenly been emphasized. The idea had been there all along. Only the means were lacking. It can be shown that the development of the broadside sailing warship was a continued process the pace of which was closely attuned to whatever was technically possible at any given time. One of the subsidiary objectives of this book is to make that point.

There was a corresponding progression in the evolution of sailing ship tactics. We shall attempt, therefore, by examining selected examples, to establish the rough outlines of that progression. Our primary interest, however, lies in the early development of the true broadside sailing warship. At what point did a vehicle emerge which was technically capable of

---

[1] D. W. Waters, 'The Elizabethan Navy and the Armada Campaign', *The Mariner's Mirror*, XXXV, No. 1 (January, 1949), 95.

[2] For example, by Garrett Mattingly, *The Armada* (Boston, 1962), p. 196.

[3] For example, see Waters, 'The Elizabethan Navy and the Armada Campaign', p. 110. To be completely fair to Waters, he states that the Spanish 'had scorned' cannon power before the Marques de Santa Cruz' victory over the French off the Azores in 1582, but that they 'had ceased to scorn it when the Armada came'.

[4] Carlo Cipolla, *Guns, Sails and Empires* (New York, 1965), p. 84.

exercising control of the sea in the Mahanian sense? Since control of the sea can be won only through battle, it is from an examination of battle tactics that we must find the answer.

Examination of the record makes it clear that even though solutions were being sought, the technical problems of the sailing warship which made it an intrinsically defensive weapon were not solved in the fifteenth century. The fight between four Genoese carracks and a body of Turkish galleys off Constantinople on 20 April 1453, was more like a siege on land than a naval engagement.[1] The Muslim galleys clustered around the carracks and attempted to board under cover of a hail of arrows while the Genoese sailors and men at arms replied from above with crossbow bolts, hand-cannon pellets and assorted heavy objects hurled down in an attempt to stave in the bottoms of the Muslim boats. Though gunpowder weapons, probably including cannon, were used in this encounter they had little effect on its outcome.

Of more interest to us is the battle of Zonchio, fought near Lepanto in August of 1499 between an Ottoman fleet centered around a large carrack under Burak Re'is[2] and a Venetian force including two armed carracks under Loredan and Armer. We are fortunate in knowing a good deal about this fight, described in some detail by Haji Kahlifeh, also known as Katib Chelebi.[3] Chelebi wrote a century and a half after the fact, but a Venetian woodcut survives which must be very nearly contemporary with the battle itself and whose details are in complete accord with those of Chelebi's account.[4] A reproduction of this woodcut appears on the dust jacket.

A careful reconstruction of a Venetian carrack *ca.* 1500 by Björn Landström[5] shows a vessel armed with a large number of small wrought-iron swivel pieces along the railings. Though more advanced in its rigging

---

[1] An account and analysis of this fight, recorded by Kritovolous, is in Lefebvre des Noëttes, *De la Marine Antique à la Marine Moderne, la Révolution du Gouvernail* (Paris, 1935), pp. 112–23.

[2] Burak Re'is was a *ghazi* seafarer recruited into the Ottoman system by Sultan Bayezid II. See A. C. Hess, 'The Evolution of the Ottoman Seaborne Empire', *American Historical Review*, LXXV, No. 7 (December, 1970), 1905.

[3] *The History of the Maritime Wars of the Turks* (London, 1831), pp. 20–1.

[4] An original is preserved in the British Museum. I am indebted to Mr Carlo Ramelli, Assistant Director of the Museo Storico Navale, Venice, for having brought it to my attention and for having rendered expert assistance in interpreting its details. Its style and manner of rendition place it firmly in the late fifteenth or early sixteenth century. In addition, its rendering of technical details agrees precisely with what is known about the details of late fifteenth-century rigging and armament. Two examples should make this clear: the Venetian carracks are depicted without ratlines. Ratlines made their appearance on Venetian ships very early in the sixteenth century but not before. The peculiar swivel mounts of the bow guns of the Turkish galleys which the woodcut shows are of a type unknown until a cannon and mount of almost precisely the same type and vintage, now on display in the Museo Storico Navale, were dredged from the bottom near Venice in recent years.

[5] *The Ship* (New York, 1961), pp. 108–9.

details and a somewhat smaller ship, it is thus nearly identical to the two Venetian carracks in the woodcut of Zonchio. But the Ottoman carrack, unfortunately partially obscured by the Venetian ships in the woodcut, seems to have been more strongly armed. Chelebi's description of it is worth repeating:

These vessels [there were two large carracks, built by one Iani who had been a ship-builder at Venice; but only one of them fought at Zonchio] had two decks, the one like that of a galleon, and the other like that of a *maona* [a large oared transport]; and on the side of each of these, according to custom, were two port holes in which immense guns were placed. Along the upper deck was a netting, under which on both sides were four and twenty oars, each pulled by nine men. The sterns were like those of a galleon . . . Each of these ships contained two thousand soldiers and sailors.[1]

We may reasonably suppose that the 'immense guns' were large cast-bronze stone-throwing cannon of the type still on display in and around Istanbul, though perhaps not quite so large. It would be reasonable to suggest that they fired stone balls of at least 200 pounds. Katib Chelebi tells us that they sank outright a Venetian galley and a 'barge' (probably a small sailing ship) early in the engagement, but no further mention is made of them. This is probably explained by the difficulty involved in loading one of these huge pieces, a process fully described by Kritovolous in his *History of Mehmed the Conqueror*. The powder chamber, about one third the diameter of the barrel, was tightly packed with powder. A closely fitting wooden rod was then inserted into the mouth of the chamber and hammered in with iron rods, 'closing in and packing down the powder so completely that, whatever happened, nothing could force it out in any way except by an explosion'.[2]

It is possible that Burak Re'is' men were unable to reload in the heat of battle. If the guns were mounted in fixed timber balks, as they probably were, the gunners would have had to lean completely outside the portholes to pound the wooden wads down, an extended and dangerous operation, and probably a suicidal one in a close boarding fight. For this or for some

[1] *The History of the Maritime Wars of the Turks*, James Mitchell trans. (London, 1831), pp. 20–1.
[2] *The History of Mehmed the Conqueror*, Charles T. Riggs trans. (Princeton, 1954), p. 44, entry 133. These firing instructions provided the key to success in an experiment testing the internal ballistics of serpentine (dry compounded) black powder or the type used in the fifteenth century. The portions of the testing program (undertaken at the H. P. White Laboratory, Bel Aire, Maryland) dealing with serpentine powder resulted in nothing more than a considerable quantity of smoke and a bad smell until, in desperation, resort was had to Kritovolous' loading instructions. The initially close confinement provided by the tight wooden plug gave the imperfectly compounded powder an opportunity to react properly, resulting in internal pressures and muzzle velocities comparable to those obtained with modern black powder.

other less obvious reason the heavy Ottoman artillery had no further effect on the battle. This is underlined by the prominent place given to the anti-boarding netting both in Katib Chelebi's description of the carrack and in the Venetian woodcut.

The Venetian carracks seem to have pressed Burak Re'is hard. Finally, in desperation, he turned to incendiary weapons. Using burning pitch, the Turks set both of their opponents afire, but the conflagration spread and all three ships were destroyed.

Gunpowder had played an important part in the battle, but that part was by no means the dominant one. This conclusion is underlined by a close examination of the contemporary Venetian woodcut. Of twenty-one Turks shown with recognizable weapons in hand, only one is using a gunpowder weapon, a relatively crude hand cannon. Two men stationed in the main fighting top of the Ottoman carrack are employing directional incendiary projectors of some sort. Twelve have composite recurved bows and six are wielding swords.

The percentage of Venetians depicted using gunpowder weapons is somewhat higher. Of twenty-one whose weapons are clearly depicted, four are using primitive arquebusses. Five are using the composite recurved bow, one has a crossbow, five have spears or javelins and three bear edged weapons. Three are simply hurling down objects of various sorts – barrels and rocks – on their opponents below. Though hardly conclusive in precise percentages, this difference between the Turkish and Venetian preferences for individual weapons is surely accurate in generally indicative terms. More will be said about national differences in the rate of adoption of gunpowder weapons in the following chapter. Suffice it to say here that in 1499 traditional weapons were holding their own in naval combat, particularly among the Turks. Combat between sailing warships was still a haphazard, hit or miss affair in which even the heaviest and most advanced weaponry offered little hope of a decisive and favorable outcome.

The half century following Zonchio saw considerable change in the design, handling characteristics, and armament of sailing warships, particularly of the nations of the North Atlantic. At some point the classic gunwale-to-gunwale donnybrook of the type exemplified by Zonchio gave way to admit the possibility of stand-off artillery action; but the effect on tactics was not at once overwhelming. This is borne out by the record of early naval artillery actions.

The earliest of these were probably those between the Portuguese and their Muslim opponents in the east.[1] But little record remains of their

---

[1] Vasco da Gama's initial victory of Calicut seems to have been the only one of those actually fought between moving fleets under sail.

tactical details and the Muslim ships involved were for the most part very weakly armed. The first full-fledged running fight between broadside sailing warships of which any detailed tactical record remains is that which took place between William Towerson's *Tiger* of London, 120 tons burden,[1] in company with a Frenchman of similar size and five Portuguese warships off the Guinea coast on 27 January 1557.[2]

The details of this engagement were instructive. Towerson in the *Tiger*, accompanied by the *Hart* of London, 60 tons, and a pinnace of 16 tons, had gone out to the Guinea coast with the main object of trading for slaves.[3] We have no knowledge of the armament of the English ships other than the significant fact that the *Tiger* carried its main battery on a lower gundeck firing through ports near the waterline. It must therefore have consisted of relatively heavy cannon. From the description of an elephant hunt which Towerson's men undertook ashore we know that his men were armed with 'harquebusses, pikes, long bowes, crossbowes, partizans, long swordes, and swordes and bucklers'.[4] In personal weapons, at least, gunpowder had not yet triumphed over traditional weapons and skills. A half century had produced little change from the armaments of Zonchio.

Upon arrival on the Guinea coast Towerson's flotilla fell in with a similar group of French ships under one 'captaine Blundel' whose flagship was evidently of a size similar to the *Tiger*.[5] Of the armament of the French ships we know only that the pinnace was armed with 'four bases'.[6]

As to the armament of the *Tiger* and Blundel's flagship, upon whom the burden of combat was to fall, we can only speculate. Our detailed knowledge of the armament of certain English ships of the following decade, principally Hawkins' *Jesus of Lubeck* captured at San Juan de Ulloa, gives us the basis for an educated guess. It is unlikely that Towerson's main

[1] That is, its rated carrying capacity was 120 'tunnes' of wine. Its modern displacement tonnage would have been somewhat larger.

[2] This is from Richard Hakluyt, *The Principal Navigations*, vol. VI (Glasgow, 1904), pp. 220–2. I first encountered reference to Towerson's fight in 'Notes', *The Mariner's Mirror*, XL., No. 3 (August, 1954), 233, through A. H. Taylor's comment that the Portuguese were first to recognize the defensive power of the line astern. See also Taylor's fine article 'Carrack into Galleon', *The Mariner's Mirror*, XXXVI (April, 1950).

[3] All of this is based upon the account in Hakluyt, *The Principal Navigations*, vol. VI, pp. 212–31, entitled 'The second voyage made by Maister William Towerson to the coast of Guinea, and the Castle of Mina in the year 1556 . . .'.

[4] Hakluyt, *The Principal Navigations*, vol. VI, 'The second voyage made by Maister William Towerson . . .', p. 215.

[5] 'Flagship' is technically a misnomer. Towerson's account uses 'admirall'. The system of tactical flag signals which gave flagships their name was still almost a century in the future. In 1557 the command and control of fleets of sailing warships was in a rudimentary stage at best.

[6] A 'base' (Spanish *verso*) was a wrought-iron, breech-loading swivel piece of perhaps 300 to 600 pounds weight and two to four inches bore diameter. It generally fired scatter shot.

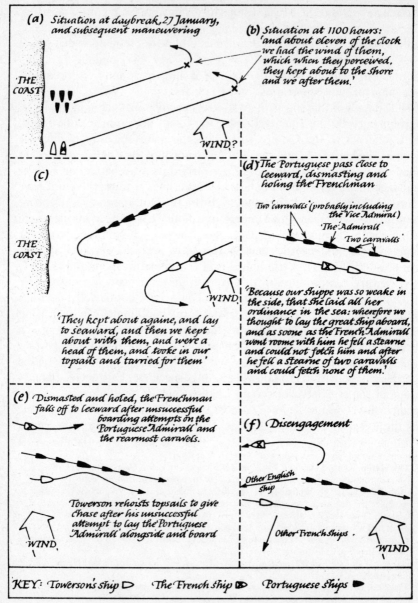

(a) *Situation at daybreak, 27 January, and subsequent maneuvering*

THE COAST

(b) *Situation at 1100 hours: 'and about eleven of the clock we had the wind of them, which when they perceived, they kept about to the Shore and we after them.'*

WIND?

(c)

THE COAST

'*They kept about againe, and lay to seaward, and then we kept about with them, and were a head of them, and tooke in our topsails and tarried for them*'

WIND

(d) *The Portuguese pass close to leeward, dismasting and holing the Frenchman*

Two 'caravalls (probably including the Vice Admiral)
The 'Admirall'
Two 'caravalls'

'*Because our Shippe was so weake in the side, that she laid all her ordinance in the sea: wherefore we thought to lay the great Ship aboard, and as soone as the French Admirall went roome with him he fell a stearne and could not fetch him and after he fell a stearne of two caravalls and could fetch none of them.*'

(e) *Dismasted and holed, the Frenchman falls off to leeward after unsuccessful boarding attempts on the Portuguese 'Admirall' and the rearmost caravels.*

Towerson rehoists topsails to give chase after his unsuccessful attempt to lay the Portuguese 'Admirall' alongside and board

WIND

(f) *Disengagement*

Other English ship

Other French ships .

WIND

KEY: *Towerson's ship* ▷ *The French ship* ◈ *Portuguese ships* ◣

Fig. 3   William Towerson's fight off the Guinea coast, 27 January 1557
All quotations are from Towerson's log, 'The Second Voyage made by Maister William Towerson . . .', in Richard Hakluyt, *The Principal Navigations*, VI (Glasgow, 1904), 221–2.

gundeck battery consisted of more than eight cannon of about 4,000 pounds weight each. These would have been at most thirty pounders, that is guns firing a thirty-pound cast-iron ball. Two or three of them might have been pedreros, guns cast for a cut stone ball of slightly greater weight and considerably greater size. The bulk of the main battery would have been somewhat smaller than this with perhaps a single pair of relatively large pieces behind the rearmost broadside ports. A few smaller pieces, perhaps four, firing balls of twelve to six pounds or less, would have been mounted on the upper deck.

In the face of a common enemy – the Portuguese jealously guarded their dominance of the Guinea coast – Towerson and Blundel agreed to share their trade, sailing together for mutual protection. On 24 January, after a period of profitable trading, they got word that a Portuguese squadron was working its way up the coast to oppose them. Therefore they set sail at dusk on the night of the 25th (apparently they had fairly detailed intelligence of the Portuguese position) and 'lay close [hauled] all night to get the wind of them'. In this they did not succeed. On the 26th, still to leeward, they caught sight of their opponents for the first time, at anchor near shore. Finding themselves unable to 'fetch' (pull to windward of) the Portuguese before dark, Towerson and Blundel anchored 'within a demiculverin shot' of them and issued out 'white scarffes' to their men as an identifying mark in case the Portuguese attempted a night attack and it came to boarding. Both sides weighed anchor at dawn on the 27th and made out to sea. Whether through superior sailing or – more likely – a fortuitous shift in the wind during the night, the allies 'had the wind of them' by eleven o'clock.

This placed the two flotillas in the situation shown in Fig. 3, position *b*. The French and English 'admiralls' had by this time been abandoned by their smaller consorts who stood well clear to windward throughout the ensuing engagement. Both sides fought in a line astern: Towerson and the Frenchman apparently as a tactic of opportunity, the Portuguese by design. The engagement was, in the event, indecisive. The Portuguese could probably have closed with and destroyed or captured at least the Frenchman; but their mission seems to have been simply to drive off the interlopers.

The Portuguese squadron consisted of five ships, three caravels and two proto-galleons.[1] Towerson's description of them is worth repeating:

---

[1] Ship design was still in a period of transition in 1557 and the definitive galleon is not known to have emerged. Their sailing characteristics make it doubtful that the two larger Portuguese ships were of the carrack type; but it is plain that they stood considerably higher in the water than the caravels. I have therefore used the term 'proto-galleon' to describe them.

three of them which were the smallest went so fast that it was not possible for a ship to boord them, and carried such ordnance that if they had had the weather of us they would have troubled 3 of the best ships that we had, and as for their Admiral and Vice admiral they were both notablie appointed.[1]

Reference to Fig. 3 should place this statement in context. It seems clear that the smaller of the Portuguese ships were designed and armed for stand-off artillery action. This is significant. So is Towerson's surprise at it. It is apparent that both the French and English considered boarding their chosen method of combat. This should come as no surprise: they were in it for loot more than for victory. Stand-off artillery action was a profoundly defensive tactic hardly suited to their habitually piratical objectives.

Towerson, for his part, found that he was unable to use his main battery against his targets to leeward 'because our shippe was so weake in the side [lacking in lateral 'stiffness'] that she laid all her ordnance in the sea'. Whether this meant that the ship's heel laid the gunports in the water so that they could not be opened or that it depressed the guns, presumably with inadequate means of elevating them, so that their fire fell short, is unclear. In any event it is plain that only the Portuguese were really prepared for the sort of fight which ensued.

Even they – and this is a point which we shall encounter again – seem to have lacked sufficient heavy ordnance to arm their two larger ships. It is evident from Towerson's account that the fire of the caravels was devastating and that of the two larger ships ineffective. Our most likely explanation is that they were armed, in the absence of enough good heavy ordnance, with numbers of relatively small swivel guns for a boarding fight where their greater height in the water would have carried the maximum advantage. This turning of necessity to advantage must have been a common phenomenon, and shows that the scarcity of artillery could play a dominant role in determining its employment. The Portuguese wisely chose to combine their heaviest fire power with their most mobile ships.

A number of general points emerge from analysis of this action (the graphic depiction shown in Fig. 3 was chosen over a narrative account for reasons of clarity and brevity); it is plain that the Portuguese understood the defensive advantages of the line ahead to windward and used them consciously. They were almost certainly the first to do so.[2] The development of this tactic is generally attributed to the period of the Anglo-Dutch

[1] Hakluyt, *Principal Navigations*, vol. VI, p. 222.
[2] A. H. Taylor's comment in 'Notes', *The Mariner's Mirror*, XL., No. 3 (August, 1954), 233.

naval wars of the middle 1600s, almost a century later, with the Dutch Admiral De Ruyter generally receiving the main credit.

While limiting the choice of action to acceptance or refusal of battle at the enemy's option, the line ahead to windward allowed for increased effectiveness of defensive artillery fire 'to which the enemy for a time was unable to reply'.[1] This was partly because the attacker, in turning in toward the defensive line to close the distance or to board, had to turn his broadside away from his intended point of contact while the defender's broadsides continued to bear. Added to this on occasions were the action of wind and waves which drove the attacker's lee gunports under, making it unsafe or impossible to open them.

All of this combines to make one major point: the initial impact of artillery on galley tactics was negligible. The galley had been an intrinsically offensive weapon before the advent of gunpowder and it remained one until its demise. The sailing ship, on the other hand, was hardly a warship at all before gunpowder. But the initial effect of cannon armament was to add not to its offensive capability, but to its defensive power. Before the broadside sailing warship could be used in a truly offensive role major technical, intellectual and tactical breakthroughs had to be made.

William Towerson's fight showed the broadside sailing warship of the mid-sixteenth century at the limit of its capabilities. Towerson and Blundel had no thought but to board their opponents – a repetition of the tactics of Zonchio. The only real improvement was in their determination to do so from an advantageous position gained by control of the weather gage if at all possible. But they were frustrated in their attempts to do so by the superior Portuguese sailing ability, tactics and firepower. When Blundel and Towerson took in their topsails to await the Portuguese and board, the Portuguese handily avoided their attempts to pull alongside. The first caravel passing from astern holed the Frenchman and the second brought down his mainmast. This effectively forecast the essentially defensive nature of broadside sailing ship tactics almost down to Nelson's day. Unless a fleet actively desired close action or was badly handled, it was difficult indeed to bring it to decisive action. This intrinsically defensive character of sailing warships does much to explain the survival of the war galley. It might not pay a galley to attack a heavily armed broadside ship; but the galley could usually avoid the sailing vessel at will until much later.

A final point bears repeating before we discuss the development of

[1] Alfred T. Mahan, *The Influence of Seapower Upon History* (Boston, 1890), p. 6, has an excellent discussion of the relative advantages of the lee and weather gages. Line ahead varied from line astern only in the position of the flagship.

gunpowder weapons and their impact on the Mediterranean system of warfare at sea. We noted an apparent difference in the degree to which Burak Re'is' men and their Venetian opponents had adopted firearms. There seemed also to have been a Turkish preference for the composite recurved bow. These national preferences in individual weaponry were not, as we shall point out in chapter 4, the product of whim or chance. Like many other regional differences between Mediterranean naval forces which we shall discuss in the following chapter, these were the product of underlying cultural, social, and economic differences

THE MEDITERRANEAN SYSTEM OF NAVAL WARFARE: PHYSICAL, ECONOMIC AND SOCIAL LIMITATIONS

In the preceding chapter we discussed the basic technical and tactical solutions to the problems of war at sea which were imposed by Mediterranean conditions. When the sixteenth century dawned the war galley – using the term in its broadest sense to include all oared fighting vessels of any size – was the principal instrument of armed violence at sea in the Mediterranean as it had been since antiquity. The introduction of effective heavy artillery during the course of the fifteenth century had done nothing to change this. The result was the tactical framework which we have just discussed. But factors other than purely technical ones were at work.

Any government or group of individuals which armed and manned a galley was diverting economic and social resources from some other task. This sort of trade-off in the allocation of resources is an integral part of any decision to create and employ armed force. The benefits expected to result from the creation of armed force must be weighed against the social, economic, cultural and political cost. But that cost is not a simple function of the total resource requirement expressed in monetary terms. This was as true in the sixteenth century as it is in the twentieth.

The type and scale of resources needed to support a galley fleet imposed, as we might expect, their own peculiar restrictions. These have never been rigorously investigated, but certain broad qualitative and quantitative observations can be made which go a long way toward establishing the nature of the conceptual framework within which armed conflict at sea was conducted in the sixteenth-century Mediterranean.

Perhaps the logical place to begin is with the fortified port. We have already touched on the nature of the tactical relationship between the fortified port and the galley fleet; now we shall undertake an analysis of the strategic relationship between the two. This hinged on logistical and socio-economic factors, that is on the quantity and quality of men, provisions, armaments and munitions which could be obtained through the fortified port. The galley was tied to its port in space by the rapid consumption of provisions and tied to its port in time by a variety of more subtle social and economic considerations. It would be no exaggeration to characterize the nature of sixteenth-century Mediterranean warfare at sea as a symbiotic relationship between the seaside fortress, more particularly the fortified port, and the war galley. The purpose of this chapter is to examine the nature of this relationship and its strategic ramifications.

This relationship is most readily apparent in its effect on the radius of action of galleys and galley fleets. Here the contrast between the galley fleet and the fleet of sailing warships is striking and complete. The main sources of a sailing warship's power were her hull, sails and guns. These consumed stores – powder and shot, pitch, tow, cordage, canvas – only on an occasional, as-needed basis. The galley had these requirements as well; but the fighting heart of the galley was the muscle and blood of her men. Where powder and shot, pitch, tow, cordage and canvas could be stored indefinitely and used at will, water, biscuit, wine, olive oil, fish, meat and cheese were consumed on a daily basis and spoiled rapidly. This combined with the size of a galley's crew, the crucial military importance of their health and vigor, and the severe limitations on storage space aboard specialized rowing vessels to limit severely the galley's radius of action and to tie it tightly to its bases.

For individual galleys and galiots operating in the *guerre de course* the limitations which this imposed were not too severe. Though the galley's cruising radius was theoretically determined by its need to take on water at intervals of two weeks or less[1] it was not too difficult for a galley or two to find an undefended beach, land, and slip a watering party ashore. Small raiding squadrons also had a reasonable expectation of being able to capture, either afloat or ashore, enough provisions to keep them going for extended periods: indeed an example of precisely this sort of thing was given in chapter 1.

But for an entire fleet, the problem was one of an entirely different magnitude. Fleets, their speed governed by their slowest ships, moved far more slowly and far more predictably. Where almost any spring would satisfy the needs of a single galley, the places where a fleet of fifty or more galleys could water in a limited period of time were well known and comparatively few in number. Where a quick raid ashore for mutton or the biscuit supply of a captured ship would keep a raiding galiot provisioned for weeks, the amounts of provisions which an entire fleet required were not simply floating around for the asking. The movements of fleets and squadrons were further restricted by outbreaks of sickness among the *ciurmi* and fighting men. We read time after time that upon reaching a particular port the commander of a squadron was forced to take various

See pp. 62–3 ff above.

of his galleys out of commission because of gaps in the ranks from disease or to halt for a number of weeks to allow his oarsmen to recuperate. In 1570, for example, the Venetian fleet was decimated by an outbreak of sickness shortly after the commencement of hostilities with the Ottoman Empire. This paralyzed it at a critical period and forced the Venetians to rely heavily upon allies whose objectives were at cross purposes with their own, thus insuring the fall of at least Nicosia and probably Famagusta as well.[1] Oarsmen, like water and provisions, were readily available only in small quantities.

All of this comes down to one basic point: the radius of action of galley fleets was restricted by logistic factors and was an inverse function of the size of the fleet or squadron involved. The larger the fleet, the shorter its radius of action. We shall show in the concluding chapters that this restriction became increasingly severe during the course of the sixteenth century and that it had an important economic dimension.

The inverse relationship between a galley fleet's size and its radius of action requires elaboration. This quickly involves us in two subsidiary problems: the requirements of galley warfare in general for ports capable of providing the manpower and the logistical and technical support required by galley squadrons and fleets, and the contrast between the support requirements of the 'little war' and those of classic naval warfare in the usual sense. These two problems are closely bound up together.

In theory, at least, fortified ports were unnecessary to the offensive prosecution of the 'little war'. Small-scale raiding operations could be launched from improvised bases in bays and along the beaches. The Muslim sea *ghazis* of Anatolia, in fact, seem to have operated in this way during the fourteenth and fifteenth centuries. In practice, however, the advantages of secure fortified ports were readily apparent and the maintenance of convenient bases was an integral part of raiding operations. The location of such bases was a prime consideration. The closer the raiders' bases were to their targets, the more effective their raids were likely to be, both in the narrowly tactical sense and in terms of cost effectiveness. Preying galiots and fustas, working close to home, could continue to operate from such bases even in the winter and the fortified port gave the raider convenient refuge from enemy warships. The limitations of galley fleets ensured that raiders would always be able to get in and out of their ports since, practically speaking, close and prolonged blockade was impossible. The Mahanian response to the *guerre de course* was therefore

[1] See the account of the campaign of 1570 given by Sir George Hill, *A History of Cyprus*, vol. III, *The Frankish Period 1453–1571* (Cambridge, 1948), pp. 892ff.

precluded and prolonged 'little wars' of economic attrition were the rule in the sixteenth-century Mediterranean. Such major naval battles of the classic sort as punctuated the sixteenth century almost invariably revolved around an attempt by one party or another to seize a strategic base for raiding.

Routine countermeasures against raiding operations also required bases. The Spanish developed a whole chain of bases along the northern coast of the Mediterranean from Gibraltar to Messina, with outposts in the Balearics and Sardinia, to support squadrons engaged in protecting the coasts from Islamic raiders. The Venetians, in their heyday at the end of the fifteenth century, had an almost continuous line of fortified ports stretching down the eastern shore of the Adriatic, around the Morea, along the northern coast of Crete, and as far as Cyprus. These ports provided safe havens for Venetian commerce and supported small squadrons of galleys involved in its protection.

These numerous small bases were well suited to the 'little war' of raid and counter raid; but it must be emphasized that the forces involved were usually modest. During the last two decades of the sixteenth century the Venetian standing fleet consisted of only 29 galleys in time of 'peace' (up from 23 in 1523) of which four or five seem to have been laid up for repairs at any one time.[1] It was broken down into squadrons, the largest of which consisted of only a dozen galleys based in Venice itself. The others were considerably smaller: the squadron based in Canea to protect Venetian commerce in Cretan waters had only four galleys on strength. Under normal circumstances the Galleys of Spain, the main Spanish squadron engaged in anti-raiding work, rarely exceeded fifteen galleys in strength and the Galleys of Sicily, based in Messina, seem never to have exceeded ten.[2] The restriction which kept such forces small in size was not so much total cost, though that was a factor, but limitations in the logistical base available for their support.

This can be placed in context by comparing the modest forces of the 'little war' with those required for a major expedition. Charles V's Tunis expedition of 1535 included 74 galleys and 30 galiots in addition to something of the order of 150 large roundships and numerous smaller ones carrying 25,000 infantrymen and 2,000 horses.[3] The Turks brought 130 galleys, 18 galiots, 8 *maonas* (large oared transports) and 14 large round-

---

[1] Alberto Tenenti, *Piracy and the Decline of Venice 1580–1615* (Berkeley, 1967), p. 121.

[2] *Colección Sanz de Barutell (Simancas)*, *Artículo* 4, dto. 265, gives the strength of the Galleys of Spain on 14 June 1562 as 12. Dto. 42 from the same *Artículo* gives their strength as 15 in 1536 and that of the Galleys of Sicily as 4.

[3] Francisco-Felipe Olesa Muñido, *La Organización Naval de los Estados Mediterraneos y en Especial de España Durante los Siglos XVI y XVII* (Madrid, 1968), vol. I, p. 363.

ships carrying about 29,000 troops and a large siege train from Constantinople to the siege of Malta in 1565.[1]

The logistical apparatus which sustained the raiding galiots and small protective squadrons of the 'little war' was inadequate to support such an effort. There were two main reasons for this. First and perhaps most obvious, only a very large port city with a rich hinterland behind it could provide the quantity of economic support which such an expedition required. Thus the number and size of the port cities of the various Mediterranean powers placed a direct limit on the size of the expeditions which they could mount. Gross quantitative differences in support facilities do much to explain the balance of armed power at sea in the sixteenth-century Mediterranean.

The second point is more complex. The high cost of maintaining a galley in commission kept galley fleets small in ordinary times, yet comparatively large forces were needed to support a major expedition such as the two mentioned above. The ability to greatly expand a small peacetime fleet at short notice was therefore essential. This required, in addition to the requisite quantity of logistic support and manpower reserves, certain specialized facilities whose size and efficiency were critical determinants of naval strength. Shipyards were needed so that the requisite number of galleys could be built and commissioned quickly. Arsenals were needed to cast cannon for them. Powder mills had to be available with the reserve capacity to supply a large expedition quickly. So did ovens for the baking of ship's biscuit in great quantities. This last requirement tells us a great deal about Mediterranean warfare reflecting the heavy emphasis upon man-power rather than machines. An examination of the way in which biscuit was handled by the various Mediterranean powers provides an interesting insight into the differences in outlook between them.

Biscuit assumed a unique importance since it was not only the backbone of the galley crew's diet, but also the only major constituent of that diet which was more or less non-perishable. The importance of biscuit to Venice is underlined by the position of the *Provveditore sopra i biscotti*, officials of the biscuit, within the Venetian naval establishment. In charge of provisioning, these *Provveditori* sat as full members of the *Collegio della Milizia da Mar*, the supreme Venetian naval planning body.[2] Even more

---

[1] The estimate of ship strength is from a contemporary document attributed to Don Juan Paez de Castro in the *Colección Navarrete*, vol. IV, dto. 19, fol. 224. See 'Malta, 1565', p. 184 below.
[2] Olesa Muñido, *La Organización Naval*, vol. II, pp. 1004–10. The *Collegio della Milizia da Mar* consisted of a representative of the Doge, 3 *Savii* representing the Seante, 3 *Provveditori all' Arsenal* in charge of the construction and repair of ships, the *Provveditori sopra i biscotti*, the *Provveditori alle Artiglierie* in charge of artillery production, and the *Pagadori all Armar* in charge of finance.

suggestive is the existence within the Ottoman provisioning bureau, the *Mevkufat Kalemi*, of a *peksimet emini*, the intendant of the biscuit. Although theoretically lower in the hierarchy than his Venetian equivalents – he had no direct counterpart in the decentralized Spanish naval bureaucracy – his position was better integrated into the operational process.[1] The *peksimet emini* kept a running account of the availability of supplies for the baking of biscuit and the production of the ovens under his control, generally coordinating procurement and production. Unlike the *Provveditori sopra i biscotti*, who were curiously disconnected from the command of the Venetian fleet, and the heads of the various Spanish biscuit ovens, who fell under the control of the Viceroys, the *peksimet emini* was in effect directly responsible to the *Kapudan Paşa* through the central bureaucracy of the Provisioning Bureau.[2] This careful attention to the coordination of the provision of biscuit by the Ottoman fleet, certainly the largest and probably the most offensively minded of the Mediterranean fleets of the sixteenth century, is a significant and suggestive fact. In contrast, the decentralization of control of the means of providing for the supply of biscuit within the Spanish possessions suggests an essentially defensive orientation and certain inherent bureaucratic limitations on the offensive capabilities of Spanish naval power.

The importance to a major expedition of specialized facilities such as biscuit ovens, cannon foundries, shipyards and powder mills cannot be over-emphasized. Since the high cost of maintaining a galley in commission kept the squadrons used in normal times small, the ability to expand the fleet rapidly through the use of such facilities to launch an invasion or to repel one was essential.

To some extent the characteristics of the galley made this fairly easy. A relatively modest number of experienced seamen were needed on each galley and galley hulls were relatively cheap. Seamen from the standing squadrons could be apportioned among newly commissioned galleys to serve as cadres and to train the new crews.[3] The same sort of built-in

---

[1] I am indebted to Professor Joel Shinder of Fredonia State University, New York, who discovered the existence of the *peksimet emini* while doing research in Istanbul in 1969 on a Ford Foundation grant under the auspices of the Department of Oriental Studies, Princeton University.

[2] The *peksimet emini* was mainly concerned with coordinating and record keeping. He was answerable to the *Kapudan Paşa* through the chain of command of the *Mevkufat Kalemi* from whom he was separated by at least two levels of the bureaucracy. The point is that there was a direct line of authority running from the operational commander of the fleet right down to the lowest levels of the Provisioning Bureau.

[3] The importance of this factor was first brought to my attention by Sammy J. Cannon's unpublished term paper submitted 9 January 1962 to satisfy the requirements of Oriental Studies 535, Princeton University (Professor Itzkowitz), 'The Condition of the Ottoman Navy in the Sixteenth Century and Some Causes of Its Decline', p. 29.

capability for expansion applied to the rowing gangs as well. Starting around the middle of the fifteenth century there was a shift in the rowing system of Mediterranean galleys from one where each oarsman pulled his own individual oar to one in which all the oarsmen on a bench pulled a single large oar. This shift, largely completed by 1550,[1] reduced the requirement for experienced oarsmen by two-thirds or more. Henceforth only one skilled oarsman, the man farthest inboard who feathered the oar and set the pace, was needed to a bench. The others did not have to be skilled, but could be 'trained' for their work in the modern sense of the word, a crucial distinction which we shall elaborate on in chapter 4. It was a relatively simple matter to embark soldiers from the land army as needed. But all of this had to be supported by an effective logistical base of shipyards, arsenals, powder mills and biscuit ovens. The size and qualitative characteristics of the logistic bases of the various Mediterranean powers did much to determine the extent and nature of their power at sea. Our discussion of these considerations leads, by the very nature of things, into a discussion of the strategic balance in the Mediterranean during the sixteenth century.

The requirements for a logistical base capable of supporting a major operation could, as previously noted, be satisfied only by a major port city with excellent harbor facilities and either a rich hinterland to its rear or a well developed trade network supporting it. During the sixteenth century only three cities of the Mediterranean satisfied these requirements beyond doubt: Barcelona, Venice, and Constantinople. It is no accident, therefore, that these cities formed the nuclei of the great Mediterranean naval powers in the age of the galley: Spain, Venice, and the Ottoman Empire. These three cities, perhaps more than the nations to which they belonged, dominated Mediterranean naval warfare.

A number of other cities might have made the list, but for one reason or another did not. Alexandria was never developed as a first-class naval base, either by the Mamluks or by the Ottomans. Salonika was a specialized provisioning base and a point of embarkation for troops, but lacked technical support facilities. Lisbon clearly satisfied all the requirements, but entered directly into the mainstream of Mediterranean maritime conflict only on rare occasions, notably Charles V's Tunis expedition of 1535. Her most significant contribution to the Mediterranean maritime struggle was indirect and far to the east, between Aden, Ormuz, and the Coramandel coast.

Of lower capability than these great port cities were a number of others

---

[1] We will have a great deal to say about this shift, highly significant as an indicator of social and economic trends, in ch. 5.

which had all the qualitative prerequisites, but were backed by fewer economic resources or, in several cases, less governmental interest: Seville, Málaga, Marseilles, Genoa, Toulon, Algiers, Naples, Messina, and Smirna. Expeditions of only moderate size could be dispatched by these cities; but they served as excellent forward staging bases for a major one.

Next we have a much larger group of ports on which a squadron could be based or which could, if adequate resources were brought along, serve as a staging base for a major expedition. Here harbor facilities and strategic location became more important than economic resources. Most of the minor ports already mentioned in discussing the basing requirements of the little war fall into this group.

There were, in addition, a number of lesser ports which, because of their unique geographic situations, had great strategic significance. All of these had two essential characteristics: first, their harbors were spacious and well protected from the elements. Consequently they were capable of staging a major expedition or at the very least serving as a major center of raiding activity. Second, and most important, access to them by hostile land armies was difficult or impossible. This was of central importance. Most of them were on islands of no great size. They could be seized and held by naval power alone.

Prominent in this group were the cities of Rhodes, Canea on Crete, Famagusta on Cyprus, Coron at the south-western tip of the Morea, the fortress city of Corfu, Tunis and the island fortress of La Goleta in its harbor, the island of Djerba, Malta, and Puerto Mahan on Minorca. All of these places derived their importance from the inability of an amphibious expedition to conquer any extensive stretch of territory very far from its bases. The nature of this limitation is perhaps best illustrated by several examples, both hypothetical and real.

An Ottoman attempt to capture and hold Messina in the sixteenth century would have been patently absurd. Experienced and competent military commanders, if not their political superiors, were well aware of this. The Turks could hardly have overrun all of Sicily with the armed strength of a single expedition and the Spanish power in Sicily was considerable and solidly based. With a vast expanse of coastline, including several ports, on which to land their forces, it would have been easy for the Spanish to get troops ashore to attack the besiegers from behind. This was particularly significant inasmuch as Naples was very close at hand and Genoa within striking distance. Very small naval forces would have sufficed for this effort, since a sixteenth-century galley could transport as many as 400 infantry on a short haul and disembark them on almost any beach. Therefore, even if the Spanish fleet had been utterly crushed in battle, the capture of Messina would have been an impossible project for an Ottoman fleet. Even if they had captured the city by a fluke it is most unlikely that the Turks could have held it for long.

The same considerations would have applied to a combined Spanish and Venetian attack on Negropont. They did not, however, apply to an Ottoman descent on Rhodes or Cyprus. The economic resources of both of these islands, particularly Cyprus, were not inconsiderable; but they were close to the sources of Ottoman power. In addition they were too far from friendly bases to be easily relieved.

About all the defenders of Rhodes or Cyprus could hope for was enough relief supplies and men to make the siege a long and protracted one and wear out their opponents. This worked for the Knights of St John in 1480, but Rhodes fell to an all-out effort by Suleiman I in 1522. Although a brilliant relief by Antonio Quirini helped to make the siege a long and costly one, Famagusta went under after a siege which lasted for almost a year, from 18 September 1570 to 1 August 1571.

The fortresses in question were very strong ones and the cost involved in taking them was high – too high for the Ottomans at Rhodes in 1480 – but the defense and mode of relief was entirely passive. If relief could be got in at all, it would consist of supplies and reinforcements for the garrison, not an independent force to break the lines from the outside and raise the siege.

A different set of considerations applied to an Ottoman descent on Malta or a Christian one on Tunis or Djerba. Here the geography of the place made it fairly easy for a superior besieging fleet to prevent any large relief force from getting ashore despite the relative proximity of hostile bases. If the relief force did get as far as the beaches the besiegers could, at relatively short notice, leave their lines briefly and meet them in the awkward act of disembarking. The thought of an opposed landing with a superior fleet baying at his heels was enough to chill the guts of the most courageous Mediterranean naval commander. The fear of getting into just such a predicament explains Don Garcia de Toledo's protracted delay in getting the final decisive relief into Malta in 1565. It also explains the great stealth involved in the first, small, relief. The final relief went in only after most of the remaining convertible Ottoman resources of oarsmen, ammunition, and infantry had been expended in a last desperate assault on Fort St Michael and Birgu. There was not enough left with which to put to sea to face the relieving fleet without breaking off the siege.

These examples suggest the principles which were the core of sixteenth-century Mediterranean naval thought. They revolved around a three-way relationship between the available forces, the distance of the objective from each side's bases, and the tactical strength and strategic significance of the objective itself. The emphasis is far different from that which the Mahanian conceptual framework would suggest.

In addition to the restrictions imposed on a galley fleet's radius of action by its need for provisions, an additional and less flexible restriction was imposed by seasonal factors. Where the provisioning problem could be overcome to some extent by forward bases and sheer logistical mass, the seasonal limits were notably unresponsive to human attempts to stretch them. The Mediterranean campaigning season was short, from mid-March to mid-October at the latest, and a galley fleet could go only a limited distance from its bases and still return home before the advent of the winter storms. The farther a galley fleet went from its bases, the less time it could spend at its objective before being forced to return. The time factor was particularly critical since the objective of a major expedition was almost invariably a major fortress the reduction of which was likely to involve a prolonged siege.

Historians have long been aware that this sort of factor exercised a decisive limitation on the campaigns of Ottoman land armies, but explicit recognition of its functioning at sea has been oddly belated. The operation of such a factor at sea was first explained in detail and its importance pointed out by A. C. Hess, appropriately enough an Ottoman historian, in 1966.[1] Ottoman awareness of the factors discussed above was keen, as Hess has effectively demonstrated. The Spanish were equally cognizant of the limitations of galley fleets, as we shall show.

We should not imagine that these limits to the campaigning season were the product of poor seamanship or of an exaggerated fear of heavy seas. Mediterranean conditions made it possible – and therefore necessary – to operate highly specialized fighting ships in the summer. The same design characteristics which made them militarily effective in the summer weakened their ability to resist the elements with any degree of certainty in the winter. On many occasions fleets were scattered and decimated by a sudden onslaught of bad weather at or just after the close of the normal campaigning season. Charles V's disaster at the hands of the great storm of 24, 25 and 26 October 1541, when fourteen galleys and no less than 130 transports of various sizes were driven ashore and wrecked, is perhaps the most spectacular example, but by no means the only one.[2] We have already mentioned the storm which caught Bar-

---

[1] 'The Closure of the Ottoman Frontier in North Africa 1574–95,' unpublished Harvard dissertation (1966).

[2] C. W. C. Oman, *A History of the Art of War in the Sixteenth Century* (London, 1937), p. 697. This was out of a total force of about 50 galleys and 150 transports according to Olesa

barossa's fleet just two days after the battle of Prevesa in 1538 and drove it up against the Albanian coast with heavy loss in hulls, though probably not in manpower.

The restriction on the length of the campaigning season placed an equally stringent restriction on the distance over which a sizeable fleet could operate without the use of a permanent wintering station. The Ottoman fleet which recaptured Tunis in 1574 left Istanbul on 15 May and returned in November. About a month and a week were consumed in travel each way, leaving just over three months of effective military action at the objective.[1] The limits of this campaign – just over a thousand miles one way from base to objective – represented the extreme limits of a late sixteenth-century galley fleet powerful enough to reduce a major objective. The limits on smaller forces were less stringent, but the force which they could bring to bear on the objective was correspondingly less. The resultant strategic framework was thus a product of seasonal and geographic factors and of the intrinsic characteristics of the galley and galley fleets.

Mediterranean naval commanders – if not their politically or religiously oriented superiors – were keenly aware of the operation of all of these factors. We are aided in our understanding of them by the survival of an evaluation of the strategic situation of the Spanish Empire which was made just following the campaigning season of 1564 and submitted to the Council of Galleys in Madrid by the Captain General of the Sea, Don Garcia de Toledo.[2] This will be of direct interest to us in our analysis of the siege of Malta following chapter 4. The report combines an estimate of the situation with a list of recommendations for action to be taken,

---

Muñido, *La Organización Naval*, vol. I, p. 364. Haji Kahlifeh, *A History of the Maritime Wars of the Turks*, James Mitchell trans. (London, 1831), p. 68, states that 106 ships were driven ashore and that 4 galleys were forced to run into the harbor and were taken.

[1] Hess, 'Closure of the Ottoman Frontier', p. 75. According to Spanish sources the size of this fleet was at least 240 galleys and 25 large galiots, 16 *maonas*, 3 galleons and about a dozen large sailing ships of unspecified type. These figures are based on three eyewitness reports: dtos. 63, 64, and 65 in the *Colección Sanz de Barutell (Simancas), Artículo* 6. They are the report of the captain of a reconnaissance *fusta*, the report of an ordinary escaped galley slave, and the report of an escaped galley slave who was a Knight of St John. All three agree fairly closely: but I have used the latter's somewhat lower totals because of his evident familiarity with naval matters.

[2] An eighteenth-century transcription of this document is in the *Colección Navarrete*, vol. XII, dto. 79, fol. 195 ff. Navarrete himself made a thorough search of the family papers of the descendents of Don Garcia de Toledo in 1792–3 with fortunate results for the naval historian. The Council of Galleys was a deliberative body which advised Philip II on naval matters. Don Garcia de Toledo had just led a major Spanish expedition in the conquest of the Peñon de Velez, a Muslim raiding base on the North African coast directly south of Málaga. This expedition, the first Spanish success to break the long chain of disasters going back to Djerba, must have done much for Don Garcia's reputation.

combining its consideration of the factors which we have just discussed in a highly sophisticated manner. It was written by a thoroughly competent and seasoned commander and deals, as a proper military evaluation should, with known enemy capabilities instead of with probable enemy intentions. Written at the high point of Ottoman power at sea it was, of necessity, concerned almost entirely with defensive matters.

The report began by considering the options open to the Ottoman fleet in order of their danger to Spain. The means of countering each possible Ottoman gambit were discussed, along with a listing of the means which each counter would require. The form which this portion of the report takes is highly revealing. It consists of a list of every Spanish port or fortress (in sixteenth-century Spanish the meaning of fortified port was carried by a single word: *plaza*) open to Ottoman attack by sea. The first of these, the point of greatest danger, was Malta.

The loss of Malta, according to Don Garcia, would 'redound to the great harm of Christendom'. The reasons for this and the reason for Malta's strategic vulnerability were not explicitly spelled out in the report; but they are quite clear and were implicit to the entire line of reasoning followed by Don Garcia. Malta was close enough to the Ottoman sources of naval power to permit a strong and sustained attack upon it, yet close enough to the Spanish sphere of interest to be a serious threat to Spain in Turkish hands. The danger was heightened by Malta's small size: Don Garcia was very explicit about this point. Since Malta was small, it would be difficult to get relief onto the island in the face of a superior fleet.

La Goleta, the island fortress dominating the harbor of Tunis, would be easier for the Ottomans to capture from the narrowly tactical point of view, but it would represent less of a gain to the Turk than Malta, a perpetual thorn in his side. It was also farther from his bases and thus a difficult objective from the strategic and logistic point of view. Because of La Goleta's peculiar geography – a tiny island fortress lying almost surrounded within a hostile harbor – relief would be almost impossible without a superior fleet, clearly something which Don Garcia did not envisage. He therefore recommended that reinforcements and materials for fortification be sent in during the winter to strengthen the place.

With Puerto Mahon on Minorca the situation was reversed. The loss of Puerto Mahon would be an enormous blow to Spain; but Minorca was so close to the Spanish bases that relief would be easy. It was so far from Ottoman bases that any siege could only be a short one. The fort there was undermanned according to Don Garcia, but he felt that the garrison would have no difficulty in holding out until help arrived.

The threat to the Spanish presidios of Oran and Mazarquivir on the African coast far to the west was even less. The campaigning problems for the Ottoman fleet would be enormous and the prospective gain marginal. If their fortresses were kept in decent shape they would be in little danger.

For completeness, the mode of response to an Ottoman attack on any of the Spanish places on the northern coast of the Mediterranean was included in Don Garcia's survey. The description of the anticipated tactical response – we must bear in mind that an inferior Spanish fleet was assumed – is so graphic as to bear quoting in full:

It seems to me that the other regions and places [literally, *plazas*, fortified ports] from Velona [a port on the Dalmatian coast opposite the heel of the Italian 'boot'] to here [Barcelona] have relief, because, placing a large force of men in the fleet, although it is dangerous and misfortune might occur, still you can disembark them near the place attacked by the enemy to try by land that which you cannot by sea.

The pattern was clear. Don Garcia's whole concept of naval strategy revolved around the attack, defense and relief of fortified ports. His conceptual framework was an amphibious one, not an exclusively naval one, as the phrase 'to try by land that which you cannot by sea' clearly indicates. His ideas were evidently closely shared by the Sultan's closest advisors and by Piali Paşa, his Ottoman opposite number. The blow fell at Malta, just as Don Garcia had predicted.

But even more important than what this report says is what it does not say: at no point was the possibility of a general fleet engagement even considered. It was not that the Spanish fleet was inferior and had to avoid contact. Don Garcia de Toledo simply did not consider the Spanish fleet a proper Ottoman objective. In his view Piali Paşa would have been either a fool or derelict in his duty to seek out and destroy the Spanish fleet instead of proceeding straight to his objective. Don Garcia plainly considered him neither.

The frequently encountered assertion that Mediterranean naval commanders of the sixteenth century were no more than land soldiers embarked aboard ship and were consequently ignorant of the ways of war at sea simply does not hold up under examination. We would have to look very far and hard to find a strategic evaluation of equal explicitness, accuracy and sophistication written by a Dutch or an English naval commander until much later. This is only to be expected, since the art of commanding fleets of galleys was a very old one in 1564 and that of commanding fleets of sailing warships hardly born.

Having investigated the factors which limited the galley's employment in space, we now turn to those which restricted its employment in time. In addition to the seasonal limits which the Mediterranean weather placed on the operations of galley fleets, there were economic restrictions which affected the timing of the galley fleet's employment and which were, in the long run, even more rigid. These operated in two ways. The sailors, oarsmen, and soldiers of galleys engaged in the perpetual little war were more or less full-time professionals. But relatively few of them – unlike the Dutch Sea Beggars or the English Sea Dogs – did nothing else at all for their livelihood. Mediterranean warfare at sea was a seasonal affair and many of those who engaged in it were employed in productive economic activity during the five winter months when galleys were habitually taken out of commission. A galley's cooper or barber would obviously be inclined to follow his trade ashore; but there were other and less obvious examples. We know that skilled French galley slaves in the early 1700s were allowed to ply their trades during the winter months and that certain of the others were allowed to perform manual labor for hire in the port towns.[1] There is every reason to expect that this was a long established custom.

Off-season economic activities were frequently of considerable economic significance. They could range all the way from an Algerian galley slave used to dig irrigation ditches, to the free Venetian oarsman or sailor who signed on board a merchant ship, to the Turkish soldier in the Morea who used the winter months to supervise the operation of his agricultural *timar*[2] holding.

The rhythms of Mediterranean war at sea were geared to this annual economic cycle. Galley fleets campaigned in the winter months upon occasion. It was a calculated tactical risk which often paid off. But it was a device which could be used only so often without resulting in serious economic dislocations. The small naval establishments which lived off the proceeds of the *guerre de course* – notably the Knights of Malta and certain of the North African sea *ghazis* – were alone in being relatively immune to this limitation.

The second form of economic restriction operated over the long term. Perhaps even more powerful, its effects were interwoven and mixed up with those of the first. The sailors, oarsmen and soldiers of the galleys engaged in the perpetual little war were more or less full-time professionals, if only on a seasonal basis. But the social complexion of a large expedition was quite different. Large numbers of men had to be called up for a limited period of service. Their absence from their habitual occupations created a degree of economic dislocation which could not be tolerated for long.

[1] Jean Marteilhe, *Galley Slave* (London, 1957), pp. 64–9.
[2] The *timar* was a non-hereditary feudatory grant of land for military service.

The major Mediterranean naval powers, Spain, Venice and the Ottoman Empire, based their capability to launch a major expedition or to repel a major threat upon their ability to expand their standing fleet quickly into a force capable of undertaking a major expedition. This was done by expanding the galley fleet itself and by mobilizing large numbers of sailing vessels, usually commandeered merchant ships, to provide logistical support and to serve as troop transports. The long-term economic effects of these two steps were much the same. This kind of effort could be undertaken only so many times in so many years before the absence of the fisherman from his village, the *timar* holder from his land, the free oarsman from his fields or flocks, and the merchant seaman and his ship from their trade routes resulted in intolerable economic hardship.

The impact of disturbing these two closely interrelated cycles of warfare at sea varied from nation to nation. The Ottoman fleet was least constant in size from year to year and was thus presumably most affected by long-term economic limitations. The Spanish fleet[1] varied least in size and thus was presumably most affected by short-term economic restrictions. There is incomplete but suggestive evidence to support this theory.

The outpouring of precious metals from the New World following the second decade of the sixteenth century gave Spain the wherewithal to employ large numbers of salaried professionals, particularly professional soldiers, on a more or less permanent basis. This was a key Spanish advantage and a very necessary one given the efficiency and flexibility of Ottoman institutions. Large numbers of soldiers could be mustered for sea duty, as in 1571-3, then released from service afloat and put to other tasks when the danger had passed.

The Spanish, unlike the Ottomans, did not have the fiscal organization and social flexibility needed to expand their naval forces rapidly every second or third year and then demobilize them at the close of the season. In a sense this was inevitable for military reasons since massive demobilization was a luxury which Spain could not afford. Moreover, the Ottomans held the initiative at sea for most of the sixteenth century. They were free to plan their offensive strokes to maximize the force behind them and to minimize the economic dislocation which they caused. Spain, however, had to respond to each Ottoman challenge whenever and wherever it

---

[1] Technically the Spanish fleet, if such an organization can be said to have existed, was a temporary combination of the various permanent squadrons of galleys with temporarily enlisted soldiers and galleys and conscripted support vessels for the undertaking of a particular task. I have used the term here to mean the combined total strength of the various major unconnected standing squadrons of galleys: the galleys of Spain, Naples, Sicily, Andrea Doria's Genoese squadron, and so on.

came. This posture demanded a larger permanent force, a force made possible by American gold and silver.

But if a relative abundance of precious metals gave Spain some immunity from the long-term economic restrictions of war at sea, they made her uniquely vulnerable to the seasonal ones. This was in part because of a curious economic backlash. The same abundance of precious metals which made it possible for Spain to maintain an adequate standing fleet raised the level of prices of all the things which a galley fleet needed. It was consequently more expensive to operate a galley along the coasts of Spain than anywhere else in the Mediterranean.[1] This disparity was well known and was compensated for by basing as many galleys as possible in Spain's Italian dominions.

The problems of seasonal economic dislocation were clearly recognized. In a document associated with the one just cited, Don Garcia de Toledo argued in 1564 that his charge as Captain General of the Sea should be merged with that of Viceroy of Sicily.[2] That, he said, would permit a minimization of economic dislocation – he was thinking primarily of the Sicilian sailors employed on his galleys – by placing economic and military planning under one head. His model, interestingly enough, was an explicitly Ottoman one: the combination of the *Kapudan Paşa's* operational control of the fleet with his extensive holdings in the Morea. Significantly, Don Garcia's request was granted and he was made Viceroy of Sicily as well as being Captain General of the Sea.[3]

The heavy Spanish dependence upon precious metals tied to their need to minimize long-term economic dislocation gave the Spanish naval bureaucracy an almost fanatical obsession with cost-cutting measures, spurred on by regular urgings from Philip II. His detailed instructions to the highest officials on the steps to be taken to prevent fraud and to safeguard money entrusted to them bordered on the comical. Ridiculous schemes to reduce expenditures were concocted by hangers-on at court,[4]

---

[1] This fact is reflected in most contemporary Spanish documents dealing with the costs of operating a galley (see Figs. 12, 13 and 14, pp. 223, 224 and 225). F. Braudel, *La Méditerranée et le Monde Méditerranéen à l'Epoque de Philipe II*, Spanish edition (Mexico City, 1953), p. 352, states that prices in Sardinia and the Balkans were low by Italian standards.

[2] This 'discourse' is in the *Colección Navarrete*, vol. XII, dto. 78, fol. 289.

[3] This experiment was not repeated however. The crisis of 1565 passed and the two posts were never again combined under a single head, probably – though this is conjecture – because of Philip's obsessive distrust of powerful subordinates. For Philip's relations with his subordinates and his methods of controlling them, see H. G. Koenigsberger, 'The Statecraft of Philip II', *European Studies Review*, I, No. 1 (1971).

[4] One of the most spectacular and least practical of these was a scheme advanced in 1570 by one Tomas de Lupian to protect the commerce of the West Indies with a massive fleet of no less than 60 galeasses. (There were only six at Lepanto.) The cost of arming and maintaining

and one royal official actually went so far as to urge the commanders of galleys to save money by reducing the expenditure of powder and shot on the Turk.[1]

It was repeatedly emphasized that crews were to be released in the winter months, whenever possible, to reduce the royal payroll.[2] From the 1530s the numbers of armed seamen aboard Spanish galleys were systematically reduced for the same reason. Regular Spanish infantry – who had in any case to be on the payroll all year round to prevent mutiny – were embarked in their place for any serious undertaking.[3]

The Spaniards, in a defensive strategic posture, had to maintain a standing galley fleet of some size on a permanent basis. They were therefore forced to rely almost exclusively upon servile rowing power to reduce maintenance costs. Only when faced with absolutely no alternative did the Spanish arm their galleys with salaried free oarsmen.[4] This was not only of military and economic importance, but had political significance as well since the Spanish consciously used condemnation to the galleys as a device for social control.[5] The use of free oarsmen was so far from the Spanish practice that the term employed to describe them, *buenas boyas*, was a direct borrowing from the Italian *di buona voglia* – of good volition – and meaningless in Spanish.

But for the Ottomans the free oarsman offered numerous advantages. The higher cost of maintaining him on campaign was offset by the fact that he needed to be employed only occasionally. The system of taxation

these was to be defrayed by the tax proceeds of a total monopoly on trade. Among other things, the galeasses themselves were to haul wine to the New World for sale at highly inflated prices. The cost accounting of this document is detailed, the technical ignorance behind it appalling. The document is in the *Colección Navarrete*, vol. VIII, dto. 96, fol. 612.

[1] The document containing this cost-cutting suggestion, dating from about 1590, is in the *Colección Navarrete*, vol. VIII, dto. 26, fol. 169. Its tone, attitude and bureaucratic jargon bear a striking resemblance to U.S. Air Force directives of the McNamara era (*ca.* 1964–7).

[2] This seems to have been emphasized increasingly from the middle of the sixteenth century on. A document of 1600, *Colección Navarrete*, vol. IX, dto. 34, fol. 360ff., section 2, paragraph 2, emphasizes that locally recruited arquebusiers should be released from service and taken off the payrolls in the winter.

[3] This transition can be seen in Spanish documents cited as the sources for Figs. 12, 13 and 14 (pp. 223, 224 and 225). See also Olesa Muñido, *La Organización Naval*, pp. 789–843, for a full discussion of the origins and role of troops embarked on Spanish galleys.

[4] This consideration was closely linked to the rise of prices. The salary of a Spanish *remero de buena boya* (free oarsman) was 1 ducat a month in 1538. By 1571, *Colección Sanz de Barutell* (*Simancas*), *Artículo* 4, vol. 2, dto. 322, fol. 420–2, it had risen to 10 ducats per months less a 2-ducat 'clothing allowance'. It is significant that no evidence of the use of *buenas boyas* between 1539 and 1571 was encountered. The Lepanto campaign, and the need for large numbers of oarsmen which it presented, no doubt forced the Spanish authorities to revert to a practice which they had long abandoned, at least on a large scale, for reasons of economy.

[5] I. A. A. Thompson, 'A Map of Crime in Sixteenth Century Spain', *The Economic History Review*, 2nd series, XXI, No. 2 (August 1968), 244–67.

was in any case geared to support him directly. In combat, the free oarsman was an asset rather than a liability. Though hardly the equal of a Janissary or a Spanish infantryman of the *tercios*, a hardened Anatolian or Greek villager could do serviceable work with a scimitar. His services in siege warfare ashore as a sapper and miner or to swell the ranks of storming parties were indispensable. '*Azabs*, irregular light infantrymen, seem to have been employed habitually in some numbers as oarsmen for just this purpose.[1]

Free *maryol*[2] oarsmen who enlisted of their own volition in return for free maintenance and a small salary, supplemented by a sizeable minority of slaves, seem to have satisfied the bulk of the Ottoman requirements in ordinary times. According to a Christian report of the mid-sixteenth century, of 130 Ottoman galleys in commission at an unspecified date, 40 were rowed by slaves, 30 by salaried volunteer Christian oarsmen and 60 by conscripted salaried Muslim oarsmen.[3] In 1556 three galleys of the squadron of Ali Burtasi were, according to Muslim sources, rowed by slaves.[4] His *Capitana* and two others were rowed by '*azabs* and the remaining 36 were rowed by salaried Greek oarsmen. Our source is specific in stating that the proportion of servile oarsmen was heavily diluted with free Muslims 'in time of war' for reasons of combat effectiveness and security.

The extraordinary demands of a major campaign were filled by a system of short-term conscription which was carefully juggled to minimize economic dislocation. Each village in the districts covered was assessed in December by representatives of the *Kapudan Paşa* to provide a given number of oarsmen for the following campaigning season, depending upon the number of households in the village and the navy's requirements. One oarsman was generally taken for every twenty to thirty households in a given year. His upkeep was paid for by the remaining households as a form of taxation. This was a general Ottoman practice and applied also to the '*azabs*.[5] According to the Ottoman naval historian Ismail Uzuncarsılı, in the fifteenth and sixteenth centuries one of each twenty taxable units in the assessed villages, presumably households, had to provide an oarsman, the remaining nineteen units providing for his wages and maintenance.[6]

---

[1] See H. Bowen, ''*Azab*', *Encyclopedia of Islam*, new edition, vol. I (London, 1960), p. 807.

[2] This term apparently applied only to Christians. See H. Kahane and A. Tietze, *The Lingua Franca in the Levant* (Urbana, Ill., 1952), entry 399, 'maryol'. The same term also applied to salaried Christian sailors.

[3] Cited by Olesa Muñido, *La Organización Naval*, vol. II, p. 1154.

[4] Ismail Uzuncarsılı, *Osmanli Devletinin Merkez ve Bahriye Teskilati* (Ankara, 1948), p. 482.

[5] H. Bowen, ''*Azab*', *Encyclopedia of Islam*, new edition, vol. I (London, 1960), p. 807.

[6] *Osmanli Devletinin Merkez ve Bahriye Teskilati* (Ankara, 1948), p. 482.

This system seems to have been applied alternately to the European and Anatolian provinces of the Empire on a year-on and year-off basis to minimize economic hardship. Evidence of this practice is found in a report of 1534 by a Spanish agent in Constantinople on the condition of Barbarossa's squadron. This states that the oarsmen on his ordinary galleys in that year were 'from Serbia and Bulgaria and had never before been to sea'.[1] The lack of Anatolian oarsmen is suggestive of the recruiting system described above. The same general system of conscription seems to have been applied to fishing districts and villages to obtain sailors.

The backbone of the Ottoman military system on land was the *timar*, a non-hereditary feudatory grant of land made in return for service by the *timar* holder and his retainers in time of war as armored horse archers. Although the extent to which it was applied to naval service remains an open question there is no doubt that to some degree it was.[2] In any case the *timar* system was entirely characteristic of the Ottoman culture and the Ottoman approach to recruitment of trained fighting men. It deserves our attention for this reason alone.

In its original and uncorrupted form, the grant of a *timar* holding was made only in recognition of military service. In return for control over the land and its inhabitants and the administration of their taxation, the surplus above a certain amount going to the *timar* holder, the *timariot* was expected to appear in the field at his own expense as a fully armed cavalryman (*sipahi*), accompanied by similarly armed retainers if his holding was a large one, when called out on campaign. *Timariot sipahis* often served dismounted as heavy infantry aboard ship and at sieges. Though they seem to have shared the true cavalryman's distrust of ships and distaste for assaulting a breach dismounted, they could – at least during the sixteenth century – be induced to do both and were first-class fighting men in every respect. They were of particular value since virtually all of them were highly proficient with the Turkish composite recurved bow. Some of them can be seen in the engraving by Mateo Perez d'Aleccio of the fall of Fort St Elmo at the siege of Malta in 1565 giving covering fire to the assault parties.[3] There is, in addition, evidence that the *timar*

---

[1] *Colección Sanz de Barutell (Simancas) Artículo* 6, dto. 20, fol. 41–2. See also Olesa Muñido, *La Organización Naval*, vol. II, pp. 1152–4.

[2] See 'Timar', *Encyclopedia of Islam*, vol. IV (London, 1924), pp. 767–76. See also Uzuncarsılı, *Osmanli Devletinin Merkez ve Bahriye Teskilati*, p. 495, for a general discussion of the sources of fighting men for Ottoman naval expeditions.

[3] Reproduced in Balbi de Correggio, *The Siege of Malta*, Ernle Bradford trans. (London, 1965), following p. 88. There is no guarantee, of course, that the individuals seen in the foreground employing their bows are *sipahis*, but their dress and equipment suggest that they are cavalry and the Janissaries are known to have gone over to firearms almost exclusively by this time.

system was applied to specifically naval service in the Morea and the islands of the Aegean.[1]

It is well recognized by Ottoman historians that the economic limitations of the *timar* system served as an important restriction to the expansion of the Ottoman Empire on land. The close relationship between the fiscal, military, and economic activities of the *timar* holder which made this inevitable was characteristic of Ottoman society. It should be evident, therefore, that the same sort of limitation was also operative at sea. Thus while the Ottomans were able – so long as they retained the initiative – to minimize the effects of the short-term economic restrictions of naval warfare, they were more inflexibly bound by the long-term ones than their rivals.

The Ottoman situation contrasts strongly with the Spanish. As the sixteenth century progressed, the Spanish increasingly manned their galleys and those of their allies with full-time professional soldiers. By the 1550s, other fighting men seem never to have been embarked on Spanish galleys for serious operations and only rarely on those of Spain's allies. By contrast, in the Ottoman system salaried professional soldiers served only as the hard core of the fleet's fighting strength. Out of a force of about 25,000 fighting men aboard the Turkish galleys at Lepanto only some 4,000 were Janissaries. There were some 12,000 *sipahis* by contrast, and it seems probable that the vast majority of them were *timariots* rather than salaried *sipahis* of the Porte.[2] By contrast, almost all the fighting strength of the galleys of the Spanish contribution to the Christian fleet at Lepanto, some 10,250 troops out of a total of 12,150, consisted of salaried Imperial troops.[3]

The Venetian problem was a special one. Venice had money, but was short of men. Her situation deteriorated slowly and steadily throughout the sixteenth century as the Ottomans progressively overran the traditional Venetian recruiting areas.[4] Since Venice depended upon seaborne commerce for her economic survival, it was obviously in her interests to make any maritime war as short and decisive as possible. This was particularly true of an Ottoman war since the most lucrative Venetian trades, particu-

---

[1] 'Timar', *Encyclopedia of Islam*, 1924 ed., vol. IV, p. 769.

[2] Of these *timariots*, 3,000 were raised from the southern Morea alone. Olesa Muñido, *Organización Naval*, vol. II, p. 1163.

[3] See Manuscript 1693, *Documentos de Lepanto*, Museo Naval, Madrid, dto. 14, fol. 73ff., for a detailed report on the strength of the Spanish–Imperial contribution to the allied fleet at Lepanto. This is covered fully in our treatment of Lepanto. Note also that the Spanish made some 5,700 salaried infantry available to the Venetians.

[4] See G. E. Rothenberg, 'Christian Insurrections in Turkish Dalmatia 1580–96', *The Slavonic and East European Review*, XL (1961–2), particularly p. 137. By 1580 Venice controlled only the coastal cities of Dalmatia.

larly the rich trade in spices, flowed westward from Ottoman ports, and since Venice, particularly in the early sixteenth century, was heavily dependent on wheat from the Greek islands of the Aegean.

A short war demanded a large fleet; but the great cost of keeping a galley in commission kept the Venetian standing squadrons small of necessity. The superb technical resources of the Venetian Arsenal, the relatively low cost of galley hulls, and the availability of capital provided a solution. Working continuously, a relatively modest force of skilled shipwrights, cannon founders, and other necessary artisans could build a large number of galleys and keep them laid up and ready for commissioning. The expense of arming these galleys and the responsibility for manning them was then apportioned out among the Venetian territories, with Venice herself taking the largest share: Venice contributed 61 galleys and 8 galeasses to the fleet which fought at Lepanto, Candia in Crete contributed 18 galleys, Canea 8, Retimo 3, Corfu 3, Cefalonia 2, Zante 2, and Lesina, Querso, Veglia, Capo de Istria, Cataro, Padua, Bergamo, Arbe, and Brescia one each: a total of 106 galleys and 8 galeasses.[1]

The mobilization of such a force required considerable manpower resources. Here the Venetian solution was similar to the Ottoman one. Its only real failing was the lack of the land power needed to protect its primary recruiting grounds in Greece, Albania and along the Dalmatian coast. Sailors presented no problem. Venice had plenty of them in her merchant fleet and only a few were needed to man each galley. Free oarsmen were enlisted on the outbreak of war. Prior to the demise of the merchant galley for economic reasons in the first quarter of the sixteenth century there was a sizeable pool of merchant oarsmen on which to draw. Subsequently, merchant seamen of the ordinary sort seem to have served just as well. In addition, the towns and villages of the Dalmatian coast were expected to provide a second quota of oarsmen on top of those sent to arm the Dalmatian galleys for which the larger towns were responsible.[2] The administration of this system of recruiting oarsmen seems to have been roughly similar to the Ottoman practice, with the assessment being made on the basis of one oarsman for every so many households.

The key point about the Venetian *ciurmi* is that they were largely – at

---

[1] Olesa Muñido, *La Organización Naval*, vol. II, pp. 999–1000.

[2] M. Joro Tadic, 'Les Sources de L'Histoire Maritime Yougoslave', *Les Sources de l'Histoire Maritime en Europe du Moyen Age au XVIIIe Siècle* (Paris, 1962), pp. 74–6. Alberto Tenenti, *Cristoforo da Canal: la Marine Vénitienne avant Lépanto* (Paris, 1962), p. 64, cites the Spanish Ambassador to Venice to the effect that in 1546 the resources of Dalmatia would serve to arm 14 galleys with oarsmen while Crete could arm 12, the Ionian islands 6, Venice proper 20, and the mainland provinces 70. Da Canal estimated, pp. 71–2, that 22 galleys could be armed with Dalmatian oarsmen in 1558.

first overwhelmingly – composed of free men. It is doubtful that true galley slaves, prisoners of war put on the chain, were ever used to any extent. Although an experimental squadron of two galleys was rowed by *forzati* in 1545, the first regularly sanctioned use of convict oarsmen aboard Venetian galleys did not occur until 1549,[1] and only six galleys of the standing squadron protecting the Gulf of Venice were involved. The reason for the introduction of servile oarsmen was one of economy, as the arguments of Cristoforo da Canal, the chief proponent of the innovation, make plain.[2] Although numerous other arguments were given, the crux of the matter was cost. This point is often missed since it was such an obvious one to the Venetian principals in the dispute that most of the debate was devoted to other issues: Da Canal's opponents seem to have conceded him the matter of cost from the first.

Even in the Venetian standing fleet the use of *forzati* gained ground only slowly, probably because of skepticism about their value in combat. In 1569 only 12 galleys were manned by *forzati* and the galleys of squadron commanders in the standing fleet continued to be rowed by free oarsmen through the end of the sixteenth century.[3] This clear preference for free oarsmen by the Venetians on any grounds but economy refutes the idea that a galley could be rowed efficiently only by servile labor.[4] Venetian galleys were known, first and foremost, for their excellent performance under oars and the Venetians could pinch a penny as hard as anyone. They also had their own tactical reasons for this preference, as we shall see in chapter 5. They turned to servile labor only when the economic situation became severe and then with notable reluctance.

The greatest Venetian deficiency was in fighting men. These seem to have been good, but there were never enough of them. They were called *scapoli* or *huomini di spada*, men of the sword, and seem to have consisted mostly of Greek and Albanian mercenaries and men from the Dalmatian coast led by a hard crust of armored Venetian nobles.

[1] Alberto Tenenti, *Cristoforo da Canal*, pp. 83, 85. Small numbers of prisoners of war seem to have been used as oarsmen of opportunity while on campaign, and service in the galleys was apparently used as a means of commuting a prison sentence for bad debts incurred by a Venetian citizen. Those in the latter category, however, seem to have been treated exactly like the ordinary salaried oarsmen: Tenenti, *Cristoforo da Canal*, p. 81.

[2] Tenenti, *Cristoforo da Canal*, pp. 78–83.

[3] *Ibid.* p. 88.

[4] See for example Jean Marteilhe's autobiographical account, *Galley Slave*, pp. 74–5. Marteilhe was a French Hugenot condemned to the galleys in the first years of the eighteenth century. Marteilhe uses an incident involving an unsuccessful attempt to arm four half-galleys with French sailors for oarsmen in 1704 as his basis for saying that 'they are never able to work galleys without slaves'. This must be qualified, as there were a number of factors involved. It is significant that the galleys of the nations which habitually employed free oarsmen were designed to be easier to row.

The Venetian solution to the problem presented by the restrictions of a system of warfare based upon the war galley was a remarkably efficient one. The major weaknesses of the Venetian defense system were neither political, fiscal nor economic in the technical sense, but military: an inability to control her recruiting grounds. The Venetian naval posture in the sixteenth century, like Venice herself, was uniquely sensitive to the long-term economic consequences of a major war.

The solutions of the various minor establishments varied. The Knights of St John used slaves extensively in their rowing gangs and seem to have supplied themselves through coastal raiding as much as possible. We know that they also used mercenary sailors, both Greek and Maltese, and salaried free oarsmen – free Greek oarsmen are mentioned at the siege of Malta in 1565 – but to what extent is not clear.[1] The small size of their establishment and the profitable nature of their 'privateering' activities made it possible for them to man their galleys, at least during the Maltese phase of their history, largely with full-time professional fighting men. These were headed by the Knights themselves and by the lesser military members of the order, who seem to have comprised between them the majority of the fighting strength aboard the galleys of the order. This gave the galleys of Malta the highest proportion of trained, armored men at arms ordinarily carried aboard any of the Mediterranean galleys in the second half of the sixteenth century. A Spanish document of 1600 survives which holds up the galleys of the Knights of St John as an example of the merits of embarking gentlemen (*gente de cualidad*) aboard galleys as fighting men.[2] Unfortunately, little is known about the nature of the Knights' naval organization during their stay on Rhodes.

Except for the unusually high proportion of experienced armored fighting men, the manning of the galleys of Malta was apparently similar to that of the galleys of Spain's Italian client states. The Papal fleet, and the Florentines when they entered the arena in the 1570s, seem also to have used servile rowing power extensively.[3] Local seamen were evidently employed on a seasonal basis and their fighting strength consisted principally of mercenary infantry.

Andrea Doria's Genoese squadron and that of his great-nephew Gian

[1] Balbi di Correggio, *The Siege of Malta*, p. 41. See also Olesa Muñido, *Organización Naval*, vol. II, p. 1106.

[2] *Colección Navarrete*, vol. IX, dto. 34, fol. 360ff, section 2, paragraph 2. See Olesa Muñido, *Organización Naval*, vol. II, pp. 1101 and 1104–6, for a discussion of the functions of the knights embarked on the Order's galleys.

[3] Olesa Muñido, *Organización Naval*, vol. II, p. 1075, states that as early as 1511 convicts were being released from prison in numbers to serve as oarsmen in the Papal galleys. Alberto Tenenti, *Cristoforo da Canal*, p. 100, cites da Canal as considering typical a Florentine galley *ca.* 1571 rowed exclusively by *forzati*.

seem to have used *forzati* almost exclusively for their rowing strength, probably for reasons of economy. We know that the Spanish were forced to employ numbers of free, salaried oarsmen in 1571; yet in the same year Gian Andrea Doria was able to rent out 200 apparently excess *forzati* to Spain at an annual cost of 35 ducats apiece.[1] The Riviera on both sides of Genoa served as a prime source of seamen and Doria's squadrons were well served in this respect. In addition to their obvious function, Genoese sailors had a good reputation for their fighting ability and were regularly embarked as fighting men on Genoese galleys. The contracts of the Genoese naval entrepreneurs generally provided for Spanish soldiers to be embarked only in extraordinary circumstances. Don Garcia de Toledo is on record as considering the Genoese sailors unique among mariners as being good men to have on your side in a fight. But this cut two ways. His royal instructions of 1564 as Captain General of the Sea explicitly urge that care should be taken to prevent outbreaks of fighting between the soldiers and sailors, 'particularly the Genoese'.[2] As time went on, increasing use was made of Spanish infantry, and by the middle of the sixteenth century the Genoese galleys habitually embarked Spanish or mercenary Italian infantry on the royal payroll to supplement or replace the armed seamen for any major enterprise.

Owing mainly to the sparseness of the economic resources behind them, the *ghazi* states of the North African coast were faced with a number of specific problems. They used free oarsmen extensively on the very smallest raiding vessels, where every available arm was needed to swing a sword and where there was a good prospect of profit for all. But on the larger vessels, galiots and galleys, slaves seem to have been used almost exclusively. This is made clear by the detailed record kept by Don Álvaro de Bazan of Muslim ships captured by vessels under his command during the period 1564–83, and by the record of the capture of a Muslim galiot in 1564.[3] We know how many Muslim captives were taken from these ships and how many Christian slaves were set free, thus permitting a comparison. Two hundred and eighty 'Turks' were taken aboard the four galiots listed, and 280 Christians were freed. The number of Christians corresponds almost exactly to the number of oarsmen needed for four galiots, assuming that they were of 18 banks. But from the 21 *bergantins* captured by Bazan's forces only 10 Christians were freed while 365 'Turks' were captured, a circumstance suggesting strongly that these smaller

---

[1] *Colección Sanz de Barutell* (*Simancas*), *Artículo* 4, vol. 2, dto. 324, fol. 430–1.
[2] *Colección Navarrete*, vol. XII, dto. 83, fol. 309, and vol. III, dto. 8, fol. 148.
[3] *Ibid.* vol. X, dto. 7, fol. 48, and *Colección Sanz de Barutell* (*Simancas*) *Artículo* 4, dto. 277, respectively. Galiots were rowed with two men to an oar and four to a bench.

craft were rowed almost exclusively by free men. There are several reasons for this.

First, there were no populous Muslim regions near at hand from which any considerable numbers of oarsmen could be drawn on a seasonal basis, so slaves had to be used as much as possible to minimize short-term economic dislocation. Second, the larger ships carried more fighting men, both in absolute and relative terms, and a hostile *ciurma* represented less of a security problem. Finally, the North African sea *ghazis* always seem to have been able to provide themselves with an adequate supply of slaves through raids on Christian commerce and, particularly, coasts. At least one of these took place in Ireland as late as the 1620s, and occasional raids were still made on northern Spain this late. Particularly worthy of note was a raid by North African ships on the Spanish coast near the Portuguese–Galician border in 1624.[1] The raid was repelled in uniquely Spanish style with the aid of a local monastery, one of whose monks was an old and experienced artillerist retired from his profession and who, if we are to believe the document, sank one of the attacking ships single-handed.

The North African manpower pool seems to have been heavily taxed simply in order to provide an adequate supply of trained sailors and soldiers. Certainly it was not comparable to the great recruiting grounds for seamen along the Andalusian coast, the Rivieras, Sicily, the Dalmatian coast, the islands of the Aegean, Greece, and the Black Sea.[2] An indirect reflection of this manpower shortage can be seen in the prominent part played in the maritime affairs of the North African states by renegade Christians, particularly those who brought nautical or maritime skills with them when they defected. The fighting strength of the North African galleys seems to have consisted of a mixture of experienced seasonal adventurers and full-time *ghazis*, many of them well equipped and proficient with the composite recurved bow. To these were added the permanent salaried retinues of the various local rulers. Algiers supported her own corps of Janissaries, in no way inferior to their Ottoman model, who served regularly aboard ship and constituted the cream of the Muslim assault force at Malta in 1565.

It should be noted in passing that the North African manpower problem was clearly not a qualitative one. Spanish documents of the middle third of the sixteenth century place particular emphasis upon the capture of Muslim – particularly Morisco – galley captains. A sizeable reward was offered by the crown for the capture of these so-called *arraezes* (a corruption of *re'is*), and strict instructions forbade their ransom or release in

---

[1] *Colección Navarrete*, vol. VI, dto. 21, fol. 120.
[2] Braudel, *La Mediterranée*, Spanish edition, pp. 117-18.

prisoner exchanges and prescribed harsh treatment aboard ship to prevent their escape. The royal instructions of 1557 to Don Juan de Mendoza, Captain General of the Galleys of Spain, deal with this in some detail. A prize of 200 ducats was offered for each *arraez* caught, a figure equal to the entire monthly sum provided for the ordinary expense of maintaining a galley in commission, and a reward of 150 ducats was offered for any 'morisco turk'. Captured *arraezes* were to be hung, Moriscos put on the oar.[1] This was an eloquent and sincere testimonial to their technical and military competence. The Spanish genuinely feared the skill and knowledge of these men right down to the captain of the lowest private *bergantin*.

By specializing in the *guerre de course* and making it a paying business, the North African *ghazi* states were able to support a fairly sizeable permanent naval establishment on a year-in and year-out basis. This in turn enabled them to get the most out of their scanty economic and manpower resources by minimizing seasonal economic dislocations. In this respect they resembled the Knights of St John. There was, however, a severe and inflexible limit on the amount of naval force which they could muster on any given occasion. By maximizing their naval power over the long term, they severely limited their short-term ability to expand it in time of need. This meant, in practical terms, that they brought a very high proportion of their available manpower into play on a yearly part-time basis during the campaigning season. This idea is supported by an analysis of the Tunis expedition of 1535 by Don Sancho de Leiva, sent to Don Juan of Austria in 1568 as a model for the conduct of a campaign at sea.[2] Don Sancho states that Barbarossa's manpower strength was high because the campaign began in July and 'at that time [of the year] all the Arabs are near the navy, among whom, by paying them well, he could raise a large number'.

In summary it is clear that economic factors did much to give sixteenth-century Mediterranean war at sea its peculiar problems and characteristics. The economic and social requirements of supporting a sixteenth-century galley fleet were profoundly different in kind from those of supporting a fleet of sailing warships. So were the consequences. We cannot expect generalizations about the nature of maritime conflict developed through a study of the one to apply to the other. Attempts to modify the generalizations based on the study of sailing fleets to fit galley fleets create as many problems as they solve. The only sure course of action was to start from scratch and develop a purely Mediterranean conceptual framework.

[1] *Colección Navarrete*, vol. III, dto. 6, fol. 133.
[2] *Ibid.* vol. III, dto. 10, fol. 162.

Within this framework we have examined the technical reasons for the galley's existence and the social and economic ramifications of its peculiar characteristics.

There are dangers in this approach, too. One investigator cannot hope to cover the entire range of studies needed to rigorously develop such a framework from primary source material. This presents a considerable problem, as there is relatively little secondary material extant which deals with sixteenth-century naval history. The investigator must therefore concentrate his primary research in the areas which he deems most critical, depending upon carefully selected secondary material in the others.

This we have done. We first outlined the relationship between geographic and climatic factors and the technical development of the methods and means of waging war at sea. We then described these means as they existed in the Mediterranean during the sixteenth century. We next briefly examined the tactical and strategic realities of sixteenth-century war at sea. These were then connected with the economic and social demands of galley warfare. What remains is to examine the galley closely within the context thus established, and then to determine what technical changes – if any – were closely bound up with the demise of the galley. It is to be anticipated that such changes, if they in fact took place and if their effects can be identified, will not be technical in the narrow sense. They are more apt to be the technical results of long-term economic and social changes.

We have thus far deliberately omitted mention of most of the technical military factors which had an impact on the nature of galley warfare. There is a reason for this omission. Our discussion up to now has been centered around the geographic, economic and social factors which shaped the nature of sixteenth-century war at sea in the Mediterranean. Most previous analyses have gone wrong by neglecting to consider these factors altogether or by assuming that they applied to galley warfare as they did to sailing ship warfare. This latter fault is particularly misleading since technical military factors were demonstrably more intimately connected with social and economic factors in galley warfare than in warfare under sails. Our general discussion of geographic, climatic, economic and social forces was therefore a necessary prerequisite for a proper consideration of technical military factors.

Perhaps the most important of these technical changes was the spread of gunpowder weapons, in particular artillery. The introduction and generalization of effective artillery armament at sea was the central fact of life of sixteenth-century naval warfare. We have structured the development of our thesis around this development and its effects. Having established the general parameters of galley warfare, we will briefly examine how and when gunpowder weapons were adopted and used, with particular attention to the cultural and economic factors. We will then establish the nature and magnitude of the impact of artillery upon Mediterranean warfare at sea.

Djerba, 1560

The results of Prevesa clearly showed that Venice stood to lose more commercially through enmity with the Turk than she stood to recoup militarily by means of a Spanish alliance. In theory Venice and the Habsburg hegemony combined should have been more than a match for the Ottoman Empire at sea. It did not – for reasons which were as much economic as military – work out that way in practice.

There followed a period of aggressiveness at sea by the Ottomans and North Africans, periodically bolstered by French assistance. The Spanish, occupied with the wars in Italy and, through the Habsburg connection, with the religious problems of Germany and with the Ottoman threat to Austria, fought with their backs to the wall.

The Turk, by contrast, was seldom to be so free of pressing difficulties. An Ottoman expedition to the Gudjerati coast almost simultaneous with Prevesa had resulted in the occupation of Aden, thus relieving the worst of Suleiman's anxieties in that quarter. The subsequent seizure of Basra in 1546 had effectively nullified the Portuguese threat. Suleiman's capture of Baghdad in the winter of 1534–5 had taken the sting of immediacy from the Safavid menace. Only twice in the following two decades, in 1548 and 1554, was Suleiman compelled to campaign to the east beyond Lake Van, and the second of these two campaigns ended with the treaty of Amasia in 1555, initiating a period of peace with Persia which was to last for almost a quarter of a century.

Barbarossa's recapture of Castelnuovo in 1539 was only the first of a series of Spanish misfortunes in the Mediterranean. Charles V's disastrous failure before Algiers in 1541 marked the beginning of a long series of devastating Muslim raids on the coasts of the Spanish dominions. These were climaxed by active cooperation between the French and Ottoman fleets in 1542–4, the latter actually wintering in Toulon. The death of Barbarossa in 1546 did nothing to relieve the pressure.

Barbarossa's lieutenant and successor, Turgut Re'is, operating from his island base of Djerba, continued to mount raids far to the north and west and succeeded in capturing and briefly occupying the Sicilian ports of Pozouli and Castellamare on the Gulf of Naples in 1548. In 1550 he captured the port city of Mahedia on the African mainland between Djerba and Tunis.

This drew a strong Spanish response. Mahedia quickly reverted to Spanish control and a naval attack by Andrea Doria on Djerba the following year nearly succeeded in trapping Turgut's squadron. Doria, with a superior force of galleys, had blockaded Turgut in the channel between Djerba and the mainland. But Turgut, in a remarkable display of Mediterranean seamanship, managed to bring his squadron out by dredging creeks on the opposite side of the island, which Doria had supposed to be unnavigable. Floating his galleys out by the back door, he got away to raid Malta and devastate Gozo in cooperation with an Ottoman fleet, and closed the season in triumph by capturing Tripoli from the Knights of St John.

At this point France resumed hostilities against Spain and active French–Ottoman naval cooperation was undertaken in 1552–4 and 1557–8. In 1556 Piali Paşa, then *Kapudan Paşa*, ventured far to the west to attack Oran and in 1558 mounted a destructive raid on the Balearics, capturing Ciudadela on Minorca with a large haul of slaves. Then in April of 1559 the treaty of Cateau Cambrésis relieved the Spanish of French pressure and deprived the Ottomans of French ports. The successful conclusion of the Schmalkaldian War in 1547 and the religious peace of Augsburg in 1555 had already lessened the danger to the Habsburg dominions in Austria. Having successfully repelled all major Muslim attacks on their coasts and having twice separated the Ottoman–Valois alliance in the nineteen years since Charles V's Algiers debacle, the Spanish felt renewed confidence, in part for technical military reasons: 'Peace has just been concluded with the King of France [wrote Philip II] which leads one to suppose that the Turks, deprived of assistance and lacking any port in the western Mediterranean to accommodate their fleet, will not send it against Christendom.'[1]

The time seemed ripe, therefore, to take the offensive against the North African corsairs. The near success of Andrea Doria's final campaign against Turgut in 1551 must have made the occasion seem particularly auspicious. The blow would, of necessity, take the form of a strike against Muslim bases. It was a question of timing, leadership and of deciding upon a specific objective.

By 1560 Andrea Doria, nearing death at 93, was too old to campaign actively. His customary place as Spain's Captain General of the Sea was therefore assumed by his great-nephew and heir-designate Gian. Philip II's reasons for accepting this transfer of authority are unknown. Perhaps he

[1] Geoffrey Parker, 'Spain, Her Enemies and the Revolt of the Netherlands', *Past and Present*, No. 49 (November 1970).

had no choice. It is plain, however, that military experience and demonstrated leadership ability were not among Gian Andrea Doria's attributes. Only 20 years old when he assumed command, he was to show himself considerably less capable tactically than his predecessor and patron.

The elder Doria's abilities as a commander were considerable, though whether or not he ordinarily exercised them to the fullest extent is a moot point. We may well suspect that he intentionally sabotaged the operations of his allies on more than one occasion; but he was never caught short tactically through incompetence or a lack of foresight, except perhaps at Prevesa. He went on record as warning Charles V against his disastrous Algiers venture of 1541 and generally showed an uncanny ability to avoid disaster. The same cannot be said for his heir. Gian Andrea Doria's record as a naval commander was to be a spotty one. At Lepanto, one of the few occasions on which he showed much tactical initiative, he was totally outclassed by Uluj Ali. It is worth noting that his detractors in the Christian camp questioned not only his loyalty and tactical skill, but also his courage.[1] This was something which had never happened to the elder Doria. Whatever else might have been said about him (and there was a great deal to be said) his personal fortitude was never seriously at issue.

This transfer of leadership was to play a critical part in the campaign of 1560. Both the timing and direction of the Spanish thrust were critically dependent upon the quality of leadership displayed by Doria, the effective commander of the expedition.[2] It is also worth noting that Gian Andrea Doria was to prove incapable of 'shielding' Chios as his predecessor had done. Chios fell in 1566 for reasons about which we can only speculate. The abysmal failure of the campaign of 1560 may well have been among them.

The timing of the Djerba expedition strongly suggests an almost mechanical connection with the end of the French threat to Italy that was formally marked by the treaty of Cateau Cambrésis in April of 1559. One of the greatest strategic advantages enjoyed by the Spanish lay in their access to numbers of first-class professional soldiers, a hard core of Spanish infantry of the *tercios* which could be swelled out to the required dimensions with Italian and German mercenaries. The flow of precious metals from America enabled the Spanish to convert this pool of superb fighting manpower into effective military force at will.

American gold and silver also gave Spain an advantage in strategic

[1] After Lepanto he was alleged to have concealed his prized crystal stern lantern below decks – thus removing his most visible sign of authority from view – to prevent it being broken in the fight and presumably to conceal his identity from the Muslims.
[2] The Duke of Medinaceli commanded the land forces and was the nominal head of the expedition, but never seems to have made an attempt to exercise operational control.

flexibility: a transfer of gold was considerably easier to effect than a transfer of troops. Soldiers could be discharged in Flanders and others hired in Naples with considerably less wastage and effort than the physical movement of the troops themselves would have involved. In addition the Spanish could press their fiscal resources to the breaking point and on several occasions did so. Neither they nor their opponents could afford to be so reckless with human resources. Spain shrugged off her repeated bankruptcies with little immediate damage; but on occasions when her pool of trained fighting manpower was severely hit, the damage was far more visible and immediate. Djerba was one of these occasions.

The Spanish reserves of precious metals were every bit as limited as the French and Ottoman reserves of manpower, but they were considerably easier to redeploy. Just such a redeployment seems to have occurred in the summer of 1559. Preparations for a major naval expedition based on Messina were well under way by July: the Spanish must have stretched their fiscal resources immediately after the treaty of Cateau Cambrésis in order to be ready by this time. The Galleys of Malta arrived in Messina on 31 July, a circumstance which strongly suggests that the initial decision to mount a naval expedition must have been nearly simultaneous with the signing of the treaty.[1]

It is also possible that the Spanish hoped for a winter sailing to forestall the possibility of an Ottoman counterstroke far from Constantinople in the season of storms. If so, however, their hopes were frustrated by the slow progress southward made by the expedition following its assembly at the end of October, a slowness probably justified by a realistic fear of bad weather (see Map 4).

The Spanish expedition was not an excessively large one. About 50 to 54 galleys, 5 galiots, 29 sailing transports of some size (including 2 *galeones*) and 35 smaller ones were involved, the sailing craft carrying a force of perhaps 5,000 Spanish, German and Italian infantry and a siege train.[2] It should nevertheless have been capable of achieving something of value. Unlike many Spanish expeditions it was in the field in strength at the very start of the campaigning season. The correspondingly small

---

[1] The details of the timing of the early stages of the Djerba campaign are based on R. C. Anderson, *Naval Wars in the Levant* (Princeton, 1952), pp. 8–13, and A. Bombaci, 'Le Fonti Turchi della Battaglia delle Gerbe', *Rivista degli Studi Orientali* (Rome), XIX (1941), 193–6; XX (1942), 279–304; XXI, fasc. II, III, IV (1946), 198–218. Bombaci's brief introduction to his Ottoman documents, vol. XIX, pp. 193–6, is the best quick summary of the Djerba campaign available.

[2] Anderson, *Naval Wars in the Levant*, pp. 5–9, William H. Prescott, *History of the Reign of Philip the Second*, vol. III (Philadelphia, 1904), p. 135. Geoffrey Parker, 'Spain, Her Enemies and the Revolt of the Netherlands', p. 76, says that 10,000 Spanish troops were lost at Djerba; but this probably includes oarsmen and seamen.

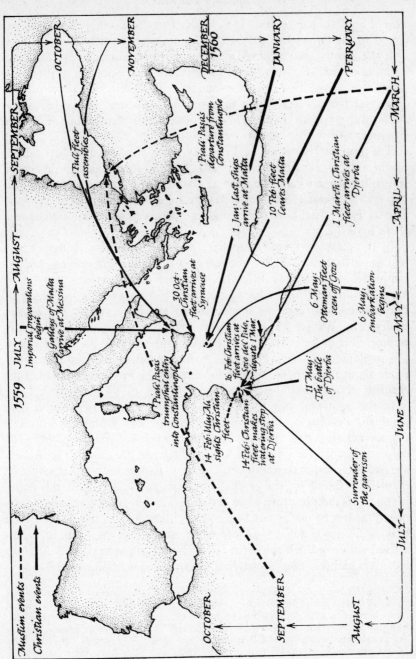

Map 4 The Djerba Campaign, 1560

Muslim events ----→
Christian events ——→

1559 JULY → AUGUST
Imperial preparations begin

SEPTEMBER
OCTOBER
NOVEMBER
DECEMBER 1560
JANUARY
FEBRUARY
MARCH
APRIL
MAY
JUNE
JULY

AUGUST
SEPTEMBER
OCTOBER

Galleys of Malta arrive at Messina

Piali Pasa's triumphal entry into Constantinople

Full fleet assembles

Piali Pasa's departure from Constantinople

30 Oct: Christian fleet arrives at Syracuse

1 Jan: last ships arrive at Malta

10 Feb: fleet leaves Malta

1 March: Christian fleet arrives at Djerba

14 Feb: Ula Ala sights Christian fleet

14 Feb: Christian fleet makes watering stop at Djerba

16 Feb: Christian fleet arrives at Soco del Faio, departs 1 Mar

6 May: Ottoman fleet seen off Gozo

6 May: embarkation begins

11 May: The battle of Djerba

Surrender of the garrison

size of the Ottoman reaction force under Piali Paşa – only 86 galleys, just over half the force which Barbarossa had mustered at Prevesa – indicates that the Spanish had achieved strategic surprise. For once the Turk was reacting instead of acting. But indecisiveness and uncertainty threw the advantage away. The Spanish – and the blame for this must be laid largely at Doria's feet – seem to have vacillated over whether or not to make an attempt on Tripoli. Their vacillation gave the well-oiled Ottoman machinery what little time it needed to react.

Touching at Djerba on 14 February 1560, the Christian fleet landed on the 15th to take on water against light opposition and then proceeded south to Seco del Palo (see Map 4) where it stagnated in indecision for two critical weeks. Not until 1 March did a council of war settle upon Djerba as the final objective. Landing operations were not commenced there until the 7th.

In the meantime three stragglers from the expedition, galleys which had sailed late from Malta because of a delay in provisioning, had attempted to water at Djerba on 18 February and were badly cut up by local Muslim land forces, losing 150 men. Even worse, the main expedition had had the supreme misfortune to brush up against two galleys under Uluj Ali on 13 or 14 February. Uluj Ali made no delay in pulling clear to the north to seek out the Ottoman fleet under Piali Paşa. His intelligence relieved Piali, who had probably sailed from Constantinople about 1 March, of whatever uncertainty he may have had about the Spanish strength and objectives.

In the meanwhile the Spanish forces had overrun Djerba with little trouble. An outbreak of sickness forced the Galleys of Malta to withdraw temporarily from 8 to 27 April, but otherwise all had gone smoothly. The construction of a fort garnished with artillery and dominating the anchorage had been undertaken, evidently under the assumption that it would be regularly relieved by sea or that its garrison could control the entire island. This did not prove to be the case. The Christian forces had completed the fort by 6 May and began to re-embark in leisurely fashion. The bulk of the force was still ashore when, at dusk on the 10th, a *fragata* arrived with word that the entire Turkish fleet had been sighted off Gozo four days earlier.[1] This electrifying news produced instant chaos.

---

[1] This, the following account of the naval battle of Djerba and the subsequent reduction of the Spanish fortress ashore are from an eyewitness account covering events from 10 May to the surrender of the Imperial garrison on 31 July. Originally in Italian, it was translated into Spanish by Navarrete's compilers in the eighteenth century. Entitled 'Relación breve y verdadera dela Jornada de Las Gelves desde el dia que arrivió el Armada Turquesca hasta quel fuerte fue tomado por los Turcos . . .' it is the *Colección Navarrete*, vol. IV, dto. 13, fol. 134–43. This account is detailed, candid and apparently quite accurate.

The German mercenaries seem to have insisted that their contract did not cover garrison duty and that they should be re-embarked first, thus diverting the attention of the Spanish leadership and delaying matters at a critical time. After a series of frenzied conferences held ashore and aboard his galley throughout the night – the contemporary account from which we have this fairly reeks with panic – Doria apparently resolved shortly before dawn to re-embark the entire force and depart. Barely started, the re-embarkation operation was in full swing when Piali Paşa's force of some 86 galleys appeared on the horizon like a thunderclap out of the blue.[1]

Our Spanish source (p. 128, n. 1, above) suggests that the Christian fleet could have held off the Turks had it preserved its discipline and formed on line to oppose them, emphasizing the known combat value of the heavy and well manned Spanish galleys in this sort of fight. He is probably correct. A sizeable force of western galleys formed on line with a friendly shore to their rear could expect to make a successful stand in the face of an enemy with a considerable numerical advantage. In one of his last fights, Andrea Doria the Elder, bound from Genoa to Naples in 1552 with a force of 39 galleys, was surprised by a force of no less than 103 Muslim galleys and galiots under Sinan Paşa and Turgut Re'is. Despite the enormous disparity in numbers, far worse than the odds of roughly five to three which the Christians faced at Djerba, Doria managed to keep his fleet in hand and got off with a loss of only seven galleys.[2]

At the very least, Piali Paşa would have had to accept high casualties to win through to his main objective – the isolation of the Christian force ashore. But Gian Andrea Doria, apparently thinking only of his skin, made no effective attempt to order his fleet in battle formation. Our contemporary account describes the results:

At this point the fleet of the Christians weighed anchor in the worst disorder which was ever seen and put itself in flight and [thus], of a sudden, breaking itself. The Paşa, seeing such a shameful thing, made sail and began to pursue the Christians' fleet and brought it to ruin without striking a blow.[3]

Piali Paşa's reaction on seeing disorder in the Spanish ranks was bold, decisive – and correct. The Ottoman galleys were apparently preparing to lower and stow their sails, yards and masts in anticipation of close combat when they sighted the Spanish fleet. This would have been a standard preparation and a vitally important one, particularly for a formal, head-on

---

[1] Prescott, *History of the Reign of Philip the Second*, vol. III, p. 137.
[2] Anderson, *Naval Wars in the Levant*, p. 6.
[3] *Colección Navarrete*, vol. IV, dto. 13, fol. 134–5.

fight. Brought down by cannon fire, the falling weight of the mast and large lateen yard could crush half the *ciurma* in a single blow.

Piali Paşa's decision to lay on sail was therefore a calculated risk with potentially disastrous results. It made the Muslim galleys considerably more vulnerable to artillery fire and made it virtually impossible for them to maintain formation as they ran down on the Spanish fleet. But it increased the closure speed with the disordered Christian galleys from a crawling two or three knots to a probable six to ten.[1] Piali's order to hoist sail and go straight in ranks among the great snap decisions in naval history. The Spanish had no opportunity to form on line even if they had been so inclined.

The loss to Spain and her allies was severe. Between 28 and 30 galleys were captured or sunk including the *capitanas* of the Pope, Sicily, Monaco and Terranova.[2] The Galleys of Sicily were nearly wiped out in this encounter and the Papal fleet was crippled for years to come. Eight or nine of the larger sailing ships were captured and almost all of the smaller ones taken or sunk. The only bright spot was the successful defense put up by several Aragonese ships and the galleon of Cigala, the latter having resisted attack by 18 Muslim galleys including Piali Paşa's *Capitana*. Among the galleys only those of Malta, Cigala, and perhaps half a dozen additional fugitives managed to get away.

The disaster was complete. The valiant defense of the garrison ashore in the siege that followed did nothing to alter the fact. Andrea Doria pulled out like a thief in the night two days later with a number of swift *fragatas* carrying certain gentlemen of his entourage in addition to himself. His promise to return and relieve the garrison must have seemed as valueless to Don Álvaro de Sande, the colonel of Spanish infantry who assumed command ashore, as in fact it was.

Turgut Re'is arrived a week or so later from Tripoli with a force of 16 galleys and galiots carrying his siege train and both sides settled down to a prolonged blockade. The Spanish resisted with courage and considerable skill. Only toward the end of May did the Turks succeed in driving a covering force of Spanish arquebusiers back from the garrison's exposed water supply, a well in a market place 'a cannon shot' from the walls. From this point it was only a matter of time. The discovery of a meager source

[1] See Olesa Muñido, *La Organización Naval*, vol. I, p. 74. Winds in the Gulf of Tunis are generally variable from the west and north-west during the spring and summer. Piali's fleet apparently stood in from the north on a beam reach, the galley's best point of sailing in light airs.

[2] This is from the account in the *Colección Navarrete*, vol. IV, dto. 13, and Anderson, *Naval Wars in the Levant*, pp. 12–13. I have depended primarily upon the latter for the size of the loss and upon the former for the identity of the more important losses and details of the fight.

of water within the walls – attributed by some to divine intervention – only served to prolong the agony.

Our Spanish source insists that a great opportunity was lost during late May or early June as Piali Paşa

had all of his men ashore, both soldiers and *ciurma*, and both his galleys and those which he had taken from the Christians were completely disarmed with less than 50 men per galley and all the oars and rudders dismounted for fear that the Christian slaves would [capture the galleys and] escape.[1]

This may well have been the case. But the means for exploiting the situation were lacking. Four galleys came out from Malta toward the middle of June to slip in and take off the wounded, losing one of their number on the return voyage. This final sortie represented the limit of Christian naval power.

The fighting ashore was prolonged and bitter. The Turks attempted amphibious assaults on the fortress on several occasions while methodically pushing their siege batteries up to within 60 to 65 yards of the walls.[2] The Spanish took such counter measures as were available to them, grounding several of their galleys and filling them with earth to serve as posts from which offshore flanking fire could be directed into the Turkish trenches.[3]

Ultimately the lack of water told. By mid June the Christians were driven to distilling sea water to supplement the inadequate flow of the small well within their lines; but there was inadequate fuel available to gain much water from this source. By mid July, despite the regular execution of attempted deserters, as many as 20 to 30 men a day were going over to the Ottoman lines, driven mad by thirst. On the 29th the garrison, down to about 800 effective men, made a final sortie. When it failed Don Álvaro de Sande asked for terms. The Djerba campaign was over.

Djerba had a profound effect on Spanish naval power. This was not, however, for reasons which an orthodox Mahanian interpretation would suggest. The most significant effect of Piali Paşa and Turgut Re'is' victory was the loss of trained manpower to Spain. The number of ships involved, relatively small by modern standards, should not deceive us. The loss of Djerba hurt Spain and her allies badly. At a minimum, some-

---

[1] *Colección Navarrete*, vol. IV, dto. 13, fol. 135. 'Disarmed', in this context means 'unmanned' in addition to its usual, North Atlantic, meaning.

[2] *Colección Navarrete*, vol. IV, dto. 13, fol. 139.

[3] H. Kahane and A. Tietze, *The Lingua Franca in the Levant* (Urbana, Ill., 1952), p. 247, entry 325, 'Garida'. Kahane and Tietze's source of information is Bombaci, 'Le fonti turchi della battaglia delle Gerbe'.

thing like 600 experienced *oficiales*[1] were lost there. These were men whose technical expertise was the critical ingredient in the successful conduct of galley warfare: captains, sailing masters, quartermasters, sergeants at arms, *remolares*, *alguaciles*, boatswains, ship's carpenters, coopers, barbers, chaplains, artillerists, and their trained assistants.[2] An approximately equal number of seasoned mariners, mariners who were not only sailors, but hardened fighting men as well, was also lost, together with some 2,000 naval arquebusiers and soldiers accustomed to service at sea plus at least 6,400 oarsmen.[3] The numbers involved, not inconsiderable by modern standards, are almost overwhelming when measured against the scale of naval warfare in the sixteenth century. That this loss crippled the effective Spanish exercise of power at sea is clearly shown by the disasters of the next few years.

The men lost at Djerba were not men 'trained' in the modern sense. They were, in the case of several of the Spanish squadrons, an entire generation of experienced fighting manpower from a given region or principality. They were men who had learned the ways of warfare at sea in the traditional fashion, the products of an entire lifetime of skill and experience. They were all that their regions could spare economically, and that – except in extraordinary circumstances – only during the campaigning season.

The loss of such men on the scale of Djerba clearly had a critical effect on the Spanish exercise of power at sea. Our indirect evidence of this is strong. Our direct evidence, though compelling, is sparse. Our sixteenth-century sources are not given to critical self-analysis. We know, however, that the Spanish had to completely alter their system of manning aboard the Galleys of Naples following Djerba. In place of the naval arquebusiers who had hitherto shipped aboard the Galleys of Naples, regular Spanish infantry had to be embarked for the first time – our source specifically

---

[1] *Oficiales* could have been rendered as 'officers' or as 'officials'; but either of these terms would have been misleading. Though most of these men were not officers in the modern sense, their duties were clearly supervisory in nature. 'Official', on the other hand, has a misleading non-combatant ring, suggesting primarily administrative duties. In fact the *oficiales*, particularly early in the sixteenth century, were the hard fighting core of the war galley. I have based my estimate of 600 on the fact that an ordinary Spanish, Genoese or Sicilian galley of 1560 carried about 15 of these men, *capitanas* carrying more. I have multiplied an estimated average of 20 *oficiales* per galley by 30, the number of Christian galleys lost at Djerba.

[2] See Appendix 5 for a list of the *oficiales* carried on western galleys in the sixteenth century, their titles (which I have rendered only approximately) and their duties. I have used the Spanish terms here, the positions and duties being about the same on all Mediterranean galleys. The *remolar*, as his name suggests, was in charge of the galley's motive power, its oars and oarsmen. His position corresponds roughly to that of chief engineer on a modern warship. The principal duty of the *alguacil* was the rationing and distribution of water.

[3] I have assumed an average of something over 50 fighting men and 160 oarsmen per galley.

says 'after Djerba' – with grave problems of efficiency and discipline – 'great confusion and much disorder' resulting. The problem of getting men used to the sea is specifically mentioned.[1] There is evidence that a similar change occurred aboard the galleys of Sicily at the same time and probably aboard those of Spain as well.[2]

The loss to Spain in trained and experienced leaders was at least as critical as that in soldiers and sailors. Both sides were habitually reluctant to exchange prisoners when experienced naval commanders were involved, a sure reflection of the pain which must have resulted when the shoe was on the other foot. We know for a fact that the ranking Spaniards (and a surprising number of ordinary soldiers) captured at Djerba were released in a prisoner exchange by the Ottomans only after their own considerable loss at Lepanto, the final transfer occurring at Ragusa in May of 1575, fifteen years after Djerba.[3]

It is therefore perhaps more than coincidence that the squadrons of Spain and her allies suffered a series of disasters in the years immediately following Djerba. In November of the same year, two galleys of the Florentine squadron (two had been lost at Djerba) were run aground and wrecked after having been surprised south-east of Elba by a fleet of 13 Algerian galiots and forced to run for it. More serious, the reconstituted Galleys of Sicily, eight in strength, were surprised off the west coast of Italy the next year by seven galleys under Turgut Re'is and captured *in toto*. Shortly before, the three galleys of the Viscount of Cigala, one of the few squadrons to have emerged intact from Djerba, had been captured too.[4] Finally, in 1562, a fleet of 32 galleys under Juan de Mendoza, 12 of them Spanish, was driven up against the Andalusian coast near Málaga by a storm with a loss of some 4,000 men and all but three of the fleet.[5]

It is impossible to trace in detail the cause and effect relationship between the loss of trained and experienced manpower at Djerba and the disasters which followed. The nature of the Mediterranean system of warfare at sea makes it certain, however, that a relationship existed. This

[1] This is from a contemporary analysis of the various *asientos* under which the galleys of Naples operated from 1552 to 1569 in the *Colección Sanz de Barutell* (*Simancas*), *Artículo* 4, vol. 2, dto. 311, fol. 382ff.

[2] We know that the changes in manning on the galleys of Naples which we have described also occurred aboard the galleys of Spain and Sicily during the period 1550–70; but we have no evidence explicitly connecting the change with Djerba except in the case of Naples. If the galleys of Naples were affected by Djerba, those of Sicily, which lost even more heavily, would have been affected even more.

[3] See M. Rosi, *Nuovi Documenti Relativi alla Liberazione dei Principali Prigionieri Turchi Presi a Lepanto* (Rome, 1901), in the Archivio di Stato Veneziano, Venice.

[4] Anderson, *Naval Wars in the Levant*, p. 14.

[5] Olesa Muñido, *La Organización Naval*, vol. I, p. 366. W. H. Prescott, *History of the Reign of Philip the Second*, vol. III (Philadelphia, 1904), p. 144.

was because the trained men on whose skills the conduct of galley warfare depended were more than just 'trained' in the modern sense of the word. Their essential skills were an art, not a memorized list of things to do and situations to avoid. There is no better example of this difference than the contrast between an eighteenth-century European infantryman and a sixteenth-century Turkish or Venetian archer skilled in the use of the composite recurved bow. Our examination of this contrast in the following chapter should make this point clear. Though the skills involved in piloting a galley or laying its main bow gun were perhaps not as difficult to master as the Turkish bow, the manner of acquiring them and the end results in terms of efficiency were very similar.

The existence of galley fleets was a precarious one at the best of times. Tactically the Mediterranean war galley of the sixteenth century was an intrinsically offensive craft. Surprised or outmaneuvered, it was at a severe – frequently fatal – disadvantage. A fragile and barely seaworthy craft, it depended heavily for its survival on the skill of its captain and pilot. It was, therefore, uniquely dependent upon the tactical and nautical skill with which it was employed. The sort of skill involved could not be picked up during a few casual summer cruises, but was the product of a lifetime of experience. Since economic factors kept the scale of Mediterranean naval warfare relatively small in ordinary times, there were few men qualified to command galleys at any given time in any given area. The loss of such men was critical.

It was because of this that Mediterranean naval battles could be decisive even when no key geographic location changed hands as a result. Piali Paşa did not gain command of the sea from his victory of Djerba. The characteristics of the Mediterranean system of maritime conflict precluded this. But he did cripple Spanish naval forces for a considerable period of time. Such was the result of Djerba. It was, as we shall see, also to be the result of Lepanto, though in an even more critical way.

But Djerba was not, in the long run, decisive. There were five main reasons for this: the economic and social limitations imposed by the long-term rhythms of the Mediterranean system of warfare at sea prevented the Ottomans from immediately exploiting the Spanish weakness. Second, the geographic limitations of galley fleets prevented a decisive Ottoman strike deep into the western Mediterranean. Third, the fighting qualities of the Spanish infantry of the *tercios* and their mercenary Italian and German brethren gave Spain a potentially decisive clout by land – if her fleet could get them to the critical point in time. The fourth reason was Malta. The fifth was Don Garcia de Toledo.

4

THE WEAPONS OF SIXTEENTH-CENTURY WARFARE AT SEA

In the preceding chapters we have outlined the overall parameters of the Mediterranean system of armed conflict at sea in considerable detail. But with the partial exception of the galley, we have said little in concrete, quantitative, terms about the technology involved. We have outlined the strategic framework of Mediterranean warfare at sea in fairly precise terms and have undertaken a general overview of tactics, particularly galley tactics, on the assumption that the strategic characteristics of any system of warfare stem from its tactical characteristics. We shall examine the tactical characteristics of the Mediterranean system of warfare at sea in detail in the next chapter; but these characteristics stemmed, in turn, from the characteristics of the weapons involved and from the abilities of their users.

This last point deserves closer examination. In an age of exotic weaponry and mass armies the second half of the equation – user effectiveness – has frequently been overshadowed and attention focused almost exclusively on the technological characteristics of the weapons themselves, an emphasis which is inappropriate to our subject. In comparing armies or navies with one another both historians and military analysts have all too often implicitly assumed an equality of user competence and effectiveness which did not, in fact, exist. In part this is a problem of science versus art. While highly sophisticated techniques have been developed in recent years for making a comparative evaluation of the technological characteristics of weapons systems – speed, range, vulnerability, destructive impact and, finally, cost – the art of comparing the soldiers and seamen of one nation with those of another remains little more advanced than it was in the days of Alexander the Great.

To a degree the modern analyst's assumption of an equality of user competence is justifiable. Current weaponry is highly complex, changes frequently and is increasingly designed to be foolproof and easy to use so that men can be 'trained' to use it in relatively short periods of time. When weapons are so designed, there is unlikely to be much difference between what one user and another can get out of them regardless of individual skill. But this emphasis on 'training' is a relatively recent phenomenon.

Until the sixteenth century warfare was dominated by men who were not trained in any meaningful sense of the word, but who learned their military skills in childhood and adolescence as a part of their total cultural environment. The advent of 'training' – the imparting of unfamiliar military skills to men who were themselves generally unaccustomed to warfare – depended upon the development of relatively simple weapons which could compete effectively with traditional methods of warfare. Gunpowder made this possible on a large scale for the first time.

But gunpowder weapons, particularly individual firearms, were first used successfully on a large scale within what looks very much like the old pattern of military skills acquired through immersion in the total cultural environment.[1] At the same time, a successful effort was made in some areas to 'train' fighting men in the use of the more effective of the traditional weapons. The results were strikingly – and misleadingly – similar. A Spanish musketeer and a *sipahi* of the Porte of the mid-sixteenth century, a small arms specialist and a trained horse archer, must have had very similar attitudes toward their weapons and their work. This is hardly surprising. New weapons are at first almost invariably used within the conceptual framework established by their predecessors.[2] Ultimately, however, the intrinsic characteristics of gunpowder weapons prevailed. A Sicilian naval arquebusier who had learned his military skills in the old way was undoubtedly more effective on campaign and in battle than a trained infantryman of the *tercios* temporarily embarked on a galley. This point was dealt with in our discussion of the effect on Spanish naval power of the losses incurred at Djerba. But infantrymen of the *tercios* were, for a variety of reasons, a good deal easier to come by than seaman-arquebusiers of the old type.

The above example represents only the beginning of a process which

---

[1] The Hussites must be noted as a partial exception. The Hussites were forced, by their social complexion and the nature of the religious wars on which they had embarked, to break with their old cultural patterns and take up new methods of warfare. It was precisely their lack of traditional military skills – and time – which forced them to train in the use of firearms. The reference here is to the Ottomans and the Spanish.

[2] This truism has been noted frequently with regard to socially and culturally based resistance to the correct tactical employment of new and novel weapons; but it is equally true with regard to expectations as to the sort of training to be employed. It is commonplace to note that aircraft were at first employed as 'cavalry' for reconnaissance. But it is equally significant that replacement aircraft were at first casually handed out to units just as remounts were assigned in the cavalry and that French pilots in World War I were allowed to teach themselves to fly by the Blériot system without benefit of an instructor. Like a boy learning to handle a docile old plug before progressing to more spirited mounts, the tyro pilot began on an underpowered, clipped-wing, 'aircraft' which was capable only of fast taxi-ing. He then progressed to an underpowered trainer which was capable of short hops and, by stages, to full-fledged aircraft, never flying with anyone but himself.

culminated in the recruiting policies of eighteenth-century Europe where armies came to be composed of guttersnipes and the derelicts of society, swept up by press gangs and forcibly trained to the king's service. This, of course, lies well outside the bounds of our study. Two points, however, must be made: the introduction of effective gunpowder weapons made possible a kind of relationship between weapons, their users, and the culture from which the users came which was, in most parts of the world, entirely new. The tension between this new kind of relationship and that which had preceded it lies at the heart of our study. In this context, the galley – propelled in battle by muscle power, but capable of making effective use of gunpowder weapons – was an important focal point in the struggle between new and old. Secondly, the relationship between weapon and user was a much closer one in the sixteenth-century Mediterranean than our experience since the industrial revolution would lead us to expect. The apparent modernity of certain of the weapons involved should not mislead us. The weapon which a man carried or served was far more likely to be a reflection of his total cultural environment than merely the product of a bureaucratic decision.

The weapons of sixteenth-century Mediterranean warfare at sea can be conveniently, if arbitrarily, divided into three categories: edged weapons, individual missile weapons, and artillery. A few highly specialized, rare, and obsolete weapons – mines, battering rams and catapults – are not covered by our categories and the boundary between individual firearms and artillery was indefinite. Individual armor, still undeniably important in warfare, was not really a weapon at all, though it can be logically dealt with in our discussion of edged weapons. Nevertheless, this categorization offers the advantage of accurately reflecting tactical reality.

We shall therefore discuss each of these categories in turn, dealing with the capabilities and limitations of the weapons in each of them in more or less quantitative terms. We will then discuss their tactical employment by the various Mediterranean nations, focusing on galley warfare. In light of the pivotal importance of artillery, considerable attention will be paid to sixteenth-century gunnery and the tactical employment of cannon. We will not, however, center our attention on purely technical matters.

In several key areas important differences existed between nations in the design, construction and use of weapons of the same class. In almost every case these differences, and the differences in tactical and strategic philosophy which they underline, were the result of social, cultural and economic factors rather than purely technological ones. The importance of understanding the interplay between these factors will become apparent in our discussion of galley tactics, the War of Cyprus and the Lepanto campaign. Finally, we will point out the importance of these same factors in governing the adoption or non-adoption of new forms of weaponry. In so doing we will challenge the usual assumption that weapons development proceeds in a straightforward fashion with technological progress steadily providing new and better weapons and rendering older, inferior ones obsolete. In fact, as we will show, the older systems were frequently superior, on a narrowly tactical basis, to those which replaced them.

As the sixteenth century began, edged weapons played an important role, in some areas a dominant role, in the art of war. The battlefields of western Europe in particular were largely ruled by armored men wielding edged weapons: sword, lance, pike, and pole arms of various kinds. By its end, even though direct shock action[1] was to remain the ultimate arbiter of the battlefield for a long time to come, individual firearms had clearly wrested cold steel from its position of dominance in Europe just as they had begun to threaten the horse archer and his composite recurved bow elsewhere.

Developments in the Mediterranean world generally paralleled those in Europe. Though the importance of missile weapons in general and artillery in particular increased during the sixteenth century, boarding remained, under ordinary circumstances, the only decisive maneuver of galley warfare and hence of Mediterranean warfare at sea. Missile weapons played an increasingly crucial role in preparing the way for boarding; but boarding itself remained essentially a shock action fought out with edged weapons. Even in siege operations, the other side of the amphibious coin which we shall examine in our treatment of the Ottoman attack of 1565 on Malta, fortified places were still generally taken by storm, not simply surrendered after bombardment had made them untenable.

In land warfare considerable variation existed between the Mediterranean nations with regard to types of edged weapons, the tactical formations within which were used, and the amount and weight of armor worn. A number of factors acted to level out these differences in warfare at sea. The close confines of a shipboard fight precluded the use of many of the most formidable weapons of land warfare, notably the pike. Variations in tactical formations were virtually eliminated by space restrictions aboard galleys. The greater need for agility at sea posed by the necessity of

---

[1] By shock action we mean combat in which the attacker attempts to gain the upper hand by bringing his troops and/or their mounts into physical contact with the defenders in order to benefit from the violent impact – the shock – of their onslaught. 'Pure' shock action, as represented by a medieval European cavalry charge or the attack of a Swiss pike square, is encountered relatively rarely in military history; nevertheless the distinction between shock and missile action is a valid one. Though too much can be made of it, troops who are exceptionally good at the one are rarely particularly adept at the other.

leaping from ship to ship and clambering over railings somewhat curtailed the use of armor. Turks, North Africans, Spaniards and Venetians alike used halberds, half pikes and other more exotic pole arms of moderate length.[1] All used one-handed swords designed according to their national preferences. The full-sized galleys of all of these nations included in their complements at least a small core of armored fighting men. All of this remained essentially constant throughout the sixteenth century.

There were, however, differences. The Spanish and their German mercenaries used long, two-handed swords upon occasion: one of these was wielded by Don Juan of Austria at Lepanto.[2] The Spanish and their allies seem generally to have worn more and heavier armor than the Venetians or Turks, who frequently carried small shields by way of compensation.[3] Though of good construction, Turkish armor was generally lighter than that of the Christian European nations, as were Muslim edged weapons in general.

In essence, we are primarily concerned here with the size and 'weight' of the specialized fighting complements carried by the galleys of the various Mediterranean nations. Without going into too much detail, these differences can be roughly summed up as follows: the galleys of the Knights of St John of Malta (we know little about the manning of their galleys before expulsion from Rhodes) carried a higher proportion of armored fighting men, men who were also as a rule individually more heavily armed and armored than their adversaries, than any others. Next in the shock power of their fighting complements came the Spanish galleys and those of the Papal States. Genoese galleys in the Spanish service, at least during the second half of the sixteenth century, seem to have carried almost as many armored fighting men as their Spanish opposites, at least when Spanish infantry was embarked; but the picture is unclear. The fighting complements of Venetian galleys included a thin crust of armored Venetian nobles, men who were as heavily armed and armored and who fought every bit as well as their Spanish and Maltese opposites. However, most of the specialized fighting men aboard Venetian galleys, the *huomini di spada*, or *scapoli*, were lightly armed Dalmatians and Greek or Albanian mercenaries. Relatively few such specialized fighting men were carried by western standards. This was partially compensated for by the fact that

---

[1] These came in a bewildering variety under an even more bewildering variety of names. Basically, they were all variations on the half-pike (for thrusting) and the halberd or pole axe (for hacking), with the optional addition of a hook on the reverse side for pulling an opponent off balance and other gruesome looking projections for aesthetic appeal.

[2] This weapon, some six feet long, is on display in the Museo Naval, Madrid.

[3] Many of these, both Venetian and Turkish, are on display at the Ducal armory and in the Museo Correr, Venice.

Venetian *ciurmi* went armed and fought as free men. Though apparently larger, at least on major campaigns, the specialized fighting complements of Ottoman galleys, *'azabs*, *sipahis* and Janissaries, were somewhat more lightly armed with respect to edged weapons and more lightly armored than their Venetian opponents. Clearly, few Muslim fighting men – if any – wore even partial suits of plate armor. Christian nobles, gentlemen adventurers and many ordinary fighting men habitually did so.[1] Once again, this was compensated for in part by the presence of at least some armed free oarsmen on Ottoman galleys, particularly aboard flagships. Finally, the provision of fighting men aboard the galleys of the North African *ghazi* states seems to have roughly paralleled Ottoman practice, a somewhat artificial point in view of the North African preference for smaller raiding craft rowed largely by free men.

Though important, distinctions between the size and 'weight' of these specialized boarding parties are largely irrelevant when viewed out of context. The lack of shock power which the complement of an Ottoman or Venetian galley could muster was balanced by an increased emphasis on missile weaponry and, as we shall discuss in the following chapter, tactical mobility.

When we turn to individual missile weapons, the relatively homogeneous picture which we observed in our treatment of edged weapons and armor disappears. The various Mediterranean nations had clear and sharply differing preferences with regard to individual missile weapons, preferences which were solidly rooted in cultural, social and economic differences. There is also an important chronological component. Where the use of edged weapons and armor in galley warfare showed relatively little change during the sixteenth century, important changes occurred in individual missile weaponry. The role of individual missile weapons in galley warfare remained essentially unchanged: to clear the way for a boarding attack and then to support it, to repel hostile boarders, to support skirmishing and siege operations ashore. But gunpowder weapons gained enormously in importance.

[1] The tapestries depicting Charles V's Tunis campaign of 1535 in the Armeria Real, Madrid, are our most concrete evidence of the general trend. Spanish nobles, like Venetian nobles and the Knights of St John, fought in essentially full plate armor: breastplate and backplate, helmet, arm and shoulder defenses, tassets and complete defenses for at least the upper leg. Many, if not most, ordinary Spanish infantrymen and German and Italian mercenaries in the Spanish and Imperial service wore at least an open helmet of some sort plus a breastplate and tassets. Ottoman *timariot* cavalrymen, who served dismounted aboard ship on major campaigns, wore an open helmet and fairly complete suits of chain mail reinforced with plate at strategic points, often including a complete breastplate; but Janissaries and *'azabs* seem to have worn very little armor, most of it chain mail, though helmets were not uncommon and breastplates were apparently worn by a few.

In purely descriptive terms the regional differences in weaponry are relatively easy to come to grips with. The Turks habitually used the composite recurved bow, supplementing it with firearms, particularly among the Janissaries. The Venetians also used the composite bow in addition to the crossbow, particularly in the earlier period, though not to the same extent as the Turks. They also turned increasingly to firearms as the century progressed. The others began with the crossbow and went over to the arquebus during the first half of the sixteenth century. The Spanish led the way in this development and went a step further than their competitors by developing the Spanish infantry musket, though never adopting it to the exclusion of the arquebus (see Appendix 1).

But this is oversimplified and leaves many very tactical problems unilluminated. The best way to undertake a comparative analysis of these weapons is to examine two areas: first, the process by which the arquebus replaced the crossbow and by which the arquebus was in turn partially replaced by the musket, and second, the relative advantages of these weapons *vis-à-vis* the composite recurved bow.

About the origins of the crossbow little is known. All that can be said with certainty is that it made its appearance in Europe toward the end of the Dark Ages. Its use quickly became generalized throughout Europe; but for various reasons it never became important elsewhere except in European hands.[1] The crossbow began as a relatively crude weapon, a simple wooden bow set on a staff. It underwent a continuous process of development as the armor which it was called upon to penetrate steadily improved, mounting a composite bow of wood and horn by the eleventh century and a steel bow during the fourteenth. As early as the twelfth century its effectiveness prompted a series of injunctions by the Church banning its use against all but infidels.[2] The reasons for this tell us much about the problem of cultural resistance to new and novel weaponry.

The crossbow and its successor, the arquebus, had one important characteristic in common: no great amount of skill was needed to become effective with either. Where a lifetime of constant practice was needed to master the use of the composite bow – or for that matter the lance – from horseback, a few hours sufficed to teach an ordinary fellow to draw and aim a crossbow. The injunctions against the crossbow cited above were

---

[1] I have ignored the Chinese crossbow since it had no influence on the events with which we are concerned here. The Arabs knew the crossbow; but only seem to have used it in siege warfare.

[2] The use of the crossbow against all but infidels was first interdicted under penalty of anathema by the Lateran Council in 1139. The prohibition was confirmed at the close of the twelfth century by Pope Innocent III, and Conrad III of Germany (1138–52) forbade its use in his territory. See Sir Ralph Payne-Gallwey, *The Crossbow* (London, 1903), p. 3.

rooted in a realization of this: the crossbow was the first personal weapon capable of killing an armored knight which could be obtained and used by almost anyone without benefit of great skill, practice or wealth. The social implications inherent in this were not lost on the ecclesiastical hierarchy.

The weapon which the Papal injunctions had sought to ban was the composite crossbow of wood and horn. This proved incapable of reliably penetrating the plate armor which became increasingly common during the fourteenth century and was replaced by the steel crossbow.[1] In many respects this was a fearsome weapon. The development of an elaborate pulley and windlass system with a considerable mechanical advantage to draw the crossbow permitted the use of a short, very stiff, bow of mild steel into which a great deal of energy could be packed. The energy which a steel crossbow imparted to its projectile was greater than that given to an arrow by even the most powerful bow – draw forces in excess of a thousand pounds were common. Because the bow was short, relatively little of the energy was expended in accelerating the tips of the bow and most of its considerable force was applied directly to the bolt.[2]

But there were two great disadvantages to this system: it was intrinsically inaccurate and the winding operation took a great deal of time and attention. The reasons for the crossbow's inaccuracy are somewhat involved. They begin with the mechanics of the release mechanism (see Fig. 4). Where an archer, by precisely controlling his release, could ensure that the energy in his bowstring was smoothly transmitted to the arrow, the crossbow release mechanism released the cord abruptly and somewhat erratically. Instead of being smoothly accelerated in a carefully controlled direction, the crossbow bolt began its voyage lying loosely in its trough, and was then 'slapped' into flight with enormous force. Crossbow bolts had to be made short and thick with a flat base in order to prevent the tremendous impact of the cord from reducing them to splinters.[3] In view of the need for strength and the basic inaccuracy of the crossbow, war bolts were often very crudely made, having a single leather

---

[1] According to Payne-Gallwey, *The Crossbow*, pp. 32, 90, the steel crossbow first appeared about 1370. This date corresponds closely to the appearance of effective plate armor on a large scale. See Sir Charles Ffoulkes, *Armour and Weapons* (Oxford, 1909), pp. 30–68. The transition from chain mail to full plate began in Western Europe about 1300 and was completed shortly after 1400.

[2] The energy stored in a tensed bow, when expended, drives not only the arrow, but also the bowstring or cord and the mass of the bow itself. It follows that a bow with less mass will be capable of driving its projectile (assuming a sufficiently small projectile mass) with greater velocity. The easiest way to reduce the mass of the bow while holding the force applied to the projectile constant is to make the bow stiffer and shorter.

[3] Payne-Gallwey, *The Crossbow*, pp. 14–15, describes shooting an ordinary arrow from a heavy steel crossbow with just that result.

fin set into a slot sawed across the base of the bolt. The aerodynamic in-
efficiency of the resultant shape sharply increased drag and therefore
reduced the maximum range. This was aggravated by the considerable and
unpredictable vibration which the impact of the cord imparted to the bolt.
By further and inconsistently increasing the aerodynamic drag of the bolt
this vibration additionally reduced both range and accuracy.

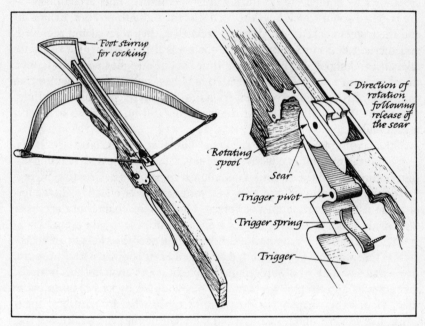

Fig. 4 The firing mechanism of a fifteenth-century, windlass-drawn steel crossbow

From the point of view of the sixteenth-century fighting man aboard
ship, the steel crossbow was a murderously effective short-range weapon.
Armed with a good stout crossbow, he need fear neither man, devil nor
armored knight – if he could hit him. But to be sure of getting a solid hit,
the crossbowman had to wait until his target was quite close: about 75
yards at most and even less if he were armored.[1] This was well and good if
the crossbowman were shooting from a secure place where he could reload

---

[1] Payne-Gallwey, *The Crossbow*, p. 10, gives 80–300 yards as a 'moderate' range for 'the destruction of a single enemy'. When he says this, however, he is thinking primarily of penetrating
power and not accuracy. Against a moving target on the battlefield we should shorten this
considerably.

at will. But in a boarding fight he had to make his first shot tell: it was the only one he was likely to get off. Drawing, cocking, and loading a crossbow was a lengthy process.

First the windlass had to be attached to the butt of the stock (see Fig. 4). Then the tackle (a four-pulley arrangement was most common) had to be relaxed and attached to the cord. Then the cord was drawn back with ten or twelve brisk turns of the crank (a foot stirrup was provided on most crossbows to hold it steady during this operation). This accomplished, the notched spool which held the cord was rotated into position behind it and the trigger cocked. The drawing tackle was then relaxed and removed and the bolt laid in its trough. Only then was the crossbowman ready to take aim and shoot. All of this took time: about one shot per minute was the maximum rate of fire possible.[1] It was best not accomplished in the company of rough fellows – even friends – who were continually jostling you about. When all else failed the crossbow did not even make a very useful club.

The maximum range of the steel crossbow was a respectable 400 yards or so; but the maximum effective range was a good deal less, depending on the conditions and the target.[2] The bolt lost most of its destructive energy to aerodynamic drag in the first 150 yards and was effective thereafter only against unprotected men or horses. The basic inaccuracy of the crossbow made shooting at long ranges a chancy business in any event.

The spread of the crossbow's use was influenced by the sort of social factors that we have already hinted at. It had been popular with European mercenaries – men who were 'trained' to fight – and civic militias from its inception as an effective weapon, and was adopted by sailors at an early date. It was the weapon *par excellence* of those who, by nature of their work, had to fight upon occasion, but who had neither the wealth nor the leisure time for the practice needed to become archers or men at arms. The crossbow reigned supreme among such groups until the first practical firearms began to appear about the end of the third quarter of the fifteenth century. These did not immediately render the crossbow obsolete, but slowly supplanted it as they became technically more efficient. The point to be made here is that the sort of social groups to which the crossbow was

---

[1] Payne-Gallwey, *The Crossbow*, p. 154.

[2] The main variables were the size of the enemy force and the degree to which the hostile troops were protected by bulwarks, armor, etc. Payne-Gallwey, *The Crossbow*, p. 20, gives 370–80 yards as his estimate of the extreme range attainable with 'the ordinary military crossbow of the fourteenth century'. This estimate applies only to normal field weapons. On p. 14 he describes shooting a heavy bolt to a range of 460 yards with a large, specialized, siege crossbow. This crossbow, however, was a monster weighing 18 pounds and still having a draw force of 1,200 pounds after four centuries of deterioration.

a useful and practical weapon were precisely those which turned to fire-arms most naturally.

The process by which the arquebus replaced the crossbow was an almost entirely technical one, with perhaps some retardation due to force of habit and custom. The cost of the two weapons must have been about the same since the value of materials needed and the amount of labor involved were closely comparable. When the matchlock arquebus appeared on the scene it fitted into a niche in the social–military system already established by the crossbow. Even more important, the crossbow had already accustomed the ruling elite of Western Europe to a certain tolerance for the existence of effective weaponry in the hands of the lower social orders. The initial shock among the lay and ecclesiastical hierarchy had slowly given way to a grudging acceptance of the crossbow. It had proved useful against the infidel: Richard the Lionheart of England had defeated the redoubtable Saladin at Arsouf in 1191 largely with its assistance.[1] Nobles had found it entertaining to hunt with the crossbow (light ones which even their ladies could use were made for use against birds and small game),[2] and had found it useful to keep a supply of them in their castles to turn the kitchen help into serviceable soldiers in the event of an unexpected siege. Thus the onset of effective firearms, though universally decried by those in high places, was not without precedent in Europe.

In the East, however, things were different. The crossbow, although known to the Arabs, had never been much used. The heavy steel crossbow was unsuitable for use on horseback and would in any case have been totally outclassed in range and rate of fire by the composite recurved bow. Here, on the great plains of Central Asia, the Ukraine, Anatolia and the Fertile Crescent, the traditional weapons of antiquity dominated. The

---

[1] C. W. C. Oman, *A History of the Art of War in the Middle Ages*, vol. I, 2nd ed. (London, 1924), pp. 305–19, gives a superb account of this most instructive battle, as does W. F. Paterson, 'The Archers of Islam', *Journal of the Economic and Social History of the Orient*, vol. IX, Parts I–II (November, 1966), pp. 83–4, with the addition of a thorough technical analysis. R. C. Smail, *Crusading Warfare (1097–1193)* (Cambridge, 1956), has perhaps the best tactical analysis of Arsouf. Most of Richard's crossbowmen seem to have been mercenaries from the great Italian mercantile cities.

[2] Sporting crossbows made for noble owners were a completely different proposition from the ordinary military crossbow and the best of them were undoubtedly more accurate. Some powerful sporting crossbows were fitted with cranequins, an expensive gear and ratchet arrangement which could be used on horseback. But the occasions on which finely made weapons of this type appeared in the field were so few and the numbers in which they were used so small as to justify omitting all mention of them from the text. The use of cranequin crossbows by Francis I's mounted bodyguard of 200 men at Marignano in 1515 (mentioned by Payne-Gallwey, *The Crossbow*, p. 134) is the only example which comes to mind and a very late one at that.

critical importance of strategic and tactical mobility to cavalry warfare on open plains precluded the use of heavy armor, and the accuracy of the bow at long ranges could tell. The technical superiority of the composite recurved bow was never effectively challenged and the military supremacy of the traditionally trained man on horseback remained secure. So did the social and political dominance which that military superiority conferred. The violent opposition of Eastern cavalry elites to the use of the arquebus – magnificently documented for the Mamluks by David Ayalon[1] – was directly connected to this situation. Only the Ottoman Turks showed the social flexibility needed to accept and foster the use of individual firearms in war.

The genesis of individual firearms was at first a slow process. 'Hand-cannon' had made their appearance as early as the mid-fourteenth century, but were awkward to serve and were useful only at sieges and the like.[2] It was not until the development of the matchlock mechanism, apparently conceived in Germany about the middle of the fifteenth century, that individual firearms came into serious competition with the crossbow.

Whereas the old handcannon had been fired by a gunner thrusting a hot coal or a length of smouldering slow match[3] into the flashpan by hand, the matchlock accomplished this mechanically. The tip of the match was grasped in a pair of adjustable jaws atop a pivoted arm (see Fig. 5). The arm was connected to a trigger so that the match could be brought into contact with the priming powder in the flashpan using only the fingers of one hand.

The matchlock was not an ideal arrangement. The burning match had to be lit before use, which took time, and then kept lit (a costly business when we think in terms of whole armies) and continually adjusted as it burned down. Tactical disadvantages were numerous as well: the glowing match was sure to give you away in a night surprise and the matchlock was manifestly unsuited for use on horseback.[4] But the matchlock was

---

[1] *Gunpowder and Firearms in the Mamluk Kingdom, a Challenge to a Medieval Society* (London, 1956). The strong resistance by mounted elites to the adoption of firearms was by no means unique to the nations of Asia and the Muslim Near East. The persistence of the lance as a primary cavalry weapon in European armies until World War I, and even after in some cases, makes this clear.

[2] Once again we must cite as an exception the use of firearms in the field by the Hussites in the 1420s and 1430s. The Hussites solved the problem of a slow rate of fire and the need of pre-matchlock small arms for multi-man crews by giving their handgunners cover in their wagon laagers.

[3] Slow match was ordinary string soaked in a saltpeter solution and then allowed to dry. It burned gradually with a bright, smouldering tip like a punk stick or a small, intense, cigarette end.

[4] Highly strung cavalry horses disliked having a length of smouldering match swinging around

simple, cheap and foolproof. These qualities kept it in almost universal service until it was finally replaced by the flint lock late in the seventeenth century.

The fully developed matchlock was on a rough parity with the crossbow

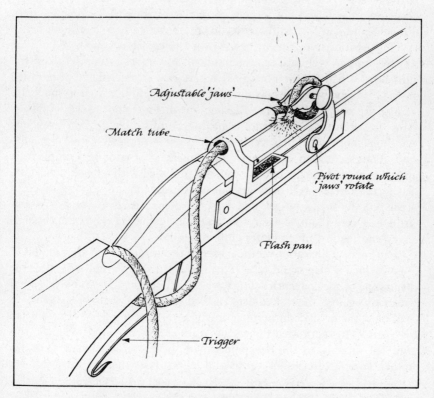

Adjustable 'jaws'

Match tube

Pivot round which 'jaws' rotate

Flash pan

Trigger

Fig. 5   The basic matchlock mechanism

Taken from sketches made of sixteenth-century Spanish infantry muskets in the Museo del Ejercito, Madrid

NOTE. Pulling up on the trigger causes the 'jaws' to rotate downward, bringing the smouldering end of the match into contact with the powder in the flash pan.

their ears. More important, the matchlock arquebus required two hands, one to hold and one to adjust the match and pull the trigger, leaving none for the reins. This problem was partly solved by the invention in the early sixteenth century of the wheel-lock, a clockwork mechanism which rotated a serrated wheel against pyrites to throw sparks into the flash pan. Though fairly reliable, this mechanism was delicate and its great cost placed it beyond the means of the average soldier. Though it made the cavalry pistol possible, it had no discernible effect on war at sea.

in Spanish armies by 1500.[1] In 1518 it replaced the crossbow on Venetian war galleys by order of the Council of Ten.[2] By 1530 crossbows were growing scarce on the weapons inventories of Spanish warships and are hardly ever encountered after 1540.[3] All in all, it is safe to say that the matchlock arquebus was known throughout Europe by the 1520s, though in many areas it was not in general use. According to Venetian sources French galleys in 1552 still carried 40 crossbowmen and 60 arquebusiers.[4]

The superiority of the arquebus over the crossbow was based almost entirely upon technical considerations. No more accurate than the crossbow, it had at best a marginal superiority in short-range penetrative power. Its advantage in maximum effective range, if any, was small. Its rate of fire was, on the average, faster; but this was not the crucial factor. Most important was its greater ruggedness and simplicity. The arquebus had no elaborate winding tackle which could get tangled, broken or mislaid. The essential mechanism of the arquebus consisted of a simple tube of wrought iron plugged at one end and provided with a touch hole and a flash pan. There was little to get out of adjustment and nothing much to wear out. As far as weight and bulk were concerned the crossbow and arquebus were about on a par, though the arquebus was no doubt easier to carry and made a much better club in a pinch.

The greatest limitation on the power of the arquebus was the amount of recoil which a man could take. This increased sharply not long after the beginning of the sixteenth century when arquebusiers began butting their weapons against their shoulders instead of against their breastbones as had been the practice hitherto, a practice which seems to have originated in Spain. This permitted the use of larger and more powerful small arms and led directly to the development of the Spanish musket. (For the rather complex series of cause and effect relationships involved, see

---

1 There is an abundance of evidence to support this point, for example Christopher Columbus' request of January 1495 for 100 *espingardas* (equivalent to arquebusses) and 100 crossbows to equip 200 troops who were to accompany him to the New World, cited by James D. Lavin, *A History of Spanish Firearms* (New York, 1965), p. 43. Bernal Diaz del Castillo, in his account of Cortez' expedition, *The Discovery and Conquest of Mexico 1517–1531*, A. F. Maudslay trans. (New York, 1956), habitually speaks of firearms and crossbows in the same breath.

2 Alberto Tenenti, *Cristoforo da Canal: la Marine Vénetienne avant Lépante* (Paris, 1962), p. 39.

3 Francisco Felipe Olesa Muñido, *La Organización Naval de los Mediterraneos y en Especial de España Durante los Siglos XVI y XVII* (Madrid, 1966), vol. I, pp. 326–8. The crossbow is still encountered in the regulations of 1550 of the *Casa de Contractación* of Seville establishing the standards of armament required for merchant ships trading with the Indies. These, however, undoubtedly contain an element of bureaucratic conservatism and probably represent a minimum standard of armament rather than what was actually carried. A dockyard requisition for the outfitting of 20 galleys at Barcelona in 1530, *Colección Sanz de Barutell (Simancas)*, *Artículo* 3, dto. 25, fol. 87, lists arquebusses but not crossbows.

4 Tenenti, *Cristoforo da Canal*, pp. 39–40.

Appendix 1.) In its fully developed form the musket had a considerable advantage over the arquebus in killing power at long ranges. The Spanish musket could reliably penetrate armor at a hundred yards and kill an unprotected man or horse at five hundred.[1]

In part this advantage was gained by sheer size. The typical sixteenth-century arquebus, if there was such a thing, weighed ten pounds or less and had a bore diameter of about 60 caliber (sixty hundredths of an inch). Spanish muskets, however, weighed at least eighteen pounds and generally had bore diameters of from 70 to 85 caliber, with a few specimens larger than 90 caliber.[2] This meant that in place of the arquebus ball of about a half ounce, the musket fired a full two-ounce lead ball. The recoil of these massive weapons, even though partly absorbed by their own great weight, must have been prodigious. Only large and powerful men could fire them, a limitation which prevented their universal use even in Spanish armies. Though it was no more accurate than the arquebus – hitting an individual man at 75 or 80 yards would have been an exceptional feat[3] – the musket's long effective range and great stopping power made it an ideal individual missile weapon for siege warfare and shipboard use. The Spanish used the musket extensively and Ottoman shoulder arms, whose effectiveness at sieges was particularly noted, approached musket proportions.[4]

The last and most misunderstood of the individual missile weapons is the composite recurved bow. Though traditionally derided by European historians as antiquated and 'obsolete', the Turkish bow of the sixteenth century was capable of delivering a higher volume of accurate and effective fire at longer ranges than any competing weapon. It is plain, in fact, that the composite recurved bow in the hands of a strong and experienced archer – a crucial qualification – was, for most purposes, far and away the outstanding individual missile weapon of the sixteenth century.

The sixteenth-century Turkish war bow seems to have been of moderate

---

[1] Robert Held, *The Age of Firearms* (New York, 1957), p. 39, estimates that the Spanish musket could penetrate armor handily up to 125 yards and 'stop in his tracks by sheer impact whatever man or beast it might hit at ranges well over 200 yards', an estimate which seems quite reasonable.

[2] This statement is based upon examination of the numerous examples on display in the Museo del Ejercito, Madrid.

[3] Payne-Gallwey, *The Crossbow*, p. 26, cites a letter from an English soldier in the Napoleonic wars which mentions the picking off of an enemy sentry with a musket at 80 yards as an exceptional feat. The accuracy of all smooth-bore small arms was about the same.

[4] The statement regarding the size of Ottoman small arms is based upon an examination of Muslim muskets in the collections of the Armeria Real, Madrid, and the Ducal Armory and Museo Correr, Venice. The effectiveness of Ottoman musketry in siege warfare is attested to by Franscisco Balbi di Correggio, *The Siege of Malta, 1565*, E. Bradford trans. (London, 1965), pp. 49–50. Balbi contends that the great length of the Muslim muskets limited their rate of fire.

size, perhaps because of its heritage as a cavalry bow. The bulk of evidence, including contemporary pictorial representations, suggests that the typical Turkish war bow was about 40 to 45 inches long and shot an arrow weighing about an ounce.[1] Such a bow could have driven its arrow to an extreme range of about 500 yards and, given a square hit, through almost any armor at 100 yards.[2] Because of its superior aerodynamic characteristics an arrow did not lose its velocity and destructive energy as rapidly as a crossbow bolt or an arquebus ball. Only the size and brute power of the musket gave it a slight advantage in maximum effective range.

A trained archer, when fresh, could get off six aimed shots in a minute with ease. Perhaps the best modern estimate of his long-range accuracy comes from W. F. Paterson, himself an experienced archer. Paterson concludes that a good shot on a calm day could be expected to hit a target the size of a man on horseback at 280 yards about once in every four shots.[3] This represents an impressive standard of accuracy and is not far below what a reasonably experienced modern rifleman can achieve firing offhand at an unknown distance over iron sights. At a hundred yards such an archer would have been able to pick his man. At fifty he would have been sure death.

This is not to say that the composite bow, even in the narrowly tactical sense, was the 'ultimate weapon'. Even in the hands of an expert it had its

---

[1] Heavier arrows give increased stopping power and penetrative power. But because of their weight they can only be driven by a relatively long bow which, because of its greater mass, is limited in the velocity – and hence range – which it can impart to them. Short bows, on the other hand, are capable of producing higher velocities and longer ranges for the same draw force, but only if used with a sufficiently light arrow since they lack the power to drive a heavier one. The rather complex trade-off between bow size and arrow weight, depending upon the range and toughness of the target, is explained by W. F. Paterson, 'The Archers of Islam', *Journal of the Economic and Social History of the Orient*, IX, Parts I-II (November 1966), 81. A bow of the size and 'weight' described here was optimized toward the light, long-range end of the spectrum. The portions of my discussion dealing with the construction, use and range of the Turkish bow are based ultimately upon Mustafa Kani, *Telchis resail er-rumat* (*Excerpts from the writings of the Archers*) (Constantinople, 1847), written during Turkish archery's final revival during the reign of Murad III. Kani's work was translated and published with limited commentary by Joachim Hein, 'Bogenhandwerk und Bogensport bei den Osmanen', *Der Islam*, XIV (1925), 289-360. This, in turn, was the basis for an expanded and technically much more knowledgeable treatment by Paul E. Klopsteg, *Turkish Archery and the Composite Bow* (Evanston, Ill., 1947), which I have used as my primary reference.

[2] This estimate of penetrative ability is from Paterson, 'The Archers of Islam', p. 86, and is based on modern experimentation. The estimate of extreme range is my own, based upon extrapolation of data given by Payne-Gallwey on pp. 18-20 of his Appendix on the Turkish bow in *The Crossbow*. I consider Payne-Gallwey's data to be somewhat conservative since it is based upon the skill and strength of an archer who would have been at best a dilettante by sixteenth-century Ottoman standards, and upon bows which were preserved by a random process of selection and are unlikely to have been representative of the best and most powerful even when new.

[3] Paterson, 'The Archers of Islam', p. 83.

disadvantages. Draw forces of 150 pounds or so taxed even a very strong man and the initial rate of six shots per minute could not be sustained for long. The composite bow was more delicate than firearms. Humidity and dampness had a detrimental effect on the composite bow's performance – a significant problem in war at sea, though one which does not seem to have been insurmountable or even particularly serious under ordinary circumstances.[1] Finally, the bow presented difficulties in firing from cover and through loopholes. Once his weapon was loaded an arquebusier or musketeer could fire over, under, or through almost anything, a considerable advantage in siege operations and warfare at sea; but an archer had to stand erect, if only for an instant, to draw, aim and release.[2]

But the Achilles' heel of the composite recurved bow was neither technical nor tactical. Archery did not consist of a series of mechanical movements which anyone could be 'trained' to execute, but of a whole complex of cultural, social, and economic relationships. Though the Ottomans could, and did, train archers – an immensely time-consuming business – the real basis of the composite recurved bow's existence was the traditional life style of the horse nomad of the steppes. The time of the steppe nomad was almost exclusively spent herding and guarding livestock, activities which kept him in the saddle but usually not otherwise occupied. He therefore had an infinity of time in which to perfect his traditional military skills. The tradesman, sailor, or farmer, by contrast, would have found it difficult to allot even a few hours a day to military exercise without suffering serious economic – or physical – consequences. Surrounded from birth by men who gained prestige and status from their ability to fight and shoot from the saddle, the young nomad engaged in constant archery practice from childhood. In view of the number of targets – human and animal, edible and otherwise – which the steppe presented, constant practice made economic sense. Constant practice was necessary, moreover, simply to master the basic rudiments of the art. Drawing a bow the 'weight' of which approached or exceeded 150 pounds involved immense skill as well as immense strength. Reversing

---

[1] Klopsteg, *Turkish Archery*, p. 53.

[2] This disadvantage of the bow was seized upon by the opponents of archery in the late sixteenth-century debate between English professional soldiers over the relative merits of the longbow and firearms. See particularly Sir Roger Williams, *A Briefe Discourse of Warre* (London, 1590), and, for the pro-longbow side, Sir John Smythe, *Certain Discourses . . . Concerning the Forms and Effects of Divers Sorts of Weapons . . .* (London, 1590). The anti-bow arguments used by Sir Roger in this highly instructive debate are frequently quoted out of context to imply that the bow was rendered obsolete by inherent technical defects. In fact, as careful analysis of this debate shows, the longbow itself had a considerable advantage over late sixteenth-century firearms in accuracy, range and rate of fire, but good archers could no longer be found in sufficient numbers to justify their recruitment.

the bend of an unstrung recurved bow to string it was thought for many years to be impossible without the use of mechanical aids, yet the Turks did this as a matter of routine with even the most powerful bows.[1] Where a few days and a good drill sergeant might suffice to train a reasonably good arquebusier, many years and a whole way of life were needed to produce a competent archer.

The same point applies with equal validity to the construction of bows. Individual firearms could be built quickly by methods which approached mass production. Bullets could be cast rapidly and in great numbers by unskilled workers. But the construction of a composite bow was a time-consuming ritual which took years (see Fig. 6). Some of the glues took more than a year to dry fully and had to be applied under precisely controlled conditions of temperature and humidity.[2] The final shaping and dynamic balancing of a composite bow involved a level of skill which could only be learned by many years of constant work under the supervision of a master bowyer. Even the arrows had to be shaped, fletched, and balanced with almost as much precision as went into the bow itself. There were no short cuts and productivity per man hour must have been extremely low. All in all, the manufacture of composite bows was labor-intensive in the extreme and would have been highly vulnerable to any upward movement of the wage–price spiral.

When we compare personal firearms with the composite bow, most of the advantages of the latter were lessened by the peculiar conditions of war at sea. The crews of warships, unlike cavalry in the field, fought at least partially under cover until the moment of boarding. Protection was provided by the sides of the ship itself or by temporary bulwarks erected before combat. Venetian galleys, for example, were fitted with pavisades (large shields along the sides of the rowing benches) as were Spanish galleys early in the sixteenth century, probably with the menace of long-range archery in mind.[3] On Spanish and Papal galleys, the raised fighting platform at the bow was covered on the sides and front before combat

---

[1] Payne-Gallwey, 'A Treatise on Turkish and Other Oriental Bows of Medieval and Later Times', in *The Crossbow*.

[2] Klopsteg, *Turkish Archery*, pp. 50–51. These glues, made of boiled-down cattle tendons and skin with small amounts of fish glue added to increase fluidity and flexibility, were as strong as the best modern glues, but were slow-drying and very difficult to handle and apply. A great deal of art was involved in their preparation and application, much of it characterized by a mystical, semi-religious approach.

[3] Olesa-Muñido, *La Organización Naval*, vol. I, p. 211. Admiral Fincati's reconstruction of a Venetian galley of the 1530s in the Museo Storico Navale, Venice, has these too. Pavisades are listed in an inventory of material needed for the construction of 20 galleys in the stocks in Barcelona in 1539, *Colección Sanz de Barutell* (*Simancas*), *Artículo* 4, vol. I, dto. 122, fol. 383-7.

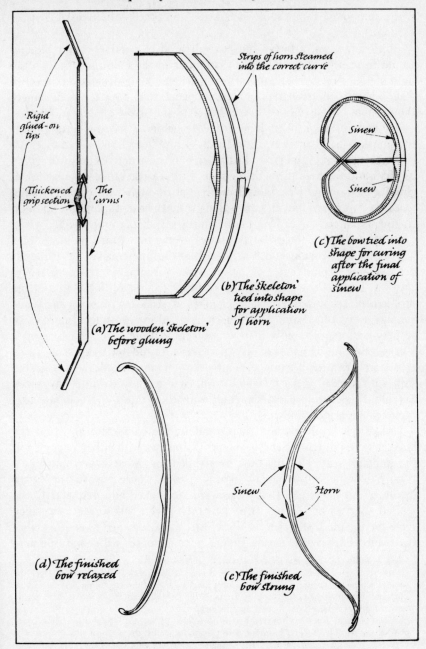

Fig. 6   The construction of a composite recurved bow

with a temporary rampart of wood, often reinforced with hides and excess cordage.[1]

At close ranges, a heavy musket ball fired at relatively high velocity would have been more effective than an arrow at smashing through the light planking of such a temporary rampart and doing damage on the other side. Though an arrow has impressive penetrative ability, this is largely the product of its superior shape. Whereas the arrow penetrates because of the concentration of its kinetic energy behind a narrow cutting edge, the musket ball smashes through by brute force and ignorance. In penetrating planking an arrow lost much of its destructive energy dragging its shaft and feathers through the hole. But at close ranges a musket ball could penetrate light planking handily, get through with enough energy to leave a gaping wound, and carry along with it a host of splinters and wood fragments which were capable of injuring eyes and other unprotected parts.

At ranges long enough for pavisades or the temporary bulwarks of a war galley to provide effective protection against musket or arquebus fire, the bow was no better off. Its supreme advantage, long-range accuracy, was lessened by the difficulty of firing from a rolling ship and the problem of accurately estimating ranges at sea.[2] Its other primary advantage, rate of fire, would have been lessened in a protracted fight since archers tired more rapidly than musketeers. All the same, the composite Turkish bow in the hands of an expert was a formidable weapon. A handful of archers with a vantage point over – or on – the deck of a hostile ship with a clear space in which to draw their bows would have been capable of executing great slaughter with their rapid and accurate fire, even against armored men.

Unlike the arquebus and the crossbow, the composite bow and the musket were not equivalent weapons. The niches which they occupied in the military history of the time overlapped, but were not synonymous. Each had its strengths and weaknesses, even where expert users were involved. An indication that these were recognized and deliberately exploited is given by the report of a Spaniard who had served as a galley slave for the Paşa of Vélez in North Africa and escaped to tell his tale.[3] He recorded that the Paşa's galiots were manned with sharpshooters

[1] Olesa Muñido, *La Organización Naval*, vol. I, pp. 188, 211–12.

[2] In the absence of mechanical range-finding devices or landmarks whose distance from the shooter is known, accurate shooting at long ranges depends directly upon accurate visual range estimation. Range estimation by eye is particularly difficult at sea where there are no terrain features between the shooter and his target.

[3] *Colección Sanz de Barutell* (Simancas), *Artículo* 6, dto. 45, fol. 117–18, entitled 'An account of what the Alcalde of Vélez has done with his galiots against the Spanish who navigate the coasts of Andalusia ... from the first of August to the end of October of 1561, related by Francisco Yañez, his captive'.

(*tiradores*), 'each one of whom carries an arquebus [*escopeta*] and a bow'. Presumably the bows were used for close-in, rapid-fire work aboard enemy ships after boarding, for raiding ashore, and for sniping at extreme ranges, while the arquebusses were used in the opening stages of an attack on a Christian ship.

What was the cumulative effect of these regional differences in individual weaponry? Before the advent of gunpowder weapons the tactical edge had unquestionably gone to the Islamic nations among whom mastery of the composite recurved bow was a traditional skill. They clearly benefited from the considerable advantage in fire power which the composite recurved bow enjoyed over the crossbow. Because of the absence of suitable materials for its construction[1] and because of the absence of social and economic conditions which would have fostered the practice of archery (except in England, a special case which has no direct bearing on our subject) the composite bow was never used in Western Europe except by the Venetians.

The Turkish composite bow had less short-range stopping power than the windlass-drawn European steel crossbow of the fifteenth and early sixteenth centuries, but this was the crossbow's only technical advantage. The impact energy of a crossbow bolt dropped off rapidly with range, giving the composite bow firing an arrow of reasonable weight an increasingly marked advantage in killing power beyond approximately 150 yards. In addition, the composite recurved bow – in skilled hands – had an enormous superiority in accuracy and rate of fire. The crossbow's main significance lies in the fact that it paved the way for individual firearms socially and intellectually.

The introduction of effective individual gunpowder weapons changed the tactical balance, but only gradually. The early sixteenth-century arquebus may have had a slight advantage over the composite bow in short-range stopping power; but it was markedly inferior in all other categories. The full-blown musket, however, had a number of advantages. Though its rate of fire was somewhat less than that of the arquebus and its accuracy not much better, its immense smashing power and long effective range served it well in naval engagements and sieges. While pavisades or a reinforced barrier of light planking provided reasonably good cover from arrow fire, they were of little value against a two-ounce lead ball impacting at close to 1,000 feet per second.[2]

---

[1] Cattle and goats with horns of sufficient length and adequate quality to provide the horn backing for the composite bow were not bred in Western Europe. Paterson, 'The Archers of Islam', p. 82.
[2] In tests conducted at the H. P. White Laboratory, Bel Aire, Maryland, on 1 July 1970, an 85

It seems clear that gunpowder weapons had, by the middle of the sixteenth century, redressed at least the Spanish disadvantage in individual weapons *vis-à-vis* their Muslim opponents. This was particularly true in formal head-on naval engagements where both sides had time to set up their pavisades and barricades on the bows and sterns of their galleys, and in siege warfare where both sides fired from behind cover most of the time and where the duration of engagements and health conditions made fatigue an important factor. But these narrowly tactical considerations, though important, were not critical.

In the end it was the expanded scale of warfare as much as anything else which shifted the balance in favor of the West. The composite bow's dependence on highly skilled manpower was its Achilles' heel. While the Spanish could convert American gold and silver almost directly into arquebusiers and musketeers at will, many years of 'lead time' were needed to raise a force of archers.[1] Likewise a force of archers lost in combat was far more difficult to replace – if it could be replaced at all. Archery depended upon the existence of a traditional socio-economic structure, in which such special skills were nurtured. Once changing conditions began to undercut the direct economic benefits of archery to a society, it could be kept alive only by direct and permanent government support. The Ottomans seem to have done this to a degree, but such a system had little elasticity. The difference can be seen in the effect upon Spain and upon the Ottoman Empire of a major defeat accompanied by severe manpower losses. The effect of Djerba on Spain's pool of trained military manpower, though severe, was temporary. There are indications, however, that the Turks never quite recovered from Lepanto. Certainly they never again displayed the same tactical aggressiveness at sea.

It was not, in sum, the technical superiority of gunpowder weapons which made the difference. Under most circumstances gunpowder weapons, even the mighty Spanish musket, were quite inferior to the composite recurved bow. Only in the specialized circumstances of a formal head-on clash between galley fleets or a siege on land did the musket's superior impact energy give it the edge. But because archery depended totally upon the economically vulnerable values of a traditional

caliber lead ball of 890 grains (about 2.3 ounces), driven by 215 grains of black powder (0.49 ounces), typically produced a muzzle velocity of about 1,100 feet per second. Sixteenth-century Spanish musketeers almost certainly used a considerably larger powder charge, as heavy as the weight of the ball according to Jorge Vigón, *Historia de la Artillería Española* (Madrid, 1947), vol. I, p. 236.

[1] This point is clearly related to that made by Braudel, *La Méditerranée*, Spanish ed. (Mexico City, 1953), p. 190, to the effect that gunpowder's ultimate effect was to shift the military balance between nomadic and sedentary peoples decisively in favor of the latter.

society the nations relying upon it were deprived of resilience in the face of adversity.

Having dealt with individual shock and missile weapons, we now turn to artillery, in many ways the most important of the three. It is generally accepted that changes in cannon technology played an important role in bringing about the decline of the Mediterranean system of warfare at sea. But this was not, as has been frequently asserted, because the introduction of effective heavy artillery rendered the war galley obsolete. The mechanism involved was far more complex and was not exclusively technological in nature. Cannon were readily absorbed by the Mediterranean system of warfare at sea – up to a point. Just what that point was will be the subject of our final chapter.

Since this whole matter is intimately bound up with tactical considerations, we will include in the following pages an examination of the tactical characteristics of sixteenth-century artillery. We will not go into the technical history of artillery except to show the origins of the main types of artillery used in the sixteenth-century Mediterranean and their relative economic and tactical advantages.

The first 'cannon' made their appearance around the beginning of the fourteenth century, small, crude, pieces throwing a weird variety of ill-assorted projectiles which were incapable of accomplishing much in the way of physical destruction. This situation prevailed until the third quarter of the fourteenth century. Then a major technological breakthrough occurred with the development of the hooped bombard, made up of wrought-iron staves and hoops much like a barrel and designed to throw a spherical projectile, usually of cut stone. This led, by the 1380s, to the construction of relatively large pieces, mostly breech loaders with detachable powder chambers of reduced internal diameter for structural reasons, throwing large cut stone balls. These quickly became gargantuan in size and were the first gunpowder weapons to have any real impact on the art of war. Their use as siege weapons became increasingly important and the traditional dates for the first use of artillery in the Mediterranean world come from this period.[1] By the second decade of the fifteenth century German cannon founders, at least, had learned to successfully duplicate the shape of the hooped bombard in bronze.[2] Cast as muzzleloaders with

---

[1] Mediterranean writers almost universally point toward Germany as the birthplace of artillery – which we can take in context to mean effective siege artillery – and to about 1300 as the date. See, for example, the statement made *ca.* 1453 by Kritovolous, *History of Mehmed the Conqueror*, Charles T. Riggs trans. (Princeton, 1954), p. 46. Later Italian writers (e.g. Biringuccio, Tartaglia and Guicciardini) were also of this opinion, echoed by Luis Collado, *Platica Manual de Artilleria* (Milan, 1592), fol. 6.

[2] Heinrich Müller, *Deutsche Bronzegeschützröhre 1400–1750* (Leipzig, 1969), pp. 28ff.

an integral powder chamber of smaller diameter than the bore, these were stronger and safer: but bronze was far more expensive than iron and the wrought-iron bombard hung on for economic reasons as long as labor remained relatively cheap. By the 1450s effective siege artillery – for the state with the fiscal power needed to command the resources – was a reality. Charles VII of France consolidated his kingdom with the assistance of the Bureau brothers' siege train from the late 1440s and Constantinople fell to the power of Mehmed II's bronze siege bombards in 1453. Effective ship-board artillery made its first, hesitant, appearance in this period.

Also about this time frame 'long' guns firing cast-iron balls appeared in competition with the older, but steadily improved, designs which threw balls of cut stone. Though at first of hooped wrought-iron construction, 'long' guns soon came to be made of bronze as well, an innovation which endured to produce the premier cannon of the early sixteenth century. The reasons for the success of long bronze cannon are curiously back-handed: increasing the length of cannon barrels yielded no significant increase in range (see Appendix 2); but the increased length helped to overcome the limitations of the imperfect casting techniques and metal-lurgy of the day, resulting in safer cannon which were less likely to burst. This was because the density and strength of bronze gun metal increase as a function of the pressure under which it is cast. European founders cast their cannon with the muzzles up; hence the density and strength of the metal at the breech – where internal pressures were greatest and where guns commonly burst – was a direct function of the length of the barrel (see Appendix 3). Though long guns required more bronze for the size and weight of ball thrown, they used cast-iron cannonballs which were cheap and easy to produce. Cannon designed to throw stone cannonballs, on the other hand, consumed less expensive bronze in their manufacture – a fact which was generally recognized – but fired projectiles which were quite expensive in terms of highly skilled labor.[1]

None of the developments which we have outlined, at least none subsequent to the development of the hooped bombard, established any clear-cut technical superiority. Tactical advantages were generally offset by economic considerations and vice versa. Thus all of the technical features which we have discussed survived into the sixteenth century, often in odd permutations and combinations. Generally, however, sixteenth-century Mediterranean artillery can be divided into four basic categories: large, wrought-iron pieces, small swivel guns, cast-bronze muzzleloaders and cast-iron artillery.

---

[1] Collado, *Platica Manual*, fol. 9. Sir Henry Brackenbury, 'Ancient Cannon in Europe', Part II, *Proceedings of the Royal Artillery Institute*, v (1865–6), 8–9.

First were the large wrought-iron cannon. These were, for both technical and economic reasons, approaching obsolescence as the sixteenth
century dawned. Large breechloaders had dropped out of favor as the
basic manufacturing problems involved in making a wrought-iron barrel
permanently sealed at one end were solved. The removable powder
chambers of cannon designed to fire a ball weighing more than a few
pounds were simply too heavy and unwieldy, particularly for shipboard
use.[1] Equivocal references to large pieces of this sort are very rarely
encountered as late as the 1530s; but by and large they were replaced by
muzzleloaders early in the century.[2] Large wrought-iron muzzleloaders
designed to fire cast-iron cannonballs were made early in the century; but
these were ultimately no more successful than the breechloaders. Built
of multiple layers of 'staves' and very closely spaced 'hoops' which gave
them a relatively smooth outer appearance, they must have been in-
ordinately expensive in terms of labor. Apparently for this reason they
were quickly replaced by cast-bronze guns. We have shown evidence that
the Ottoman basilisks used at Jiddah in 1517 were of this type; but this is
our last relatively unequivocal evidence of their use. Numbers of old
wrought-iron bombards (by definition stone-throwers) soldiered on into
the sixteenth century; but corrosion took a steady toll and by the middle
of the century they were found only aboard small merchant ships and in
fortifications. Such pieces tended to be unsafe, partly because of the
effects of saltwater corrosion and partly because they were built for
stone projectiles (which were increasingly hard to find), and the high
internal pressures which resulted from the use of iron cannonballs caused
them to burst. Consequently wise artillerists underloaded them and their
effective ranges must have been very short, probably no more than 200
yards at the outside. Their importance in warfare at sea, never great,
diminished throughout the sixteenth century.

More successful were the small wrought-iron breechloaders, called
versos by the Spanish and Portuguese, which appeared late in the fifteenth
century. Incorporating many of the characteristics of the very earliest
successful cannon these, because of their cheapness and tactical efficiency,
lasted on through the sixteenth century to be increasingly refined and even
copied in bronze. Made originally of a single layer of wrought iron 'staves'
with a dozen or so reinforced 'hoops' shrunk on to the reverse-tapered
barrel at regular intervals (see Fig. 7), one of these could have been made

---

[1] L. G. Carr Laughton, 'Early Tudor Ship Guns', Michael Lewis ed., *The Mariner's Mirror*,
XLVI (November 1960), 242ff., 258.
[2] L. G. Carr Laughton, 'Early Tudor Ship Guns', pp. 242ff. See below, 'Lepanto', pp. 230–31,
for evidence of large wrought-iron cannon mounted aboard galleys *ca.* 1536.

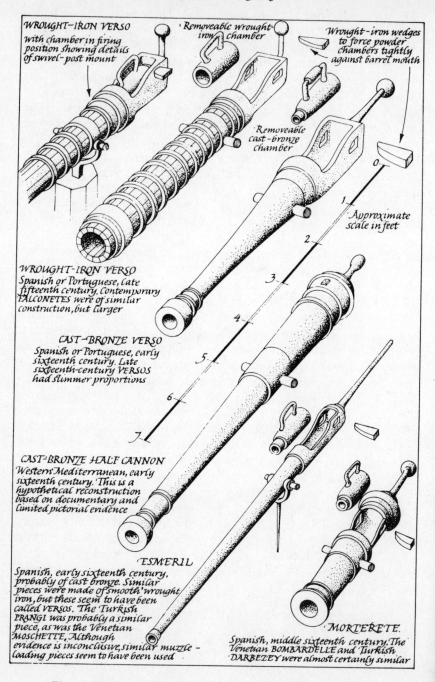

WROUGHT-IRON VERSO with chamber in firing position showing details of swivel-post mount

'Removeable wrought-iron' chamber

Wrought-iron wedges to force powder chambers tightly against barrel mouth

'Removeable cast-bronze chamber'

Approximate scale in feet

0
1
2
3
4
5
6
7

WROUGHT-IRON VERSO
Spanish or Portuguese, late fifteenth century. Contemporary FALCONETES were of similar construction, but larger

CAST-BRONZE VERSO
Spanish or Portuguese, early sixteenth century. Late sixteenth-century VERSOS had slimmer proportions

CAST-BRONZE HALF CANNON
Western Mediterranean, early sixteenth century. This is a hypothetical reconstruction based on documentary and limited pictorial evidence

ESMERIL
Spanish, early sixteenth century, probably of cast bronze. Similar pieces were made of smooth wrought iron, but these seem to have been called VERSOS. The Turkish PRANGI was probably a similar piece, as was the Venetian MOSCHETTE. Although evidence is inconclusive, similar muzzle-loading pieces seem to have been used

MORTERETE.
Spanish, middle sixteenth century. The Venetian BOMBARDELLE and Turkish DARBEZEY were almost certainly similar

Fig. 7   Naval swivel guns of the sixteenth-century Mediterranean

by a competent blacksmith and his helpers in perhaps a week. With bore diameters ranging from under two inches to over eight, these pieces were generally about four to six feet long. Their weights varied from under a hundred pounds to over four hundred. Invariably swivel mounted, they came equipped with two or three removable powder chambers which closely resembled beer mugs in form. These could be loaded and fired in rotation, permitting a maximum rate of fire of perhaps two shots per minute for short periods. Though the size, weight and basic characteristics of these swivel guns remained essentially unchanged, their design and construction was progressively refined: 'smooth' wrought-iron and cast-bronze construction were introduced early in the sixteenth century and slowly supplanted the earlier breechloaders of hooped construction (Fig. 7).

The swivel-mounted breechloaders with barrels made of finely wrought iron like large musket barrels tended toward smaller bore diameters and proportionately longer barrels than their hooped predecessors. In Spanish naval service these were called, in order of decreasing size, *versos dobles*, *versos*, *ribadoquines* and *esmeriles*, the *esmeril* being roughly equivalent to the Turkish *prangi*.

With cast-bronze swivel guns the picture was more complex. The bronze *verso* was much like the iron *verso*; but the naval *medio cañon*, though clearly a swivel piece larger than a *verso* (see Appendix 6), was probably a muzzle loader and the *morterete* (the Turkish *darbezen*) was a very short piece designed to throw scatter shot exclusively. Confusingly, the term *falconete* was more or less simultaneously applied to a cast-bronze swivel piece (possibly a muzzleloader) intermediate in size between a *medio cañon* and a bronze *verso*, a large wrought-iron swivel gun of hooped construction, and an orthodox small bronze muzzleloader of the culverin class used ashore. Similarly, the term *mosquete* (musket) designated, in addition to the shoulder arm with which the term is usually associated, a larger naval swivel piece of similar construction and a small 'long', cast-bronze swivel piece for naval use.

Because of their unquestionably modest muzzle velocities, the product of the reverse taper of their bores, the effective ranges of the early hooped *versos* must have been about 200 yards. That of the short *morteretes* would have been even less. The later *verso* types with longer untapered bores and tighter chambers would have had considerably longer effective ranges when used with solid shot, probably approaching 500 yards against personnel in the open or men lightly protected by pavisades.

Swivel pieces of this general type were used as railing pieces on large merchantmen and were the basic armament of smaller ones.[1] Loaded with

[1] *Colección Navarrete*, vol. XII, dto. 76, fol. 271-9, a Spanish government inventory made in

scattershot and fired down into the rowing benches of a raiding galiot at close range they must have been horribly effective, particularly in light of their high rate of fire. The larger swivel guns formed an integral part of the bow artillery of the war galleys of all the Mediterranean nations while the smaller types were mounted at the stern and along the railings.

Before turning to our discussion of cast-bronze artillery proper, a few words on gunnery and ballistics are necessary in order to lay the tactical groundwork for our discussion of technical and economic considerations. Here, as in many other areas, modern preoccupations have influenced our view of sixteenth-century Mediterranean conditions and it is necessary to set the record straight. The modern fixation on long-range accuracy is an example. Modern works dealing with sixteenth-century ballistics and gunnery have devoted considerable attention to the theory of shooting at long ranges, yet it is probably accurate to say that most sixteenth-century gunners knew little (at least little that was correct) and cared less about accurate long-range shooting. The reason for this is not hard to find: sixteenth-century artillery was quite ineffective at long ranges.

It is fair to say that the maximum effective range of sixteenth-century artillery was between two and five hundred yards, depending on the conditions and the nature of the target. Any sound bronze cannon larger than a swivel piece could throw its projectile several thousand yards; but for a number of reasons this was of little practical consequence. First of all, a smooth-bore gun firing a spherical projectile is intrinsically inaccurate, not least because spherical projectiles which spin in an unpredictable fashion do not fly true. On top of this, undersized cannonballs were used to compensate for variations in ball size and shape, for bores which were slightly out of true and for the hard powder deposits which quickly built up on the inside of the bore with firing. This meant that the cannonball rebounded from one side of the barrel to the other and left the muzzle at a slight – and unpredictable – angle from the centerline of the bore. In addition it acquired an indeterminate amount of spin from dragging

1564 of privately owned ships of certain of the Biscay ports and their armament. Fourteen of the 36 ships inventoried (they were mostly quite small, ranging from 35 to 150 tons burden) carried something larger than small arms, mostly wrought-iron railing pieces. Eight of the fourteen carried something larger than a *verso*. Of the eight, three carried a single piece of cast bronze plus from four to eight wrought-iron bombards on deck mounts. Two carried bombards only. Other Mediterranean nations may have armed their smaller merchant ships less heavily, but *versos* were clearly used extensively as railing pieces on the larger ones. See also *Colección Navarrete*, vol. III, dto. 4, fol. 55–132, a compilation of royal ordinances written in 1543 and amended in 1554 and 1556, prescribing the standards of armament required for merchant ships trading with the Indies. The ships of the largest class, 220 to 230 tons burden, were to have a single bronze cannon or half culverin, two *sacres* and a *falconete* of bronze, 10 wrought-iron bombards and no less than 24 *versos*. This document appears to mirror accurately the actual availability and use of ordnance, at least as of the earlier date.

against the walls of the barrel and, like a sliced golf ball, had its trajectory curved in one direction or the other by aerodynamic forces. Secondly, because inaccuracy prevented concentration of fire and because a spherical projectile quickly loses its destructive energy to aerodynamic drag, inert cannonballs could not cause much damage to any target which they were capable of hitting at long range. Exploding cannonballs were known; but since they were fused with a simple piece of slow match which had to be lit *before* firing – a hair-raising procedure which called for delicate timing and consistently good luck – they were used only in short-barreled mortars and then rarely.

Consequently, long-range artillery fire played a very small part in sixteenth-century warfare. Like his successors for the next two and a half centuries, the sixteenth-century gunner did the overwhelming majority of his work well within musket range. Occasionally massed formations in the field presented a worthwhile long-range target: at the siege of Malta in 1565 gunners firing from Fort St Angelo helped to repel an assault on Fort St Elmo nearly 1,000 yards away across the Grand Harbor.[1] Venetian gunners at the siege of Famagusta in 1570–1 disrupted a general review of troops by Mustafa Paşa, the Ottoman Commander, with fire from 60-pound culverins at an estimated range of three miles.[2] But these were exceptional occurrences. At sea an escape might be made good or a prize captured by means of a long shot which brought down some important part of the enemy's rigging; but there was an important element of luck in such exploits. Significantly, the English expression 'a long shot' has come to be associated primarily with gambling.

The gunners on Venetian galleys, all in all probably the best naval gunners in the Mediterranean, seem to have had a reasonable expectation that they could hit an oncoming hostile galley, given calm sea conditions, at about 500 yards, about the effective limit of naval gunnery. More will be said about this in chapter 5; but it is clear that Venetian gunners could hit at ranges which were considered excessive by others.[3] For tactical reasons which we have already touched on most artillery fire in galley engagements was within what the Spanish, with characteristic directness, refer to as 'clothing-burning range' (*quemaropa*).

[1] Francisco Balbi di Correggio, *The Siege of Malta, 1565*, E. Bradford trans. (London, 1965), pp. 81–2. Note that the gunners were firing at a known range, a considerable aid to accuracy.
[2] From a contemporary Italian source cited by Sir George Hill, *A History of Cyprus*, vol. III (Cambridge, 1948), p. 997.
[3] Alberto Tenenti, *Piracy and the Decline of Venice* (Berkeley, 1967), p. 79, gives an account of an engagement between Venetian galeasses and Dutch freebooters early in the seventeenth century in which the former were able to cannonade the latter into submission by accurate gunnery from beyond the Dutchman's range in a flat calm. This must have involved a range of at least 500 yards.

Nor were effective gunnery ranges much longer on land. For 'battery', the breaching of fortress walls by cannonfire – by far the most important role played by artillery through the middle of the sixteenth century at least – about 60 yards was considered the optimum range.[1] Good heavy artillery was rare and massed counterbattery fire was seldom encountered, so it made good sense to go straight at the main fortress walls from less than a hundred yards out for maximum destructive impact. These tactics, expensive in casualties and cheap in material and munitions, stand in direct contrast to siege tactics in the days of Vauban when cannon were relatively plentiful and manpower expensive. More will be said about this in our examination of the siege of Malta.

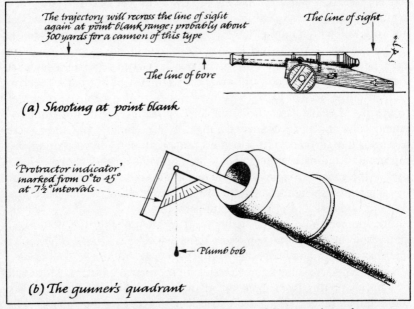

The trajectory will recross the line of sight again at point blank range; probably about 300 yards for a cannon of this type

The line of sight

The line of bore

(a) Shooting at point blank

'Protractor indicator' marked from 0° to 45° at 7½° intervals

Plumb bob

(b) The gunner's quadrant

Fig. 8   Shooting at point blank and the use of the gunner's quadrant

NOTE. Aiming 'by the line of metals' at a target level with the gun results in a positive angle of elevation of the bore of the gun of 1–3°, depending on the geometry of the gun.

The cannon shown is a Spanish or Neapolitan falcon recovered from the wreck of the galeass *Girona* by M. Robert Sténuit. The carriage is a late sixteenth-century naval mount according to J. D. Moody, 'Old naval gun carriages', *Mariner's Mirror*, XXXVIII (November 1952), 303. Such mounts were probably used in the Venetian galeasses at Lepanto.

[1] Collado, *Platica Manual*, fol. 43. This was not some theoretical ideal, but the range actually used wherever possible. The use of Ottoman siege batteries '70 to 80 paces' (about 60 to 65 yards) from the walls of the final Spanish redoubt on Djerba in 1560, already noted above, is a case in point.

For both siege and naval warfare simple aiming techniques sufficed. Sighting down the top of the barrel between his upthrust thumbs,[1] a good gunner could get all the accuracy that, practically speaking, his cannon was capable of producing. If the target was at or near point-blank range (from the Spanish *punto de blanco*, pointed at the target), usually about two to three hundred yards, the gunner simply aligned the top of the barrel directly with the target (see Fig. 8). This system, called sighting by-the-line-of-metals (*por el raso de los metales* in Spanish), continued to be used almost exclusively by naval gunners everywhere through the second decade of the nineteenth century,[2] an eloquent commentary on the intrinsic inaccuracy of smooth-bore artillery. If the target were beyond point-blank range the gunner simply elevated his line of aim slightly above the target, judging from experience how much elevation was required, and let drive. At any range where there was a reasonable expectation of hitting the target at all this system was quite accurate. Though the gunners' quadrant (see Fig. 8) was known, it was rarely used in practice. In the absence of any remotely realistic data connecting range with angles of elevation, it must have been of little or no value to the practical gunner.[3]

The sixteenth-century gunner did, on the other hand, exercise considerable care and precision in the loading operation. Christian gunners, at least good ones, seem to have been proficient in using elaborate rules to compute the correct ball size and powder charge for a cannon, depending upon its type, size, proportions and condition. Careful measurements of the cannon's dimensions were converted, according to these rules, to a maximum safe powder charge which was then adjusted for the cannon's condition. A ladle was constructed to throw a charge of the computed weight using measurements based on simple multiples of the ball diameter depending on the type of gun. Luis Collado's *Platica Manual de Artilleria* is devoted primarily to such calculations and references by Biringuccio and Tartaglia among others make it evident that similar methods were

---

[1] This technique is described by Vannoccio Biringuccio, *The Pirotechnia*, Cyril S. Smith and Martha T. Gnudi trans. based on the 1540 Venice edition (New York, 1941), p. 419.

[2] Sir Howard Douglas, *A Treatise on Naval Gunnery* (London, 1860), p. 100, states that the practice of firing 'by the line-of-metal' was still common in his day.

[3] For methods of aiming see Biringuccio, *Pirotechnia*, pp. 419–20, and Collado, *Platica Manual*, fol. 41–2, 51. The gunners' quadrant was used, if at all, only as a means of duplicating a correct angle of elevation found by trial and error. Tartaglia, a mathematician and not a gunner, has mislead many with his emphasis on the gunners' quadrant. As is explained in Appendix 2, many of the so-called 'range tables' (tables purporting to give the relationship between angle of elevation and range) which were attached to most early works on artillery have little or no discernible basis in fact. Such tables have nevertheless been religiously repeated and taken as gospel by many modern authors.

actually used by ordinary gunners.[1] Similar calculations of this type were made for Ottoman guns by arsenal personnel who engraved the correct ball size and weight of powder directly on the breech.[2]

The reason for these elaborate calculations, often derided by modern writers because of their lack of any theoretical foundation,[3] was a very real and compelling one. Sixteenth-century cannon-founding techniques were imperfect, particularly early in the century, and improved only slowly (see Appendix 3). Many cannon 'failed proof' (burst under test with an oversized charge) at the foundry; but many more passed, only to burst on active service with terrible consequences for the gunners involved.

Thus while the sixteenth-century gunner was not much worried about long-range accuracy, he was intensely concerned with internal pressures. He went to great lengths to predict them, after a fashion, and to control them. His careful measuring of the proportions of cannon and the size of cannonballs, his careful construction of powder ladles to throw the proper charge and his care in loading his gun, were all directed to this end. His computations were entirely empirical and were ultimately based only upon past experience. All that can be said for them is that they usually worked – and that is a great deal.

Having dealt briefly with gunnery, we now turn to the guns themselves. As the sixteenth century dawned, heavy artillery of cast bronze had established, if only just, a decisive superiority over its older wrought-iron competition. Bronze cannon of the sixteenth century can be divided into two large categories: those designed to fire a stone projectile and those designed to fire a projectile of cast iron. The first of these, called *pedreros* by the Christians, were cast with an integral powder chamber of reduced diameter, usually about a third to a half that of the bore (see Fig. 9). Because the sectional density of a stone cannonball is only about a third that of an iron one, the internal pressure – and therefore the amount of gunpowder – needed to produce a given muzzle velocity was less. This

---

[1] These rules are painstakingly explained by Collado for each of the three basic types of cannon: the culverins, the cannons and the pedreros, *Platica Manual*, fol. 14ff., 29ff., and 35ff.

[2] These markings can be seen on all the Ottoman cannon and many of the captured Christian pieces in the cannon park of the Askeri Musesi near St Irene's Church, Istanbul.

[3] For example, A. R. Hall, *Seventeenth Century Ballistics* (Cambridge, 1952), p. 36, says that '[sixteenth-century] gunners were weighing and measuring charges and distances before measure became the great instrument of physical science, in fact we can see in their activities a conspicuous example of the truth that accuracy with balance and ruler will prove very inadequate without the framework of an intellectual system'. In terms of long-range accuracy – essentially a modern preoccupation – Hall is quite correct; in terms of internal ballistics and safety he is much less so.

was reflected in the practice of sixteenth-century gunners who, at least in the West, loaded a *pedrero* with one half the powder charge of a cannon of battery throwing an iron ball of the same weight.[1] The barrel walls of a *pedrero* could therefore be made thinner than those of an iron-throwing gun, with attendant savings in weight and in the amount of expensive bronze required. The Turks, at least, cast their *pedreros* muzzle down, thus putting the strongest, densest, metal where the barrel was thinnest and relying on sheer mass for strength around the chamber. The moulds contained a large 'bell' above the breech (this was cut off after the metal had cooled) to increase the pressure of molten metal during casting. This permitted relatively short barrels of about eight calibers (eight times the bore diameter, not counting the chamber) without sacrificing strength (see Appendix 3). As a result, *pedreros* were considerably shorter and lighter than cannon designed to throw an iron cannonball of equal weight.

The design characteristics of *pedreros* made it possible to cast them quite large: fifteenth-century Ottoman siege and fortress pieces designed to throw a ball weighing in excess of a thousand pounds are still extant[2] and siege *pedreros* which threw balls of six and seven hundred pounds must have been common in the sixteenth century. Smaller *pedreros*, usually from twelve to fifty pounders, were used extensively at sea. Luis Collado speaks highly of them in this context and no less an expert than John Hawkins seems to have used them by preference.[3] The modern belief that *pedreros* were anti-personnel weapons whose stone projectiles shattered on impact with a wooden hull must be discounted entirely. Evidence that the impact of a stone cannonball on a warship was at least as destructive as that of an iron cannonball of equivalent weight is overwhelming and explicit.[4] Nor did the *pedrero* suffer a disadvantage in range: the limiting factor in naval warfare was not range, but as we have explained, accuracy

---

[1] Collado, *Platica Manual*, fol. 14, 29, 36.

[2] Many of these are still on display in Istanbul, particularly in the small park near the Deniz Musesi and in the fortress of Rumeli Hisar on the Bosporus.

[3] Collado, *Platica Manual*, fol. 9, 11. Careful examination of the Spanish inventory taken of the ordnance of Hawkins' flagship, the *Jesus of Lubeck*, after her capture at San Juan de Ulloa, given by Michael Lewis, 'The Guns of the *Jesus of Lubeck*', *The Mariner's Mirror*, XXII, No. 3 (July 1936), 324–35, and of a contemporary painting of the ship by Anthony Anthony, reproduced by D. W. Waters, 'The Elizabethan Navy and the Armada Campaign', *The Mariner's Mirror*, XXXV, No. 2 (April 1949), 96–7, makes it clear that three of the eight main broadside pieces were *pedreros*.

[4] See, for example, Michael Strachan, '*Sampson's* Fight with Maltese Galleys, 1628', *The Mariner's Mirror*, LV, No. 3 (August 1969), 281–90, who quotes Captain William Rainsborow of the *Sampson* to the effect that the 25 pound stone shot from the galleys, unlike the smaller iron projectiles which did little damage, 'staved on our lower decke two barrels of beef, two of pease, a Butt of Wine; some of the shot passing through nineteen inches of planke and timber . . . They bare in whole plankes, shooke and split the timbers and . . . made us leakie'.

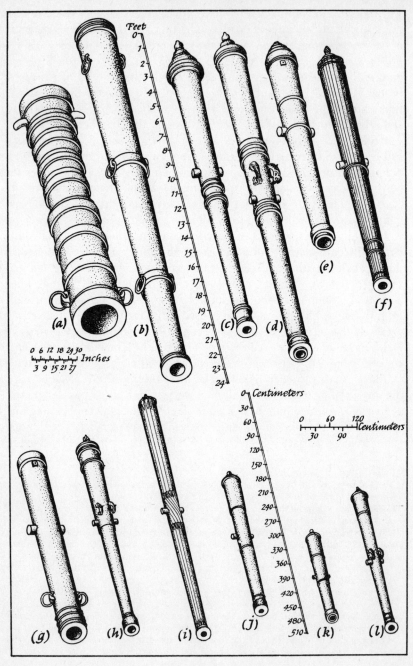

Fig. 9

Fig. 9 A comparison of the main types of cannon used in Mediterranean warfare at sea

KEY

(*a*) Ottoman basilisk, *ca.* 1453, cast for a stone ball of about 930 lb. Guns similar to this may have been used by the Ottomans at Zonchio and Jiddah. After an existent cannon in Rumeli Hisar, Turkey.

(*b*) Ottoman 120 pdr, wrought-iron basilisk. After an existent piece in the Deniz Musesi Park, Istanbul. The Ottoman basilisks used at Jiddah in 1517 were possibly similar pieces, perhaps 40–50 pdrs, of the same construction. This monster was probably a specialized siege/fortress gun.

(*c*) Spanish 36 pdr culverin, mid-sixteenth century. After existent pieces and Luis Collado's proportions.

(*d*) Spanish 50 pdr full cannon, mid-sixteenth century. After existent pieces and Collado's proportions.

(*e*) Venetian 52 pdr full cannon, based on existent pieces.

(*f*) Ottoman 56 pdr *baş topu*, mid-sixteenth century. After an existent piece in the Askeri Musesi Cannon Park.

(*g*) Ottoman 56 pdr *pedrero*, *ca.* 1570. After an existent piece in the Askeri Musesi Cannon Park.

(*h*) Spanish 14 pdr half culverin, mid-sixteenth century. After a gun by the German founder Gregory Leoffler in the Museu Militar, Lisbon. This is the gun referred to in Fig. 17. Similar pieces by Spanish founders tended to be larger and heavier for their bore diameters.

(*i*) German 12 pdr half culverin, *ca.* 1516. After an existent piece in the Askeri Musesi Cannon Park, Istanbul. This piece is probably representative of many similar Spanish pieces by German founders. Earlier Spanish–German pieces tended toward greater bulk and length and more elaborate ornamentation.

(*j*) Venetian 12 pdr *sagre*, early to mid sixteenth century. An Ottoman *šayka topu* (sidepiece) would have been of similar dimensions.

(*k*) Venetian 12 pdr *aspide*, mid to late sixteenth century. Note the short length of this later piece.

(*l*) Spanish 6 pdr half *sacre*, mid-sixteenth century. Most *sacres* used on galleys would have been somewhere between this piece and the 14 pdr half culverin (*h*) in size and proportions.

Pieces (*c*) to (*g*) are probably representative of most cannon used as main centerline bowgun on Mediterranean war galleys from the 1530s until Lepanto.

which affected iron- and stone-throwing cannon alike. In siege warfare a stone projectile – at least a large one – made up in close-range smashing power whatever it lacked in penetrative ability.

The *pedrero*'s weak point was the amount of highly skilled labor which went into the manufacture of stone cannonballs. A cannonball cutter had been a very highly paid artisan from the earliest times.[1] It is reasonable to suppose, therefore, that the wage–price spiral of the sixteenth century acted to increase the price of stone cannonballs more sharply than the prices of less labor-intensive products and, at the same time, to reduce the cannonball cutter's real wages.[2] The cannonball cutter, like the maker of composite bows, was thus caught in an economic squeeze, particularly where free market conditions prevailed, with predictable long-term results. It is a matter of record that *pedreros* dropped out of use first in those areas where the upward movement of wages and prices began – England and north-western Europe – and hung on longest in economic backwaters where the onset of the wage–price spiral was delayed – Portuguese India and the Ottoman Empire.[3]

In the sixteenth-century Mediterranean the *pedrero* was fighting a rearguard action, its tactical advantages being slowly but surely undercut by its economic vulnerability as bronze and gunpowder became increasingly cheap relative to skilled labor. Large stone-throwing guns for siege and fortress use were employed extensively only by the Ottomans and by the Portuguese in the east. Both, however, continued to use them throughout the sixteenth century. The smaller *pedreros* extensively used by all the Mediterranean nations as shipboard artillery slowly became less common as the century wore on. The Ottomans and – curiously – the Knights of Malta seem to have clung to them longest and the Venetians to have abandoned them first.

Cannon designed to fire a cast-iron cannonball fell into two categories. We have already discussed the origins of the first of these, the long guns

---

[1] Sir Henry Brackenbury, 'Ancient Cannon in Europe', Part II, *The Journal of the Royal Artillery Institution*, v (1865–6), 8–9, cites a French document of 1375 giving the cost of a small stone cannonball, probably of no more than six inches diameter, since the cannon for which it was cut weighed only 500 pounds, as two shillings and sixpence. The most costly wrought iron used in the manufacture of the cannon involved cost only sixpence a pound, the difference in price surely being attributable entirely to labor costs.

[2] See B. H. Slicher van Bath, *The Agrarian History of Western Europe A.D. 500–1850* (London, 1963), pp. 113–15, for a concise explanation of the wage–price movements of the sixteenth century.

[3] *Pedreros* are rarely heard of on English ships after the 1560s and were an anachronism in England, and probably Holland as well, by 1600. *Pedreros* continued to be cast in Portuguese India through the mid-seventeenth century (many excellent examples are on display in the Museu Militar, Lisbon) and lasted on in the Ottoman Empire into the eighteenth.

or culverins.[1] Culverins came in a wide variety of sizes, from two-pound *falconetes* weighing less than 150 pounds (exclusive of the carriage) to sixty-pound double culverins, with barrels weighing close to 9,000 pounds; but all had straight, unchambered bores which were at least 26 calibers long (26 times the bore diameter) and sometimes a great deal longer. In order of increasing size, the most common sub-types within the culverin class were the *falconete* (usually a two or three pounder), the half *sacre* (about a six pounder), the *sacre* (about a ten pounder), the half culverin (usually about a twelve pounder), and the culverin (normally a 24 to 26 pounder).[2] Double culverins, bastard culverins, and the like, of considerably greater size and sometimes as large as 70 and 80 pounders, were occasionally encountered.

In competition with the culverins were the cannons (here we use the term in its specific, technical, sense), or 'cannons of battery' as they were known in the sixteenth century. Like culverins, cannon were of cast bronze and fired iron cannonballs; but their bores were shorter, usually about 18 calibers long, their barrel walls were thinner and they customarily used a smaller powder charge. The fact that many early cannon were 'chambered', that is fitted with a powder chamber of reduced diameter, suggests a bombard ancestry. This feature made loading difficult (with *pedreros*, which were also chambered, this was less of a problem since *pedrero* barrels were relatively wide-mouthed and short) and became progressively less common as the century wore on. Cannon were less elaborately categorized than culverins, the main sub-types being the half-cannon (normally a 22 to 24 pounder whose barrel weighed from 4,000 to 5,000 pounds) and the full cannon (usually a 40 to 60 pounder with a barrel weighing from 5,000 to over 8,000 pounds in the sixteenth century).[3]

---

[1] From the Italian *colubrina* (snake), the term culverin or its equivalent was used in all major Mediterranean languages. See Henry Kahane and Andreas Tietze, *The Lingua Franca in the Levant* (Urbana, Ill., 1952), entry 210, 'colubrina'.

[2] This simplified and somewhat arbitrary categorization reflects fairly accurately mid-sixteenth-century Spanish practice and, with minor modifications, Venetian practice. See Olesa Muñido, *La Organización Naval*, vol. 1, pp. 318–23. The reader should be cautioned that the use of these terms, even by contemporary Mediterranean authors, was anything but consistent. Not only were there regional variations in the size and type of gun to which a particular term was applied, but usages changed with time. There is only the most general correlation between the definitions given here and contemporary English usage. The Spanish *sacre*, Venetian *sagre* and Turkish *šayka ṭopu*, for example, while roughly equivalent to each other, were equivalent not to the English saker as we might expect, but to the English demi culverin.

[3] These values represent Mediterranean practice and are confirmed by the observation of surviving examples in the collections of the Museo del Ejercito, Madrid; the Museu Militar, Lisbon; the Askeri Musesi and Deniz Musesi, Istanbul; and the Museo Storico Navale, Venice. Then, as now, the term 'cannon' had a general meaning which overlapped the specific, technical meaning. The Turkish equivalent, *baş ṭopu*, simply meant 'main cannon'.

References to quarter cannon, roughly equivalent to a half culverin, but shorter and throwing a larger ball, are occasionally encountered. Monster 'double cannon' and 'cannon royal' were cast to throw balls of from 80 to as much as 150 pounds, particularly early in the century; but these weighed more relative to their projectiles than smaller cannon, were considered unwieldy and inefficient in the West, and are rarely heard of except in the Ottoman siege train.[1]

The main advantage of the culverin early in the sixteenth century was its reliability and the confidence which it inspired in gunners. Whether this was explicitly recognized or not, the culverins' great length gave them added strength at the breech. This was initially a very important safety factor. That many early cannons were 'chambered' is clear evidence that weakness at the breech was recognized as a major problem. That this feature became less common as time went on, finally disappearing toward the end of the sixteenth century, must be attributed to gradual improvements in smelting and casting techniques and in the quality of cannon metal.

Though initially less reliable and more dangerous, cannons required only about two-thirds the bronze needed for a culverin cast for the same ball weight and used a powder charge which was smaller by at least a third, powerful economic incentive for further development.[2] Not surprisingly, as manufacturing standards improved throughout the sixteenth century, culverins became progressively less popular and the barrels of cast-bronze cannon in general became shorter.[3] It is difficult to avoid postulating a cause and effect relationship between these developments and the general improvement in manufacturing standards.

This progressive reduction of barrel lengths has been variously interpreted by naval historians, usually as an effort to improve ease of shipboard handling by sacrificing range.[4] Instead it seems evident, in light of our knowledge of the characteristics of cast bronze, that length was an undesirable but initially necessary means of strengthening the breech. Because of the intrinsic characteristics of black powder, increasing the length of a cannon's bore beyond about 12 calibers yielded only a slight increase in muzzle velocity and range and increasing it beyond 18 calibers

---

[1] Collado, *Platica Manual*, fol. 32.
[2] Biringuccio, *Pirotechnia*, p. 417, Collado, *Platica Manual*, fol. 11-12, 14-18. This is also confirmed by observation of surviving specimens.
[3] M. A. Lewis, *Armada Guns* (London, 1961), pp. 199-201 presents a thorough marshalling of the evidence for this change in English ordnance. Olesa Muñido, *La Organización Naval*, vol. I, pp. 302ff., presents fragmentary data which suggest that a similar process began somewhat later in Spain and (p. 318) data suggesting that such a process may have begun in Venice as early as the 1540s.
[4] e.g. Lewis, *Armada Guns*, p. 201.

yielded effectively no increase at all (see Appendix 2). The maximum ranges of all sixteenth-century cannon firing cast-iron projectiles were therefore essentially the same regardless of barrel length (the extreme ranges of *pedreros* were somewhat less because of the greater aerodynamic drag of a stone cannonball per unit of mass; but as we have indicated, this was of little practical significance).

The cannons ultimately triumphed over the culverins because of their greater economic efficiency. The relative unwieldiness of the longer, heavier culverins was undoubtedly a consideration; but there can be little doubt that the crucial factor was the saving in bronze and gunpowder. Using considerably less of both, a cannon could throw an iron ball of equal weight just as far and just as hard as a culverin. The completeness of the cannons' victory is illustrated by the application of the term 'cannon' to virtually all modern gunpowder weapons larger than a machine gun.

Though relatively little systematic study has been devoted to the subject, there were a number of clear-cut regional differences in the construction and use of bronze ordnance at sea by the Mediterranean nations. Though we will go into the matter in more detail in our discussion of galley tactics, a few general observations are in order here. Venetian cannon, regarded by contemporary experts as the best in the Mediterranean,[1] were markedly shorter and lighter than equivalent Spanish or Ottoman pieces, a fact of considerable tactical significance in galley warfare as we shall see. The difference in bulk and length between equivalent Spanish and Venetian naval pieces was particularly marked, Venetian culverins being almost equivalent to Spanish cannons and vice versa. A Venetian 52-pound cannon of 1556 cited as typical by Cristoforo da Canal had a bore length of only 16½ calibers and weighed 5,180 pounds.[2] We can take it as a fairly representative example since Venetian guns – unlike Spanish ones – were reasonably closely standardized. A contemporary Spanish naval cannon which weighed almost exactly the same, 5,050 pounds, and about which we have precise information was just over 21 calibers long and threw a ball of only 40 pounds.[3] Spanish cannon (technically half cannon) of about the same weight and vintage survive which were bored for a ball of only 26 pounds.[4] The general tendency of Spanish guns

1 Collado, *Platica Manual*, fol. 8.
2 Cited by Olesa Muñido, *La Organización Naval*, vol. I, p. 318. The cannon in question, the main centerline bow gun of a galley, was a '50 pounder'; but the pounds in question were large Venetian pounds of 477 grams as opposed to the modern English pound of 453.6 grams.
3 *Ibid.* vol. I, p. 318.
4 For example the four matched half cannon in the Museo del Ejercito, Madrid, by the German founder Gregory Leoffler. These beautifully executed guns, cast between 1543 and 1546, vary in weight from about 5,100 to 5,300 pounds and are bored for balls varying in weight from 26 to 28 pounds.

toward relatively great length and weight is explicitly confirmed by Luis Collado, an experienced and informed Spanish artillerist.[1] Interestingly, while Collado considered Spanish cannon to be sound, if somewhat unwieldy, he considered Genoese cannon, apparently of about the same proportions, to be of defective construction and positively dangerous.[2] Portuguese naval artillery was among the best in the world, if not the best, early in the sixteenth century. The Portuguese, however, hardly ever intervened directly in Mediterranean affairs after the 1530s. French artillery, particularly field artillery, was highly regarded, but had little impact on Mediterranean warfare at sea – the use of French artillery by the Barbarossa brothers to reduce the Spanish-held Peñon of Algiers in 1529 is the only major example following the French abandonment of Venice in 1499 which comes readily to mind.[3]

The Venetians seem also to have had a clear-cut superiority in the efficiency of their naval gunners, particularly aboard galleys. Their galleys were designed, as we shall see, with the efficient use of their heavy ordnance as a primary consideration. Ottoman and Spanish naval gunnery seem to have been roughly on a par with each other. Though the general level of practice was apparently not as high as that of Venetian naval gunners, the best Turkish and Spanish gunners were very good indeed. Ottoman siege batteries seem to have been particularly well handled, techniques having been developed to combine systematically the superior penetration of iron cannonballs with the tremendous smashing power of the large stone-throwing cannon.[4]

One final point about sixteenth-century gunnery must be made. The sixteenth-century gunner was not, unlike his eighteenth- or ninteeenth-century successors, a mere private soldier or able seaman who had been trained to perform certain mechanical movements under fire. Gunnery was still – like race-car driving before World War I or commercial flying in the 1920s – an uncertain business with a certain grimy glamor and a tangible aura of mystery about it. It was all very much 'seat of the pants'. Experience, basic intelligence, and a 'feel' for the business paid off more surely than precision in following a rigid set of procedures. Sixteenth-century gunnery was an art, not a science; and attempting to evaluate it as if it were a science can lead to serious errors. Its finest practitioners were

[1] Collado, *Platica Manual*, fol. 27–8, indicates that barrel lengths of 26–28 calibers were common for Spanish half cannons and 22–24 calibers for Spanish cannons. Olesa Muñido, *La Organización Naval*, vol I, p. 318, says that Spanish cannons and half cannons with barrels as long as 26 and even 30 calibers were not unusual.

[2] *Platica Manual*, fol. 8: 'The cannon founding of Genoa is the worst in Europe.'

[3] Olesa Muñido, *La Organización Naval*, vol. II, p. 1117.

[4] Collado, *Platica Manual*, fol. 13, 32.

men of unusual ability and daring who were attracted to gunnery by the mystery of the esoteric knowledge involved, by the danger, and by the prestige. It is worth noting that a number of great artists were cannon founders and gunners as well – Benvenuto Cellini and Leonardo da Vinci come immediately to mind. It is not surprising, then, that the best sixteenth-century gunnery surpassed that of the eighteenth and early nineteenth centuries, the lack of any scientific apparatus notwithstanding.

But the elitist character of sixteenth-century Mediterranean gunnery was essentially a cultural holdover from pre-gunpowder days, soon to be smothered by an outpouring of cheap cast-iron cannon from the north. As long as cannon were unique, individually made pieces, few in number and extremely expensive, this sort of relationship between gun and gunner was viable. A single good cannon, properly placed and skilfully served, could make the difference in almost any sixteenth-century engagement on land or sea. The applicability of this observation to galley warfare is obvious. But when cheap, standardized, cannon became available in large numbers, crude mass replaced selective precision and the Mediterranean war galley found itself in serious trouble, militarily as well as economically.

This brings us to our last type of artillery, properly almost beyond the bounds of our subject – cast-iron cannon. Successfully made for the first time by an English parson in the service of Henry VIII in 1543,[1] artillery of cast iron had, by the 1580s, become common in northern waters, the Dutch, the Swedes and the Germans in turn having acquired the technology from the English. The Mediterranean nations, however, did not do so until much later.

Cast-iron ordnance was not superior to bronze: it was heavier, bulkier and far more dangerous to use. But it had one overwhelming advantage – it cost only a third as much.[2] The manufacture of iron ordnance in the north on a scale approaching mass production from the 1580s on sounded the death knell for the traditional methods of acquiring military skills, however effective they may have been in the narrowly tactical sense. It also sounded the death knell for the war galley, marking the ultimate triumph of gunpowder's essential characteristics over those of the Mediterranean system of warfare at sea.

[1] H. R. Schubert, 'The First Cast Iron Cannon Made in England', *Journal of the Iron and Steel Institute*, CXLVI (1942), 137.

[2] Carlo Cipolla, *Guns, Sails and Empires* (New York, 1965), p. 42, n. 3. See also Braudel, *La Méditerranée* (Paris, 1966), p. 460. Braudel's data, drawn from English and German sources, shows the price of raw copper slowly descending to a low of about three times that of iron in the 1520s, then rising steadily to about nine times that of iron by 1600. This cannot be taken as a quantitative indication of Mediterranean conditions; but there was something approaching a world market in iron and copper, particularly the latter, and Braudel's data is surely indicative of general conditions.

Malta, 1565

Following Djerba, the Ottomans were presented with an opportunity. The Spanish fleet was severely crippled. As long at it remained so, the Ottomans had as free a hand as they were ever likely to enjoy in the central Mediterranean. But time was critical. The Ottoman opportunity, though not a fleeting one, was one which diminished steadily with each passing year. The Spanish loss was primarily in quality and experience, not numbers. Each year of campaigning which her crews and soldiers experienced lessened the danger for Spain. The significance of the opportunity presented the Ottomans by Djerba was not lost on the Spanish. Their naval weakness left their coasts and island dominions within the Mediterranean exposed to the attacks of an enemy whose strength, skill and competence were never in doubt. But while each passing year made the Spanish more able to defend their coasts and possessions, each year after Djerba also saw the Ottomans in a better position to exploit the advantage with their full strength.

The timing of the Ottoman thrust seems to have been largely taken for granted. Evidently the rhythm of Mediterranean warfare at sea had an inner logic which was far more apparent to sixteenth-century naval commanders than it is to the modern historian of their art. It was clearly apparent to experienced observers in the summer of 1564 that the blow must fall the following year. The warning sent by Don Garcia de Toledo, Captain General of the Sea and Viceroy of Sicily, to Philip II did not even bother to explain the particular need for urgency in that year above all others.[1] The realization of the need for urgency showed up in other areas as well. In 1564 as in 1539, the year after Prevesa, the Spanish took the unusual step of taking àn inventory of private ships and their armament in preparation for mobilizing them as a last-ditch defensive fleet.[2]

---

[1] *Colección Navarrete*, vol. XII, dto. 79, fol. 295ff. This warning was commented upon at length and analyzed in ch. 3.

[2] The 1539 inventory of ships is in the *Colección Sanz de Barutell (Simancas), Artículo* 4, dto. 121. This inventory was taken in November with an eye to the campaigning season of 1540. The 1564 inventories are in the *Colección Navarrete*, vol. I, dtos. 76 and 77. That for northern Spain is on fol. 271–9 and that for Andalusia is on fol. 281–7.

That the Ottoman blow would fall in 1565 was taken for granted; the only question was where?

The Ottoman choice of targets depended upon a number of relatively inflexible physical restrictions imposed by the inherent limitations of galley fleets. Based in Constantinople, a mid-sixteenth-century galley fleet could go no farther than Tunis and still carry the strength needed to mount a protracted siege of a first-class fortified place which was competently defended. Though an Ottoman fleet could, in theory, have wintered over at its objective in full strength, this would have imposed an insupportable logistic burden. It would also have left the Ottoman forces exposed to certain decimation by exposure and disease or the possibility of a sudden descent by the Spanish. The first of these risks could on occasion be reduced and tolerated by staying on with reduced forces, as was done at Rhodes in the winter of 1521–2 and at Famagusta on Cyprus in the winter of 1570–1; but both of these places were deep in the eastern Mediterranean.

All worthwhile targets in the western Mediterranean were within easy reach of Spanish bases; the second risk was therefore too great. The Turk could carry a siege of Rhodes or Famagusta through the winter, but not a siege of Malta, Tunis, or Puerto Mahon.

Another option was to winter the fleet in a friendly port in the western Mediterranean, then strike early the following spring. But Algiers did not have the resources needed to support the manpower of a major expedition and Toulon was unavailable.[1]

A descent on the Andalusian coast was therefore ruled out. If the Moriscos were to be succored and their sympathies turned to military advantage, it would have to be through the prolonged attrition of *ghazi* warfare, not a decisive blow struck by a single expedition. This would require a base from which Ottoman raiders could strike at the coasts of Spain in support of the North African Muslims. If, however, such a base were directly accessible to Spanish land power the cost of holding it – if it could be held at all – would be excessive. This was one of the lessons of Otranto in 1481 and a valid one. It ruled out Sicily and the Italian coasts.

These considerations, visible to militarily experienced Turks and Spaniards alike, pointed toward Malta. Malta was close enough to the Ottoman bases to be attacked with force: yet it was far enough west for Islamic raiders based there to be able to do the Spanish real harm. Its superb

---

[1] The Ottoman fleet wintered at Toulon in the winter of 1543–4. Though Piri Re'is ventured far to the west in his raids on Spanish dominions in the 1550s, neither he nor anyone else seems to have used Algiers as a wintering base for the entire Ottoman fleet.

harbor was an ideal base for the *ghazi* war, as every successive raid of the Knights of St John into the eastern Mediterranean demonstrated. Its small extent and the scarcity of good beaches insured that getting a relieving force ashore would be no easy task for the Spanish. All of these factors must have been dealt with at length in the deliberations of the Divan. We know that they were presented in roughly this form to Philip II by Don Garcia de Toledo.

The Spanish naval forces, in the midst of their post-Djerba build-up, were still unreliable. Spain had a single trump card – the infantry of the *tercios* and their mercenary German and Italian comrades in arms. The Spanish reserve of trained soldiers had been dented at Djerba but, unlike that of sailors and *oficiales*, it had not been virtually wiped out. It was a card that would have to be played carefully – very carefully in light of the weakness of the naval instrument which would have to transport it – and at exactly the right time, It was around this consideration that the campaign of 1565 revolved.

Thrown in too soon, a Spanish relieving force might be caught while still at sea by a skilled, numerically superior, and still fresh Ottoman fleet. But if Don Garcia waited until the bulk of the Ottoman resources of manpower, guns, and munitions had been ground down and expended in the inexorable attrition of a hard-pressed siege, the relief might arrive after its object had fallen. His first problem, therefore, was to insure that whatever place the Turk attacked could hold out for long enough to reduce the strength of the Ottoman forces to the point where relief could be introduced. This was a game which required precise estimation of a wide range of variables, strong leadership and exquisite timing. Don Garcia de Toledo possessed all three. Jean Parisot de la Valette, Grand Master of the Order of the Knights of St John of Jerusalem and commander of the garrison of Malta, possessed the second, at least, in abundance.

In many respects the Malta campaign of 1565 represented the apex of sixteenth-century amphibious siege warfare. The force which the Ottomans mustered in the spring of 1565 was not the largest of its kind of the sixteenth century, only one of the largest. Nor was its target the farthest from its port city of origin – the Ottoman expedition of 1574 against Tunis travelled some 200 miles more each way. The 1522 siege of Rhodes and the siege of Famagusta of 1570–1 were, if it is possible, even more bitterly contested. But in none of these campaigns were all the elements of amphibious siegecraft used so fully by both sides. Both sides stretched their material and human resources to the limit. Both Muslim and Christian commanders showed impressive virtuosity in their command of the technical aspects of their art. Virtually everything that could be tried was tried: destruction of walls by direct battery, assault by land, amphibious assault in small boats, amphibious relief of a besieged fortress, mining, countermining, sapping operations under cover of artillery, small arms and arrow fire, siege towers, defensive sorties by both cavalry and infantry, incendiary devices of all descriptions, and even the use of swimmers to clear away underwater obstacles to amphibious assault – and other, armed, swimmers to prevent them from accomplishing their task.

Perhaps because of interest stimulated by the siege of 1940–3 which came about for strikingly similar geographic and military reasons, the 1565 siege of Malta has attracted more recent scholarly attention than any other sixteenth-century Mediterranean campaign. Much of what has been written, however, can be seriously misleading when read out of context. Much as modern scholars have missed the skill and subtlety of sixteenth-century galley tactics by analyzing them within a Mahanian context, they have missed the science of sixteenth-century siege warfare by viewing it in terms of Vauban. At first glance, this tendency to evaluate sixteenth-century siege tactics by late seventeenth-century standards seems valid since the weapons used and their capabilities remained almost identical. Given an assumed equality of means, Vauban's rational, 'scientific', approach seems far more impressive than the blunt directness of Luis Collado, his sixteenth-century counterpart.[1] Where Vauban would begin by marking out the locations of successive siege parallels on a map with geometric precision, Collado normally advocated trundling the most effective cannon available up to within 60 yards of the walls, blasting the biggest hole possible in the shortest possible time, and assaulting the breach without delay.[2] This difference in approach is not entirely attributable to Vauban's presumably superior intellect – where conditions permitted (as in the case of a poorly sited, poorly manned, or weakly gunned

---

[1] Luis Collado's *Platica Manual de Artilleria*, which appeared first in Italian (Venice, 1586), then in an expanded Spanish edition (Milan, 1592), is in many ways a direct parallel to Vauban's work on siegecraft. The difference which a century had made in fortress architecture, manpower, motivation, and logistics causes them to emphasize different aspects of siegecraft and their styles are, as might be expected, different; but the approach of these two men to technical problems is remarkably similar. Sadly, there is no modern edition of Collado. I have used the 1592 edition throughout for consistency.

[2] Collado, *Platica Manual*, fol. 53–4 (*Tratado* 3, *Capitulo* XXXIII), puts it as follows: 'The distance of the battery [from the fortress wall] will depend upon the circumstances of the [best] site which you can find near the fortress; but the best and most proper distance (if you can do it) is 80 paces from the wall. A distance of 100 paces would be excellent and 150 very good. A distance of 200 paces is not so good and 300 is, without a doubt, too far.' I have assumed that Collado's pace is the *passo comun* of Castile, about 2.285 feet; thus, 80 paces is about 60 yards, 100 paces about 70 yards, 150 paces about 110 yards, 200 paces about 150 yards and 300 paces about 230 yards. Collado states that the breach should be wide enough for nine men to enter abreast.

fortress) his preferred approach was much the same as Collado's.[1] Indeed, there is considerable overlap between the two: where Vauban recognized the value of going straight at the main wall by direct battery when possible, Collado recognized the necessity of advancing his batteries slowly under cover of trenches and supporting artillery and musket fire where necessary.[2]

The difference between them, then, is primarily a matter of emphasis. This difference is only partially attributable to improvements in fortress architecture which made main fortress walls less vulnerable to artillery fire. It is primarily the result of a single factor: there was much less artillery around in Collado's day than in Vauban's. Defensive artillery fire in Vauban's day was, on the whole, far more intensive and sustained much longer than in Collado's. Vauban and his contemporaries adopted the method of advance by methodically laid out siege parallels not because of the logical beauty of the scheme, but because they had no choice. The proliferation of cannon and the attendant increase in fire power had, by Vauban's day, forced back the besieger, pinned him down and forced him to proceed by digging his way toward his objective under cover of heavy artillery fire. This gradual, but striking change in siege tactics is, in fact, one of the strongest indications we have of the sixteenth-century shortage of artillery, a shortage which had important ramifications in purely naval matters as we shall note in our discussion of Lepanto.

That this shortage of ordnance was a general one is evidenced by the military architecture of the early sixteenth century. Though the utility of artillery was universally recognized and although artillery had already forced radical changes in fortress design, fortresses of the sixteenth century were cut to emplace far fewer guns than those of succeeding centuries. A classic example is the Spanish fortress of Salses in the western Pyrenees, built between 1497 and 1503. By the standards of Vauban's day this squat, powerful fortress was nearly devoid of both artillery and artillerists, less than a company of whom were regularly assigned to the garrison.[3]

---

[1] Sebastian Le Prestre de Vauban, *A Manual of Siegecraft and Fortification*, trans. George A. Rothrock (Leiden, 1740), pp. 59, 83. Though Vauban does not explicitly specify an ideal range for direct battery (his 'method' normally involved pushing sapping parties into the ditch under cover of artillery fire to bring down the main wall by mining) he clearly indicates that this method is preferred in the rare instances where little defensive artillery fire is encountered. Plate XVII illustrates this point and shows the main battery working at a range of about 80 yards from the fortress wall.

[2] Collado, *Platica Manual* fol. 53.

[3] For the appearance of Salses, see the photograph in Jaques Boudet and Francesco Valori (eds.), *Armi e Eserciti Nella Storia Universale* (Milan, 1966), p. 228. The manning data is from Jorge Vigon, *Historia de la Artilleria Española*, vol. 1 (Madrid, 1947), p. 118, who cites a royal document of 1501 establishing the number of artillerists assigned to Salses as *algunas artilleros ordinarios*, that is less than a company of artillerists without officers or non-commissioned officers.

Its walls and bastions are cut with less than forty gunports, all of them apparently for large pieces. The cannon of Salses were placed with skill and care; but there were hardly enough of them to arm a single bastion in one of Vauban's major places of two centuries later. This shortage of defensive artillery made it possible for a determined attacker to go straight at the walls with the directness which Collado took for granted. Only in the rare case where a heavy concentration of defensive artillery fire was effected was a gradual, Vauban-like approach required. The most reasonable explanation for the directness of sixteenth-century siege tactics is therefore that there simply wasn't much artillery around.

Evidence for this general shortage of artillery is manifold, particularly for the early 1500s: in 1538 the total defensive artillery of Santo Domingo, a major port city in the Caribbean under constant threat from French privateers, consisted of only four culverins and four half culverins mounted in five bastions. This provision of defensive ordnance was considered adequate, though only just, the numbers of guns being considered sufficient, but the ordnance somewhat light for its task.[1] The same source tells us that an armament of two half culverins, two *sacres* and several smaller bronze pieces, supplemented by ten wrought-iron bombards salvaged from wrecks, was sufficient to repel a French raiding force of considerable strength from one of the smaller Caribbean port towns. As late as 1562 the fortifications of Oran were garnished with only 27 pieces of artillery.[2]

This scarcity of artillery is clearly not an indication that its advantages in the defense were not appreciated. It is apparent that by the middle of the sixteenth century, if not before, at least some military men understood how to handle a heavy concentration of defensive artillery fire, as we shall see in our discussion of the siege of Malta.

In light of our postulated general shortage of good bronze ordnance, the quantity and quality of artillery used at the siege of Malta in 1565, about which we are fortunate in knowing a great deal, assumes considerable significance. Malta was a full-scale contest between two empires whose military leadership exhibited a generally high level of competence and whose financial resources were, by the standards of the day, almost overwhelming. If our theory is correct – if sixteenth-century siege tactics were in fact highly sophisticated, given the general level of ordnance available – then Malta should be the proof of the pudding.

Of particular interest is the provision of defensive artillery. Taken from

---

[1] This is from the *Colección Navarrete*, vol. XXV, dto. 4, fol. 10ff., relating to the defensive measures taken against French corsairs by Spanish officials in the Caribbean.
[2] W. H Prescott, *History of the Reign of Philip the Second*, vol. III (Philadelphia, 1904), p. 145.

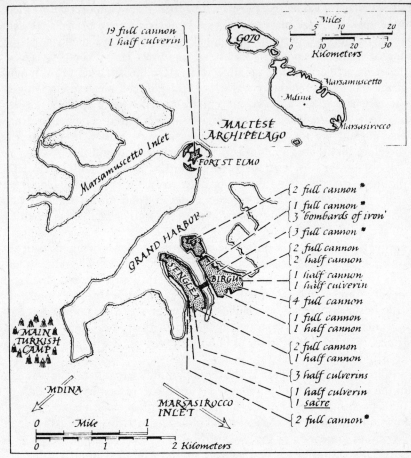

19 full cannon
1 half culverin

GOZO

Miles
5 10   20
0   10   20
10   20   30
Kilometers

Marsamuscetto

Mdina

MALTESE
ARCHIPELAGO

Marsasirocco

FORT ST ELMO

Marsamuscetto Inlet

{ 2 full cannon *

{ 1 full cannon *
{ 3 'bombards of iron'

{ 3 full cannon *

GRAND HARBOR

{ 2 full cannon
{ 2 half cannon

SENGLEA

BIRGU

{ 1 half cannon
{ 1 half culverin

{ 4 full cannon

{ 1 full cannon
{ 1 half cannon

MAIN
TURKISH
CAMP

{ 2 full cannon
{ 1 half cannon

{ 3 half culverins

MDINA

{ 1 half culverin
{ 1 sacre

MARSASIROCCO
INLET

{ 2 full cannon *

0   Mile   1

0   1   2 Kilometers

* cannon whose exact location is uncertain

Map 5   Malta, 1565, the distribution of defensive artillery

a detailed account of the siege written shortly afterward by one Don Juan
Paez de Castro, who was present during the siege, the following list is
probably very nearly inclusive:[1]

Cannon mounted in the defense of Birgu and Senglea (see Map 5):

17 full cannon (probably 40–50 pounders)

[1] *Colección Navarrete*, vol. IV, dto. 19, fol. 224ff., entitled 'Relación del sitio que puso el Turco
a la Isla de Malta y del Socorro que introdujo Don Garcia de Toledo . . . Ano 1565', authenti-
cated and transcribed from the original in the library of the Escorial by Fernandez de Navarrete himself in November 1791. In the form of a diary or an operations log, this account was
clearly written by a competent and experienced military man. De Castro's manner in listing the
type, number, and location of the various pieces of ordnance inspires considerable confidence.

5 half cannon (probably 20–30 pounders)
5 half culverins (probably 9 pounders, give or take a little)
1 *sacre* (probably about a 6 pounder)
3 *lombardas de hierro* (old wrought-iron bombards) ‗

Cannon mounted in Fort St Elmo:

19 full cannon
1 half culverin

Bearing in mind that the Knights of St John of Malta were neither totally impoverished nor ignorant of the art of siege warfare, we may assume that any lack of artillery reflected in the above list was the result of non-availability, not of ineptitude, penury or ignorance. Indeed, there is no indication that the amount of artillery available to the defense was considered inadequate at the time. Francisco Balbi di Correggio, a participant whose account of the siege was published just a few years later, tells us that the Grand Master had 'plenty of artillery', though he was somewhat short of powder.[1] We will have to modify this in light of La Valette's actual dispositions; but in terms of general expectations among soldiers of the time, Balbi is undoubtedly correct.

It is equally clear, however, that La Valette could have usefully employed many more cannon had they been available. The weight of artillery which would ideally have been sited in the defense is shown by the fact that over half of the full cannons available were assigned to the small outlying position of Fort St Elmo which dominated the entrance to the harbor of Marsamuscetto, the nearest safe anchorage available to the Ottoman fleet (see Map 5). It was there that La Valette estimated – correctly – that the first blow would fall. It was there that he would have to take toll of the still fresh Ottoman forces if the main positions of

---

[1] Francisco Balbi di Correggio, *The Siege of Malta*, 1565, trans. Ernle Bradford (London, 1565), from the 2nd edition (Barcelona, 1568), which was edited by several prominent survivors of the siege (p. 61). Balbi, an ordinary arquebusier in the garrison of Senglea, gives a long and generally accurate, but technically uninformed and occasionally confusing account. He was clearly ignorant of the finer points of gunnery and only mentions artillery in general terms when describing the damage done by the Turkish batteries and in specifics only when relating anecdotes, such as prominent leaders being killed by a cannonball, etc. For the following account of the siege I have depended primarily upon Balbi and Don Juan Paez de Castro (above, p. 182, n. 1). De Castro's account, though much shorter (only 10 folios in the original) is much more knowledgeable technically. Prescott, *History of the Reign of Philip the Second*, vol. III, pp. 174–272, still gives the best account of the siege in English, drawing on Balbi, Spanish sources and historians of the Order. Fernand Braudel's discussion of the siege in *La Méditerranée*, vol. II (Mexico City, 1953), pp. 319–29, though general, is very good and is almost unique in defending Don Garcia de Toledo against his detractors. Ernle Bradford, *The Great Siege* (London, 1961), is useful in reflecting the bitter (and in my opinion unfair) accusations that the Viceroy was needlessly dilatory in launching the relief expedition.

Senglea and Birgu were to survive. St Elmo was therefore armed as it should have been. The land walls of Birgu and Senglea were armed as best they could be with what was left over. The disparity is a striking one which strongly suggests a shortage of ordnance.

We should also note the predominance of full cannon in de Castro's list. Faced with limited financial resources and a need for scarce and expensive artillery, the Knights of St John had put their money where it would do the most good, largely ignoring smaller pieces less useful for coastal defense and in siege warfare. A shortage is also suggested by the inclusion of three old wrought-iron bombards, thoroughly obsolete by 1565 and probably well over a half century old, in the artillery of the defense. We shall see this survival of old, obsolete, and probably unsafe wrought-iron ordnance – strongly suggestive of a general shortage – again in our analysis of galley armament.

The Ottoman siege artillery was, as we would expect, more powerful, though not overwhelmingly so in terms of numbers. According to Paez de Castro, the Ottomans brought two 'large basilisks' and 60 'double cannons of battery' to Malta (an estimate which is substantiated by what we know of the siege) along with 40,000 *quintals* of gunpowder (over 2,000 short tons) and 70,000 iron cannonballs. This is amplified by Balbi di Correggio's statement that the Ottomans brought a huge 100 pound siege gun weighing 18,000 pounds (this gun and its ammunition comprised the entire load of a single galley), two eighty pounders weighing 13,000 pounds each, four 60 pounders weighing 11,000 pounds each and a 'large cannon which fired stone shot' (almost certainly one of de Castro's basilisks).[1] These monsters were plainly intended for knocking down walls by direct battery and were, so far as we can tell, used in precisely that role. We know from de Castro's account, for example, that two basilisks were emplaced hard up against the south-west corner of Birgu in the final stages of the siege when Christian powder was running short and counter-battery fire, as a consequence, was rarely employed.

The balance in manpower was far more one-sided. The Ottoman fleet of some 130 galleys, 18 galiots, 8 *maonas* (large merchant galleys) and 11 large sailing vessels left Constantinople in February with around 30,000 fighting men, including as many as 9,000 *timariot sipahis* and as

---

[1] Balbi di Correggio, *The Siege of Malta*, pp. 31–7. Balbi, apparently ignorant of the technical vocabulary of gunnery, calls all cannon of great size 'basilisks'. To de Castro and Prescott's sources, cited in *History of the Reign of Philip the Second*, vol. III, p. 179, a basilisk was a particular kind of gun, almost certainly a very large Ottoman *pedrero*. The technical meaning of this term varied over time, being used earlier in the sixteenth century to designate a large, 'long', gun designed to throw an iron projectile; but the generic meaning, 'a large gun', remained constant.

many as 6,000 Janissaries.[1] This total was swelled by some 600 men under the Governor of Alexandria who arrived with 4 galleys on 27 May, by a contingent of 2,500 North Africans under Turgut Re'is who arrived at Malta with 43 galleys, 2 galiots and a siege train on 2 June, and the Algerian contingent of 2,500 (including perhaps as many as 500 Janissaries) in 7 galleys and 20 galiots which arrived on 12 July. The Ottoman force thus ultimately included some 36,000 fighting men, well over half of them Janissaries, *sipahis* or experienced *'azabs, akinjis,* or *lewends,* in addition to numbers of oarsmen, both free and slave, who could be used as sappers and laborers.

The garrison of Malta, by contrast, comprised no more than 2,500 professional fighting men, including 500 Knights and two companies of Spanish infantry of 200 men each, bolstered by 700 or so mercenary oarsmen and armed Greek and Italian residents of Malta plus 5,000–6,000 Maltese of whom perhaps 1,000 were armed.[2]

After making several stops in the Greek islands to embark additional troops and supplies, the Ottoman fleet arrived off Malta early in the evening of 18 May. The Ottoman force apparently arrived earlier than anticipated, only six days after the arrival of a company of 200 Spanish arquebusiers, earmarked by Don Garcia de Toledo for the garrison of Fort St Elmo. The next day the Turks, barred from the anchorage of Marsamuscetto by St Elmo's guns, began disembarking at Marsasirocco inlet, five miles from Senglea and Birgu across the south-eastern corner of the island.

After some debate among the Muslim leadership (some Christian sources to the contrary, it is not clear who pressed for what course of action) it was decided that Fort St Elmo should be captured before proceeding to the siege of the main positions of Birgu and Senglea. Western analysts have generally held that the capture of Fort St Elmo was unnecessary since the bay of Marsasirocco would have served as well for an anchorage as Marsamuscetto which St Elmo dominated.[3] This view

[1] Balbi's detailed breakdown (*The Siege of Malta*, p. 36) gives 9,000 *sipahis* who were probably *timariots* (as opposed to salaried *sipahis* of the Porte), most if not all of them archers, and 6,000 Janissaries, 'all musketeers'. De Castro's estimate of 4,500 Janissaries is still impressive. Balbi's 9,000 'adventurers' and 6,000 'corsairs and adventurers' were probably mostly *'azabs* and *lewends.*

[2] Though their breakdowns vary, Balbi, de Castro and Prescott's sources are in general agreement regarding the strength of the garrison.

[3] Bradford, *The Great Siege*, pp. 71–2, presents this argument. I am indebted to Wing Commander R. A. Mason, Royal Air Force, a fellow faculty member in the Department of History, U.S. Air Force Academy, for having clarified the geography of Malta to me. Though he is not a sixteenth-century military historian, Wing Commander Mason's educated military eye for terrain provided me with an instant and comprehensive reference source for Maltese topography. Much of the following analysis is a direct result of his assistance.

is based on a misunderstanding of the role played by a galley fleet in the siege of a major seaside fortress.

In fact, Piali Paşa and Mustafa Paşa (commander of the Ottoman land forces) needed Marsamuscetto as a base to keep their amphibious forces near their logistic and manpower reserves and to avoid having to haul heavy cannon (the largest must have weighed well over 20,000 pounds with their carriages) overland any farther than necessary. This latter consideration was a critical one in view of the unavailability on Malta of large numbers of draft animals.

Close cooperation between fleet and army in siege operations was an essential ingredient of the Mediterranean system of warfare at sea, a point which many modern analysts have missed. A fleet based at Marsasirocco would have been unable to cooperate effectively with an army engaged in operations before Senglea and Birgu. As long as fleet and army were widely separated, the Muslims had to leave large security forces behind to guard the ships. These could not have participated in the siege. While acceptable early on, such a situation would have become rapidly untenable as more and more men were employed in the attrition of a hard fought siege and as dray animals were consumed as food. Similarly, the fleet would have been poorly positioned to cover the siege forces from a sudden attempt by the Spanish fleet to get in supplies or to raid the Ottoman siege lines. Committing oarsmen to hauling supplies and digging siege parallels would have entailed a permanent loss of mobility to the fleet, not a temporary deficit which could be made good at a moment's notice. Likewise, cooperation in bombarding the Christian positions by the Muslim galleys (as was actually undertaken against St Elmo on several occasions, notably to cover the assault of 15 June) would have been more involved at best. Finally, we know that the water supply in the vicinity of Marsasirocco was inadequate for the entire Ottoman fleet – the Ottoman galleys were sent to get water at the Bays of St Paul and Salinas to the west of Marsamuscetto less than two weeks after their arrival[1] (see Map 5).

The bombardment of St Elmo by Ottoman batteries emplaced 'about 600 paces' [460 yards][2] up the peninsula from the ditch of the fortress began on 25 May. That the Ottoman batteries began work at such long range despite the poor siting of St Elmo against overland attack – the fortress was positioned primarily to deny Marsamuscetto to hostile fleets and to defend the entrance to the grand harbor – is probably attributable to effective Christian counterbattery fire. We know that the bulk of St

---

[1] Balbi di Correggio, *The Siege of Malta*, p. 61.
[2] *Ibid.* p. 56.

Elmo's ordnance was emplaced to defend against attack by land.[1] St Elmo held out for the unexpectedly long period of twenty-eight days, falling on Saturday, 23 June, after nearly three weeks of intensive bombardment and four major assaults.

In part the long resistance was due to the Turks' inability to cut St Elmo off from reinforcement across the harbor by small boat until 18 June, when they finally succeeded in driving a trench down to the water's edge below the fort under the direction of Turgut Re'is, newly arrived with his contingent from Tripoli. In part it was undoubtedly because the Ottoman leadership underestimated St Elmo's strength and, concerned with their logistic problem (which the capture of St Elmo was intended to solve), seem to have held back their heaviest artillery for the final attack on Birgu and Senglea. However this may have been, St Elmo's artillery plainly played a major role in the defense: directly through counterbattery fire and in repelling assaults with fire into the main ditch and indirectly by denying Marsamuscetto to the Ottoman fleet.

According to Balbi di Correggio's sources, St Elmo cost the Turks some 18,000 rounds of artillery ammunition and 6,000 casualties, including the great Muslim commander Turgut Re'is, whose battery bombarded St Elmo across the mouth of Marsamuscetto from the point which still bears his name – Drugut Point.[2] Though this estimate is probably high in light of the Christian casualties of around 1,500 men killed, it is clear that the Ottoman casualties were heavy, particularly among the Janissaries and *sipahis* who played a much less prominent role in subsequent operations.

Robbed of time, fighting manpower and resources by the prolonged resistance of St Elmo, the Ottomans quickly occupied Marsamuscetto with their fleet and shifted their main batteries around to face the land walls of Birgu and Senglea. Almost simultaneously, Don Garcia de Toledo dispatched a small, hand-picked relief force carried in his four best galleys. Though it would not come ashore until the night of 3–4 July because of a storm encountered en route and because of the difficulties in finding a safe spot for a covert night debarkation on the tiny island, the timing was surely less than accidental.

The Ottomans at first concentrated their attention on Senglea. Though the land walls, bolstered by the bastions and artillery of Fort St Michael, were more than adequate in their intact state to resist direct assault, the water defenses along French Creek were weak and the shore adjacent to them gradual and smooth, an obvious invitation to amphibious assault. Serious bombardment of Senglea began on 3 July, concentrating on the

---

[1] Prescott, *History of the Reign of Philip the Second*, vol. III, p. 178.
[2] Balbi di Correggio, *The Siege of Malta*, p. 91.

south-west corner of the land walls and on the already weak defenses along the creek. The Turkish preparations were obvious to the defenders – numbers of boats, some of them fairly large, were dragged overland from Marsamuscetto to the head of the Grand Harbor opposite the main Muslim camp – and underwater obstacles, stakes connected with chains and the like, were planted in the shallows. On 11 July Muslim swimmers attempted to clear these away, but were repelled by numbers of Maltese under cover of arquebus fire.

On 15 July, with Muslim artillery firing at a range of less than 400 yards having nearly levelled the defenses along French Creek in spots, a major assault was launched, spearheaded by the Algerian contingent which had arrived only three days before, and covered by a simultaneous land attack on Fort St Michael.

The main force of the assault was broken by the underwater obstacles which stopped the Muslim boats short of the beach and snared the robes of the fighting men. Nevertheless the fighting along French Creek was severe, lasting about five hours with perhaps 3,000 attackers involved. At the peak of the assault ten Muslim boats carrying about 1,000 men, seeing their predecessors entangled in the underwater obstacles, shifted their attack to the low-lying tip of Senglea, hoping to get ashore unopposed with the Christian reserves committed elsewhere – as in fact they were. Instead, they were taken in flank by a battery firing from a platform at water level beneath the tip of Fort St Angelo. Firing at a range of about 300 yards, the Christian guns killed hundreds of Muslims outright with their first volley and sank nine of the ten boats, drowning most of the survivors.[1] A better example of the effect of accurate and effective gunnery is hard to find. The result was a bloody Muslim débâcle. The survivors of the assault force in French Creek retreated to their boats in disorder, pursued by the garrison.

The next day the Muslims shifted their attention to the land defenses, opening a violent frontal bombardment of Fort St Michael. Mining against the land walls of both Birgu and Senglea had begun by 17 July (though it was never very effective, apparently because of the hard soil) and trenches were advanced under cover of an increasingly intense bombardment and heavy musket fire which forced the defenders to keep their heads down and their guns out of action most of the time. An attempted surprise attack on Fort St Michael was beaten back on the 28th.

Then, at noon on 2 August, following an extended bombardment which

---

[1] This incident is mentioned both by Balbi and Paez de Castro. Balbi, p. 115, colors his account, stating that this force was specially chosen from among non-swimmers to insure against retreat.

had done considerable damage to the walls, the Ottomans launched a mass assault which succeeded in gaining a temporary lodgement in several places. It was beaten back with great difficulty after five hours of intense fighting, most of it hand-to-hand. Apparently encouraged by indications that Christian manpower reserves were running thin – the Muslim artillery seems to have established an almost total fire superiority by this point, the Christian guns being kept under cover except when actually needed to repel an assault – Mustafa Paşa tried again on the 7th.

Hoping to catch La Valette without reserves, the Muslim attack began all along the line at dawn, concentrating on Fort St Michael and the south-west corner of the land wall of Birgu where the ditch was almost completely filled with rubble brought down from the walls by Turkish cannonballs. Here the Muslims gained a sizeable foothold and a number of Muslim standards were planted along the wall. La Valette himself led the counterattack at Birgu with his last reserves and the battle hung in the balance for nearly nine hours.

Then, as the Muslims had victory nearly within their grasp, the un-expected happened: Dom Pedro de Mezquita, the Portuguese governor of the old citadel of Mdina in the center of the island, had apparently watched the progress of the attack with close attention. His tiny force had harassed Muslim foraging parties throughout the siege and had repelled the half-hearted attack on Mdina with which their efforts had been rewarded during the preceeding week. Now their moment was at hand. Mezquita launched the handful of horsemen and arquebusiers which he had available, surely no more than 100 of each, against the Ottoman base camp, stripped clean of ablebodied men for the assault. Shouting 'victory and relief' the shoestring force piled into the Muslim camp slashing the wounded, cutting down tents, and burning everything they could lay hands on. The timing was perfect. Just when one more supreme effort might have overcome Christian resistance, terrified survivors from the camp came streaming into the siege lines and broke the Muslim resolve. Whether on Mustafa Paşa's orders or as a simple reflex movement, the Ottoman assault force, half convinced that a Spanish relief force was between them and their fleet, pulled back from the walls of Birgu and Senglea. The threat was never again to be so severe – though this was hardly apparent at the time to the hard pressed defenders.

The siege settled down to a deadly game of sniping, sapping, mining and countermining. Showing considerable skill, Ottoman sappers worked their trenches in closer and closer to the south-west corner of Birgu and the half-ruined 'spur' of Fort St Michael under a steady protective hail of musketry and cannonballs. The defenders used every means at their disposal, at one point cutting a surprise gunport low in the wall of Birgu to enfilade a particularly menacing Turkish trench. On 20 August Mustafa Paşa launched a major assault against Fort St Michael – and led it in person despite his advanced age, a sign of demoralization among the Ottoman shock troops. Another violent assault took place the next day, spearheaded by the few remaining Janissaries and – according to Balbi di Correggio – '*azabs* and laborers dressed in the clothing of fallen Janissaries to exaggerate their numbers and demoralize the defenders.

On the 24th the wind blew up cold from the north, bringing rain with it and extinguishing the arquebusiers' slow matches, a harbinger of the approaching end of the campaigning season. The defenders broke out crossbows to discourage an assault in the rain with cold steel.

On the 27th the Turks pushed a siege tower – a throwback to the Crusades – against Fort St Michael only to have it destroyed by a masked cannon firing through a newly cut gunport low in the wall. That they could even attempt such a maneuver shows the completeness of the Ottoman fire superiority.

Though still dangerous, the Ottoman besiegers had plainly had much of the fire taken out of their bellies while the defenders, even if nearing the end of their tether both physically and logistically, could see the end in sight. Defensive sorties were launched into the Turkish trenches and bread and cheese were thrown into Muslim sap heads to convince the sappers that Christian supplies of food were unlimited. Muslim assaults were made on the 29th, again on the 30th, and on the first of September a final moveable siege tower was tried, its upper story filled with Janissary arquebusiers to clear the walls of defenders, only to have it burnt and destroyed. Mining was increasingly resorted to, but with little effect.

Given another month, the müezzin's call might well have sounded – indeed, given the exhausted condition of the garrison, probably would have sounded – from atop Fort St Angelo. But, as Mustafa Paşa and Piali Paşa undoubtedly knew, Don Garcia de Toledo would give the Muslims considerably less than a month. Piali's fleet, its best fighting manpower and much of its motive power ground into raw meat and dust against the walls of Birgu and Senglea, drowned in French Creek and buried in the ditch of Fort St Elmo, was barely a match for the fresh and untried Spanish fleet which it could have handled with ease a month and a half earlier.

Mining through the rubble brought down by cannonballs was increasingly resorted to in a vain attempt to blast a clear way into the Christian defenses, but to no avail. The heart had gone out of the Muslim forces. By 4 September the Janissaries had to go into the trenches to beat the

sappers to force them to their work. Then, on 7 September, a galiot
entered Marsamuscetto with news that the Christian relief was at hand.
Slowly and methodically, taking until the 11th to finish the job, the
Ottomans pulled out their artillery and withdrew. Piali's great fleet,
unable to confront the Spanish and Genoese galleys head on, allowed
Don Garcia's relief force of 11,000 men[1] to disembark unopposed. The
great siege was over.

Behind the two primary reasons for the Ottoman failure, the staunch
defense and successful relief, are a number of lesser ones. The Ottoman
failure to take the lightly defended citadel of Mdina, the old capital of
Malta, early in the siege had serious repercussions. Though the approaches
to Mdina were difficult, it was an old place defended by an inadequate
garrison. It is unlikely that it could have held out for long had the Ottomans attacked it in strength when fresh. As it was, their attempt came
almost as a last resort after most of their strength had been worn down in
the capture of St Elmo and in several assaults on Birgu and Senglea. In
the meantime, the modest force of Christian cavalry based at Mdina had
been effective in curtailing the activities of Turkish foraging parties. More
important still was the diversionary attack on the Ottoman camp just as
the attack on Senglea and Birgu which came nearest to success was
reaching its climax on 7 August. Without the diversion produced by this
highly destructive raid, the Muslim assault on Fort St Michael directed
by Mustafa Paşa in person might well have succeeded. The subsequent
repulse disheartened the Turks just when the edge had begun to wear off
their freshness. Subsequent assaults do not seem to have been delivered
with the same élan. It is worth noting that the Ottomans in 1570 systematically cleared Cyprus of all opposition, taking the strong inland fortress
of Nicosia in a full-scale siege at considerable cost, before attacking
Famagusta, their main objective.

The major question remaining concerns the timing of the Spanish
relief efforts. Contemporary partisans of the Knights of St John roundly
condemned Don Garcia of Toledo for his slowness in introducing relief
into Malta.[2] Modern analysts, with the notable and almost solitary exception of Fernand Braudel, have followed their lead. There may be some
validity to this charge. Only one thing can be said in defense of Don
Garcia's tactical judgment: it worked.

Closer analysis suggests that Don Garcia had good reason to be cautious. Because of the heavy losses suffered by Spanish naval forces in 1560

[1] Prescott, *History of the Reign of Philip the Second*, vol. III, p. 238.
[2] Echoed by Bradford, *The Great Siege*, p. 210, and particularly p. 107 where he states that Don
Garcia has been treated harshly by historians for his 'dilatory behavior . . . with good reason'.

and again in 1562, the level of experience and state of training of his galley crews cannot have been high. He was outnumbered nearly five to one by the Ottoman fleet at first – the final relief expedition contained only some 28 galleys – a situation which deteriorated further with the subsequent arrival of Muslim contingents from Alexandria, Tripoli and Algiers. The spectre of being surprised in the act of disembarking a relief force – the entrance to the Grand Harbor was too narrow and closely guarded to be forced even before Fort St Elmo fell into Muslim hands – must have hung heavily over his head. So must the thought of what had happened to Gian Andrea Doria off Djerba five years before at the head of a larger and better trained fleet.

Delay – unless the place actually fell – would only add to the suffering of the garrison. But the loss of the Spanish fleet would have insured their doom. It was all a matter of timing. The evidence is that Don Garcia's was intelligent and calculated to a nicety. He made an accurate estimate of the factors involved. He then backed up his estimate by reinforcing the garrison's staying power at the critical point, putting in a company of 200 Spanish arquebusiers for the garrison of Fort St Elmo – for he too understood the importance of the place – on 13 May, six days before the siege began. His first aid to the garrison after the siege had begun, the so-called 'little relief' of 29 June, got onto the island just in time to make good the loss incurred by the fall of Fort St Elmo. A night operation put in on the only practicable beach on the island out of reach of the Ottoman fleet, a small stretch of level shore on the north-west corner of the island, the relief of 29 June was of necessity a small one. It involved two Spanish galleys and two of the galleys of Malta, probably the best ships and crews available at the time, carrying about 700 infantry. Significantly, the galleys of the 'small' relief transported only about 175 infantrymen apiece, while the soldiers of the final relief were crammed in nearly 500 to a galley.

The final 'big' relief went in on 8 September when the Ottoman fighting strength had been ground down by La Valette's defenders to the point that Piali Paşa could no longer oppose Don Garcia by sea. Don Garcia had played his hand close to his chest – and won. He had, with the staunch defenders of Malta, triumphed over the forces of the Ottoman Empire commanded by Piali Paşa, Mustafa Paşa, and Turgut Re'is who, perhaps symbolically, died in the siege just before the fall of Fort St Elmo. He had also triumphed over the lingering after-effects of Djerba. In an operation where unnecessary risks were the surest road to ruin, he had taken none. For this, the Noble Order of the Knights of St John of Malta never forgave him. The verdict of history should be more generous.

From the technical point of view, the most notable features of the

Malta campaign involved the use of artillery. The initial Ottoman point of attack, Fort St Elmo, was determined by the control which the guns of St Elmo exercised over the entrances of the Grand Harbor of Malta and of Marsamuscetto inlet, the only nearby protected anchorage large enough to accommodate the Turkish fleet. This strategic position clearly established Fort St Elmo as the initial Ottoman objective and a vitally necessary one. The failure of the final attacks on Birgu and Senglea was a direct consequence of the inability of the Turkish gunners to open a breach sufficiently wide for the *'azabs* and Janissaries to mount an assault. All in all, Malta was a gunner's fight.

But of more consequence than such narrowly tactical considerations is the matter of quantity. Though tactically effective, the cannon used on Malta in 1565 were employed in small numbers. Except at Fort St Elmo – a highly significant exception – the Christians never seem to have used as many as half a dozen cannon at any one place and time. The Ottomans, able to pick the time and place of their attacks and having all the resources of a vast Empire behind them, never seem to have had more than about 70 large pieces in their siege batteries.

This shortage of good ordnance presents a striking contrast with the conditions which prevailed a century later and does much to explain the peculiar characteristics of the Mediterranean system of warfare at sea in the sixteenth century.

5

THE GALLEY

After having discussed the reasons for the galley's existence, its general characteristics, the strategic framework within which it operated, the composition of its crew and the nature of their armament, we come to the central question. What could a galley actually do? What were its tactical characteristics and capabilities? How fast and maneuverable was it and how much shock effect and fire power did it have? What degree of tactical control could the commander of a galley fleet exercise?

Here, as in so many areas before, we come up against our ingrained North Atlantic prejudices. In any treatment of sailing warships or their steam- or oil-driven descendants the term 'armament' would refer to the ship's guns, the gear and tackle immediately associated with them, and perhaps their stores of ammunition. But a war galley was 'armed' not just with guns, but with men and oars as well. Though a bit odd to the modern ear, the use of the word in this sense is self-explanatory. We are not apt to misunderstand its use in such phrases as 'armed with 144 oarsmen to row 3 by 3 from poop to prow'. Nevertheless the Mediterranean idea of armament deserves additional explanation.

The Mediterranean military man of the sixteenth century made no distinction between a warship's motive power and its combat power. To him the two were part of an inseparable whole. The speed under oars of a warship and its effective military power were so closely interrelated that neither could be viewed in isolation. Neither could the factors which contributed to them. He would not have attempted to isolate them for analysis and neither shall we.

In the preceding chapters we have repeatedly emphasized the over-riding importance of speed under oars. The time has now come to make an estimate of just what that speed was. This is not as easy as it might seem. Contemporary sources have little to say about speed as we usually think of it, and with good reason.

To a sixteenth-century galley captain the concept of speed as an instantaneous velocity was an almost valueless abstraction. He probably knew with great precision just how his galley compared with the other galleys in his squadron at a given time. Depending on the condition of his *ciurma,* whether or not the bottom was freshly scraped and greased, the state of the sea and weather and a thousand lesser factors, he knew what kind of a showing his ship was likely to make against the various foreign galleys he was apt to come up against. But his interest was mainly in differences in speed over the short haul, not in absolute values. He prospered or perished on the basis of his ability to make quick and accurate estimates of the speed differential between two oared fighting craft. The odds are that he was very good at it. But it is most unlikely that he knew within 10 per cent of the actual figure just what velocity his galley was capable of at flank speed.

His only interest in absolute speed was over the long haul. Even here he was not really interested in speed, but with elapsed time over distance, a rather different sort of thing. He could probably estimate with considerable accuracy how long it would take him to get from a given point to another if the weather and sea state held constant or if they changed as expected. But both this and his appreciation of relative speed differences were empirical estimates based on the rule of thumb. Neither really involved the concept of instantaneous velocity so dear to the hearts of modern navigators and physical scientists. In any case, he had no means of determining instantaneous velocity if he had wanted to. Even a precise average was beyond him for he had no means of accurately measuring short periods of time or long distances. This effectively precluded the use of any means of measuring speed directly, by the drag force on a trailing line for example, since this would have required an accurate means of calibration. Such means did not exist until the development of the chronometer in the eighteenth century.

The best modern estimate of the speed of galleys under oars is one derived by the application of hydrodynamic theory by Admiral W. L. Rodgers in 1937.[1] Rodgers began with U.S. Navy twelve-man racing cutters (similar to an ordinary lifeboat, but about 31 feet long) whose hydrodynamic drag as a function of speed had been found experimentally. Rowed by a championship crew, these craft could maintain an average speed of 7 knots (seven nautical miles per hour) over a three-mile course.

Power is the product of force times velocity. Rodgers was therefore able to combine the known speed of 7 knots with the experimentally found hydrodynamic drag force of 114 pounds to compute the total propulsive power required. This worked out to 2.94 horsepower. Since there were twelve oarsmen, this meant that each was producing about one-sixth effective horsepower. Note that this was *effective* horsepower, the amount of the oarsmen's effort which actually went toward overcoming the hydro-

[1] *Greek and Roman Naval Warfare* (Annapolis, 1937), pp. 29ff.

dynamic drag of the hull. The oarsmen's total power output was considerably more than the effective horsepower, the balance being absorbed by the inertia of the oars, the inertia of the oarsmen's bodies, slippage of the oars in the water, friction losses in the oarlocks and so on.

Rodgers then went on to estimate that the oarsmen of medieval galleys would have been capable of producing about one-eighth effective horsepower. Though Rodgers' expressed reasons for reducing the figure are questionable (he assumed that the modern oarsman was necessarily larger and better fed, forgetting that the medieval oarsman would have been much more thoroughly conditioned) he was probably roughly correct because of efficiency losses due to the longer oars on medieval craft.

Working from the set figure of one-eighth effective horsepower per oarsman and using established empirical hydrodynamic formulas for drag (see Appendix 4) he arrived at a maximum speed of just under 7 knots for a Venetian trireme *alla sensile* based on Fincati's reconstruction in the Museo Storico Navale, Venice.[1] Though possibly a half knot or so on the low side, this is a sound estimate, representing approximately the maximum dash speed of the typical sixteenth-century galley under oars.

But this was a dash speed and nothing more. Oarsmen tired rapidly at the accelerated stroke (about 26 per minute) needed to maintain it. From his knowledge of the performance deterioration of the crews of racing cutters, Rodgers estimated that this speed could be maintained for no more than 20 minutes.

If propulsion under oars were to be maintained for any extended period of time a reduced speed had to be accepted. This was an essential characteristic – perhaps *the* essential performance characteristic – of oar-driven fighting vessels. The longer and harder the *ciurma* was worked, the lower the reserves of energy dropped for use in an emergency. This was not only true over the short haul, it was cumulative in nature. Oarsmen who were worked to the limit for a matter of hours might require days to recover their full strength and stamina. As a matter of common sense no competent commander abused his *ciurma* without good reason. This consideration was particularly critical if the oarsmen were armed and formed an important part of the galley's fighting force as they did on Venetian galleys and many Ottoman ones. In this case the combat capability as well as the mobility of a galley declined sharply and steadily every minute that the oarsmen rowed hard. This does much to explain the complaints of the Venetian commanders several days before Lepanto that Don Juan had needlessly driven the fleet too long and hard under oars. The Spanish, with plenty of soldiers and largely servile *ciurmi*,

[1] W. L. Rodgers, *Naval Warfare Under Oars* (Annapolis, 1939), pp. 230–31.

would understandably have been less concerned about their oarsmen than the Venetians.[1]

As a galley's speed under oars was reduced, the oarsmen tired progressively less rapidly. In the absence of experimentally derived data on human power output over time it is impossible to be precise, so we will have to accept Rodgers' estimates. Based as they are on the actual performance of men propelling vessels, they are probably as good as anything which could be derived experimentally short of actually building a reconstruction of a galley. By applying his method to the same hypothetical Venetian trireme we arrive at a cruising speed of about 4 knots.[2] This agrees closely with one of the few indications of galley performance in absolute terms which we have from contemporary sources.

This is contained in a document which is of considerable interest in its own right since it contains a remarkably comprehensive exposition of galley tactics and provides a framework for our discussion. Dating by internal evidence from the late 1560s and attributed to Don Garcia de Toledo, it is entitled 'Discourse on what a galley needs to navigate well armed, both with *ciurma* and with other people'.[3]

Don Garcia began by recommending that 20 oarsmen be added to the standard *ciurma* of 164. The reasons which he gave for this recommended measure tell us a great deal. The prime reason for *not* doing it – cost – is ignored; but Don Garcia's evaluation was written at a dangerous time for Spain. The extra 20 oarsmen would ensure that none of the benches would ever have to be worked two by two, a succinct commentary on the expected state of health since 164 oarsmen were enough to work a 24-bank galley three by three throughout with twenty left over. The additional oarsmen would permit better sustained speed under poor conditions. They would also permit the commander of a squadron to arm several of his galleys to row four by four throughout by stripping the others of their surplus oarsmen if a higher dash speed were needed 'to effect something of importance'.

[1] Archivo di Stato Veneziano, *opusculo* 3000, p. 16. This is Sebastian Venier's *Relazione* as delivered to the Venetian Senate after the completion of his tour of duty on 29 December 1571.

[2] See Appendix 4. Rodgers works this out only for a classical Greek trireme of about 45 tons displacement, a considerably smaller boat. He estimated that such a vessel, mounting 15 banks on a side, would have had a maximum speed of 7.2 knots and a cruising speed of 4.8 knots.

[3] *Colección Navarrete*, vol. XII, dto. 83, fol. 309ff. This document uses 164 oarsmen to an ordinary galley as a standard figure. This figure was common to the period between 1560 and Lepanto. The document is almost certainly from the period following Don Garcia's retirement from active service in 1565 and was probably among the various suggestions and summaries of his experience which he sent to Don Juan of Austria upon the latter's assumption of the post of Captain General of the Sea in 1568.

Of more immediate concern to us is the advantage which the presence of the additional oarsmen would give in raiding hostile coasts in summer 'when the nights are short'.[1] To avoid detection by lookouts posted on high vantage points near the objective it was necessary to start the run-in from 'eight or nine leagues' offshore just after dusk. This permitted a surprise attack just before dawn. With the 20 extra men, said Don Garcia, the *ciurma* would be tired; but without them they would be completely shot and without reserves of strength for an emergency. We can assume, therefore, that the speed involved was very near the absolute maximum.

If we assume eight hours of darkness and 18 leagues to a degree of latitude (60 nautical miles)[2] this works out to a speed of $3\frac{1}{2}$ or $3\frac{3}{4}$ knots, depending upon whether a distance of 8 or 9 leagues is used. There are too many approximations involved in the calculation to expect any great degree of precision in the result, but they are all good ones and we are unlikely to be very far from the truth.

The difference between this speed and the cruising speed of about 4 knots for a Venetian trireme derived from Rodgers' figures can partly be explained in terms of regional design variation: Don Garcia explicitly stated that Spanish galleys were not as fast under oars as Muslim ones and we know from other sources that Venetian galleys were faster under oars than Ottoman galleys. But this opens the Pandora's box of regional variations in galley design which we shall leave closed for a few pages more.

Our general idea of a galley's performance characteristics under oars is summarized in Fig. 10. Under good conditions with a fresh and healthy *ciurma* and a clean bottom the very fastest of galleys could cover about $2\frac{1}{3}$ nautical miles in 20 minutes (about 4,700 yards at 235 yards per minute) but only by driving the oarsmen to the limit. This had a direct bearing upon galley tactics.

It is axiomatic that the tactical employment of a weapon system is ultimately determined by the relationship between its mobility characteristics, vulnerability, and firepower characteristics. In most cases battlefield speed, rate of fire and armament effectiveness as a function of range are the principal determinants of tactics. This was as true of sixteenth-century galley warfare as it is of twentieth-century tank warfare.

[1] This passage is on fol. 310 of the document cited above, p. 197 n. 3.

[2] The eight hours is reached by assuming that night lasts from twilight to first light. Eighteen leagues to a degree of latitude works out to three and a third nautical miles to a league. This compares closely with the value of 3.34 nautical miles to the Portuguese league given by J. Villasana Haggard, *Handbook for Translators of Spanish Historical Documents* (Austin, 1941), p. 78. This was probably the league used for navigating. In any case, the values given by Haggard for the Spanish league, from 3 to 3.19 nautical miles, are nearly the same.

A galley could cover 200 yards, ordinarily about the maximum effective range of sixteenth-century artillery at sea, in about a minute, considerably less time than was needed to load a cannon. In a head-on fight, galleys were therefore limited to a single shot from their bow artillery before it came to boarding unless both sides deliberately held off within range, an unlikely contingency except in a large formal fleet engagement where neither side wished to engage and neither side broke formation. It was usually impossible to reload the main battery after boarding contact was made since the cannon muzzles were at the most exposed part of the

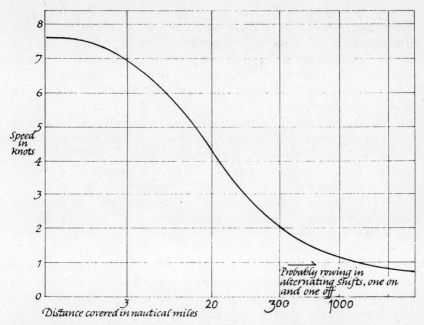

Fig. 10 Rowing speed of a galley as a function of the maximum distance which can be covered at that speed

forward deck. Consequently in a head-on clash galley captains held their fire, trying to discharge all their forward firing ordnance simultaneously at the shortest possible range. Firing first was unlikely to yield any tactical advantage since the chances of dismounting the opposing galley's artillery were almost nil and fewer men would be killed at longer range. Since their main battery cannon were only going to get off one shot each, it behoved them to make sure that that one shot counted to the maximum possible extent. Since the probable effects of the fire increased geometrically as the range shortened (inaccuracy was the main problem), there was a powerful incentive to fire at the actual moment of impact when bow touched bow. There is evidence that the Ottomans loaded their main centerline bow guns with scatter shot for galley versus galley encounters, a clear indication of the tactical mentality of galley warfare.[1]

This presents a parallel with the linear infantry tactics of eighteenth-century Europe which is so marked as to bear extended comment. There, a very similar relationship between battlefield mobility, rate of fire and maximum effective range produced strikingly similar tactics. A man at the double could cover the maximum effective range of an eighteenth-century infantry musket, under 100 yards, in less time than it took to reload. The essential inaccuracy of eighteenth-century musketry, like that of sixteenth-century naval gunnery, combined with its potentially devastating impact to make fire exponentially more effective as the range was shortened. Well trained infantry regiments held their fire until the last instant and the shortest possible range, generally within fifty yards. The byword, 'Hold your fire until you see the whites of their eyes', was no mere figure of speech. The tactical ideal was to fire after the enemy had fired and only when so close that every shot would tell, then go in with the bayonet before the enemy – disordered, decimated and blinded by the smoke – could close ranks and reload. There was considerable disadvantage in firing first unless the volley could be followed up immediately – a matter of a very few seconds – by a bayonet charge. This corresponds, of course, to the boarding rush in a galley fight. Once the enemy had expended his volley there was nothing to prevent closing in to an arm's length before firing.

It was perhaps more difficult to bring off a successful retrograde movement under fire with a disordered squadron of galleys than with a broken infantry regiment, but otherwise the similarity in tactics is marked. It is hardly remarkable when viewed from this perspective that the basic tactical formation – a thin, straight line abreast – was the same. This was a natural consequence of the three-way relationship between speed, rate of fire and armament effectiveness as a function of range mentioned above. In both cases the combination of inaccuracy, a slow rate of fire and the devastating close-range effect of the weapons involved conspired to make formal engagements a one-shot, eyeball-to-eyeball affair.

The results in galley warfare were often as devastating as we would expect. In 1528 Antonio Doria killed more than 40 men aboard Don Hugo de Moncada's galley with a single volley from the basilisk, two

---

[1] Katib Celebi, *Tuhfet-ul Kibar il Esfar-ul-Bihar* (Istanbul, 1329 A.H.), pp. 150–1. I am indebted to Professor Andrew C. Hess of Temple University for this citation.

half cannons, two *sacres* and two *falconetes* which his galley mounted forward.[1]

Tactically the line abreast formation placed a further restriction on speed. Each galley had to make its movements conform not only to those of the flagship, but also to those of the galleys between it and the flagship. Since galleys far out on the wings could not see the flagship clearly and since each galley had to maintain its position relative to its immediate neighbors no matter what, errors in position keeping were cumulative. If the galley next to the flagship lagged a bit and then surged ahead, the error was transmitted and magnified all the way down the line. Consequently the galleys on the extreme ends of a sixty-ship line abreast (the flagship was normally in the middle) must have used a geat deal of their power simply jockeying around to stay in position. A turn would have magnified their problems enormously – the usual results of the child's game of crack-the-whip come immediately to mind. The skill and effort involved in pivoting a line of fifty galleys to face the enemy on a new heading twenty or thirty degrees from the old one – the maneuver actually accomplished by the Christian Left under Agostin Barbarigo at Lepanto – must have been considerable.

In addition to this 'crack-the-whip' effect, there was another basic difficulty in maintaining a proper line abreast formation. This was the 'accordion' effect, caused by cumulative errors in precisely maintaining the desired lateral separation between galleys. If, for example, the second galley out from the center of a long line abreast moved in a bit too close to the flagship, the galleys beyond it would be forced to close in, too, in order to maintain the desired separation. This tendency would become exaggerated as it progressed out toward the end of the line. Then, as the original offender moved back into correct position, the whole cycle would start over again with the first, 'unnecessary' correction leading to over-corrections and causing gaps to suddenly open up between galleys on the flanks. An alert enemy could exploit these gaps to penetrate the line and outflank individual galleys. Considerable skill and constant vigilance on the part of the helmsmen must have been needed to keep this tendency from getting completely out of hand, a problem which seems to have affected both Christian wings at Lepanto.

As a guess, one would suppose that if the flagship of a formation of sixty galleys maintained a steady 2 knots straight ahead, the ships on the

---

[1] This story is in a letter from Paulo Giovio to Pope Clement VI in *I Diarii Marino Sanuto* (Venice, 1897), vol. XLVI, fol. 666–7. The basilisk was probably an orthodox 40 or 50 pounder, perhaps of wrought iron; the half cannons were probably large swivel guns of the *verso* type; the *sacres* orthodox 8 or 10 pounders; and the *falconetes* swivel pieces.

extreme flanks would have had to vary their speed between a near stand-still and 5 or 6 knots in order to hold position. Much of this speed variation would have been due to lateral jockeying. There was no relief from these difficulties. The galley's terrible vulnerability to attack from the side made the maintenance of a line abreast formation a matter of life or death, particularly for western galleys facing faster and more agile Muslim craft. The overriding need to maintain formation placed, in turn, a rigid and almost inflexible upper limit on the size of galley squadrons. The center squadron in the usual sixteenth-century order of battle of three squadrons on line was required to maneuver least since both of its flanks were protected. It was consequently the largest, containing a maximum of 65 galleys.

The two flanking squadrons were required to maneuver more and therefore had to be smaller – an inflexible limit of 53 or 54 galleys seems to have been the rule. The Muslims seem occasionally to have used a somewhat looser crescent formation which permitted their squadrons to be larger, a natural consequence of their greater agility which gave them the advantage in a mêlée situation; but when a rigid line abreast was used these limitations applied with equal force to the galley fleets of all nations.

This remarkable formation-keeping ability – both sides put some 170 galleys on line at Lepanto – was partly a consequence of Mediterranean methods of command and control. At the beginning of the sixteenth century Mediterranean naval commanders could exercise a considerable degree of control over galley fleets through a comprehensive set of standing operating instructions supplemented by a system of sail, flag, cannon, trumpet and lantern signals.[1] These signals served primarily to transmit information and to supplement the remarkably effective basic formation discipline which centered around a tightly enforced conformity to the flagship's movements. They were inadequate to order elaborate tactical evolutions on the spur of the moment; but these would have been rendered impossible in any event by the galley's severely limited endurance at flank speed. Sophisticated tactical variations – of which we shall see several superb examples at Lepanto – had to be arranged well in advance.

[1] See the *Colección Sanz de Barutell* (*Simancas*), *Artículo* 3, vcl. 1, dto. 2, fol. 25–35, a set of sailing instructions for the galleys of Castile *ca.* 1430, and *Colección Navarrete*, vol. XII, dto. 80, fol. 229ff., a set of similar instructions issued by Don Garcia de Toledo *ca.* 1564. There are remarkably few differences between the two. Basically these sailing instructions cover two main areas: enforcement of formation discipline (heavy penalties were laid down for fouling another galley's oars, taking the lead from the flagship, lighting more than the proper number of stern lanterns at night, etc.) and transmittal of information (on sighting unknown sails in daylight the main sail was dipped once for each sail sighted, two lanterns were displayed by the galley which was first in locating a channel at night, etc.). Discipline aboard ship, treatment of *ciurmi*, maintenance of royal funds, etc. are also covered.

This should not blind us to the fact that the Mediterranean nations were well in advance of those of the North Atlantic in the area of command and control of fleets under way in the sixteenth century. Though the Dutch and the English were eventually to evolve an effective and comprehensive system of flag signals capable of controlling the movements of fleets of sailing warships in battle, this was not until the seventeenth century. There is no evidence of the existence of any English equivalent to the sailing orders discussed above until after the reign of Elizabeth.[1] Only the Portuguese seem to have made any real progress in this area during the sixteenth century.

Our estimated speed of about 2 knots straight ahead for a sizeable fleet fully deployed in line abreast probably represents an upper limit. The appearance of speed given by the war galley's low, lean, functional look is thus entirely misleading. A major engagement between galley fleets fully deployed must have been excruciatingly slow to develop. The only display of real speed would have been in the last few yards before closing when contact was inevitable. Each galley would have surged ahead attempting to exploit gaps in the enemy line to get a favorable attack angle on the enemy craft opposite it, much in the manner of American football linesmen breaking from their three-point stance at the snap of the ball to try to get the best blocking angle on the on-rushing defensive players.

This brings us back to our starting point: the galley maximum dash speed of about 7 knots. Here a brief résumé is in order. By driving the *ciurma* very close to the limit, a cruising speed of some 3 to 4 knots could be maintained for about eight hours. By splitting the *ciurma* into two watches which rowed and rested alternately, a speed of perhaps half that much could be maintained[2] (see Fig. 10). All these figures are theoretical values which were rarely attained in practice. The unplated wooden bottoms of galleys fouled rapidly and *ciurmi* were frequently under strength, both in numbers and vigor. On top of this, fleets were chained to the speed of the slowest vessel in them.

About all we can expect from our brief investigation of the absolute speed characteristics of galleys under oars is the acquisition of an added dimension in our ability to visualize a galley fight. The speeds which we have settled on are anything but precise, nor would they be very meaningful if they were. But they give us a useful peg on which to hang our knowledge of tactics. Having established an absolute reference point –

---

[1] A. H. Taylor, 'Carrack into Galleon', *The Mariner's Mirror*, xxxvi, No. 2 (April 1950), 149.
[2] This speed of about 2 knots is more or less confirmed by the performance in 1546 of a Venetian galley of exceptional size, 29 banks rowed 4 by 4, cited by Alberto Tenenti, *Cristoforo da Canal* (Paris, 1962), p. 46. This galley could, under ideal conditions, make 50 miles in 'a day' (presumably of about 12 hours) under oars alone.

even an approximate one – we can turn to relative performance differences with more assurance. Since these were the main concern of the sixteenth-century Mediterranean naval commander it is appropriate that we devote the balance of our attention to them.

Here contemporary evidence, if not over-abundant, is explicit and reliable. We know that from the earliest times the galleys of the western family – French, Spanish, Papal, Genoese and, later, Maltese galleys – had been considered slower under oars than either Venetian or Muslim galleys.[1] The Venetian naval commander Cristoforo da Canal, writing around the middle of the sixteenth century, clarified and amplified this: although highly critical of their characteristics in other areas, he had nothing but praise for the turn of speed of Venetian galleys under oars. We have it on his authority that the galleys of Venice were faster under oars than those of either the Ottoman Empire or Spain (which we can take to include Malta, the Papal States and Genoa).[2]

The picture is rounded out by a passage from Don Garcia de Toledo's 'Discourse', from which we have already drawn in our analysis of the galley's absolute speed capabilities. One of his reasons for reinforcing the normal *ciurma* of 164 which ordinary Spanish galleys carried in the 1560s with an additional 20 oarsmen was that:

Although it will not be enough with the advantage of the above-mentioned 20 men to overhaul under oars any Turkish galley, at least of the good ones (since they go [armed in such a way so] that there will be few *capitanas* [flagships] which could pull even with them no matter how heavily reinforced [their *ciurmi* are] in quantity and quality), at least it will give you a chance [to catch them] if you can begin even with them and [thus the ability to] exploit the many opportunities which will arise.[3]

The wording is difficult; but the meaning is clear. Under oars alone any Muslim galley in halfway decent shape (Don Garcia's 'Turks' were mostly North Africans), let alone a galiot or a *fusta*, could outrun a Spanish galley hands down. A clean Spanish galley with a healthy, heavily rein-

---

1 This is from D'Albertis, *Le Construzione Navali . . . al tempo di Colombo* (1693), cited by R. C. Anderson, *Oared Fighting Ships* (London, 1962), pp. 25–6.

2 Tenenti, *Cristoforo da Canal*, pp. 33–4.

3 The passage, *Colección Navarrete*, vol. XII, dto. 83, fol. 310, is as follows in full: 'La tercera es, que aunque no hayan de ser bastantes con la ventaja de los 20 hombres arriba dichos para alcanzer al remo ningun Navio de Turcos, a lomenos delos buenos (pues segun ellos caminan no harán poco los Capitanas que los alcanzares por mas reforzados que bayan en quantidad y qualidad) a lomenos lo seran para que el que las lleva a cargo pueda amanecer sobre ellos y gozar de muchas occasiones que suelen ofrecerse.' Don Garcia's Spanish is always unconventional and frequently obscure, but this passage is particularly difficult. I am indebted to Mrs Lilian Polyzoides of the Firestone Library Staff, Princeton University, a good Catalan, for having rendered invaluable service in helping me to puzzle through the intracacies of Don Garcia's wording.

forced *ciurma* and surprise on its side stood only a reasonably good chance of bringing a Muslim galley to battle before it could get away. If the chase were even a moderately long one, the Muslim galley was expected to be able to pull clear, a circumstance which tells us that the Spanish paid a heavy price in efficiency for the competitive dash speed which they got by reinforcing their *ciurma*. Additional oarsmen increased propulsive power, but not quite as much as they lessened efficiency. Rowing efficiency decreased as more men were put on each oar and every additional oarsman – or soldier – taken on board made the ship ride a bit deeper in the water, increasing hydrodynamic drag. While they might have been capable of producing the same top speed, the oarsmen on a heavily laden and heavily reinforced galley tired more quickly than those on a lighter one. Spanish galleys, as we shall see, carried on the whole a greater weight of artillery and more fighting manpower than any others. They paid a heavy penalty for this in speed under oars.

The relative speed difference between Venetian and North African galleys is unclear. There is a possibility that the latter were as fast under oars as the former. But in view of the North African preference for large, fast galiots (presumably because their greater speed under oars and their lighter demands on a limited manpower supply made them a more attractive choice for offensive raiding operations) this is an academic question. The Algerian contingent at Malta in 1565 had only seven galleys out of a total force of 34, the rest being galiots, a ratio which seems to have been abnormally heavy on galleys.[1]

In sum, Venetian galleys were faster under oars than Ottoman ones. Muslim galleys of all varieties were faster than those of Spain. By extension they were faster than the other western galleys as well since differences in design and manning within the western family were minimal. The differences in speed which we have noted were tactically significant and remained consistent throughout our period of concern. They were not the product of some fortuitously clever design or some accidental superiority in hull lines (though the Venetians, working a bit harder at it, seem to have had a slight advantage); rather they were the inevitable consequence of basic differences in tactical requirements and design philosophy. In saying this we have already – and inevitably – crossed the artificial boundary between performance and combat capabilities. A gain in either one of these areas generally entailed a sacrifice in the other.

The next critical area of performance was speed and efficiency as a sailing vessel. The brief space which we shall give to analysis of this factor does not lessen its importance. Efficiency as a sailing vessel was the prime

[1] *Colección Navarrete*, vol. IV, dto. 19, fol. 224.

determinant of a galley's strategic radius of action. Oared fighting ships were not outstanding performers under sails. Their unavoidably narrow beam and shallow draft left them without the stiffness needed to carry a heavy press of canvas. Their lack of effective keel area made them leewardly and inefficient on a beam reach or when beating to windward, the only points of sailing where their large lateen sails were particularly effective. Something of the order of 12 knots with a stiff following breeze and a fairly calm sea probably represented about the most that a galley could do.[1] Because of their long narrow hulls, lack of lateral stiffness and low freeboard, galleys were unsafe in high winds and heavy seas. About all that could be done under these conditions was to put up a storm sail (on the foremast if there were one) and run for it before the wind, jettisoning the heavy forward ordnance to keep the low bows from driving under.[2]

The Venetian galleys, optimized for speed under oars, were notoriously poor sailors. We have this on the authority of Cristoforo da Canal. In straight contests of a more or less friendly nature he found his galleys badly outclassed by both Ottoman and Spanish ones.[3] This difference has been noted by other authorities too.[4] The difference in sailing capability between Ottoman and western galleys seems to have been relatively slight with the palm going to the Muslim craft.[5] Since the Muslim galleys were generally lighter and with lower freeboard one suspects that their advantage would have been greatest in calm seas and relatively light airs. Smaller oared vessels such as the North African galiots would have suffered under any other conditions from a sheer lack of size in addition to the usual faults of specialized rowing craft. Not only would they have been more vulnerable to heavy seas, their necessarily shorter masts would have left their sails partly blanked out by the waves in even a moderate swell.

No nation's galleys held a superiority in both performance under oars and performance under sails, clear if indirect evidence that design compromise within narrow limits was involved. The order of superiority in

---

[1] This estimate, cited by Rodgers, *Naval Warfare Under Oars*, p. 232, comes from Alberto Guglielmotti, *Storia della Marina Pontifica* (Rome, 1604).

[2] This seems to have been a standard expedient. See, for example, an account of four of the galleys of Malta caught by a sudden storm off La Goleta in 1624 in the *Colección Navarrete*, vol. VI, dto. 25, fol. 126. Only two of the four survived and then only by jettisoning all of their ordnance.

[3] Cristoforo da Canal, in Tenenti, *Cristoforo da Canal*, p. 43, cites as exceptional the transit of Jafer Re'is' squadron from Algiers to Corfu in 22 days in 1557. Note that this averages out to only slightly under 2 knots. See also pp. 31–2 and the references to Jafer Re'is' scorn of the Venetian galleys' sailing ability on p. 33.

[4] See above, p. 204, n. 1.

[5] Tenenti, *Cristoforo da Canal*, p. 43, cites various specific instances of the superior sailing capabilities of western and Ottoman galleys given by da Canal. On balance, the Muslim craft seem to have been faster.

rowing speed – Venice, the Ottomans, Spain – was reshuffled in sailing efficiency with Venice dropping from first to last place. The reasons for this phenomenon become apparent as we examine the next area of galley design, effectiveness as a fighting platform. This area was peculiarly important since it gave the others their relevance. The purpose of the galley, after all, was to fight.

At this point the issue becomes more complex. Effectiveness as a fighting platform cannot be treated intelligently without simultaneously dealing with tactics and certain aspects of galley design. The reason for this is straightforward: the way in which a galley was built revealed the tactical concerns of its designers.

The overriding importance of speed under oars and the great cost and bulk of good heavy artillery left the designer little room for variation in mounting the galley's main battery. There were only so many ways in which a 5,000 pound cannon fifteen feet long could be mounted on a twenty-foot wide hull crammed with soldiers and oarsmen. The details of main centerline bow gun mounts were therefore roughly similar for all Mediterranean galleys. At first rigidly mounted on heavy timber balks, the main centerline cannon came to be mounted on a recoiling carriage by about the second decade of the sixteenth century.

The main centerline bow gun was set on its trunnions in a solidly constructed wooden box, similar in appearance to a standard eighteenth-century naval carriage but with a flat bottom and without wheels. This box was allowed to slide back and forth in a wooden track running along the centerline of the hull. Space was so restricted that on recoil it ran back inside the *corsia*, the raised gangway running between the rowing benches. This ingenious method of mounting the centerline bow gun is shown on the only surviving contemporary model of a sixteenth-century galley, a model of a Venetian galley in the Museo Storico Navale, Venice. A contemporary Spanish model of a small galley or galiot of the seventeenth century in the Museo Naval, Madrid, shows the centerline cannon mounted in this way and we know that Franch galleys early in the eighteenth century still used the same arrangement.[1] Though the arrangements on Muslim galleys are not clear, it seems likely that this method of mounting was shared by all Mediterranean galleys.

During the early 1500s the rest of the forward-firing artillery seems to have been mounted on rigid vertical posts, apparently with provisions for varying at least the elevation (see Appendix 6). Later the two largest side pieces were apparently given sliding mounts similar to the main centerline guns.

[1] Jean Marteilhe, *Galley Slave* (London, 1957).

The main area of regional variation in sixteenth-century galley design involved the provision of specialized fighting superstructures. The design and location of these superstructures on the galleys of the various Mediterranean nations tell us a great deal about their respective design philosophies and tactical concepts.

The most overt structural difference between Mediterranean galleys involved the provision of a large, permanent, fighting platform above the bow artillery. The western galleys, those of France, Spain and her allies and the Papacy, had such a platform. Muslim galleys and those of Venice did not. Our earliest truly positive evidence of this structure, called the *arrumbada* in Spanish, is from the Flemish tapestries depicting Charles V's conquest of Tunis in 1535 in the *Armeria Real*, Madrid.[1] It seems plain, however, that the *arrumbada* was by that time an established design feature.

Occupying the space just forward of the two foremost rowing benches and just behind the most sharply tapered forward portion of the bow, the *arrumbada* ran the full width of the hull and was no more than ten feet long.[2] It stood approximately a man's height above the forward deck and was partially supported on its flanks by sloping sides which extended down to the *apostis*. This raised fighting platform and its supports were thus trapezoidal in shape when viewed from the front.

The primary function of the *arrumbada* was to serve as a boarding platform, its height conferring a crucial advantage in the assault. On Spanish and Maltese galleys, the massed fire of the musketeers stationed there was habitually used to supplement the final volley of the bow artillery just before contact. The *arrumbada*, protected on the front and sides by a temporary barricade of light planking erected before combat, also provided a useful redoubt and gave the arquebusiers and musketeers posted there superior defensive fields of fire.

The space beneath the *arrumbada* must have provided cramped and poorly ventilated quarters for the artillerists; but this was apparently acceptable since the main battery was normally fired only once in a serious boarding fight. If the initial attack were successful, friendly boarders would immediately mask the main battery's fire. If it were not, the enemy would be dominating – if not actually occupying – the area forward of the guns that the gunners needed to work in to reload. In a running fight the

---

[1] The best reproductions of these magnificent tapestries are in Tennyson's *Elizabethan England* (London, 1940). Because of the poor lighting in the Armeria Real, these are in many ways a more useful source than the tapestries themselves.

[2] This figure is based on the Charles V tapestries, cited above, and on the dimensions of the fighting platform given by Jean Marteilhe, *Galley Slave*. The ten foot value given by the latter is probably high for a sixteenth-century galley.

problem was not so critical since the gunners could work openly out on the deck forward of the guns.

From such contemporary pictorial evidence as we have, it seems clear that none of the eastern galleys had a permanent structure corresponding to the *arrumbada* during the sixteenth century. It is doubtful that Muslim galleys ever acquired one. The evidence supporting these conclusions is given in Appendix 6.

Despite general agreement that a raised fighting platform was absent, the actual structural details of the bows of Islamic galleys are in doubt. There is some evidence that the bow guns of Ottoman galleys were covered by a short half-deck of sorts.[1] This would have been a very low structure, more like a raised hatch cover than a deck, probably at about the level of the *corsia* and extending forward no more than five or six feet. There would have been just enough clearance between it and the tops of the cannon to permit the gunners to sight and fire them. The bow guns would have been loaded from the open bow in front of the 'half-deck' and fired from behind it.

The absence of a raised fighting structure forward suggests that Islamic galleys were not designed primarily for a tactically offensive role in formal, head-on fleet engagements. This impression is reinforced by the fact that the principal fighting superstructure on Ottoman galleys was at the stern, a profoundly defensive arrangement. This redoubt was based on the awning which, on Ottoman galleys, was constructed of leather nailed to a solid wooden frame instead of cloth as was usual on Christian galleys. The leather awning provided overhead protection and reduced the danger of fire while the similarly reinforced sides of the stern structure below it gave cover to the archers and musketeers.[2]

One final structural detail of Ottoman galleys deserves comment. Although the bows of Ottoman galleys were lower than those of Christian galleys, the beak or 'spur' of Ottoman galleys was particularly stout. Iron-shod to assist it in penetrating light upper planking, it was angled upward to allow it to ride over and break down the *apostis* of an enemy galley (Spanish galleys had a similar spur with a strengthened tip; but since they rode higher in the water the upward tilt was not so pronounced). This feature was much admired by Cristoforo da Canal who urged its adoption on Venetian galleys, ultimately with success.[3] This upward angled spur must also have made the Ottoman galleys somewhat safer when hard driven under sails, an important strategic consideration. The Venetians,

---

[1] See Olesa Muñido, *La Organización Naval*, vol. I (Madrid, 1968), p. 226.
[2] *Ibid.* vol. I, pp. 226, 227.
[3] Tenenti, *Cristoforo da Canal*, p. 32.

on the other hand, used a completely horizontal spur until after the middle of the sixteenth century, probably because it interfered less with the field of fire of the centerline bow gun.

The design of Venetian fighting superstructures was completely separate and distinct from either western or Ottoman practice. Before 1500, Venetian galleys seem not to have had a raised bow superstructure. Then at some point early in the sixteenth century, probably before 1530 and more or less concurrent with the adoption of effective bow artillery, Venetian galleys acquired a temporary fighting platform at the bow.[1] This structure eventually, though well after the period of our concern, evolved into a permanent structure more or less along western lines. The temporary structure which preceded it was unique to Venetian galleys. This was based on four heavy support beams running fore and aft which were set on vertical posts at about shoulder height above the front end of the *apostis* and on either side of the main centerline bow gun. The rear of these beams was slightly higher than the front, giving the platform a slight forward tilt. Planks could be laid across these beams (that is at right angles to the long axis of the ship) forming a raised platform about ten feet long above all of the bow guns except for the main centerline piece.

This arrangement offered the advantage of being dismountable at will. When taken down it did not, unlike the permanent structures on western galleys and the low half-deck on Ottoman ones, hamper the gunners in loading and laying their pieces. Even when the platform was erected, the opening above the main centerline gun gave the gunners good ventilation and a clear working space. This emphasis on the efficient use of artillery was characteristically Venetian, characteristic because the Venetians, always short of manpower, had to place particularly heavy reliance on gunnery. They were quite prepared for the boarding fight, as the presence of the raised fighting platform showed; but artillery was their favored instrument.

This emphasis is further underscored by the high quality of Venetian ordnance. Without exception, surviving examples of sixteenth-century Venetian cannon show no evidence of inexpert workmanship or inferior metal.[2] They are invariably cleanly functional in design and entirely

[1] There is evidence that it may have appeared somewhat later. Admiral Fincati's reconstruction of a Venetian trireme of the 1530s in the Museo Storico Navale, Venice, shows only about half of the essential supporting structure of the platform described below. If accurate, this reconstruction represents an intermediate step in the evolution of the Venetian fighting platform. The uniqueness of the Venetian bow superstructure is attested to by Tenenti, *Cristoforo da Canal*, p. 38, particularly nn. 56 and 57.
[2] This statement is based on examination of the collection of Venetian ordnance belonging to the Askeri Musesi, presently on display in the courtyard of St Irene's Church, Istanbul, and

devoid of the elaborate raised ornamentation characteristic of many of the best German, Spanish and Portuguese guns. Most important, Venetian guns were, as we noted in chapter 4, considerably lighter and shorter than equivalent Spanish guns in particular. For a given amount of firepower, Venetian galleys were therefore lighter and easier to row.

The shorter and lighter Venetian guns must also have been easier to handle in combat and it is worth noting that Venetian methods of gunnery seem to have been ahead of practice elsewhere. There is evidence that Venetian galley captains preferred combat under conditions approaching a flat calm so that their gunners could shoot more accurately.[1] If true, this constitutes strong evidence that Venetian naval gunners were shooting at 500 yards and over with serious expectation of hitting their mark, a remarkable performance by sixteenth- or eighteenth-century standards. Long-range accuracy, even if possible, made little sense in galley warfare unless the guns could be reloaded in time for a final discharge at the moment of contact just prior to boarding. Since two small squadrons of galleys would have had a head-on closure rate of at least 8 knots (270 yards per minute) and since about two minutes were needed to reload, a distance of more than 500 yards is indicated. For a good gun and a good gunner who was familiar with his piece shooting in a flat calm, this range is well within reason.

Direct comparison between Venetian and Ottoman naval artillery is difficult to make. There are indications that the Ottomans used *pedreros* extensively as main bow guns as late as the 1540s.[2] The Christian spoils of Lepanto, however, included only 17 *pedreros*, clearly smaller than the main centerline bow guns which were separately enumerated, out of a total of 390 captured guns included in the formal division of spoils.[3] This suggests an apparent conformity with contemporary western practice where the main centerline cannon was often flanked by two smaller *pedreros*.[4] If we apportion the captured Turkish guns out among the 117 captured galleys and 10 galiots we arrive at a level of armament very near established western standards.

that in the Museo Storico Navale, Venice. The latter collection includes many ordinary operational cannon used in the defense of Famagusta in 1570–1, captured by the Turks and later repatriated. The former collection is a general grab bag of captured Venetian cannon, including many captured at the fall of Candia in 1659.

[1] See Alberto Tenenti, *Piracy and the Decline of Venice* (Berkeley, 1967), p. 79.
[2] *Colección Sanz de Barutell (Simancas), Artículo 6, dto. 20.*
[3] *Colección Sanz de Barutell (Simancas), Artículo 5*, vol. 2, dto. 317, fol. 406–7.
[4] For example, the standard of armament for Florentine galleys *ca.* 1574, cited by P. A. Gugliel-motti, *Storia della Marina Pontifica*, vol. IV (Florence, 1871), p. 166, given in Anderson, *Oared Fighting Ships*, pp. 69–70. This same arrangement is given by Anderson for Papal galleys as late as 1664.

Since western galleys were often less heavily armed than the 'standard' would lead us to expect – we shall give an example of this in the final section dealing with the battle of Lepanto – there may have been an even more marked similarity in armament than this would suggest. On balance, Spanish galleys were probably more heavily armed with artillery than Ottoman ones. It is generally conceded, however, that Islamic galleys were lighter and more agile under oars than Spanish galleys, in addition to being faster. They would therefore presumably have been more adept at bringing their guns to bear.

It is partly a matter of educated speculation; but the palm for efficiency as an artillery platform surely went to the Venetian galleys. Though probably not as maneuverable as Muslim galleys, they were faster flat out and seem to have been more heavily armed. They had better arrangements for serving the guns than galleys of the western family and packed as much fire power as the best of them. In addition, the lighter and less bulky Venetian cannon were more efficient than those of their rivals.

The characteristics of Venetian ordnance and galleys were determined by the chronic Venetian shortage of manpower. Perpetually short of trained fighting men, the Venetians had to depend heavily upon their free oarsmen to augment their fighting strength. This had certain advantages. Since they carried less men, Venetian galleys were lighter and therefore faster than they would have been otherwise. The relative lightness of Venetian ordnance also made a significant contribution to performance.

The Venetians were not unskilled in the boarding fight nor were they necessarily reluctant to enter into it; but the decision to board was a peculiarly irrevocable one for a Venetian galley captain. The Venetians would board willingly, but only with the prospect of a short, decisive fight and with every advantage that their superior speed and ordnance could give them. This gave Venetian galley tactics an explosive, all or nothing, quality. We shall see this emerge strikingly in the conduct of the predominantly Venetian left wing at Lepanto.

These tactical characteristics dovetailed neatly with Venetian strategic requirements. The usual tactical problem for a Venetian fleet or squadron was the relief of a fortress under Ottoman attack or a sudden descent on some isolated Ottoman fortified place. In neither case was a head-on clash with the Ottoman fleet desirable. The aim was to make a quick dash for the objective, blasting a way into the place if necessary, but not to get closely engaged unless it was absolutely unavoidable.

An excellent example of the sort of operation for which Venetian galleys were tailored was the relief of Famagusta by Mark Antonio Quirini in the winter of 1570-1.[1] This operation is a useful starting point for our discussion of tactics proper. The Ottomans had commenced hostilities by invading Cyprus in the spring of 1570. The Venetians, stretched thin everywhere, had pulled their available forces into Nicosia, the capital of the island, and the key port of Famagusta. Perhaps remembering the successful Spanish attack on their rear at Malta five years before just as the final assault was going in, the Ottoman commanders resolved to clear the interior of the island of all resistance before tackling the powerful fortifications of Famagusta. Nicosia was therefore attacked first, falling to a massive assault in August. Though it was too late in the season to begin a major siege, the Ottomans established lines of circumvallation around Famagusta on land and held their fleet ready to counter a possible relief. When the combined Christian fleet broke up for the winter in November without having accomplished anything, the Ottomans left a small blockading force behind covered by seven or eight galleys under the Bey of Rhodes and sent the bulk of their fleet home to prepare for an all-out effort the next spring. Quirini, *Capitano in Golfo* the preceding year, was left at Candia in Crete with a small force with the responsibility of relieving Famagusta.

Assembling a force of four large sailing ships loaded with 1,600 fighting men plus stores and munitions for the garrison and an escort force of 13 galleys, he sortied from Candia on 16 January. Because of their different sailing characteristics the sailing vessels and the galleys proceeded independently, effecting an apparently preplanned rendezvous off Famagusta on the 23rd – an impressive feat of seamanship in itself. At this point Quirini displayed exquisite tactical judgment. The full details of the engagement that followed are not known, but this much is clear: Quirini sent the four sailing ships in toward the harbor first, following at a distance with his galleys. This presented the seven galleys of the Ottoman blockading force with Hobson's choice. They could let the supply ships through uncontested – an obviously unacceptable course of action – or they could expose themselves to a flank attack by Quirini's galleys in attempting to stop them.

If they were to remain faithful to their mission there was only one alternative left open. Their casualties make it plain that they took it. They had to repel Quirini's relief by prompt and direct action or perish in the attempt. Three of their number were sunk outright, almost certainly by the bow guns of Quirini's galleys, and the rest forced up against the beach

[1] I have taken this account of Quirini's relief from Sir George Hill, *A History of Cyprus*, vol. III, *The Frankish Period, 1432–1571* (Cambridge, 1948), pp. 943-7.

under cover of the Ottoman land forces.[1] This gave Quirini a free hand. He had accomplished his primary mission and had an overwhelmingly superior force for the moment. He was able to capture a sizeable prize, a *maona* loaded with munitions and a crew of 300, and destroy the remaining four Turkish galleys on the beach while his supply ships unloaded. This accomplished, the combined force left Famagusta on 16 February and was back in Candia by the 21st. At no time during the operation do the Venetian galleys seem to have come to a formal boarding fight with their Ottoman opponents. Their artillery and mobility had done the whole job. The Bey of Rhodes exaggerated the size of Quirini's force in his report to Constantinople – he said it comprised 22 galleys – and sought to explain away his defeat on the grounds that he 'had no reserves of rowers and was short of bread'.[2]

The Spanish tactical problem was quite different. Spanish galleys and tactics evolved around a protracted war of coastal raiding. The need to transport troops rapidly and deposit them in out of the way places predominated. To relieve a village hit by Muslim raiders, infantry was needed, not artillery. The same consideration applied to a raid on a Muslim base. Though shipborne artillery could provide invaluable support, it was of little use in itself without infantry to do the necessary dirty work.

Both, however, were needed. This had the effect of loading Spanish galleys down with guns and troops and reducing their speed under oars. But speed under oars was rarely a crucial requirement. With a fighting platform packed with hardened infantry of the *tercios* and a good battery beneath their feet, a Spanish galley rarely had to run from anything. All it needed was enough mobility to turn bows on to its opponent. For the purpose of getting to some threatened point on the coast or to raid a Muslim base, efficiency under sail was more useful than rowing speed in any case. Oars were useful for providing tactical mobility, not speed.

An example of the sort of operation in which Spanish naval forces habitually engaged serves to illustrate the point and presents an interesting contrast with Quirini's relief of Famagusta. In the dead of the winter of 1564–5 Don Álvaro de Bazan, Captain General of the Galleys of Spain,

---

[1] The details are given by Hill. The analysis is my own. Hill states explicitly that Quirini sent his supply ships in first with his galleys in support a considerable distance astern, according to one Italian source just out of sight around a promontory close inshore. The Venetian supply ships, being more stoutly constructed, were less vulnerable to the Ottoman bow guns than the Ottoman galleys, taken in flank, were to the Venetian. It would seem likely that the surviving Turkish galleys pulled up to the beach stern first as a defensive measure though Hill offers no special details to confirm this theory.

[2] Ismail Uzuncarsılı, 'Some documents concerning the activities of the Allies and Venice with the Turkish State between the battle of Lepanto and the conquest of Cyprus', *Turkiyat Mejmuasi*, III (1926–33), 257–92, cited by Hill, *A History of Cyprus*, vol. III, pp. 1161–2.

undertook a counter raid against the North African coast.[1] His objective was the mouth of the river of Tetuán, an important base of Muslim raiding activity. We cannot be entirely sure of the reasoning behind this operation, but we can reasonably suppose that it was intended as a spoiling attack. With the memory of the disaster of 1562[2] still fresh and with the certainty of a major Ottoman campaign far to the west in the coming season, Don Álvaro was no doubt eager to pull the fangs of the North African raiders while he still had a local superiority of forces with which to do so. Like most winter operations it was conducted on a shoestring.

Leaving Seville with six galleys three days after Christmas, Bazan picked up four *bergantins*, essential for the kind of operation which he was about to undertake, at Puerto de Santa Maria at the mouth of the Taugus. Sending one of them out to reconnoiter, he sortied for Gibraltar on 16 February. There his scratch force picked up four caravels and three *chalupas*, probably all armed fishermen,[3] and a galiot. The Spanish ranks were swelled, in the words of the account, by 'almost 150 arquebusiers and crossbowmen, friends of ours, from the towns of Tarifa, Ximena, and Gibraltar, who out of friendship alone [i.e. without salary] ... went on the said expedition'. A further stop was made at Tangiers where another group of arquebusiers, perhaps 75 strong, was picked up. All of this took time. Finally on 3 March Bazan sortied from Tangiers after having stripped one of his six galleys of oarsmen to arm the other five and leaving it behind. Stopping briefly at the presidio of Ceuta on the North African coast he obtained two more *bergantins* and several pilots familiar with the local area.

The attack on the Muslim raiding base took the form of a cutting-out

---

[1] The account of this operation is from the *Colección Navarrete*, vol. IV, dto. 28, fol. 218ff.

[2] A combined fleet of 28 galleys under Juan de Mendoza (Olesa Muñido, *La Organización Naval*, vol. I, p. 366, gives a strength of 32 for Mendoza's squadron shortly before the disaster) running from Málaga before an easterly gale at the end of the campaigning season was caught by a sudden shift of wind to the south and run up against the Spanish coast with a loss of 4,000 men and all but 4 of the galleys. See R. C. Anderson, *Naval Wars in the Levant* (Princeton, 1952), p. 15. The composition of Mendoza's force at the beginning of the season given in the *Colección Sanz de Barutell* (*Simancas*), *Artículo* 4, dto. 265, suggests that 12 of the galleys of Spain, 6 of Naples and 6 under Antonio Doria were involved in the disaster.

[3] These *chalupas* (literally, 'sloops') and their fisherman–sailors were not to be taken lightly. Kenneth R. Andrews, *Elizabethan Privateering* (Cambridge, 1964), relates a hair-raising tale of an all-night fight between a Basque fishing boat and an English privateer which took place in the 1580s. The English ran alongside and boarded just before dusk; but the out-numbered Spaniards held out in the forecastle until rising seas forced the English vessel to release its grappling irons and sheer away, leaving the boarding party behind. The struggle continued until dawn with the Spaniards at one point attempting to blast the stern, in which the English had barricaded themselves, off the boat with their final keg of gunpowder. They capitulated only after dawn when they had run completely out of ammunition and the English boarded afresh.

party of soldiers and sailors in armed skiffs supported by the three *chalupas* whose shallow draft enabled them to work close inshore. Their attempt to bring out two 'Turkish' raiding vessels or burn them at their moorings quickly drew a strong response. Large numbers of Muslim cavalry, arquebusiers and crossbowmen engaged the skiffs at close range as they attempted to approach their victims. This brought the *chalupas*, small enough to be rowed, close inshore to help out with their breech-loading swivel guns. They in turn became heavily engaged, actually coming to hand strokes with the Muslims and suffering some fifty wounded in the process. Finally Bazan was forced to bring his galleys in almost to the beach to cover the withdrawal of the *chalupas*. Only the fire power of the galleys' main batteries permitted the extraction of the raiding force without serious loss. Until the galleys intervened, the Spanish raiders were being drawn in deeper and deeper with little hope of reprieve.

This action cannot be considered entirely typical. A small Muslim raid on the Spanish coast by a galiot or two opposed only by local ground forces was probably a more common sort of engagement. But larger raids were not unknown. The year 1564 in fact seems to have been a particularly bad one on the Spanish coasts with Muslim raiding forces of as many as 16 galiots and galleys coming ashore near Barcelona.[1] An elaborate network of signal and warning towers was established along the coasts of Spain, Sardinia, and the Kingdoms of Naples and Sicily to warn the inhabitants of threatened villages and to bring land and naval forces to the scene.[2] The tactics employed by these forces in clashes with Muslim raiders must have been similar to those described above. Certainly the use of galley bow artillery to cover the landing or extraction of an infantry force was standard Spanish practice. In a strikingly modern action, the Marques of Santa Cruz employed his galleys in direct support of an amphibious infantry assault on field fortifications garnished with artillery in the attack on Terciera in the Azores in 1583. Santa Cruz' account of the opposed landing is worth quoting in full as a magnificent, though not entirely typical, example of Spanish galley tactics:

receiving many cannonades ... the [flag] galley began to batter and dismount the enemy artillery and the rest of the galleys [did likewise] ... and the landing boats ran aground and placed the soldiers at the sides of the forts, and along the trenches, although with much difficulty and working under the pressure of the furious artillery, arquebus, and musket fire of the enemy. And the soldiers mounting [the trenches] in

---

[1] Olesa Muñido, *La Organización Naval*, vol. II, p. 940.
[2] *Ibid.* vol. II, ch. 17, pp. 938–89, covers this in detail. The Spanish organization in the West Indies was of necessity less elaborate, but essentially similar in its details.

several places came under heavy arquebus and musket fire, but finally won the forts and trenches.[1]

The Ottoman employment of galleys was strikingly different. Where Spanish galleys were designed around the amphibious skirmishes of the 'little war', their Ottoman opposites existed principally to transport siege forces to their destination and to cover their operations once there. The Ottoman galleys of the small standing squadrons frequently operated in a strategically defensive role, but this was not the *raison d'être* of Ottoman naval power. The characteristic Ottoman naval operation was a serious attack on a major fortified place. The list of such operations is a long one: the attack on Negropont in 1476 and its capture in 1479, the siege of Rhodes in 1480 and the capture of Otranto in 1481, the capture of Lepanto in 1499, the successful sieges of Coron and Modon in 1500, the siege of Rhodes in 1522, the unsuccessful attempt on Corfu in 1537, the capture of Castelnuovo in 1539, the starving out of the Imperial garrison on Djerba in 1560, the siege of Malta in 1565 and the recapture of Tunis in 1574.

These operations demanded an amphibious capability, but not necessarily a tactical one. Galleys were used to transport troops and guns and to get them ashore expeditiously. The larger cannon of the siege train in particular seem to have been transported in galleys to facilitate getting them ashore.[2] Opposed landings, however, were not ordinarily needed or attempted. The main thing was strategic mobility, to get the siege force to the objective and to cover it once there. The superior sailing characteristics of Ottoman galleys were clearly no accident.

Where does this leave us? What conclusions can we draw from our discussion of regional variation in galley construction, armament and tactics? The gross external differences between the galleys of the various Mediterranean nations were comparatively slight. Even the performance differences were small in absolute terms. We should not exaggerate them. But the high degree of standardization within the various Mediterranean fleets made these differences all important.

Though we run the risk of overstating our case, it is possible to characterize briefly the overall nature of these differences. If we had to sum it all up in a single phrase we would describe the Spanish galley as a tactical

[1] *Colección Navarrete*, vol. v, dto. 1, fol. 3. This is Santa Cruz' own account and includes a complete inventory of the forces involved. The Azores campaign of 1583 is well covered by a number of contemporary Spanish accounts including that of Cristoval Mosquera de Figuerola, *Comentarios Militares y Jornada a las Islas de los Azores* (Madrid, 1596).
[2] Luis Collado, *Platica Manual de Artilleria*, fol. 32. Balbi di Correggio, *The Siege of Malta* (1565), p. 33, states that a 100 pounder Ottoman cannon weighing 180 cwt. (about 9 tons) was loaded, with its ammunition, on a single 25-bank galley for the Malta expedition.

infantry assault craft. It was short on flat out speed under oars, but long on raw combat power – remember that we are making no attempt to differentiate between the galley and its complement – for the crunch of a boarding fight. It had quite enough tactical mobility to properly exploit its combat power and enough strategic mobility to place its complement of troops where they were needed. Designed for the amphibious war of raid and counter-raid, the Spanish galley was almost accidentally equally well suited for the knock-down, drag-out of a formal fleet engagement.

The North African galleys and galiots can be viewed as strategic raiding craft. Designed for lightning raids on Christian coasts and commerce, they needed speed under oars above all else to escape from Spanish, Genoese, and Papal patrols. Where the proper objective of the Spanish galley was the North African raider's base or the raider himself, the North African's proper objective was the isolated and lightly defended coastal village or merchant ship. A true guerrilla of the sea, he behaved and fought like one. Lower in the water and less heavily armed with artillery because of their size, North African galiots were at a severe disadvantage in a formal fleet engagement with western galleys. In battle, the North Africans attempted to create and exploit mêlée situations where their superior speed and agility could be used to neutralize the superior head-on power of the western galleys by delivering flank attacks. When these failed, only fanatical courage remained.

The Venetian galley can be viewed as a heavily armed tactical attack transport. Like the Spanish galley it evolved within the conceptual framework of a defensive strategic role. But there was an important difference: where the Spanish galley could only accomplish its mission by engaging hostile naval and amphibious forces in battle, the Venetian galley ideally did so with light contact or none at all. The usual job of the Venetian fleet or squadron was the relief of a seaside fortress besieged by the Turk or, if the opportunity arose, an offensive dash at a similar Ottoman place. In neither case was engaging the hostile fleet in battle likely to aid in accomplishment of the mission.

Since the Venetian defensive mission was to preserve the integrity of a line of closely spaced bases, strategic mobility – efficiency under sail – was not a prime requisite. A nearby staging base was generally available for a relieving squadron. But since the relief operation almost invariably had to be undertaken in the face of a superior Ottoman fleet, tactical mobility – speed under oars – was of the essence. This combined with the chronic Venetian manpower shortage and technological superiority to give the Venetian galley its peculiar characteristics. Where the Spanish galley was a platform for infantry, the Venetian galley was a platform for artillery.

But there were complications: the Ottomans knew the score quite as well as the Venetians. They were adept at interposing their fleet, usually superior in strength, between a Venetian relieving force and its goal. The Venetians, therefore, often found themselves in the position of having to fight their way into a beleaguered fortress or see it fall. This meant attacking the Ottomans in a position chosen by them. Venetian galleys were therefore equipped with provisions for fitting a temporary raised fighting platform at the prow. But where the boarding fight was the first choice of the Spanish, it was the final alternative for the Venetians.

The Ottoman galley, by contrast, was designed for a strategic role which was profoundly offensive and a tactical role which was profoundly defensive. Its job was to get the siege forces to their objective and to prevent interference with their activities by enemy naval forces once there. This might mean receiving an attack from an enemy fleet; but it rarely meant delivering one. An Ottoman fleet victory could do little to help the progress of the siege, but a defeat could do much to impair it.

In sum, it is apparent that national trends in galley design were the product and the accurate reflection of the tactical and strategic requirements of the nations involved. Galley design was therefore an accurate reflection of geographic considerations. This was true of sailing warships as well: Dutch men-of-war of the seventeenth and eighteenth centuries, for example, had flatter bottoms and shallower draft than their French and English counterparts because of the shallowness of most Dutch ports. But because of the uniquely close relationship between human and technical considerations in galley warfare, galley design was also a reflection of each nation's social, political and economic situation. There was no single optimum galley design from the technical point of view, even for a particular set of geographic circumstances. Galley design was determined as much by human and economic considerations as it was by technical ones.

This characteristic of sixteenth-century Mediterranean warfare at sea, perhaps more than any other, has rendered it largely incomprehensible within the traditional Mahanian framework of naval history. Because of a failure to understand the importance of the human factor in Mediterranean naval tactics and technology, modern naval historians have missed much of the science and subtlety in Mediterranean warfare at sea, particularly at the tactical level.

Of this there is no better example than the battle of Lepanto. Viewed by generations of western naval historians as 'a land battle at sea' (whatever that means), Lepanto has emerged as an enormous free-for-all, an unscientific brawl in which the aim of the opposing commanders was

simply to come to grips with their opponents in as quick and uncompli-
cated a manner as possible. In fact, nothing could be farther from the
truth. On both sides Lepanto was tactically one of the most carefully
planned and best fought battles in the annals of warfare. But this becomes
apparent only through careful analysis of the tactical ramifications of
regional variations in galley design – variations which were largely the
product of social and economic considerations rather than purely technical
ones.

LEPANTO, 1571

Despite the repulse before Malta in 1565, the Ottoman Empire retained both its power and the initiative at sea. Though Malta was clearly a major turning point, this is more apparent in retrospect than it was at the time. Ottoman losses in manpower at the siege of Malta had been considerable, but most of those lost had been irregulars and impressed oarsmen. Reserves of trained seamen and commanders had remained intact. It is significant, therefore, that the next Ottoman thrust was not delivered outward into the western Mediterranean against Spain, but inward against Venice. The Moriscos still presented a serious problem of internal security to Spain, but the moment for exploiting that opportunity had passed. The explanation for the shift in the direction of Ottoman expansion is largely a technical one.

In the three decades since Prevesa the technical facts of life of warfare at sea had shifted in such a way as to markedly reduce the offensive strategic capabilities of the galley fleet. This was particularly true after the middle of the sixteenth century. While becoming more powerful tactically, the galley suffered a gradual diminution of its strategic mobility. Like the carnivorous dinosaur, the war galley dominated its environment. But, like the dinosaur, it grew progressively larger and more powerful to compete with its own kind until, like the dinosaur, it became increasingly immobile. The tactical power of the Mediterranean war galley, like the teeth and jaws of *Tyrannosaurus rex*, depended upon a continuous supply of flesh and blood. Eventually the logistic demands of the war galley, like those of the thunder lizard, grew too large for its environment to support and it was ultimately replaced by competitors which, though less impressive tactically, were considerably more efficient logistically.

The decrease in strategic mobility combined with a shift in the balance between offensive and defensive firepower, largely the result of a gradual increase in the amount of available artillery in the Mediterranean world, to induce strategic stasis. This occurred at an early stage in the galley's decline, while its tactical monopoly was still complete. With the War of Cyprus and the battle of Lepanto the Mediterranean system of naval warfare reached its apex. The reliance upon human muscle power had shunted the development of the galley into an evolutionary dead end. This war and this battle mark the peak of the galley fleet's tactical power and, at the same time, the onset of strategic paralysis.

The most important causal factor behind both trends was an increase in the size of galleys and an increase in the size of their complements which were directly connected to one another. Because of the limitations of human muscle as a source of propulsive power, the ratio between the size of a galley and the size of its crew began to diverge rapidly. The

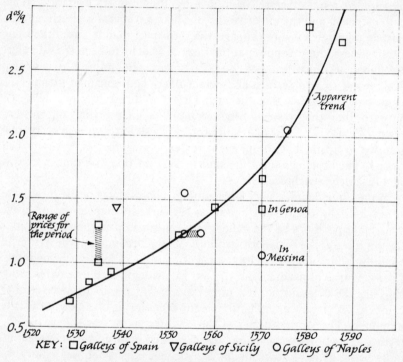

Fig. 11   The rising cost of biscuit, 1523–87
(Cost is given in ducats per *quintal* of about 101.4 English pounds)

NOTE. During the period in question biscuit rose from just under 25 per cent of the total cost of operating a galley to between 30 and 50 per cent. Prices in Spain were consistently higher than those in Sicily or Naples. Genoese prices were intermediate.

SOURCES. 1523: *Colección Sanz de Barutell (Simancas)*, *Artículo* 5, dto 2; 1529: *Artículo* 3, vol. I, dto 17, and *Artículo* 5, dto 3; 1533: *Artículo* 3, vol. I, dto 42; 1533: *Artículo* 5, dto 12; 1537: *Artículo* 4, vol. I, dto 59; 1538: *Artículo* 5, dto 16; 1552: *Artículo* 5, dto 29; 1552–9: *Artículo* 4, vol. 2, dto 311; 1553: *Artículo* 5, dto 34; 1560: *Colección Navarrete*, vol. XII, dto 84; 1571: *Colección Sanz de Barutell (Simancas)*, *Artículo* 4, vol. 2, dtos 322 and 323; 1575: *Artículo* 5, dto 44; 1580: *Colección Navarrete*, vol. XII, dto 100; 1587: vol. VIII, dto 11.

reasons for this are straightforward. An increase in a galley's size with a proportionate increase in fighting manpower resulted in an obvious and direct increase in combat power. But unless speed under oars were to be sacrificed, each increase in size had to be accompanied by increasingly disproportionate increases in the size of the *ciurmi*.

The result was a slight increase in the size of galleys and a sharp increase in the size of their complements after 1550. This had a direct and immedi-

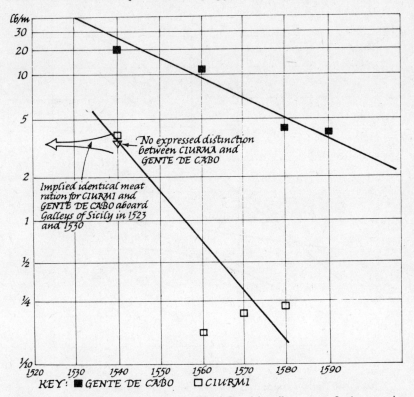

Fig. 12   Changes in the meat ration aboard Spanish galleys, 1523–87 (meat rations of *ciurmi* and *gente de cabo* in pounds per month per man)

NOTES

Ration for *ciurma*, galleys of Sicily, 1538: 26 oz biscuit (hardtack) per day; 4 oz meat three days a week; a 'stew of vegetables' four days a week (2 oz portions).

Ration for *ciurma*, galleys of Spain, 1580: 26 oz biscuit per day; 8 oz meat five days a year; about one-eighth of a cup of *garbanzos* per day.

SOURCES. 1523 and 1530: *Colección Sanz de Barutell (Simancas), Artículo* 5, dto 2; 1538: *Artículo* 5, dto 16; 1539: *Artículo* 5, dto 17; 1560: *Colección Navarrete*, vol. XII, dto 84; 1571: *Colección Sanz de Barutell (Simancas), Artículo* 4, vol. 2, dto 322; 1580: *Colección Navarrete*, vol. XII, dto 100; 1587: vol. VIII, dto 11.

ate effect upon strategic mobility by reducing the amount of storage space per man available aboard a galley for water and provisions. It helped to produce strategic stasis in the long run by acting in combination with the price revolution to increase sharply the cost of operating a galley. This consideration, upon which we will comment only briefly, looms large among the factors which ultimately combined to deliver the *coup de grâce* to the Mediterranean system. Because of the extremely detailed and

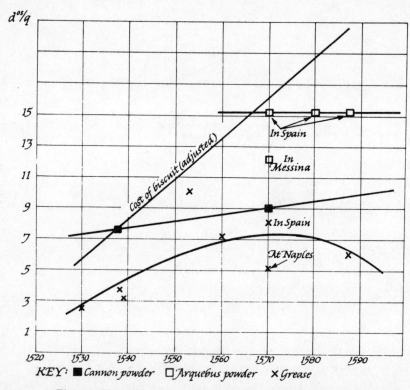

Fig. 13 Changes in the cost of gunpowder and grease, 1529–87

NOTE. The line showing the price of biscuit for comparison was taken from the data shown in Fig. 11. A constant multiplier was applied to the biscuit prices. This multiplier was selected for convenience to give equality of gunpowder and biscuit prices in 1538. This permits a comparison of the relative rise in price. Note that arquebus powder was considerably more expensive than cannon powder, which had less salt-peter, the most expensive ingredient, until late in the century.

SOURCES. 1538: *Colección Sanz de Barutell (Simancas), Artículo* 5, dto 16; 1571: *Artículo* 4, vol. 2, dto 322 and 323; 1580: *Colección Navarrete*, vol. XII, dto 100; 1587: vol. VIII, dto 11.

complex nature of the mass of evidence supporting this conclusion, a graphic presentation has been employed. This is shown in Figs. 11, 12, 13 and 14.

In summary, the increase in the size of a galley's complement combined

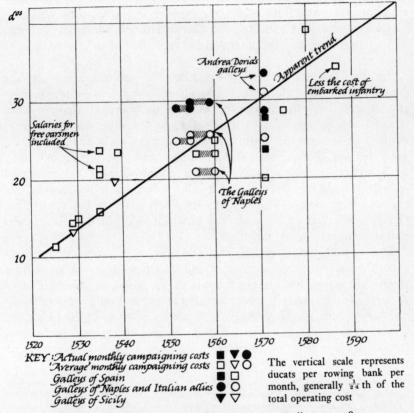

Fig. 14   The rising cost to Spain of operating a galley, 1523–87

NOTE. The figures for actual campaigning costs include, as far as possible, the true cost of maintaining and paying the oarsmen, sailors and soldiers actually carried on campaign. The 'average' monthly cost is a prorated average, the total yearly cost divided by twelve. It therefore reflects the savings effected by releasing most of the soldiers, sailors and *oficiales* in the non-campaigning months. From 1550 on there is an increased divergence between actual campaigning and 'average' costs. This is a reflection of heavier manning while on campaign coupled with shorter campaigning seasons. In the earlier period galleys seem to have campaigned most of the time during the period from March to September. Later on this was not the case; but the average was computed as if it were.

SOURCES. As for Figs. 11, 12 and 13.

with an increase in the prices of the commodities needed to keep a man alive and in good fighting trim at sea to make a galley prohibitively expensive to operate. This was certainly true in terms of combat effectiveness per unit cost when compared to a broadside sailing warship. It was probably true in absolute terms as well. Galley fleets declined in size after the War of Cyprus. This was surely as much for fiscal as for logistic or tactical reasons. The appetite of the Mediterranean war galley, like that of *Tyrannosaurus rex*, had outgrown the capability of its environment to sustain it.

From its appearance until the middle of the sixteenth century, the Mediterranean war galley changed hardly at all in external dimensions or in the size of its complement. Before 1550 the standard Mediterranean warship was the trireme *alla sensile* of 24 banks[1] with, minus shortages because of sickness, an unvarying 144 oarsmen, each pulling his own individual oar. Then about 1552, for reasons which are not entirely clear, a change in the rowing systems of galleys was introduced which permitted augmentation of the *ciurma* almost at will. On Spanish galleys this changeover can be pinpointed as having occurred between 1552 and 1557.[2] This change was to the system *a scaloccio* in which all of the men on a bench pulled a single large oar together.

This, in turn, permitted the construction of larger galleys. By the mid-1560s the *ciurmi* of ordinary Spanish galleys, still of 24 banks but slightly larger than before, had increased in size from 144 to an optimum of 160.[3] By 1571 this figure had further increased to 174 and the galleys of Spain and her western allies had their *ciurmi* reinforced to no less than 200 for the Lepanto campaign.[4] This increase mirrored an increase in the total complements of galleys, an increase which was particularly sharp aboard lantern galleys.

[1] That is, of rowing benches per side. There is some difficulty in comparing bank counts. The rowing bench omitted on the starboard side of a galley for the skiff and on the port side for the cooking area were sometimes included in the total, but usually not. Early in the sixteenth century the standard western galley had 25 banks, not counting the empty benches, though galleys of as few as 21 banks were built. By 1530, the standard was established at 24 banks where it remained throughout the Mediterranean until after 1550 although triremes *alla sensile* of 21 banks and even less continued to be built. Triremes *alla sensile* with more than 25 banks were extremely rare.

[2] The primary document leading to this conclusion is a summary of the *asientos* of the Galleys of Naples from 1552 to 1569 in the *Colección Sanz de Barutell (Simancas), Artículo* 4, vol. 2, dto 311. This is independently supported by reports mentioning the rowing systems aboard Spanish galleys in 1556 made by Cristoforo da Canal, Alberto Tenenti, *Cristoforo da Canal* (Paris, 1967), p. 34.

[3] See the document previously cited and Don Garcia de Toledo's remarks *ca.* 1564, *Colección Navarrete*, vol. XII, dto. 83, fol. 309. These are the most relevant of a host of documents bearing on the subject.

[4] *Colección Sanz de Barutell (Simancas), Artículo* 4, vol. 2, dto. 323, fol. 424–6.

In 1535 an ordinary galley of Spain had carried about 65 *gente de cabo*[1] in addition to her oarsmen. In 1536, Don Álvaro de Bazan's *capitana* carried the usual complement of oarsmen (but with shortages filled from the other galleys in the squadron), plus three *oficiales* and 120 *gente de cabo* including 100 arquebusiers.[2]

By 1571 the level of manning had increased markedly. An ordinary galley of Spain carried a normal complement of about 80 *gente de cabo* who were reinforced with regular Spanish infantry for major expeditions.[3] In addition to their 200 oarsmen the ordinary Spanish galleys which fought at Lepanto carried an average of 112 *gente de cabo* plus gentlemen adventurers and about 150 attached soldiers.[4] But if the level of manning of ordinary galleys had increased sharply, that of lantern galleys and *capitanas* had risen astronomically. Don Juan's *Real* (flagship) at Lepanto had 35 rowing banks and must therefore have carried some 420 oarsmen rowing six to a bench. Its fighting complement centered around no less than 400 Sardinian arquebusiers.[5] In this, it was closely matched by its Ottoman opposite number. Ali Paşa's flagship carried 300 Janissaries and 100 arquebusiers.[6] The tremendous crowding involved is highlighted by the limited size of even Don Juan's *Real*: only about 160 feet long by perhaps 25 feet across the *apostis*.

Venetian tests with a quinquireme *alla sensile* in 1529 had shown that a 50 per cent increase in hull displacement had to be accompanied by a 100 per cent increase in the size of the *ciurma* unless a reduction in dash speed were to be accepted.[7] Such a reduction in speed under oars was

---

[1] This is from Don Álvaro de Bazan's *asiento* as Captain General of the Galleys of Spain in the *Colección Sanz de Barutell (Simancas), Artículo* 5, dto. 11, fol. 43-4. The term *gente de cabo* covered sailors, artillerists, and fighting men who formed a regular part of the galley's complement. Though technically *gente de cabo*, attached infantrymen were usually enumerated separately. The three highest *oficiales*, the *patrón*, *sotapatrón* and *comitre*, were enumerated separately at first, then later lumped together with the *oficiales* and sailors under the overall heading of *gente de cabo*. This and the three following examples were carefully selected as being representative. The manning aboard a given galley for, say, a mission reinforcing a besieged fortress might be considerably higher. The figures I have given represent a galley's usual complement, the minimum considered adequate to sustain regular operations.

[2] *Colección Sanz de Barutell (Simancas), Artículo* 4, vol. 1, dto. 41, fol. 121-7.

[3] *Ibid.* vol. 2, dto, 323, fol. 424-6.

[4] *Ibid.* vol. 2, dto. 322, fol. 420-2. Lantern galleys carried a considerably larger complement, as we shall show a few pages on.

[5] Olesa Muñido, *La Organización Naval*, vol. 1 (Madrid, 1968), p. 194.

[6] Baron Purgstall von Hammer, *Histoire de L'Empire Ottoman*, vol. VI, J. J. Hellert trans. (Paris, 1835), p. 427.

[7] We have this from the results of speed trials conducted on Vettour Fausto's quinquireme which was rowed by five oars and five oarsmen to a bench, R. C. Anderson, *Oared Fighting Ships* (London, 1962), p. 67. We know from the vessel's dimensions that its displacement was increased by about half. It carried exactly twice as many oars and oarsmen as a normal trireme and was only marginally faster in speed trials.

tactically unacceptable. This meant that as galleys grew in size the amount of hull space per man available for storing provisions diminished geometrically.

There was no way out of this difficulty. The increase in the size of galleys, made possible by the adoption of the rowing system *a scaloccio*, was forced by tactical considerations. To triumph strategically it is necessary to survive tactically. Because of the geographic and climatic peculiarities of the Mediterranean, the galley remained tactically viable for as long as artillery was relatively scarce. But the galley had to compete not only against targets ashore and lightly armed merchant ships; it had to compete against other galleys as well. If the enemy built larger and more heavily manned galleys (which had to carry a larger *ciurma* in order to retain their tactical mobility) larger and more heavily manned galleys would have to be built to meet him in battle. Head-on fights with other galleys were far from being the galley's most important role. But it was a role which the galley had to be able to perform.

Only the Venetians, backed by the (albeit declining) availability of skilled, free oarsmen who were willing and able to fight and by the excellence of their artillery, went against the trend for a time. Venetian triremes *alla sensile* fought at Lepanto and perhaps a few Ottoman and North African ones did as well.[1] But Venetian lantern galleys – larger than ordinary galleys, carefully armed and manned to serve as tactical focal points in battle – though few in number, were as large as anybody's. That the Venetians understood the tactical issues involved at least as well as their competitors is shown by the fact that they went beyond the lantern galley to develop the galeass. We shall have more to say about this shortly.

The increase in the size of galleys and their crews did not immediately eliminate the possibility of a powerful offensive strategic stroke. Don Juan captured Tunis in 1574 and the Ottomans got it back the following year. But it is worth noting that the deep penetrations of the western Mediterranean by the entire Ottoman fleet in the 1540s and 50s were never repeated. The Ottoman recapture of Tunis in 1574 was, in fact, the last major strategic accomplishment of a galley fleet.

But the strategic stasis which began to set in was the result of more than the reduction of the galley fleet's radius of action. The augmented manning which cut so heavily into the galley's strategic mobility also gave important

---

[1] This statement is based upon the established fact that the Venetians retained the system *alla sensile* longest and upon an engraving of Lepanto by Giovanni B. Camocio (reproduced in C. W. C. Oman, *A History of the Art of War in the Sixteenth Century* (London, 1937), p. 734) which clearly shows several triremes *alla sensile*. It is apparent that Camocio intended to depict the triremes *alla sensile* as just that, since several galleys rowed *a scaloccio* – much less difficult to depict – are shown nearer in the foreground.

tactical advantages to the galley fleet operating defensively near its own bases. This, like almost any advantage accruing to the defense, worked to produce stability. But a consideration of almost equal importance was a gradual increase in the amount of available artillery.

Logically, this increase in fire power should have shifted the balance of war in favor of the attacker. But here, as in many other cases before and since, theory failed to triumph over secondary factual considerations. The modest and gradual increase in the amount of artillery available in the Mediterranean world during the sixteenth century was more than offset by developments in fortification. Seaside fortifications in particular were becoming more numerous and improving in design.

By the 1520s the temporary ascendancy of siege artillery over fortification design which had prevailed in the Mediterranean world in the last decades of the fifteenth century and first decades of the sixteenth had been neutralized. Caught momentarily at a loss by the enormous smashing power of Ottoman siege cannon in particular, fortress designers had responded to the challenge quickly and well. The brevity of the sieges of the Venetian fortresses of Modon and Coron in the Morea in 1500 stands in sharp contrast to the extreme difficulty encountered by the Ottomans in taking Rhodes in 1522.

From the 1520s on the proliferation of well designed first-class seaside fortifications seems to have gradually exerted a powerful strategic stabilizing influence. Venetian fortress design in particular quickly attained a high level of perfection. If we take into account the relative scarcity of defensive artillery around which they were designed, the fortifications of Nicosia and Famagusta on Cyprus were at least on a par with Vauban's designs.[1]

The increase in the amount of available artillery, logically the natural counter to more powerful fortifications, actually worked in the other direction by increasing the defensive fire power of fortresses relative to that of siege trains. The only other likely way out of the developing strategic stasis, a radical improvement in artillery design and tactical capabilities, was beyond the technology of the times and was not to come about for another two and a half centuries. In addition there was a buffer mechanism which served to reduce the impact of the increased availability of ordnance on the conduct of Mediterranean warfare at sea: the bow of a galley could hold only so much artillery.

As early as the 1530s many galleys were already carrying as much ord-

---

[1] Sir George Hill, *A History of Cyprus*, vol. III, *The Frankish Period, 1432–1571* (Cambridge, 1948), pp. 844–64, contains a thorough and concise technical evaluation of the fortifications together with much information concerning their design and construction.

nance as they could practically hold. We have already mentioned the armament of Filippino Doria's galley of 1528: a basilisk, two half cannons (large swivel guns), two *sacres* and two *falconetes* (also swivel guns).[1] This level of armament was only a short step from that of the galleys which fought at Lepanto. This isolated example is placed in context by our knowledge of the armament of the galleys of Spain and her Italian allies some eight years later.

Because a detailed and apparently complete inventory made of the armament of the Galleys of Spain, Sicily, Monaco, Terranova and Antonio Doria in 1536 is preserved in the Museo Naval, Madrid, we are able to make a number of generalizations about the state of galley armament at that time. This document also gives us a basis for comparison with what we know about Spanish, Venetian and Ottoman galley armament at Lepanto. Covering a total of 23 galleys (13 of Spain, 4 of Sicily, and 2 each of Monaco, the Marques of Terranova, and Antonio Doria), it gives the full armament of each in the Mediterranean sense of the word including exact totals of oarsmen, *oficiales*, *gente de cabo*, and artillery all the way down to the number of arquebusses carried.[2]

This document allows us to reconstruct the ideal armament of a western galley of the 1530s with some confidence. This would have included a full cannon firing about a fifty pound ball mounted on the centerline, flanked by a pair of nine to twelve pound half culverins, a pair of *pedreros* of about the same size or, at the least, a pair of large *sacres*. These were flanked in turn by a pair of smaller *sacres*, probably six pounders. In the gaps between these five main bow guns were four heavy vertical timbers about four feet high on top of which were mounted large swivel pieces (see Appendix 6). An additional, smaller pair of swivel pieces was mounted on a lighter pair of vertical timbers outboard of the *sacres*. On western galleys a number of light swivel pieces were mounted atop the *arrumbada*, the fighting platform above the main battery.

At least insofar as the five main pieces are concerned, this ideal armament was a common standard throughout the Mediterranean. But on the galleys of our 1536 sample this ideal was only partially realized. The distribution of ordnance aboard the 23 galleys, in fact, strongly suggests a shortage of artillery. Old wrought-iron pieces (though apparently exceptional ones of great size) were evidently pressed into service as main centerline bow guns on two of the galleys of Spain. These pieces, called a

[1] *I Diarii Marino Sanuto* (Venice, 1897), vol. 46, col. 666–7.
[2] *Colección Sanz de Barutell* (Simancas), *Artículo* 4, vol. 1, dto. 42, fol. 121–7. The unique value of this document lies in the fact that it gives the actual armament of a large number of galleys at the same time, not an ideal standard armament which may or may not have been representative as most such documents do.

cañon verso pentino and a *cañon serpentino* respectively, were mounted on the third and fourth most heavily gunned of the galleys of Spain. The distinction made between these pieces and the *cañones* and *culebrinas* of the other galleys suggests a constructional difference. The terminology *verso pentino*, in fact, suggests a breechloader, reinforcing the idea that these two cannons were probably 'long' closely built wrought-iron pieces, similar in construction to the pair of large wrought-iron guns built in 1516 and on display in the park surrounding the Tomb of Barbarossa in Istanbul. Only 8 of the 23 galleys had their full complement of half culverins and *sacres* and it is illuminating that all of these were among the Galleys of Spain. On one galley, the only piece which was larger than a swivel gun was the main centerline bow gun.

But the strengths must be noted as well as the shortages. All of the 23 galleys listed had at least a full cannon or the equivalent – a gun weighing from 4,500 to 7,000 pounds and firing a 30 to 50 pound cast-iron ball – as the main centerline gun. The main bow guns of no less than 8 of the 13 galleys of Spain are explicitly listed as 'large' cannon and that of one more as a 'large' culverin, probably a more massive piece still. With the one exception noted above, all of the 23 had at least a pair of *sacres* as flanking pieces.

Nevertheless the shortage of secondary armament is striking. The quantity of ordnance available to Spain and her allies in 1536 was sufficient to satisfy the main requirement of arming a fleet of galleys – barely. No standardization, however, was possible. The fact that the galleys of Spain were more heavily armed than those of the lesser allies suggests that great cost, indicative of short supply, was a factor.

By Lepanto enough ordnance had become available to fill in the gaps in the secondary armament. Christian sources list all of the galleys of the Holy League as having five cannon apiece.[1] This corresponds exactly to a main centerline bow gun and two pairs of flanking pieces as large as a *sacre* (the smaller swivel pieces being ignored), the partially realized ideal of 1535. This standard of armament was apparently matched by the Muslims.

This is made clear by an analysis of surviving accounts detailing the division of spoils, including the captured ordnance, among the victors after the battle.[2] Excluding the sixty or so Muslim galleys which were so badly damaged that they sank shortly after the battle, 117 galleys, ten galiots and three *fustas* were included in the division of spoils. These

---

[1] Althea Weil, *The Navy of Venice* (New York, 1910), p. 263.
[2] Our information is from a Spanish account of the division, *Colección Sanz de Barutell* (*Simancas*), *Artículo* 4, vol. 2, dto. 317, fol. 406–7. This agrees in all of its particulars with the figures given from Venetian sources by Weil, *The Navy of Venice*.

yielded 117 main centerline bow guns (*cañones de crujia*, that is cannon suitable for mounting as the main centerline bow gun of an ordinary galley), 17 'pedreros' and 256 'smaller pieces'. The raw numerical average of three cannon per galley which this gives would seem to imply that the Muslim galleys had only a single pair of flanking pieces. In fact, this was probably not so. On all except the most heavily armed lantern galleys the second pair of flanking pieces would have been at most small *sacres* weighing no more than 1,500 pounds, light enough to manhandle out of their mounts and carry off as loot. The high value attached to bronze makes it all but certain that this is precisely what happened. The pieces light enough to be carried off without block and tackle (and perhaps a few that weren't) would have been removed by whoever got to them first and thus excluded from the formal division of spoils which did not take place until three days after the battle. It is probably fair to estimate, therefore, that each Muslim galley carried at least two cannon which were as big as a large *sacre* or bigger in addition to its main centerline bow gun. If we allot ten of the 'smaller pieces' to the galiots as their main centerline bow guns, we still have enough left over to give each of the 117 Muslim galleys a pair of flanking pieces and, by including the *pedreros*, to give 21 of the 117 galleys two pairs of flanking pieces larger than a small *sacre*. It is surely more than coincidental that the figure 21 corresponds almost exactly to the number of Christian lantern galleys, of which there were 25 at Lepanto. The correlation in the number of lantern galleys is probably even closer than this would suggest since a number of the Muslim lantern galleys were surely among those sunk. This compares closely with what we know of Christian standards of armament. If the Christians had an advantage in fire power on a galley-for-galley basis, it was only in the size of the smaller flanking pieces and in swivel guns.

Although the strategic parameters of Mediterranean warfare at sea had become somewhat constricted by the time of Lepanto, tactics remained essentially the same. However heavily it was manned and armed, a galley still carried its fighting power forward and was maneuvered and fought in the same way. Lepanto was, if anything, a classic textbook example of Mediterranean galley tactics. There was, however, a technical innovation which had a significant impact on the battle of Lepanto: the galeasses.[1]

---

[1] The English word derives from the Spanish *galeaza*, a large galley. The usual English dictionary definition, a composite warship using both sails and oars for propulsion, is misleading. The galeass differed from the ordinary galley mainly in having more and heavier cannon. It was almost incidentally a better sailing vessel, the product of a larger hull. Mediterranean military men viewed the galeass as precisely what it was – a big galley. They were far more concerned with its poor rowing characteristics than with its relatively good performance under sail.

A Venetian development, the galeass can be viewed as a manifestation of the increased availability of good bronze artillery in the final decades of the sixteenth century. A magnificent improvisation, the galeass was nothing more than a merchant galley provided with a heavy artillery armament and specialized fighting superstructures at the bow and stern to hold it.

Somewhat longer than an ordinary galley and with a much more spacious and seaworthy hull, the merchant galley had originally evolved as a vehicle for transporting precious cargos over long distances. In the age before artillery the merchant galley's large crew provided an effective defense against pirates. In the age before the perfection of sails and rigging its limited mobility under oars provided a relatively sure means of making port. All in all, the merchant galley was a well designed and seaworthy ship. But in the course of the sixteenth century, rising labor costs and competition from ever more efficient sailing ships combined to render the merchant galley – efficient as it was technologically – a losing proposition from the economic point of view.

The Venetians seem, however, to have recognized its military potential – or perhaps they were served by innate conservatism. Instead of being sold or broken up, at least ten merchant galleys were laid up in the Arsenal against future need. When war with the Turk broke out in 1570, these were given a heavy artillery armament and converted into warships.

The Venetian galeass of 1571 was a relatively large ship, about 160 feet long by a shade over 40 feet wide (as opposed to about 135 feet by 23 feet for an ordinary galley), rowing 26 banks and probably six men to an oar.[1] It was, as we would expect, exceedingly slow under oars. With the same number of oarsmen and oars (though longer and heavier oars and thus mechanically less efficient ones) as a reasonably large lantern galley, the galeass had roughly four times the hull displacement. Its mobility under oars was, however, sufficient for it to cooperate effectively with a carefully handled galley fleet, something which a sailing warship could not do. This assumed significance because of two factors: its high freeboard which made it relatively immune to boarding attacks, and the weight of its artillery fire.

The galeasses' artillery armament was very respectable indeed. Though no detailed armament lists of the Venetian galeasses which fought at Lepanto have come to hand, the galeass changed relatively little in its career of just over a century and we know a good deal about other galeasses. The four Neapolitan galeasses which sailed with the Spanish Armada of 1588 carried an average of five full cannons, two or three half cannons

[1] Anderson, *Oared Fighting Ships*, has a full discussion of the galeasses' technical development.

(these were clearly not the small swivel guns which went by the same name), eight *pedreros* of indeterminate size, four half culverins, seven *sacres*, four half *sacres* and around twenty sizeable swivel pieces each.[1] This was almost exactly enough to arm completely five ordinary galleys and still have a pair of half cannons, not carried on galleys, left over. There is every reason to believe that the Venetian galeasses which fought at Lepanto were just as well armed. We have sound evidence, indirect but positive, that the Venetians had a surplus of good artillery in 1571 and that the Spanish did not. When siege operations were contemplated shortly before Lepanto, Don Juan was forced to beg cannon from the Venetian *Capitano Generale de Mar*, Sebastian Venier.[2] Because of the greater deck space aboard a galeass and because all of the heavy cannon were not pointed immovably forward, they could be more effectively employed in a mêlée. The shelter which a galeasses' high freeboard and protective superstructures offered the gunners allowed them to reload and continue firing even after the boarding fight had been joined in earnest. This was to have considerable impact on the outcome of Lepanto.

It is generally considered that the battle of Lepanto was one of the great turning points of history, but modern historians have been hard pressed to explain why. Militarily the Holy League derived little immediate advantage from their victory. No territory changed hands in the wake of the battle and Uluj Ali appeared the next year at the head of a sizeable fleet to face off the Christians in the strait between Cerigo and the southeastern tip of the Morea. The Ottomans had wanted Cyprus, they took Cyprus, and that was that.

It is apparent that in the short-term military sense Lepanto accomplished little or nothing. Western military historians – not looking beyond the short-term implications except within an orthodox Mahanian framework – therefore have generally taken one of two positions:

> Lepanto should have been decisive, but the Christian failure promptly and decisively to exploit their hard won 'command of the sea' threw the victory away.

> Lepanto was indeed decisive – but only in the psychological sense.

We have already demolished the first of these. Galley fleets simply could not exercise command of the sea in the Mahanian sense. The second, though deserving of serious consideration, is at once too ephemeral and

---

[1] Michael Lewis, *Armada Guns* (London, 1961), p. 138.
[2] This is from Venier's report to the Venetian Senate, delivered on 29 December 1572, *opusculo* 3000, p. 13, Archivo di Stato Veneziano, Venice.

too complex to be commented upon intelligently in a work devoted primarily to more concrete considerations.

This much can be said: Lepanto was viewed as a major triumph throughout Christendom. There is evidence that the Ottomans viewed it as a major disaster.[1] In this context, the sheer numerical magnitude of the Christian victory cannot be ignored. The capture of no less than 127 galleys and galiots (minus a considerable number that were in too bad a condition to be brought away) was an event unprecedented in Mediterranean history. This in turn suggests a massive loss of trained Muslim manpower, the same factor which crippled Spain and her allies after the disaster at Djerba in 1560. The ill effects of Lepanto on the Ottoman Empire did not become immediately apparent because of two essentially unconnected events: the revolt of the Netherlands and the Portuguese defeat in Morocco at Al 'Cazar in 1578. The former diverted Spanish attention and resources northward and ultimately resulted in the dissipation of Spanish and Portuguese naval power with the defeat of the Invincible Armada of 1588. The latter decimated the Portuguese nobility, resulted in the death of the Portuguese king, and brought the Portuguese Empire under the dead hand of Philip II. From the Ottoman point of view, the effect was the same in both cases: a mortal enemy was effectively neutralized for a prolonged period of time. Had the Portuguese remained a viable and independent force in Africa and the east and if the religious outbreak in Holland had been forestalled for a decade, Lepanto would surely have assumed a more prominent place in world history.[2] We shall say more about this in concluding.

First we should note that Lepanto represented, in the technical sense, the ultimate development of the Mediterranean system of armed conflict at sea. Lepanto showed that system at the peak of its tactical power. But that tactical peak had been achieved by a degenerate line of development which was shortly to result in strategic paralysis. The aftermath of Lepanto shows that this process of decay had already begun to set in by 1571. There was no other viable option for the Mediterranean nations:

[1] Demetrius Cantemir, *The History of the Growth and Decay of the Othman Empire*, N. Tinda trans. (London, 1734), pp. 223–4. Cantemir, a *millet* official under the Ottomans, refers to Lepanto as 'the greatest blow the Ottomans received since the defeat of Ildirim Bayezid [Bayezid I, the Lightning]'. That Cantemir, writing only several generations after Lepanto and depending on Ottoman sources should have classified it with Bayezid I's crushing defeat at the hands of Timur the Mongol before Angora in 1402 is surely indicative.

[2] Professor Andrew C. Hess of Temple University, the only trained Ottomanist – indeed, virtually the only modern historian – to have seriously addressed himself to the question of Lepanto's historical significance, has concluded that Lepanto was not, within the framework of the Ottoman–Habsburg and Ottoman–Portuguese struggle of the sixteenth century, decisive. Within this historical framework, we are in agreement.

because of its heavy reliance upon human muscle both for tactical mobility and for combat power, the war galley had carried the seeds of its own destruction from the first.

Both of these trends are shown in relief by the War of Cyprus and the battle of Lepanto. Frustrated before the walls of Senglea and Birgu five years before, the Ottomans had sought a target closer to their bases. With their greater strategic scheme of 1565 rendered impracticable by the increasingly restrictive intrinsic limitations of galley fleets and by Spanish power in the kingdoms of Sicily and Naples, Cyprus became the most logical target. Its considerable geographical extent must have seemed particularly attractive to the perpetually land hungry Ottomans. The need of the Ottoman Empire for continued expansion to provide fresh lands for incorporation within the *timar* system has been well documented. The continued availability of new *timar* land was, in fact, one of the essential ingredients for the health of the Ottoman body politic. It is logical to assume, therefore, that a similar mechanism was tied to Ottoman expansion by sea. The other alternative considered by the Divan in 1570, offensive action in North Africa, would have been less attractive than an attack on Cyprus from this point of view since the lands involved were already legally in the hands of Muslims.[1]

As an objective Cyprus offered powerful strategic advantages to the Ottomans. It was relatively close to their bases, about 750 nautical miles from Constantinople and hard up against the friendly coast of Asia Minor. Conversely, it was a full 1,300 miles from Venice and nearly a thousand from Messina. Canea in Crete, the nearest Venetian staging base, was just over 500 miles away. This neatly reversed the ratio of the Malta campaign of 1565.

After presenting an ultimatum to the Venetian Senate in February of 1570 demanding that Cyprus be ceded – a demand which could only be rejected – the Turk struck. Landing on Cyprus in force early in July, the Ottoman army under Lala Mustafa Paşa quickly overran the entire island except for the fortress cities of Nicosia and Famagusta. Nicosia, well inland and thus deprived of any hope of relief except by a full-scale counter-invasion of the island, was overwhelmed by assault on 9 September after a siege of just over two months. During this period the Ottoman fleet under Piali Paşa had awaited the appearance of the Venetian fleet, first by itself and then in loose combination with the newly reconstituted

---

[1] According to Andrew C. Hess, 'The Moriscos: An Ottoman Fifth Column', *American Historical Review*, LXXIV, No. 1 (October 1968), 12, the Grand Vizier Mehmet Sokollu favored expansion in North Africa while Lala Mustafa Paşa, Piali Paşa, and Hoca Sinan Paşa favored the invasion of Cyprus.

Papal fleet under Marc Antonio Colonna and a Spanish contingent under Gian Andrea Doria, Philip II's Captain General of the Sea. Piali Paşa's decision to land troops from the fleet to mount the final assault on Nicosia represented a calculated risk based on the assumption that inter-allied dissension would paralyze the combined Christian force, an assumption which was richly justified by events.

Sickness in the Venetian fleet had forestalled any early decision by Zane, Venetian *Capitano Generale de Mar*, to go it alone. Then the non-cooperation and obstructionism of Gian Andrea Doria had effectively paralyzed the combined Christian force until the fall of Nicosia and continued to do so until the close of the campaigning season.[1] The year ended with the Turks blockading Famagusta covered by a skeleton fleet of some eight galleys under the Bey of Rhodes, awaiting the onset of spring for a major effort on the city.

Marc Antonio Quirini's relief of Famagusta in January ensured the prolonged resistance of the garrison, ably commanded by Antonio Bragadino, and set the stage militarily for the campaign of the following season. It also brought about the replacement of Piali Paşa as Kapudan Paşa by his second in command, Müezzinzade Ali Paşa.[2]

Meanwhile, the Pope had been working to rectify the obviously unsatisfactory command arrangements of the previous year. The result was the formation of the Holy League of Spain, Venice and the Papacy, finally consummated through a treaty of alliance on 25 May 1571.[3] This document was primarily a treaty of naval cooperation. Don Juan of Austria, bastard half-brother of the King of Spain, was named Captain General of the League's fleet with Colonna, the Pope's Captain General, his second in command. The expenses of the League were to be divided among Spain, Venice and the Pope on a 3:2:1 ratio. Messina was designated as the fleet's rendezvous point.

Preoccupied with a major Morisco revolt, the Spaniards were slow to act. Don Juan, in command of operations against the Moriscos, did not leave Barcelona until 20 July. He arrived at Messina with 24 galleys on 23 August – nineteen days after Antonio Bragadino, following a heroic

[1] Hill, *A History of Cyprus*, vol. III, pp. 892 ff, includes a magnificent account of this campaign.

[2] Literally, 'Ali, Son of the Müezzin'. Ottoman names, in the absence of family names, were ordinarily prefixed with a nickname. These might be derived from the father's occupation (as in this case – Ali, son of the caller to prayers in a mosque), the individual's appearance (Kara Mustafa Paşa – swarthy Mustafa), birthplace (Merzifonlu Ali Paşa – Ali from Merzifon), personal habits (Yavuz Selim – Selim the Grim), or relationship with the Sultan (Lala Mustafa Paşa – Mustafa, the childhood tutor and companion of the Sultan).

[3] The full Latin text of the agreement is available in photocopy in the Museo Naval, Madrid, MSS 1693, *Documentos de Lepanto*.

and skilful defense, surrendered Famagusta to Lala Mustafa Paşa.[1] Don Juan had been preceded on 20 July by the Papal contingent of 12 galleys under Colonna and by the subsequent arrival of the Venetian main body of 58 galleys and 6 galeasses under Sebastian Venier, the new *Capitano Generale da Mar* (Zane having been returned to Venice and imprisoned following the débâcle of the previous year). The arrival of sixty Venetian galleys from Crete on 1 September brought the fleet of the League up to something approaching its full strength of about 207 galleys and six galeasses.[2] It should be noted here that the Venetians, recognizing the inability of their fleet to accomplish anything significant operating alone once the Ottomans had fully mobilized, had risked everything on the success of the League. The fortifications of Venice were virtually nonexistent and only a small squadron of 14 galleys and four galeasses stood between the Ottoman fleet and the upper Adriatic.[3] A sudden descent on Venice by the Ottoman fleet, a bold decision but by no means an unthinkable one, could have brought ruin. The decision to concentrate the bulk of Venice's naval power at Messina, where it would be at the tender mercies of Gian Andrea Doria's delaying tactics, was a bold strategic move.

Even before the fall of Famagusta, the Ottoman fleet had begun working its way westward, capturing and sacking Retimo on Crete in July and then overrunning Cerigo before pausing to career and grease the galley's bottoms at Navarino.[4] Aware of the impending formation of the League's

---

[1] Hill, *A History of Cyprus*, vol. III, pp. 943ff., has a full and excellent account of the siege.

[2] There is general agreement concerning the approximate total, but nearly complete confusion concerning the precise make-up of the Christian fleet. The Venetians at Lepanto are variously credited with having had 105 galleys (Weil, *The Navy of Venice*, p. 263), 106 galleys (Olesa Muñido, *La Organización Naval*, vol. II, p. 1000), and 108 galleys (Anderson, *Naval Wars in the Levant*, p. 38). A major source of confusion is the classification of the galleys of the various naval entrepreneurs fighting under the Spanish flag, sometimes listed with the galleys of Sicily or Naples and sometimes independently. Finally, and most confusing, galiots are occasionally included in the total. To compound matters, a fair number of galleys joined the Christian fleet between its sailing from Messina on 16 September and the day of battle on 7 October. Don Juan's sailing orders of 9 September, MSS 1693, *Documentos de Lepanto*, doc. 4, fol. 8–26, show a total of only 188 Christian galleys, yet as many as 225 are held to have entered into combat on 7 October. Olesa Muñido, *La Organización Naval*, vol. I, p. 371, has an intelligent discussion of this problem.

[3] The Venetians were fully alive to the menace. See the *Relazione Misier Vicenzo Morosini*, Busta 55, *Collegio V (Secreta), Relazioni*, in the Archivio di Stato Veneziano, Venice. Morosini was appointed *Provveditor Generale del Lido*, the commander of the main land defenses of Venice against attack from the sea, on 9 September, 1571. He shows a realistic appreciation of the Ottoman amphibious capability and the defensive measures to be taken against it.

[4] As we noted in Fig. 13 (above, p. 224) grease for galleys' bottoms was a major expense of galley warfare. Lead sheathing was known (it had been used by the Greeks in classical times), but a galley's need for lightness precluded its use and something had to be done to forestall the growth of barnacles and the work of the teredo worm. Frequent greasing of the bottom with tallow was the only practical solution, though an expensive one.

fleet, the Ottomans had effected a rendezvous with a North African contingent of about 40 galleys and galiots under Uluj Ali Paşa, to bring the total Muslim strength up to some 230 galleys and 70 galiots.[1]

Müezzinzade Ali Paşa had proceeded as far north as the Gulf of Prevesa when word came of the unification of the various contingents of the League's fleet at Messina. In the War of Cyprus the fleet commanders of both sides seem to have taken particular care to prevent the arrival of an enemy fleet along the coast behind them, that is between their own fleet and its bases. Apparently for logistical reasons, a way clear had to be maintained along the coast to the rear. In addition, it would have been exceedingly difficult and dangerous for a Muslim fleet caught in the north Adriatic to work its way back to Constantinople past the watchful eyes of a Christian fleet at Corfu.

Thus when the Christian fleet sortied from Messina on 16 September, the Ottoman fleet was in the process of moving south from Prevesa to the forward base of Lepanto on the northern shore of the Gulf of Corinth. When Don Juan, urged on by Venier with Colonna's support, crossed over from Corfu to the eastern shore of the Adriatic and headed cautiously south, the Ottomans were solidly established at Lepanto. Don Juan's decision to sortie seems to have represented a victory of sorts for the Venetians in the allied councils. Disputes between the allied contingents and particularly their commanders had been frequent and bitter. The Venetians were intensely suspicious of Gian Andrea Doria who had attempted to use the Venetian shortage of manpower as an excuse for inaction at every step. Venier's *Relazione* speaks well of Colonna and suggests that he and Venier were frequently in agreement on tactical matters. It speaks disparagingly of Don Juan's technical expertise in spots and accuses Doria of everything from habitual obstructionism to personal cowardice. Contemporary Spanish accounts generally speak well of Colonna, give Venier and Barbarigo (the Venetian commander of the Christian Left who was killed in the battle) grudging praise for their courage and tactical skill, and say as little as possible about Doria. These disputes were to be submerged in the battle which followed.

Though both commanders, particularly Ali Paşa, were aware of the movements of the opposing fleet, both seem to have underestimated the strength of their opponent. Thus it was that when Gian Andrea Doria's

[1] Cantemir, *The History of the Growth and Decay of the Othman Empire*, pp. 223–4, gives the Ottomans credit for 270 to 170 'ships ... depending on the source'. Olesa Muñido, *La Organización Naval*, vol. I, p. 371, following Rosell Cayetano's authorative estimate in his *Historia del Combate Naval de Lepanto* (Madrid, 1853), p. 99, gives a total Ottoman strength of 230 galleys and 70 galiots. Not all of these, however, engaged in the battle. I have followed Rosell Cayetano's breakdown throughout.

squadron, rounding Point Scropha at the north-western entrance to the Gulf of Corinth early on the morning of 7 October, sighted the Muslim fleet away to the east up the Gulf, both sides entered battle willingly and without hesitation.

Lepanto is a rarity in military history: a battle in which both sides fought skilfully and well, where the random strokes of chance which infest the battlefield were largely neutralized by the skill of the commanders against whom they fell, and where the stronger side won – though by a narrow margin and not in the expected way. Galley warfare was a chancy business. A moment of indecision, panic or a lack of thorough planning could bring sudden and complete disaster upon a superior fleet, as Gian Andrea Doria had found off Djerba eleven years before. Neither Don Juan of Austria nor Müezzinzade Ali Paşa was guilty of any of these failings.

This is shown by the quality of their planning and the calm directness of their execution. The only questionable decision made by either was Ali Paşa's decision to fight the Christian fleet at all. There are indications, however, that he was under orders to engage and his decision would have been correct in any case if his intelligence had been accurate. It is worth noting too that the considerable size of the fleets involved presented a logistic problem of the first order to both sides. That a fleet with more than 60,000 men could be supplied at all with the primitive means of the sixteenth century is surely indicative of a high level of competence and organization.

We have mentioned that each commander had the firm intention of keeping his fleet interposed between the enemy and his own line of retreat. The main fact upon which we base this assertion has a direct bearing upon the conduct of the battle of Lepanto: the remarkably assymetrical order of battle of both fleets. The respective orders of battle make it apparent that Ali Paşa had every intention of keeping his right wing and Don Juan his left wing hard up against the shore. We have unimpeachable evidence that Don Juan had made concrete plans to this effect on 9 September, long before he had any specific idea of where the battle would be fought.[1]

In establishing this point – for the Christian and Muslim dispositions were quite different – a number of facts must be kept in mind. Muslim galleys, by and large, were lighter and lower in the water than at least the western galleys of the Christian fleet and probably those of Venice as well. This explains Don Juan's celebrated order to cut off the spurs of the

---

This is from Don Juan's order of 9 September establishing the order of battle of the allied fleet, MSS 1693, *Documentos de Lepanto*, dto. 4, fol. 8–26.

galleys of the allied fleet before the battle.[1] The slightly upturned spurs would have kept the Christian main centerline bow guns from bearing down on the lower lying Muslim craft at 'clothing burning' range for a discharge at the moment of impact. Against a first-class opponent who could be trusted to form a steady line abreast before the crunch the spurs, primarily of value in a flank attack, would have been mere decoration, unlike the blast of a fifty pound cannon at zero range.

Though less maneuverable and unable to accelerate as quickly as the Muslim galleys, those of Venice were faster and better gunned. The western galleys – those of Spain, Malta, the Papal States, Genoa, and Spain's lesser Italian allies – were marginally slower and less maneuverable than their Muslim opponents or Venetian allies; but they rode higher in the water, were at least as heavily gunned, and were provided with better superstructures for the boarding fight. They were also, at least on the morning of 7 October 1571, more heavily manned. The North African galiots (there were relatively few Christian galiots present and they were kept carefully out of direct contact with the enemy) were at a severe disadvantage in a head-on boarding fight. It would seem, in fact, that Ali Paşa held them out of the main line of battle. But in the swirling confusion of a mêlée their agility and speed under oars made them dangerous opponents, able to outflank and gang up on individual Christian galleys, thus neutralizing their superior head-on fighting power. If the Christian fleet became disordered or if gaps opened in the line, the swift Muslim galiots would be able to move in among the Christian galleys – particularly the more ponderous western galleys – like wolves in a sheepfold.

With these factors in mind, the order of battle of the two fleets assumes a peculiar significance. Both fleets at Lepanto were divided into a left wing, a center and a right wing. This organization, corresponding to the vanguard, 'main battle', and rearguard of medieval armies, was a traditional one. An advance guard and reserve squadron were added to this basic arrangement as the available forces permitted and the situation demanded. The balance between the squadrons of the Christian fleet on the day of battle was as follows:[2]

---

[1] Luis Collado, *Platica Manual de Artilleria* (Milan, 1592), fol. 50. This detail is shown in at least one contemporary painting of the battle, that by Vasari in the Vatican, reproduced by Robert F. Marx, *The Battle of Lepanto, 1571* (New York, 1966), p. 36. Collado's comments on naval gunfire strongly emphasize the potential effect of the main centerline bow gun and the crucial importance of firing low.

[2] This is from Olesa Muñido, *La Organización Naval*, vol. I, p. 370. The same totals are given for Doria's and Barbarigo's squardons by von Hammer, *Histoire de L'Empire Ottoman*, vol. VI, p. 424. Essentially the same figures are given with minor variations by Weil, *The Navy of*

The Left (Agostin Barbarigo)	53 galleys, 2 galeasses
The Center (Don Juan of Austria)	64 galleys, 2 galeasses
The Right (Gian Andrea Doria)	54 galleys, 2 galeasses
The Reserve (Don Álvaro de Bazan)	30 galleys

This appears to be a symmetrical order of battle until we consider the percentage of Venetian galleys, about 52 per cent of the total, in each of the four squadrons. Without bothering to split hairs over exactly how many galleys were present in each squadron on the day of battle (the totals given by most authorities vary by one or two), Venetian galleys made up about 42 per cent of the Reserve, 42 per cent of the Center, 47 per cent of the Right, and no less than 77 per cent of the Left.

There is a partial political explanation, but it does not go far enough: one of Don Juan's earliest and most successful decisions was to separate the various national contingents and to spread them out among the four squadrons. The idea was to prevent the mass withdrawal of one or more of the national contingents as a unit under its commander at some critical point, an eventuality which was effectively prevented. But this being the case, why was an overwhelming majority of Venetian galleys assigned to one wing – under a Venetian commander?

It is worth considering in this context that the Venetian galleys which fought at Lepanto were not only lighter and faster than their western comrades in arms, but were more lightly manned as well. Venier had arrived at Messina with less than 40 *scapoli* (fighting men) per galley, 20 below what he considered an adequate minimum of 60 in the light of the fact that his *ciurmi* were armed and fought. He subsequently hired some 5,200 Italian mercenaries under the Duke of Acri and Prosper Colonna to raise his total to about 85 per galley.[1] Under pressure from Doria and the Spaniards who, partly out of conviction and partly for political reasons, argued that his galleys were inadequately manned, Venier accepted 1,614 Spanish and 2,489 mercenary Italian infantry in the Spanish service aboard his galleys.[2] This gave the Venetian galleys an average of about 120 fighting men apiece. This was still well below the level of the western galleys.

Venice, p. 263, and Anderson, *Naval Wars in the Levant*, p. 38. The inconsistencies between these authors are generally the result of reliance upon sources which give the strength at different points in time before the battle. The League's fleet gained some 20 galleys between 9 September and 7 October as stragglers came in. The total of 201 galleys which I have given here probably omits several galleys which fought in the Reserve on 7 October.

[1] Venier's *Relazione, opusculo* 3000, *Archivo di Stato Veneziano*.

[2] Venier's *Relazione* and MSS 1693, *Documentos de Lepanto*, dto. 14, fol. 73ff., a detailed listing of the total Spanish contribution to the League entitled 'Relación de las fuerzas con que el Señor don Juan se hallava'.

Don Juan had established a minimum of 150 *gente de cabo* per galley between soldiers and gentlemen adventurers for the galleys fighting under the Spanish flag (technically, this included all of the western galleys except for the Papal and Maltese galleys and the three galleys of Genoa). Many contingents ran well over this. The galleys of Naples, for example, shipped an average of about 150 Spanish infantry and 30 gentlemen adventurers per galley, a total of about 180.[1]

The disproportionate number of Venetian galleys on the Left, therefore, emerges as a deliberate weighting of the Right to provide more speed and mobility on the inshore flank of the Christian fleet. Don Juan apparently recognized that his Left, up against the shore and opposed by fast Muslim galleys of shallower draft, ran a much greater risk of being out-flanked and disordered than his Right or Center. He therefore put his swiftest and most maneuverable galleys there, reserving his heavier galleys for the right half of the line where the need to maneuver would be less and where they could deliver the superior weight of their attack in an ordered line abreast.

This becomes even more apparent when we consider the distribution of lantern galleys in the Christian order of battle, a point which has been studiously ignored by modern analysts. There can be no doubt that the distribution of lantern galleys, like the distribution of Venetian galleys, represented a conscious and well thought out tactical decision. Their superior armament, heavy manning and careful employment make it clear that they were considered a means of achieving superiority at critical tactical focal points. Their proper employment was considered an important component of victory and correctly so.

All of the *capitanas* and *patronas* of the various contingents were not rated as 'galleys of lantern', nor were all lantern galleys necessarily the flagships or vice-flagships of their respective contingents. It is therefore fortunate that Don Juan's directive of 9 September prescribing the order of march and battle order of the Christian fleet (the two were nearly the same) has survived.[2] Don Juan's order lists only 188 galleys, the most notable omissions being Gian Andrea Doria's eleven galleys, the four galleys of the Negroni, and (apparently – the writing is unclear) the two ordinary galleys of Genoa. These omissions may well have considerable political significance. Particularly fascinating is an apparent split in the Genoese contingent. Hector Spinola in the *Capitana* of Genoa, significantly the only one of the three galleys of Genoa listed in the order of 9 September, was given command of the Christian Right, ultimately

---

[1] MSS 1693, *Documentos de Lepanto*, dto. 14, fol. 73.
[2] *Ibid.* dto. 4.

Doria's post. There are several possible explanations for this: Doria may simply have arrived late at Messina, thus carrying on an old family tradition. More likely, the dispute between Doria and Venier had grown so acrimonious and Doria's delaying tactics so obvious that Colonna – ever interested in the military success of the League as a whole – was able to persuade Don Juan to press on without Doria. This presumably brought about a split in the Genoese contingent with Spinola adhering to Colonna and Don Juan and the politically less prominent captains of the two ordinary galleys of Genoa going along with Doria.

But the tactical details of Don Juan's order are of at least equal importance. The directive of 9 September lists the entire fleet in order, with lantern galleys identified as such. Differences between this order and that observed on 7 October are, with the omissions noted above, minor. Gian Andrea Doria replaced Hector Spinola in the *Capitana* of Genoa in command of the Right, Spinola moving into the Center to the immediate right of Don Juan's *Real*. The *Capitana* of Malta was displaced from its position to the right of the *Real* by the *Capitana* of Genoa and moved to the extreme right flank of the Center. It is clear, however, that the tactical concept governing the marching order of 9 September was the same as that which determined the order of battle on 7 October.

Of the 24 lantern galleys in the Christian array on 9 September, only three were assigned to the Left.[1] Even within the Left, the weight was on the right flank. Two of the Left's three lantern galleys were on the extreme right flank and eight of the ten ordinary western galleys assigned to the Left were in the right half of the line. Of perhaps equal significance, the lantern galley of Agostin Barbarigo, commander of the Left, was posted on the extreme left flank. We shall have more to say about this later.

The Center, by contrast, had thirteen lantern galleys. Two of these were on the right flank and one on the left flank. The remainder were grouped around Don Juan's *Real* in the center. Here too, the weighting of the line to the right prevailed. Twenty of the 28 Venetian galleys assigned to the Center were in its left half; ten of the thirteen lantern galleys were in its right half.

The Right was relatively evenly balanced with two of its five lantern galleys on the left flank, one on its right flank, and the other two slightly left of center. The Right's Venetian galleys were also evenly distributed, twelve being right of center and ten left of center.

---

[1] Two of these were Venetian. This is particularly significant since only 4 of the 99 Venetian galleys listed were lantern galleys, a much lower proportion of lantern galleys to ordinary galleys than in any other contingent.

It seems evident from this that Don Juan planned to use the superior weight of his own Center to crush that of the Muslims in a formal head-on fight. If the two galeasses assigned to the Center could be posted out ahead to disorder and hopefully decimate the Muslim Center before it closed, so much the better. This was the crux of his battle plan.

The Right would meet the Muslim Left head-on if possible. If not, it would do whatever was necessary to prevent the Center from being taken in flank by the swifter Muslim craft and to avoid being disordered in the process.

The problem was on the Left. Here the light Muslim craft, drawing less water than their Christian opposites, could slip by inshore to turn the battle into a disorganized mêlée where their superior agility could tell and the head-on combat power of the western galleys would be neutralized. The Christian Left was a holding operation. Here straightforward power would be of little avail. Mobility and gun power were of the essence. It was a script written for Venetian galleys.

These arrangements were curiously mirrored by the Muslim order of battle:[1]

The Right (Mehmet Suluk Paşa)	54 galleys, 2 galiots
The Center (Müezzinzade Ali Paşa)	61 galleys, 32 galiots
The Left (Uluj Ali Paşa)	87 galleys, 8 galiots
The Reserve	8 galleys, 22 galiots, 64 *fustas*

A number of facts stand out: first, both the Muslim Center and Right matched their Christian opposites almost exactly in number of galleys. This was probably because of the intrinsic limit in the number of galleys which could maintain a line abreast. Since there is no indication from any source that the Muslim Center overlapped the Christian Center, the galiots of the Muslim Center were almost certainly used as a second line to feed reinforcements into the galleys of the first line wherever needed. They are, in fact, depicted in this way in several contemporary illustrations of the battle. Finally we have the disproportionate size of the Left under Uluj Ali to deal with.

Ali Paşa must have known that he would get the worst of the head-on clash in the Center if both sides held formation. With reinforcements fed in from the reserve galiots he had a fighting chance to hang on until Mehmet Suluk or Uluj Ali turned the Christian line, but no more. There was limited room for maneuver on the inshore flank: superior Muslim agility and lighter draft might bring about a mêlée there or outflank the

---

[1] This is from Rosell Cayetano, *Historia del Combats Naval de Lepanto* (Madrid, 1853), given by Olesa Muñido, *La Organización Naval*, vol. I, p. 371.

Christian line altogether, but this was not something to bank on. On the seaward side, however, the Muslim Left could be extended beyond the Christian right flank. This could not be done in good formation – it is doubtful whether a line abreast of more than sixty galleys could be maintained while maneuvering. But good formation would be of little account if the line could be turned. Uluj Ali could maintain enough galleys on line to meet the Christian Right (Ali Paṣa must have been aware of his superiority in numbers of galleys). The surplus galiots would then be able to break off around the outside Christian flank, catch-as-catch-can, to precipitate a mêlée.

To a surprising extent the battle went according to plan – a particularly remarkable outcome given that it was a surprise encounter[1] (see Map 6). The two galeasses assigned to cover the Christian Right had the farthest to go and were still behind the Christian line when the opposing fleets met. They, not surprisingly, never seem to have become engaged. Those attached to the Left and Center, however, managed to get to their assigned stations in front of the Christian line and did considerable execution among the on-rushing Muslims.

The fight began on the inshore flank where Mehmet Suluk abandoned formation to outflank the Christian Left along the shoreline. In this he was only partially successful. A number of his galleys seem to have completely rounded the Christian left flank and Barbarigo, whose *capitana* was on the extreme left end of the line, was killed early in the fight. First, however, he succeeded in pivoting the entire Christian Left, door-like, to the left to meet the Muslim attack.

Just how this maneuver was accomplished is unclear. It is probable that the Christian galleys nearest the shore, the faster and more maneuverable Venetian galleys, actually had to back water to maintain formation. Barbarigo's physical presence at the critical point must have played a key role in the successful completion of the Left's change of heading. The difficulty of the maneuver is attested to by the ferocity of the combat: gaps seem to have opened in the Christian line (for reasons readily understood by anyone who has ever attempted to maintain a line abreast formation in a turn) through which Muslim galleys worked their way in

---

[1] I have used Venier's *Relazione* and the Spanish account entitled 'Relación delo que hizo la Armada de la Liga Christiana desde los trienta de Setiembre 1571 hasta diez de Octubre . . .' MSS 1693, *Documentos de Lepanto*, as my major sources for reconstructing the battle. Though brief, Oman, *A History of the Art of War in the Sixteenth Century*, pp. 723–37, is the best account of Lepanto in English. Prescott, *History of the Reign of Philip the Second*, vol. IV, pp. 276–306, gives a long and informative account based on Spanish sources. Olesa Muñido, *La Organización Naval*, contains a large amount of information about Lepanto scattered throughout both volumes and W. L. Rodgers, *Naval Warfare Under Oars* (Annapolis, 1939), does a workmanlike job, though one distorted by the usual Mahanian bias.

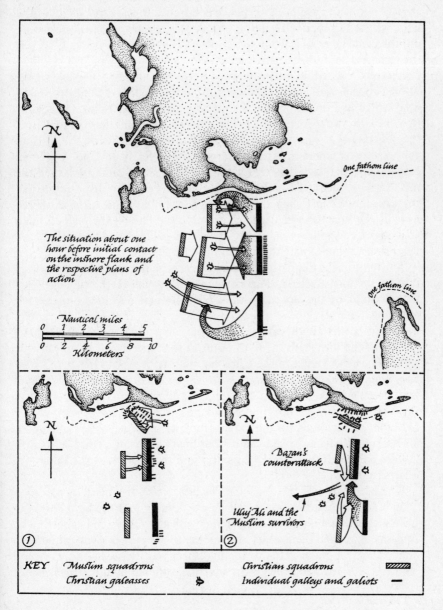

The situation about one
hour before initial contact
on the inshore flank and
the respective plans of
action

Nautical miles

Kilometers

one fathom line

one fathom line

Bazan's
counterattack

Uluj Ali and the
Muslim survivors

① ②

KEY   Muslim squadrons   Christian squadrons
      Christian galeasses   Individual galleys and galiots

Map 6   The battle of Lepanto, 7 October 1571

several places to overwhelm Venetian galleys from the flank. The Muslim archery seems to have been particularly effective in the early stages of the fight where its superior accuracy was able to tell, firing on the relatively unprotected Venetians from the flanks and rear. Ultimately, however, the greater weight of Christian metal and galleys – for Venetian skill had preserved the essential integrity of the Left's line abreast – prevailed. One of the two galeasses assigned to the Left, probably that of Agostin Bragadino which had done considerable damage to Mehmet Suluk's galleys as they initially swept past, managed to struggle back into the fray to deliver the *coup de grâce*. The fight on the Christian Left ended with the Muslim galleys driven ashore and their crews running for it on land. Christian casualties were heaviest here, for the battle in spots had approached the mêlée which Mehmet Suluk desired. But the Christian dispositions had been made with just such an eventuality in mind. Though they suffered heavily, the Venetians managed to preserve the line on the Left through skill, speed and agility where heavier western galleys would probably have been overwhelmed individually from the flank.

The fight in the Center got underway perhaps thirty minutes later than that on the inshore flank. The slowness with which the battle developed is underlined by the fact that although the fleets had sighted one another not long after daybreak, it was 'mid day' when the opposing centers locked in battle.[1] Both sides seem to have put their weight toward the middle of the line, with the Christians, at least, overbalanced toward the right. The exact center of the Christian line lay between Don Juan's *Real* and Venier's *capitana* to its left.[2] To Venier's left lay another Venetian lantern galley, that of Marco de Molin. To Don Juan's right lay, in turn, the *capitana* of the Pope under Colonna, the *capitana* of Genoa, the *capitanas* of Nicolo Doria and David Imperial, and the *patrona* of Naples, all 'galleys of lantern'. Next came an ordinary galley of Venice, a Spanish lantern galley, an ordinary Papal galley and the *Patrona* of the Pope, also a lantern galley.

The battle around the opposing flagships was particularly fierce. Don Juan's *Real* locked bows with Ali Paşa's flagship and the fight seems to have inclined initially toward the Turks with six 'galleys and galiots' (who must have wedged themselves into minute gaps in the line) investing Don Juan, some of them actually forcing their way between the *Real* and Venier's *capitana*.[3] But the height advantage offered by the *arrumbadas* of

---

[1] MSS 1693, *Documentos de Lepanto*, 'Relación delo que hizo la Armada', fol. 4.

[2] This is all from Don Juan's order of 9 September, cited above, p. 243, n. 2, with adjustment for known changes in the order of battle. There is unfortunately no record of how the Muslims posted their lantern galleys.

[3] 'Relación delo que hizo la Armada', fol. 5.

the western galleys and the greater weight of Christian metal ultimately told. For over an hour, the Muslims hung on desperately under the inspired leadership of Müezzinzade Ali Paşa.[1] Twice boarding parties from Don Juan's *Real* fought their way as far forward as the mast of Ali Paşa's flagship only to be driven back by fresh Muslim reinforcements fed in by the galiots astern. The Christians, however, were doing the same thing. The *Patrona* of Spain from the Reserve pulled up to the stern of the *Real* and, joined by the *Capitana* of the *Comendador Mayor* of Castile, fed in a steady stream of reinforcements. Finally the Muslims, fighting an uphill battle the whole way against the heavier western galleys, broke. More or less simultaneously, Ali Paşa was killed by a musket ball and a Spanish boarding party, led by Don Juan and covered by a steady rain of lead and arrows from Venier's *capitana*, overwhelmed the last resistance aboard the Turkish flagship. Defeat spread outward from this central focal point to engulf the entire Ottoman Center. Few Muslims escaped.

Meanwhile, things had gone quite differently on the seaward flank. Gian Andrea Doria, rightfully fearful of being outflanked to seaward by Uluj Ali's superior numbers, had edged out to the right, opening a sizeable gap between his own division and the Christian Center. This was aggravated by the fact that he had started out behind the Center. There are indications that, in the process of maneuvering, the strength of formation of the Christian Right had begun to weaken, allowing the intervals between galleys to widen.[2] Finally, there are indications that some of the Venetian galleys on Doria's left, suspicious of Doria's intentions and seeing the Christian Center locked in battle, broke formation to join the fight. In this they were pre-empted by Uluj Ali.

It is barely possible, of course, that Gian Andrea Doria was playing a double game. It is likely that he was quite content to keep his squadron intact while Barbarigo's Venetians on the left were getting chewed up. It is possible that he hesitated to come to grips with the Muslim Left out of cowardice, though this is unlikely both for technical reasons and in view of the fact that he fought well when he finally became engaged. The more plausible explanation is that he was simply outclassed by a superior tactician. Frustrated in his attempt to outflank the Christian Right by Doria's seaward movement, Uluj Ali allowed the distance between Doria and the Christian Center to widen, then shot the gap to fall on the right

[1] For the fight in the Center I have drawn on the 'Relación delo que hizo la Armada', fol. 4–5; Venier's *Relazione, oposculo* 3000, Archivo di Stato Veneziano; and the account in von Hammer, *Histoire de L'Empire Ottoman*; vol. VI, pp. 424–7, which is based in part on Ottoman sources. All of these are substantially in agreement.
[2] Von Hammer, *Histoire de L'Empire Ottoman*, p. 428.

flank of the Christian Center. If he had been a half hour earlier he might have turned the tide of battle. To that extent Doria had been effective.

As it was, Uluj Ali's squadron, coming fresh into the fight, piled into the victorious but exhausted Christian Center with considerable impact, quickly capturing the *capitana* of Malta and perhaps a dozen other galleys. But Ali Paşa had already fallen and the Muslim Center was in the process of collapse. Don Álvaro de Bazan came up with the still largely uncommitted Reserve and halted Uluj Ali's rush for just long enough to allow Doria's Right to make a belated appearance. Seeing the writing on the wall, Uluj Ali pulled out with perhaps a dozen galleys, the largest single Muslim contingent to escape.

The Christian victory can be attributed to three primary factors: the greater weight of the Christian Center, the inability of the Muslims to outflank the Christian fleet and precipitate a mêlée (for which Barbarigo and his Venetians on the Left must take the lion's share of the credit), and the disruptive effect of the fire of the galeasses on the Muslim array, particularly on the inshore flank.

Muslim sources have suggested that Ali Paşa's fleet was inadequately manned because of manpower losses suffered on Cyprus.[1] If this is so, and it sounds reasonable on the face of things, then Lepanto can be viewed as posthumous revenge for Antonio Bragadino, mutilated, tortured, and finally flayed alive by Lala Mustafa Paşa after his surrender of Famagusta. It would also help to explain the apparently wildly disproportionate revenge which Lala Mustafa Paşa wrought on Bragadino for his long and costly resistance.

The campaign of the fleet of the Holy League the following year came to nothing. Uluj Ali Paşa, at the head of a completely rebuilt Ottoman fleet of some 200 galleys and galiots, successfully barred the eastward progress of the Christians by taking refuge under the cliffs and batteries of Modon in a manner reminiscent of Salman Re'is' defense of Jiddah over half a century before.[2] But there are indications that the Ottoman

---

[1] Cantemir, *The History of the Growth and Decay of the Othman Empire*, p. 223, n. 19.
[2] The essential details of this campaign are given by Cantemir, *The History of the Growth and Decay of the Othman Empire*, p. 225. The *Relazione* of G. Foscarini, who followed Venier as *Capitano Generale da Mar* and led the Venetian contingent of the League's fleet in 1572, also in *opusculo* 3000, Archivo di Stato Veneziano, gives an analytical and well thought out account of the 1572 campaign. The total figure of 150 is from Cantemir while Foscarini gives the Turks credit for 140 to 210 galleys. This compares well with the report of Gil de Andrada of 16 August 1572, in the *Colección Sanz de Barutell* (*Simancas*), *Artículo* 4, dto 368, which gives Uluj Ali 140 galleys and 60 *fustas* and galiots according to one observer and 160 'large galleys' according to another. Accounts of the action off the cliffs of Modon are found in the *Colección Sanz de Barutell* (*Simancas*), *Artículo* 4, dtos. 379, 380, 381 and 382. Dto. 379 is a general account of the action which compares well with Cantemir and dto. 380 is a letter from Don

losses of skilled manpower in the War of Cyprus were severe – perhaps permanently crippling.

Spanish agent reports of the Ottoman fleet of 1572 are unanimous in stating that its personnel, particularly its fighting personnel, were untrained and inexperienced. These evaluations contrast sharply with those of only a decade earlier. One report in particular, that of a Spaniard who had been a galley slave in the Ottoman fleet and escaped, stresses the inexperience especially of the arquebusiers and archers.[1]

It is only a hypothesis, but if the Spanish still felt the adverse effect of the loss of 600 *oficiales* and 2,000 experienced naval fighting men five years after their loss at Djerba, then the Ottomans must have been severely crippled by the War of Cyprus. Even without taking into account their losses before the walls of Nicosia and Famagusta, the price which the Ottomans paid for Cyprus was high in terms of manpower. As many as 30,000 of the Ottoman force which fought at Lepanto were killed.[2] Not until the slaughter of the British levies on the 'corpse-field of Loos' in 1915 was this level and rate of butchery surpassed.

By the very nature of things, at least half of the 30,000 must have been experienced soldiers – most of the 6,000 Janissaries present surely perished – sailors, and archers. This final point is a crucial one. The preservation by the Ottomans of a sizeable corps of men who were skilled with the composite recurved bow was one of the strongest features of their naval and military establishment. At Lepanto this weapon had, as we have noted, brought the Ottomans very close to victory on the inshore flank. The loss of a sizeable proportion of the Ottoman Empire's skilled naval archers would have been a severe blow.

While the Spanish were able to train new arquebusiers fairly rapidly in the wake of Djerba, a generation was required to replace a lost bowman. If, as we suppose, the social and economic base of Ottoman archery had already been eroded significantly by 1571, then the loss incurred at Lepanto may never have been made good. All of this is tentative and a great deal of research will be required to confirm or deny the validity of the hypothesis advanced here. Nevertheless it would be reasonable, indeed almost mandatory, to begin with the working assumption that the losses of traditionally trained manpower suffered by the Ottomans in the

Juan to Philip II describing the 'difficulties which had to be confronted in order to fight the Turkish fleet beneath the Artillery of Modon'.

[1] *Colección Sanz de Barutell (Simancas), Artículo* 4, dto. 368.
[2] This estimate is from von Hammer, *Histoire de L'Empire Ottoman*, vol. VI, p. 429. All estimates of Ottoman ship and manpower losses agree closely. Some 15,000 Christian galley slaves were freed and a mere 3,468 prisoners were taken, only about 15 for every galley the Ottomans lost.

War of Cyprus signified the end of the golden age of Ottoman power at sea. Lepanto thus marked the death of a living tradition which could not be reconstituted.

More than this, however, Lepanto and the War of Cyprus showed that the war galley had reached an evolutionary dead end. The war galley had risen in response to the peculiar conditions of the Mediterranean. Those conditions left it a viable role in Mediterranean waters long after the advent of effective artillery. But as the scale of conflict grew, the war galley found itself pitted more and more against opposing fleets of war galleys. To compete tactically with its own kind, the war galley – like *Tyrannosaurus rex* – grew larger. But this growth did not enhance the war galley's strategic capabilities, rather it curtailed the galley's radius of action and sharply increased its operating costs. These trends – the inevitable consequences of dependence upon an animate source of propulsive energy – combined with the increased size of galley fleets to produce strategic stasis. The final inconclusive gropings off Modon in 1572 showed just how far this process had gone. Like the dinosaur, the galley fleet had collapsed under the burden of its own weight.

6

THE DECLINE OF THE MEDITERRANEAN SYSTEM OF WARFARE AT SEA: TECHNOLOGICAL CHANGE, SOCIAL AND ECONOMIC CAUSES AND EFFECTS

We initially approached our task with three basic objectives in mind: to trace the flow of Mediterranean naval warfare in the traditional sense (the 'big war' of major battles and campaigns), to attempt to gage the importance and trace the general outlines of the 'little war' of economic attrition, and to relate the importance of changing military and naval technology in the sixteenth-century Mediterranean to both of these.

It should be evident by now that there is a high degree of overlap between these three categories. Any attempt to deal with them independently imposes an artificial order upon a highly complex subject. The naval battles and campaigns which have received the bulk of the historian's attention – Prevesa, Djerba, Malta, Lepanto and the rest – make little sense except within the broader context of the incessant maritime war of economic attrition. The siege of Malta, for example, was an Ottoman attempt to secure a raiding base within striking distance of Spanish possessions in the western Mediterranean while, at the same time, eliminating the source of the raids of the Knights of St John of Malta into the eastern Mediterranean. Djerba resulted from a Spanish attempt to neutralize one or more of the bases of the North African sea *ghazis*.

But we must go beyond simply explaining the significance of the 'big war' in terms of the 'little war'. Both were greatly affected by changes in technology. This last point is worth emphasizing. The age of the galley was not, as has been generally assumed, a period of technological stasis. The patterns of armed conflict at sea within the Mediterranean changed markedly during the sixteenth century as a result of technological change. Technological change was an important causal factor behind the sudden growth of the great Mediterranean empires at the beginning of the sixteenth century. It was an important causal factor behind their decay at its end.

This has generally escaped notice for a number of reasons: though they were highly significant, technological changes in the sixteenth century took effect gradually, not with the dramatic suddenness which a modern conceptual orientation would lead us to expect. Secondly, changes in technology generally had their most significant impact upon the conduct of warfare at sea as a result of quantitative, not qualitative, factors. Effective heavy cannon had been around for more than a century before there were enough of them to have any significant impact upon the way in which galley fleets were handled on campaign or in battle.

This presents the historian with at least two basic difficulties: quantitative changes of the sort with which we are concerned and which occurred as far back as the sixteenth century are notoriously difficult to perceive, let alone measure. In addition, gradual quantitative changes in military technology generally exert their major influence indirectly, through interaction with social and economic factors. One of the most important effects of the generalization of heavy bronze artillery in the Mediterranean during the sixteenth century was to further increase the already rising cost of warfare at sea. The main impact of the development of efficient small arms upon warfare at sea came not, as we would suppose, directly through an increase in fire power, but indirectly through a sharp reduction in training requirements. This gave the nations which depended upon the arquebus greater resilience in the face of heavy manpower losses than those which depended upon the composite recurved bow. While it was fairly easy to turn Spanish villagers into musketeers, it was virtually impossible to turn Anatolian peasants into masters of the composite recurved bow.

All of this can be put in perspective by briefly tracing the flow of armed conflict at sea in the Mediterranean during the sixteenth century. It will become evident as we condense and assemble the points which we have already made that the impact of changing technology was decisive.

The maritime wars of the fifteenth century were, like the land wars of the fifteenth century, largely isolated from one another. They were predominantly local both in inspiration and in conduct. They fall into five categories, categories which were almost entirely independent of one another:

the overflow from land to sea of the wars of Aragon and Castile with their neighbors, Granada, France and Portugal, and with each other;

the commercial wars of the Italian maritime city states;

the wars of the Ottoman Empire against Venice in the eastern Mediterranean;

the raids of the Muslim sea *ghazis* of the various North African port cities against Christian commerce and coasts within striking distance of their respective bases, particularly the raids of the Muslims of western North Africa against Spain;

the raids of the Knights of St John of Rhodes against Muslim coasts and commerce in the eastern Mediterranean.

These maritime conflicts existed in isolated compartments which, if not quite watertight, were clearly separate one from another.[1] Even where religious motivation caused an apparent overflow between compartments, the French support of Venice in 1499 for example, the results were predominantly local.

The first years of the sixteenth century saw a series of developments which were to destroy forever this isolation, with profound economic and military consequences. These developments were predominantly, at least in the early stages, prompted by technological developments.

As the fifteenth century drew to a close, the Ottoman Empire and the nations of the Iberian peninsula were consolidating their power at opposite ends of the Mediterranean in preparation for an unprecedented expansion of their military might and geographical extent. In both cases, this expansion was the direct result of the early and widespread adoption of gunpowder weapons.

The development by the Ottomans in the middle of the fifteenth century of huge cast-bronze siege *pedreros* directly supported the creation of their empire and sustained its growth for some seven decades. From the capture of Constantinople in 1453 until the second decade of the sixteenth century, the Ottoman sultans clearly possessed the finest siege train in the world. Their tactical employment of siege artillery and, particularly, their methods of transporting and supplying it, were well in advance of those of any other nation. Their only close competition was from the Portuguese and the French. We shall say more about the Portuguese shortly. The French, like the Ottomans, consolidated their kingdom through the use of siege artillery. Though the French played the major role in the development of field artillery we have made little mention of them since their impact on Mediterranean naval technology was minimal during the sixteenth century.

The Ottoman use of field artillery was equally advanced when the sixteenth century dawned. If we neglect the highly localized wars of the Hussites in the fifteenth century and consider the first five battles in which

---

[1] C. W. C. Oman, *A History of the Art of War in the Sixteenth Century* (London, 1937), pp. 3–4, points out the isolation of the wars of the fifteenth century from one another. As I analyzed the changes which the sixteenth century brought about in warfare at sea, the aptness of his description to my subject became increasingly plain. For this and for the phrase 'watertight compartments', I am indebted to him.

field artillery played a decisive role – Ravenna (1512), Tchaldiran (1514), Marignano (1515), Merj Dabik (1516), and Ridanieh (1517) – we find that three of the five were Ottoman victories.[1] Small arms played an important role in these three victories as well.

But if the Ottomans were ahead of their competitors in the use of field and siege artillery, the Spanish had an even more commanding lead in the use of small arms. For reasons which are far from clear, the Spanish had, in the closing years of the fifteenth century, adopted the use of individual gunpowder weapons to an extent unmatched by any other nation with the possible exception of the Portuguese. By 1500 the arquebus was well on its way to replacing the crossbow in Spanish service. Gonsalvo de Cordova's victory over a French army at Cerignola in southern Italy in 1503 was the first battle since the Hussites in which small arms played a decisive role. The Spanish mastery of small arms continued to develop. In 1522 Gonsalvo's arquebusiers decimated a Swiss army in French pay at La Bicocca, the first unequivocal defeat of the Swiss pike square in open battle, and in 1525 Spanish arquebusiers operating independently and in relatively open country defeated the French army of Francis I at Pavia.

The impact of gunpowder weapons on the pre-existing international order was a profoundly destabilizing one. The Ottomans brought down the Byzantine Empire, closed the Black Sea to Christian commerce,[2] and loosened the Venetian hold on the Morea and the islands of the Aegean with the wall-smashing power of their siege *pedreros*. With the fire of the cart artillery[3] and the Janissaries' arquebusses they drove the Shii Safavids back into the interior of Iran and conquered the Mamluk Sultanate of Egypt.

[1] Ravenna was the French General Gaston de Foix's victory over the Imperialists on Easter Sunday 1512 in which the Duke of Ferrara's guns, firing in enfilade from across an unfordable canal, precipitated a fatally premature charge by the Spanish and Papal cavalry. At Tchaldiran small arms and artillery fire from behind Selim I's barricaded center, defended by the Janissaries, broke the charge of Shah Esma'il's fanatic Shii horsemen. The same general tactical recipe worked for Selim against the Mamluk cavalry at Merj Dabik and Ridanieh. Marignano was the victory by Francis I of France over a mercenary Swiss army in the Milanese service. Francis pinned the Swiss pike square in place with cavalry charges from the flanks while his prized artillery tore the Swiss ranks apart from the front.

[2] Ragusa, a Christian city but a vassal of the Porte, was the only exception. The position of Ragusa in Mediterranean history is a curious one. Though technically Ottoman vassals, the Ragusans at one time provided the bulk of Spain's naval power in the New World under contract.

[3] The Cart Artillery Corps was a uniquely Ottoman military institution. One of the five Imperial corps directly under the Sultan (the others were the Janissaries, the Sipahis of the Porte, the Sappers, and the Bombardiers or siege artillerists), the Cart Artillery Corps operated the guns which fired from atop the baggage carts chained together in the Ottoman Center. This tactical device bears more than a passing similarity to the old Hussite wagon laager.

Between them, the Spanish and the French (who were probably more advanced than the Ottomans in field artillery design, though not in siege artillery, tactics or logistics) totally upended the political shape of Italy.

But it was the Portuguese who were to strike the most profoundly destabilizing blow of all by taking gunpowder weapons to sea. All through the fifteenth century the Portuguese had systematically and experimentally expanded their knowledge of cartography, trans-oceanic navigation, and ship design. Of equal significance, the Portuguese seem to have been in the forefront of artillery development. There is good reason to believe that the design of Portuguese artillery was at least as advanced as that of any other nation in the world when the sixteenth century dawned.[1]

The combination of all of these was decisive. Before the advent of gunpowder weapons maritime commerce had been effectively restricted to the transport of luxury goods over short distances. This was because of the high cost and heavy logistic burden involved in manning a merchant ship with enough men to defend it against the attack of predatory galleys. But gunpowder upset the terms of the old equation. The limited storage space available for food and water aboard a ship capable of trans-oceanic navigation dictated a small crew. That small crew now had the wherewithal for successful defense.

The Portuguese could have reached India without gunpowder; but they could never have maintained themselves there or brought their cargos back. The same general considerations apply to the Spanish in the New World. There was a great deal more to it than just gunpowder; but without gunpowder weapons Cortez and Pizarro would have been doomed to failure from the start and the Spanish would hardly have left more of an imprint on the Western Hemisphere than the Vikings.

Why the Ottoman Empire and the nations of the Iberian peninsula, the Portuguese in particular, should have achieved so decisive a technological breakthrough in the last half of the fifteenth century is obscure at best. But the role played in both cases by a continuous and prolonged military challenge is at least worth noting. The similarity of the *Reconquista* to the process of continuous *ghazi* warfare by which the Ottomans expanded at the expense of the Byzantine Empire is a striking one.

Such an environment was a demanding one, a white hot crucible in

[1] This statement is based on the author's examination of surviving early sixteenth-century cannon, particularly in the Museu Militar, Lisbon, in addition to the usual literary sources. Not only were early sixteenth-century Portuguese cannon different in design from those of other European countries, they had – or acquired at an early date – a marked similarity to Ottoman guns. The uniquely Portuguese and Ottoman cannon designs dropped from use in the course of the seventeenth and eighteenth centuries respectively. This will be explained further on.

which militarily inefficient institutions and ideas were burned away and their remnants alloyed with superior ideas and institutions from the world beyond. In such an environment, resistance to technological innovation on cultural grounds because the innovation in question originated with a hated enemy was a luxury which could not be afforded. Both the Ottomans and the Iberian Christians were adept at cultural borrowing, though they left their own unique stamp on each borrowed idea and institution in molding it to their own purposes.

The Ottomans probably borrowed the idea of using a barricaded array of carts chained together and garnished with artillery in the center of their line of battle from ex-Hussite Bohemian mercenaries in the service of Hungary. The design of their enormous siege *pedreros* may have originated with the legendary Hungarian (or German or Czech, depending on the source) cannon founder Urban. The Janissaries, unique among Muslim military élites in that they fought on foot, may have been inspired by the Catalan Grand Company.[1]

The Spanish and Portuguese, for their part, drew heavily from their Muslim opponents in their military traditions and style of fighting. Many Spanish and Portuguese military terms and titles were taken bodily from the Arabic, for example *almirante* (admiral) and *alférez* (ensign, lieutenant). There is some evidence that the Christian Iberians may have obtained gunpowder itself from the Spanish Muslims.

However this may be, the Portuguese appearance in the Indian Ocean in the last years of the fifteenth century set in motion a chain of events which were to break down the economic compartmentalization which had kept the maritime wars of the fifteenth century isolated from one another. Upon their appearance in eastern waters the Portuguese launched a two-pronged attack. On the one hand they attempted at first to control all seaborne commerce in the Indian ocean by barring it to Muslim ships

---

[1] This, of course, is speculation. The following considerations are, however, suggestive: the Grand Company, a group of Catalan mercenaries, were released from the Aragonese service around the beginning of the fourteenth century and entered the Byzantine Empire at the request of the Emperor. They shortly turned against their new employer, devastating portions of his realm and eventually settling in southern Greece. In the meantime, however, they had soundly defeated a body of Turkish horse archers from one of the frontier emirates, an unaccustomed setback for the Muslims. Though the record is far from clear, the Catalans seem to have fought primarily on foot as crossbowmen, halberdiers and sword and buckler men. Combining effective missile fire with the staying power of first-class infantry, the Grand Company was the most effective European opposition which the Turks came up against on land between Manzikert in 1071 and the siege of Vienna in 1529. Though the theory of cultural borrowing can easily be pushed too far, it may well be more than coincidence that the only Muslim infantry élite ever created within a purely Islamic cultural framework made its appearance in an area contiguous to the scene of the Grand Company's triumphs almost immediately afterwards.

except those sailing under Portuguese permits. This attempt was doomed to failure as much for economic reasons as for technical ones. Even if the Portuguese had had sufficient resources to achieve their goal – which they did not – the resultant collapse of the commercial economy of the Indian Ocean would have hurt them more than their main Muslim opponents.[1] On the other hand they attempted to block, through the capture of Ormuz and the seizure of Socotra, the old Mediterranean spice routes through the Persian Gulf and the Red Sea.

This immediately involved them in a maritime war with the Mediterranean world. First the Mamluks, with Venetian and Ragusan technical assistance, moved to eliminate the threat by attacking the Portuguese bases in India. This brought about the merger of the new maritime war in the east with the old war of the Knights of St John of Rhodes in the form of a spoiling attack – led by a Portuguese knight – on the Mamluk staging base of Laizzo near Alexandretta in 1510.

After repelling the Mamluks at Chaul and Diu, the Portuguese went over to the attack themselves only to be repelled before Jiddah in 1517. For the next half century or so the Ottoman Empire, inheritor of the Mamluk stake in the spice routes through Cairo, Damascus and Aleppo, persisted in its attempts to drive the Portuguese from the approaches to the Red Sea and the Persian Gulf with, in the former case, a measure of success. The Ottomans, however, never threw their whole weight into this conflict. Tax revenues based on land ownership were more important to them than commercial profits and Suleiman I consequently elected to move against Hungary rather than the Portuguese in the Indian Ocean.[2] The Portuguese distaste for overland conquest made their presence there seem tolerable to the Ottomans. Still, the Ottomans had no desire to see total Portuguese control of the commerce of the Indian Ocean and the conflict ground on for nearly a century. Only when the arrival of the English and the Dutch in far eastern waters made control of the old, partly overland, spice routes increasingly irrelevant did the Ottoman–Portuguese conflict begin to wind down.

Almost simultaneously with the Portuguese opening of the spice route around the Horn of Africa, the Spanish began the conquest of the New World. Less carefully planned and less premeditated than the Portuguese expansion, the Spanish conquests had little direct impact on the Mediter-

---

[1] I am indebted to Professor Andrew C. Hess of Temple University for having pointed this out to me.

[2] See Andrew C. Hess 'The Evolution of the Ottoman Seaborne Empire in the Age of the Oceanic Discoveries, 1453–1525', *American Historical Review*, LXXV, No. 7 (December 1970) 1892ff, a brilliant exposition of the differences in outlook and objectives briefly touched on here.

ranean world. Their indirect impact, however, was overwhelming. Beginning in the 1520s, shipments of precious metals, first gold from the Indies then Peruvian and Mexican silver in increasing quantities, poured into Spain. These financed, among other things, the eastward expansion of the old Aragonese Empire and its maintenance in the face of Ottoman opposition.

In the meantime, the richness of the Spanish colonies and the commerce which they supported had attracted the attention of the French. Swarms of French privateers began to infest the Caribbean from the 1520s on, thus opening an entirely new arena of naval conflict.

As the economic effects of the Portuguese appearance in the east began to be felt and as the Spanish and Ottoman Empires expanded on a collision course, the 'watertightness' of the compartments within which the isolated naval wars of the fifteenth century had been waged began to break down.

First to go were the Genoese. Cut off from their rich Black Sea colonies by the Ottomans and therefore unable to continue the struggle with Venice on an openly military basis, the Genoese opted for economic and military absorption, first within the French sphere and then within the Spanish. The old commercial rivalry with Venice was still there, but the resources with which to pursue it were lacking. In the protracted bickering of Andrea Doria and his great nephew Gian with their Venetian allies in the Holy Alliances of 1538 and 1570, we can see the final afterglow of the Chioggian wars of the fourteenth century.

The Venetians hung on by a thread. Overmatched initially by Ottoman technology, the Venetians replied in kind only to find themselves outweighed by Ottoman resources. The initial Ottoman successes against Venice – the capture of Negropont in 1479, the capture of Lepanto in 1499, and the capture of the main Venetian fortresses in the Morea of Modon and Coron in 1500 – were largely a product of the Ottoman breakthrough in siege artillery technology. The Venetians do not seem to have had siege guns of comparable power and their fortresses, built on the old medieval pattern, could not stand up to the Turkish guns.

By the 1530s, if not sooner, the Venetians had more than caught up qualitatively. Their fortresses were as good as any in the world and their cannon were almost certainly the best, pound for pound, in the Mediterranean. But the Ottoman conquest of Egypt in 1517 had given the House of Osman an economic stranglehold on Venice. Now, war with the Ottoman Empire meant the closure of the spice routes through Damascus, Aleppo and Cairo, Venice's economic lifeline. This was a particularly grave threat in view of the presence of a competing Portuguese spice market in Antwerp ready to take up any slack which appeared in the German market. Though the tax revenues generated by the Venetian spice trade were important to the Ottomans, they were not a matter of life and death as the trade itself was to Venice. Consequently the Venetians fought the Ottoman Empire only infrequently, under severe provocation, and, if at all possible, as part of an alliance with Spain.

Spain, meanwhile, had begun to expand her perimeter to the south and east. At first this was simply an extension of one of the compartmentalized wars of the fifteenth century, an attempt by the Spanish to neutralize the North African sea *ghazis*, denying them bases by methodically establishing defensive *presidios* along the North African coast.

Two years before the fall of Granada the Spanish had occupied Alhucemas and Fedalla in Morocco. By 1510 they had occupied the Peñon de la Gomera, Oran, Bougie and Tripoli. By 1517 they had largely neutralized Algiers through the capture of the Peñon dominating the entrance to the harbor. This process of advance along the North African coast was climaxed by the capture of Tunis by Charles V in 1535.

But the Spanish advance did not go unchallenged. The North African sea *ghazis* – as opposed to the sedentary local dynasties such as the Beni Hafs of Tunis – were a hardy and dedicated breed. They had few misgivings about their ability to meet the Spanish on a man-for-man, ship-for-ship basis. Fresh and even more dedicated manpower had been added to their ranks following the first of the expulsions of Moriscos from Spain in 1500. But following the loss of the Peñon of Algiers in 1517 and Tlemcen in 1518, this last defeat being followed by the death of Khaireddin Barbarossa's brother Uruj, the shrewder among them recognized the magnitude of the threat posed by the increased scale of Spanish operations and heightened Spanish self-confidence. Outside help was needed.

In 1534 Khaireddin Barbarossa, then ruler of Algiers, solemnized a process of cooperation which had already begun by traveling to Constantinople at the head of a North African fleet to place himself in the service of the House of Osman. He had already begun the counter attack with the recapture of the Peñon of Algiers – with the aid of French artillery[1] – in 1529. His capture of Tunis from the ineffectual Beni Hafs was overcome by Charles V's expedition the following year, but Barbarossa, as Kapudan Paşa of the Ottoman Empire, defeated the combined Spanish, Papal, Genoese and Venetian fleet at Prevesa in 1538, thus repelling the Spanish from the Adriatic and further isolating Venice. Prevesa, as much as any other single event, is a clear illustration of how thoroughly the old compartmentalized wars of the fifteenth century had become intermingled.

[1] Olesa Muñido, *La Organización Naval*, vol. II (Madrid, 1968), p. 1118.

Fifty years earlier the thought of Venice, Genoa and Spain fighting together in a common cause would have been unthinkable. We should not wonder that the alliance did not work as well as modern analysts might wish.

The second prong of the Spanish advance had meanwhile brought them up against the Ottomans earlier and in a more direct fashion. In 1481 King Ferdinand of Aragon had responded to the Ottoman capture of Otranto by sending a sizeable expedition to Naples. When Otranto fell, a casualty in the struggle between Bayezid II and his brother Jem for the Ottoman succession, the Spanish moved across the straits from Apulia to Greece in almost a reflex action. Responding to Venetian requests for assistance – they had been abandoned by the French following two French–Venetian defeats before Lepanto in 1499 – an expedition under Gonsalvo da Cordova was dispatched to cooperate in the reconquest of Cefalonia in 1501.

The Ottomans, who were slowly cutting into the Venetian recruiting base along the Dalmatian coast – a land war with profound naval consequences – had thus come into contact with the expanding Spanish perimeter. By 1530 the period of rapid imperial expansion was over. The giants – Spain and the Ottoman Empire – had effectively absorbed the lesser Mediterranean powers, with the single exception of Venice, and had come into direct conflict with each other at every point. Concurrently, the compartmentalization of naval affairs characteristic of the fifteenth century had been almost completely broken down, both militarily and economically.

A key indication of the trend toward the stabilization and generalization of maritime conflict was the siege of Rhodes in 1522. Unlike the sieges of Modon and Coron in the Morea less than a quarter of a century before, it was a long, drawn-out affair and a costly one for the attacker. This was for two major reasons: fortress architecture had risen to the challenge of the siege gun and a gradual increase in the number of cannon had made artillery available for defense as well as attack.

There can be no doubt about the long-term direction of this second trend or of its importance. By the time of Vauban, cannon were available in such numbers that they could be employed in massed batteries as an integral part of permanent fortifications. The increased fire power drove the besiegers back and forced them to ground, necessitating the slow and tedious process of advance by siege parallels. The earliest stages in the slow development of formal eighteenth-century siege warfare, reflecting an equally slow growth in the number of available cannon, can be seen in the Ottoman siege of Rhodes in 1522 – expensive but successful – and

Corfu in 1537 – expensive and unsuccessful. The ultimate failure of six-teenth-century siege technique in the face of improved fortress architecture and defensive artillery fire can be seen in the Ottoman failure before Malta in 1565.

The sieges of Modon and Coron in 1500 had been quick and relatively cheap. From Rhodes on, major sieges were neither. Even the reduction of the Christian field fortifications on Djerba in 1560 was a slow and tedious business. The initial technical destabilizing influence of the development of effective gunpowder weapons had been overcome.

The destabilization which broke down the watertight integrity of the compartments which had kept the maritime wars of the fifteenth century isolated from one another was largely the product of technological change. Most of that technological change was essentially qualitative in nature. This was true of Ottoman developments in artillery design and tactics, French artillery design, and the Portuguese developments in artillery and trans-oceanic navigation.

The number of siege guns which the Ottomans were able to bring to the walls of Constantinople in 1453 or of Modon in 1500 was of secondary importance. Their mere presence there, combined with the absence of counterdevelopments in fortress design, was decisive. The Portuguese could build and equip only a small number of armed, ocean-going caravels and carracks. Though this became important later on, in 1500 it too was largely irrelevant. The Portuguese had mastered the basic techniques of trans-oceanic warfare and none of their opponents had – that was enough.

From the 1520s on, strategic gains in the Mediterranean became incremental in nature and increasingly expensive. This process, like the period of destabilization which preceded it, was largely the result of technological change. But where the earlier period of imperial expansion was primarily the product of qualitative breakthroughs in technology, the latter period of increasing stabilization was the product of quantitative changes. Unlike qualitative technological changes, these cannot be viewed in isolation since they were, almost without exception, the reflection of economic and social factors. Except in a few rare cases the resultant changes came about slowly. The only exception which comes readily to mind – and that the initiator of another era of destabilization – is the development by the English about 1543 of an industrial technique for manufacturing cannon of cast iron, a development which marked the beginning of the end of the Mediterranean system of maritime commerce and warfare.

In the period of increasing stabilization in the Mediterranean, the impact of changing technology came about primarily through its effect on the basic tool of Mediterranean warfare at sea, the war galley and its smaller derivatives. These could be used to bring about the defeat of an enemy in two basic ways: through the little war of coastal raids and economic attrition and through seaborne invasion. In practical terms these boiled down to the same thing: the attack and defense of seaside fortresses and port cities by galley fleets and the troops and siege trains which they carried.

No invasion by sea leading to permanent occupation could be contemplated without gaining control of a major port. But in practice, major invasions by sea were too expensive to be seriously considered except against an enemy who had been seriously weakened by the little war along his coasts or by internal rebellion.

The closest approach to a full-scale amphibious invasion by a sixteenth-century Mediterranean power was the Ottoman raid into Apulia in 1537. There is every reason to believe that Suleiman the Magnificent considered it the prelude to a full-scale invasion; but as long as Corfu remained in Venetian hands, there was no way to support such an invasion. When the siege of Corfu proved a bloody fiasco the threat was effectively terminated.

The cutting edge of Mediterranean warfare at sea from the 1520s through the end of the sixteenth century was therefore the little war. Raids upon coasts and commerce could directly weaken a nation economically and militarily – in the case of Venice this was eventually to prove decisive – and, at least in theory, set it up for invasion. But because of the logistically imposed range limitations[1] of the war galley and its smaller derivatives, bases nearby were needed. These had to be captured, usually from a major enemy who was fully aware of their importance and had gone to great expense and trouble to fortify and garrison them. Thus the little war, like the 'big war', depended upon the attack and defense of seaside fortresses and port cities. This meant a heavy emphasis upon siege warfare on the one hand and upon raiding on the other.

All of this boiled down to the galley. Galleys, galiots, and *fustas* conducted the raids of the little war. Other galleys defended against them. Galley fleets transported the troops and cannon needed to conduct a major siege. Roundships provided the necessary logistic support; but the amphibious capability of the galley was the critical factor in getting guns and men ashore and in standing off relief attempts by sea. Galley squadrons were detailed in response to get relief into besieged seaside fortresses.

---

[1] This was not, properly speaking, a simple range limitation but a limitation on military effectiveness as a function of range. The farther from its base a galley raided, the more space on board had to be devoted to water and provisions and the less was available for fighting men and munitions. The farther from its base it had to travel, the less effective it would be when it got there.

Where the scale of conflict was large and the number of effective heavy cannon small, as was the case in the sixteenth-century Mediterranean, the galley provided the only viable answer to the requirements of both maritime siege warfare and the little war. It made sense for the Portuguese to place large numbers of heavy and expensive bronze cannon on a single ship. It did not make sense – economically, technically, or tactically – for the Spanish, the Venetians or the Ottomans.

Arming a single large carrack or proto-galleon with an effective broadside armament would, to a Mediterranean power, have meant disarming ten or a dozen galleys. This was not an attractive choice for a number of sound reasons. Because of the peculiar characteristics of the Mediterranean, galleys could operate safely very close to the shore. They could come right up to the beach to disembark troops or guns, or right up to the walls of a seaside fortress to serve as floating siege batteries. Both of these functions were part and parcel of the Mediterranean system of armed conflict at sea. A broadside sailing warship could perform neither. It could not, moreover, prevent the galley from doing so. In addition, and perhaps most important, the ten or twelve galleys gave useful employment to some 800–1,500 *scapoli*, *'azabs*, or infantrymen of the *tercios*.

If entire fleets of broadside sailing ships capable of exercising command of the sea in the Mahanian sense could have been built and armed, the situation would have been different. But they could not. Until the advent of cast-iron cannon, a development in which the Mediterranean nations did not participate, there were simply not enough cannon available. The expense was too great. Even though the Portuguese made a valiant attempt to achieve it, command of the sea was not truly possible for a nation which relied solely upon bronze cannon.

When the period of strategic stabilization in the Mediterranean world began, the war galley had remained essentially unchanged in size, design and manning for over a century. Gunpowder changed all this. The first wrought-iron *cerbatanas* and *pasavolantes* had made their appearance on the bows of galleys in the fifteenth century (see Appendix 6). By the 1520s good pieces of heavy bronze artillery were commonly mounted as main centerline bow pieces. Numbers of light, breech-loading, swivel guns were also being mounted aboard galleys, particularly at the bow. By the 1530s, a sizeable main centerline bow gun of bronze with at least one pair of smaller bronze flanking pieces was standard. Though not all galleys were so well armed, some were armed significantly better. An educated guess would have Venetian galleys with the most complete and most nearly standardized armament in the 1530s. Spanish *capitanas* would have been the most heavily armed galleys of all, but some Spanish galleys were sadly underarmed by Venetian standards and the degree of standardization was low. The Ottoman level of armament is not clear; but it probably lay somewhere between the Venetian and Spanish standards in both total weight and standardization.

This had little impact on galley versus galley tactics or on galley versus roundship tactics. The galley had had to turn head on to its opponent to deliver an attack or to receive one even before the appearance of effective gunpowder weapons; it had to do so afterwards. Small galley versus galley fights became even more sudden and decisive than before and galleys became efficient siege weapons under certain conditions. This lack of immediate tactical impact has deceived historians. Though gunpowder weapons did indeed have a decisive impact upon Mediterranean warfare at sea during the sixteenth century, that impact took effect only over the long haul and for essentially quantitative reasons.

The Mediterranean war galley of the first half of the sixteenth century was an efficient raiding craft. Highly mobile tactically, it could work close inshore as a sort of gunboat/assault landing craft with ease. Strategically, individual galleys and galiots could mount raids as far as two thousand miles from their home ports. Entire galley fleets could engage in raiding operations nearly as far away. A galley fleet could travel a thousand miles with enough men, artillery and munitions to lay siege to a major place and return. Galley warfare was a seasonal thing; but a fair amount of raiding was done in the winter and major campaigns were occasionally launched in the months between October and March.

The symbiotic relationship between the war galley and the fortified port around which the Mediterranean system of warfare at sea revolved was, in the first half of the sixteenth century, a viable one. Then around 1550 or a little later, a number of technical, social, and economic trends which were ultimately to result in strategic stasis began to manifest themselves. All were at least indirectly connected to the appearance of effective gunpowder weapons.

Though we can trace these trends individually with some precision, we are unsure as to how they interreacted with each other. We are therefore unsure of the mechanism through which they affected galley warfare. Though we can trace several clear-cut trends which plainly had a profound impact upon the operations of galleys and galley fleets, it is impossible to say which was cause and which effect – if in fact the relationship were that simple.

But whatever the relationship between the technical, social, and economic changes involved, the net result is clear: an increase in the tactical power of galleys and galley fleets coupled with a severe loss of strategic mobility and a sharp increase in operating costs. These were directly tied in with one another. The increase in tactical power was the product of a slight increase in the size of galleys, a sharp increase in the size of their complements, and an increase in the size of galley fleets. We have already shown the increase in the size of galley fleets. The fleets which fought at Prevesa in 1538 were less than half the size of those which fought at Lepanto in 1571, an accurate indication of the general trend. The increase in the size of galleys' complements was, if anything, even more important. It was a primary factor in reducing strategic mobility and a secondary one in raising operating costs. The increase in the size of galley fleets was a primary factor in both cases.

The primary trends affecting galley warfare in the second half of the sixteenth century can be summarized under five headings:

technical changes in the construction of galleys;
a gradual increase in the amount of available artillery;
an increase in the scale of warfare at sea, leading directly to a shortage of traditionally trained manpower;
an increase in the social gap between officers and *oficiales* and between soldiers and *oficiales* accompanied by an almost complete loss of status on the part of oarsmen;
a steep rise in the cost of provisions and commodities needed to keep a man alive and healthy at sea, leading, among other things, to a marked deterioration of diet, particularly of oarsmen.

At first glance, the first of these would seem to have been dominant. The change in the rowing system of Mediterranean galleys, which took place abruptly on western galleys after 1550 and gradually on eastern galleys through the end of the century, had the effect of permitting an increase in the size of galleys without sacrificing tactical dash speed under oars. This growth in the size of galleys entailed a far more rapid increase in the number of oarsmen needed to propel them. The result was a decrease in the amount of provisions per man which could be carried and therefore a loss of strategic radius of action, the basic problem which as much as anything else produced strategic stasis. But this did not come about for purely technological reasons.

Social considerations seem to have had a bearing on the changeover since the old system of rowing, using individual oars in groups of three instead of a single large oar to a bench, though more efficient, placed a premium on oarsman skill. There is a marked correlation between the use of slave and convict *ciurmi* and the adoption of the new system and an even stronger correlation between the use of free *ciurmi* and retention of the old system.

It would be a mistake to assume *a priori* that the change in rowing systems provided the initial impetus behind the process of strategic stasis. There is reason to believe that the changeover to the new rowing system was a necessary adjustment to changes which had already taken place. A gradual increase in the weight of artillery carried on galleys, highly desirable for tactical reasons, may have combined with a decline in the quality of oarsmen to make the change imperative. It is certainly worth noting that the Spanish, whose galleys seem to have carried a greater weight of ordnance than any others and who abandoned the use of free *ciurmi* at an early date, made the changeover first, and that the Venetians, whose artillery was relatively light and who used free *ciurmi* extensively through the end of the century, were the last to abandon the old system. The deterioration of oarsmen's diets may have made the theoretical efficiency of the old system unattainable and thus irrelevant.

The gradual increase in the amount of available bronze artillery may thus have helped to bring about the change in rowing systems, accelerating the trend toward strategic stasis which it had already begun by augmenting the defensive power of fortifications. It is clear that a gradual increase in the amount of available artillery was largely responsible for the appearance of the galeass, the final degenerate step in the development of oared fighting ships and one which plainly exemplifies the technical aspects of the onset of strategic stasis.

In addition, the increased availability of cannon seems to have lowered the status of the gunner, reducing him from an elite professional surrounded by an almost mystic aura at the beginning of the sixteenth century, to an ordinary soldier or seaman by the end of the eighteenth. This seems, understandably, to have been accompanied by a decrease in skill and professionalism which is clearly evident when we compare the tactical record of sixteenth-century naval artillery in particular with that of eighteenth-century artillery. At the beginning of the sixteenth century, small numbers of cannon were used – generally decisively – with almost surgical precision both in siege warfare and on the bows of galleys. By its end, crude mass was starting to replace skill, though not to the extent that it would later on.

The high degree of skill often exhibited by sixteenth-century naval gunners becomes apparent when we compare sixteenth-century naval engagements with those of the eighteenth and early nineteenth centuries. In our discussion of William Towerson's fight off the Guinea coast in 1558, we pointed out the accuracy and effect of the Portuguese gunnery.

Hawkins' gunners at San Juan de Ulloa in 1568 used their cannon with uncanny skill, sinking two Spanish ships in less than an hour. By contrast, at Nelson's great victory of the Nile, where conditions for gunnery were nearly as perfect as those at San Juan de Ulloa, not a single French ship was sunk by gunnery (one caught fire and was destroyed when its magazine exploded) despite the tremendous number of cannon employed. This general lack of effectiveness of cannon fire, characteristic of virtually all eighteenth-century sea fights, was despite a considerable increase in the number of guns carried and in the absence of any radical improvements in ship construction. Venetian gunners of the sixteenth century seem to have been particularly good. Marc Antonio Quirini's galleys sank three Turkish galleys outright with gunfire alone in fighting their way into Famagusta harbor in the winter of 1571 – this would have been an extraordinary achievement in the eighteenth century – and nobody seems to have thought it all that remarkable.

The increase in the scale of warfare had a particularly strong impact because of the peculiar characteristics of galley warfare. When the sixteenth century dawned, galley warfare seems to have been conducted for the most part by persons of considerable experience in warfare whose lives revolved around the sea. Their traditional skills gave them a high degree of competence and an ability to operate independently. Perhaps the finest examples of this type of man were the North African *arraezes*, as the Spanish called them. Many of these men, ordinary *ghazi* captains of raiding *fustas*, galiots and galleys, rose to display extraordinary ability as naval commanders in the Ottoman service, Khaireddin Barbarossa, Turgut Re'is, and Uluj Ali being the most outstanding examples. The same sort of conditions which produced outstanding commanders such as these also produced highly skilled gunners, sailors, archers, and oarsmen.

As the size of galley fleets increased during the sixteenth century, the dominant effect on tactics and strategy of the skill of traditionally trained men was diluted. Many of these men became casualties – perhaps the most powerful effect of the major naval battles of the sixteenth century. Because their skills had been acquired in the traditional manner over the course of a lifetime, they had to be replaced by men of lesser ability and galley warfare lost much of its explosive, decisive character.

The increased scale of warfare in the sixteenth-century Mediterranean was itself a reflection of a general increase in population which affected warfare at sea in other ways. As population increased, so did the cultivation of grain. As the cultivation of grain expanded, pasture lands were plowed under and the production of meat decreased accordingly.[1] The impact of this upon galley warfare can clearly be seen in the virtual disappearance of meat from the diet of Spanish galley crews, particularly oarsmen, during the last half of the sixteenth century. It is surely more than mere coincidence that the shift in rowing systems took place as the European economy entered a period of agricultural boom during which the price of grain rose and meat became increasingly scarce. Before 1540 the oarsmen aboard Spanish galleys were allotted about four pounds of meat per month.[2] The *gente de cabo* were allotted a whopping twenty pounds a month. By 1560 the oarsmen were down to an eight-ounce ration four times a year, but the *gente de cabo* were still getting about thirteen pounds a month, a difference which is surely indicative of the social distance opening between them. By 1580, even the *gente de cabo* were down to a meager four and a half pounds a month. The writings of Cristoforo da Canal confirm that this problem was not unique to Spain. The serious deterioration in the diet of oarsmen must have brought about a serious decline in sustained rowing performance, not to mention an increase in mortality on campaign. These were surely instrumental in reducing the strategic mobility of galley fleets.

The increase in population also played a role in the general rise in prices throughout the sixteenth century. This affected galley warfare by bringing about a sharp increase in the cost of the provisions needed to keep a man healthy when at sea. Because of the unique susceptibility of price data to quantitative analysis and because of the completeness of the Spanish records in this area, we are able to trace the impact of rising prices on galley warfare with some precision.

On the obvious level, the increase in prices and the increased scale of warfare combined to place an immense financial burden on the Mediterranean nations. In Spanish service the price of biscuit, the single largest expense in the operation of a galley, quadrupled between 1529 and 1587.[3] The rise in the prices of the other edibles purchased for consumption on board ship – bacon, garbanzos, salt cod, cheese, tuna, vinegar, wine and olive oil – though not so spectacular as that of biscuit, was substantial.

The general increase in prices combined with the increased size of galleys' complements to slightly more than treble the cost of operating a fully manned Spanish galley on campaign between 1523 and 1587.[4] The other Mediterranean powers were probably not as greatly affected by the price rise as was Spain, but it is quite clear that Venice, at least, was

---

[1] This series of relationships is brilliantly explained by B. H. Slicher van Bath, *The Agrarian History of Western Europe A.D. 500–1850* (London, 1963), particularly pp. 204, 115.

[2] See Fig. 12 above, p. 223.   [3] See Fig. 11 above, p. 222.

[4] See Fig. 14 above, p. 225.

strongly affected and the trend was unquestionably in the same direction everywhere. This helped to make galley warfare an even more seasonal thing than it had been. That campaigns became less frequent and their goals less ambitious as the sixteenth century wore on is surely connected with the rise in the cost of galley warfare.

On another level, however, a change in the ratio of certain of the costs of operating a galley was far more significant than the increase in the cost of any one item in absolute terms. During the period in which the cost of operating a Spanish galley on campaign trebled and the price of biscuit quadrupled, the price of gunpowder to the Spanish crown in *marevedis* per pound barely doubled.[1] This is particularly significant when we consider that gunpowder was hideously expensive compared with the other costs of warfare at sea when cannon first made their appearance.[2]

The mechanism by which the changing ratio of prices between manufactured goods and agricultural produce affected Mediterranean warfare at sea is an almost complete unknown. It would appear, however, that the relative drop in the cost of gunpowder – about which we can make a few educated guesses – is only the tip of the iceberg. A concrete and relevant example of the impact of the change in the ratio of prices of agricultural products to those of manufactured goods, the latter reflecting the cost of labor more directly, can be found in cannon technology. We have mentioned on several occasions that Portugal and the Ottoman Empire led the world in cannon technology at the beginning of the sixteenth century. Their only close competitor was France, whose designs ultimately triumphed. The reason for the triumph of French cannon design was not technological superiority, but price, and in a remarkably indirect way.

The biggest and best of the Ottoman and Portuguese guns of the early 1500s were designed to fire stone cannonballs. French cannon were designed to throw cast-iron balls. Though most modern historians have assumed *a priori* that stone projectiles were technically inferior – a seemingly logical assumption since cast-iron cannonballs won out in the end – this was not the case.

The only technical advantage of the cast-iron projectile was in absolute maximum range, a meaningless superiority in view of the notorious inaccuracy of smoothbore cannon firing a spherical projectile. The stone cannonball, because of its lesser sectional density, created less internal

---

[1] See Fig. 13 above, p. 224.
[2] Lieutenant Henry Brackenbury, 'Ancient Cannon in Europe', Part I, *The Journal of the Royal Artillery Institution*, v, 294, cites French documents of about 1375 giving the cost of the various items connected with the manufacture of cannon. The cost of gunpowder works out to almost exactly four times as much, pound for pound, as the cost of a finished wrought-iron cannon.

pressure within the gun for a given muzzle velocity. This permitted a lighter, thinner, gun for a given projectile weight, a major advantage in view of the high cost of bronze. In addition, a stone cannonball left a larger hole than an iron ball of the same weight, a considerable advantage in naval warfare.

The problem lay in the large amount of highly skilled labor which was needed to cut a smooth, perfectly spherical ball. Cannon ball cutters were highly skilled, highly paid artisans as early as the fourteenth century.[1] The high labor cost of stone cannonballs was acceptable, even desirable, so long as labor was cheap and bronze was expensive. Eventually, however, wages rose so high that cannon firing stone cannonballs, however desirable they may have been for technical military reasons, were priced out of competition.

This thesis is borne out by the fact that cannon firing stone cannonballs were abandoned first in areas where labor was expensive – England, Holland and the rest of north-western Europe – and retained longest where it was cheap – the Ottoman Empire and the Portuguese possessions in India.

It seems apparent that this was not an isolated development, but one of many technical dislocations brought about by the creation of a worldwide money economy. The Mediterranean world, geared to a different rhythm of warfare and commerce by its own highly specialized institutions and technology, was the loser in almost every case. Ironically the Portuguese, who began the whole process, were hoist on their own petard, destroyed by the world economy which they had done so much to create.

Lepanto and the War of Cyprus marked the beginning of the end of the Mediterranean system of armed conflict at sea. The factors which we have enumerated had begun to have a decisive effect. The strategic failure of 1572 clearly showed this. The capture and recapture of Tunis in 1573–4 was the last gasp of a system slowly suffocating under its own weight. The fiscal and logistic burden of maintaining a galley fleet powerful enough to accomplish anything of note strategically had grown so large as to be prohibitive. Spain withdrew by stages into the western Mediterranean, her supply of gold and silver from the New World having lasted just long enough to stem the Ottoman tide. Venice continued to decay in place, preserved by the waning military vitality of the Mediterranean system for nearly a century until Sultan İbrahim, in a final prolonged show of Ottoman power, seized Crete. The only nation remaining with the fiscal and physical resources needed to mount a major expedition, the Ottoman Empire, was left paralyzed by the loss of the cream of its skilled manpower

[1] Brackenbury, 'Ancient Cannon in Europe', Part II, pp. 8–9. See p. 271 above.

at Lepanto. Before this loss could be made good – if it ever could have been made good – developments outside the Mediterranean intruded.

The Mediterranean system was not permitted a peaceful death. Just as it was reaching the peak of its power and efficiency, developments were taking place along the North Atlantic coast which were to overcome the intrinsic limitations of the sailing ship armed with expensive bronze cannon and were ultimately to undermine the Mediterranean system altogether.

The most significant of these was the development by the English of a method of casting relatively inexpensive iron cannon. This development was to have its impact in an essentially quantitative manner – by permitting a proliferation of heavy artillery. By the end of the sixteenth century the technique of casting cannon from iron had spread throughout much of northern Europe. As a direct consequence, the merchant ships of England and the Netherlands began to sprout growing numbers of increasingly heavy cannon. This gave them an answer to the depredations of the predatory galiots of the Mediterranean and opened to them the rich trades of the Middle Sea. Even more important, it allowed them to introduce into the Mediterranean world the bulk trades of the north, made profitable by the economy of human energy which the replacement of swords and oars by sails and cannon permitted.

The Mediterranean system of armed conflict at sea ultimately rested upon the military viability of the galley or galiot as a privateering vessel. This in turn rested upon the relative scarcity of heavy cannon in the Mediterranean world. Put in another way, a system of armed conflict based upon the intrinsic limitations of human muscle as a power source could absorb only so many cannon without losing its essential characteristics.

The war galley did not immediately lose its tactical utility with the appearance of the broadside sailing ship in the Mediterranean in numbers. But the appearance of increasing amounts of heavy ordnance mounted on the broadsides of sailing ships forced it into an increasingly specialized role. In order to maximize the galley's remaining tactical advantages – the ability to bring increasingly heavy bow guns and larger boarding parties into action in a calm – it grew increasingly larger and more unwieldly until, by the beginning of the eighteenth century, it was little more than a specialized harbor guard and short-range commerce raider. In the process, the war galley lost its amphibious capability, perhaps its most important strategic and tactical characteristic. When this stage in the technical development of the war galley had been reached – it would be impossible to pinpoint an exact date and pointless to try – the Mediterranean system of armed conflict had ceased to exist.

APPENDIX 1

THE DEVELOPMENT AND TACTICAL EMPLOYMENT OF INDIVIDUAL FIREARMS IN THE SIXTEENTH CENTURY

In the text we discussed at length the process by which the arquebus replaced the crossbow. We then dealt with the relative advantages and disadvantages of the arquebus and the sixteenth-century musket when compared to the composite recurved bow. We said little, however, about the process by which the musket developed from the arquebus, mainly because the tactical factors which influenced the growth of the arquebus into the musket were those of land warfare. Though not of primary importance to our thesis, this process of development provides an excellent example of the interplay between tactical demand and technological response.

For some time following the development of the matchlock mechanism, individual firearms remained fairly small in size. This was because individual firearms, for some obscure reason related to man's natural love of symmetry, were butted against the breastbone for firing. This placed severe limitations on the amount of recoil which a man could take and, hence, on the size and muzzle velocity of the projectile which he could fire.

Then, shortly before the beginning of the sixteenth century, men began butting their weapons to the shoulder. Like many developments of importance to the early development of practical military small arms this custom seems to have originated in Spain though we cannot be sure. The net result was the relaxation of a significant constraint governing the design of small arms: arquebusses could now be made to shoot a considerably heavier projectile than before at velocities which were at least as high.[1]

At first, however, there was little change in the size and power of at least Spanish small arms. They seem to have generally paralleled the

---

[1] Black powder small arms, like artillery, have a relatively inflexible upper limit of attainable muzzle velocity imposed by the limitations of black powder's burning rate; but because of the scale effect and because small charges burn less efficiently than larger ones, a much longer barrel, relatively speaking, is needed to approach this upper limit of muzzle velocity.

crossbow in penetrative power and effective range, gaining in popularity from their greater reliability and simplicity and perhaps from their effectiveness at frightening horses.

Then, in the waning years of the fifteenth century, Spanish armies entered Italy under the renowned Gonsalvo de Cordova. Here they encounted tactical conditions far different from those to which they were accustomed. Their Moorish opponents on the open plains of Andalusia and North Africa had been mainly lightly armored cavalry who relied on short-range missile fire and tactical mobility. But their principal opponents in Italy had weapons and tactics tailored to the more constricted battle-fields of northern Europe. They were heavily armored troops who relied almost exclusively upon direct shock action and were the finest fighting men in the world for that purpose: French heavy cavalry and Swiss and German mercenary pikemen and halberdiers.

The early chapters in the history of the development of the Spanish musket are undocumented. At first the musket was simply a 'large arquebus' to observers and it was not identified as a clearly differentiated weapon until much later. Still, it is apparent that the urgent need for increased stopping power and penetrative ability at long ranges had an almost immediate impact on Spanish small arms design. The fifty picked arquebusiers who accompanied Pedro Navarro at Ravenna in 1512 and who fired their weapons from forked rests were musketeers in fact if not in name.[1] By the battle of Mühlberg in 1547, effective small arms fire at unexpectedly long ranges was solidly established as a Spanish trademark.

That the Spanish musket of the sixteenth century was equally well suited for Mediterranean warfare at sea should not obscure the fact that it originated as a specialized infantry weapon, awesome in its power, designed to penetrate armor and stop a charging Swiss pikeman or French gendarme in his tracks at the longest possible range. While serving this purpose magnificently, the musket placed heavy demands on its user, imposed a heavier logistic burden than an ordinary arquebus and was slower to load and fire. Still, as long as armored shock action remained important on the battlefields of Europe, the Spanish musket retained its place in warfare and small arms elsewhere grew in size and power in imitation of it. The standard small arm of the late sixteenth century in northern Europe was the 'caliver' (from the French, *arquebuse du calibre de M. le Prince*, a large arquebus) of about 74 caliber.[2]

---

[1] Mentioned from Italian sources by Frederick L. Taylor, *The Art of War in Italy 1494–1529* (Cambridge, 1921), p. 46.

[2] The virtues of 'calivers', as opposed to ordinary arquebusses, were extolled by Sir Roger Williams in his *Briefe Discourse on Warre* (London, 1590).

Then, as the use of armor began to decline – to a large extent because of the effectiveness of the larger shoulder arms – the musket itself began to diminish in size until, at the end of the seventeenth century, it was no larger or more powerful than the arquebus it had initially supplanted. With the tactical demand removed, technology returned to its original level. The eighteenth-century infantry musket was lighter, easier to load, and – because of its flintlock mechanism – faster firing and more reliable than the sixteenth-century arquebus; but in effective range and stopping power it was essentially the same.

Though we know little about it, the process of development which produced the Turkish musket of the sixteenth century must have closely paralleled that which produced its Spanish equivalent. Certainly, the tactical stimuli and technological results were remarkably similar. If anything, the Janissaries – small arms specialists from an early date – may have had a head start since their opponents were armored specialists at shock action all along. This generalization applies with equal accuracy to Serbian and Hungarian knights and to Venetian and Genoese noblemen. The Mamluks, though less heavily armored than contemporary French gendarmes, were pure shock specialists and wore reasonably complete suits of mail reinforced with plate at strategic locations. In addition, the Ottomans had been opposed from the 1440s by mercenary Bohemian and Moravian infantry in the Hungarian service, forerunners of the Lands-knechts of the sixteenth century and probably just as heavily armored.

APPENDIX 2

THE EXTERNAL AND INTERNAL BALLISTICS OF SIXTEENTH-CENTURY CANNON

Many of the most commonly held misconceptions concerning warfare at sea in the sixteenth century are rooted in the seemingly obvious but mistaken belief that the range of sixteenth-century cannon was proportionate to the length of the barrel. In the text, the main thrust of our argument was to point out that the essential inaccuracy of smooth-bore weapons firing a spherical projectile combined with the terminal ballistics of an inert cannonball to make the whole question of maximum range essentially irrelevant. But while tactically valid, this argument is inadequate from the scientific and technical point of view. Military and naval historians have attached sufficient importance to the supposed range advantage of 'long' cannon to make it necessary to lay this misconception to rest once and for all.

The idea that long guns meant long range in the sixteenth century stems from two main sources: the commonly held sixteenth-century belief that this was true (at least in theory) and the fact that for modern artillery pieces using smokeless propellants it *is* true.

The first of these is essentially a matter of external ballistics, the behavior of the projectile after leaving the gun. Our most useful evidence of the external ballistics of sixteenth-century cannon should be the range data contained in most published sixteenth- and early seventeenth-century works on artillery. Ballistic analysis of this range data has shown, however, that such figures must be regarded with extreme caution if they can be used at all. This is true both of range figures in absolute terms and of the relative value of ranges given for various types of cannon.

There is no valid ballistic explanation, as we will show, for the supposed range advantage of the culverins over the cannons which the range tables in such works invariably show. If culverins did, in fact, fire at greater ranges – and there is no solid evidence that they did – it was not because of any intrinsic ballistic advantage, but for the structural reason that they could safely withstand a larger powder charge. Even this seems unlikely since all sixteenth-century cannon (except perhaps for the *pedreros*)

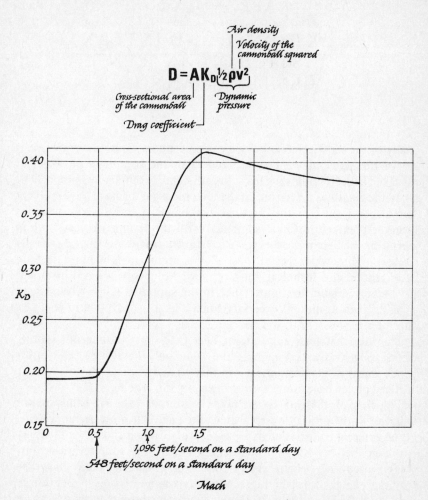

Fig. 15   The aerodynamic drag on a spherical cannonball

The drag, D, on any object is a force equal to the product of the area of the object, its drag coefficient and the dynamic pressure according to the relationship shown in the formula above. The drag coefficient changes depending on how closely the velocity of the ball approaches the velocity of sound. At velocities below about half the speed of sound (Mach 0.5 on the graph below) K_D is a constant and D varies only with the square of the velocity.

NOTE. Mach 1 = the speed of sound; Mach 0.5 = half the speed of sound, and so on.

278

appear to have been overcharged to the point that a further increase in charge would have resulted in an actual reduction in muzzle velocity and range. For reasons which we discuss in Appendix 3, culverins were rightly considered in the sixteenth century to be stronger and safer than members of the cannon class. As such, they were probably assigned to better gunners and used for 'long shots' more often than their shorter and less safe competitors; but their actual range capabilities – safety aside – were no greater than those of the shorter cannons. The unreliability of sixteenth-century range data was demonstrated by an analysis of the values given by Collado and by Diego Prado y Tovar, *Encyclopedia de Fundición de Artilleria y su Platica Manual* (1603), undertaken by Mr J. W. Kochenderfer and his co-workers in the Firing Tables Branch, U.S. Army Ballistic Research Laboratory, Aberdeen Proving Ground, Maryland, under the direction of Mr Charles H. Lebegern, Jr., Chief, Firing Tables Branch, in the spring of 1970, using orthodox external ballistic theory as stated by Robert F. Lieske and Mary L. Reiter, *Ballistic Research Laboratories Report No. 1314, Equations of Motion for a Modified Point Mass Trajectory* (Aberdeen Proving Ground, March 1966), and the accepted drag coefficients for spherical projectiles. They determined that the maximum ranges given by Collado, fol. 27, and all of the ranges given by Prado y Tovar which were subjected to analysis would have been attainable only with muzzle velocities in the neighborhood of 6,000 feet per second, nearly five times the speed of sound and almost three times the muzzle velocities of modern small arms. The general relationships involved are shown graphically in Fig. 15.

Experimentally derived mid-nineteenth-century data, most authoritatively given in the published work of Captain Thomas Jefferson Rodman, makes it plain that any muzzle velocity for black powder artillery in excess of 2,000 feet per second must be held suspect, particularly for the larger pieces. It would be premature to state categorically that all range data given by early sources is totally untrustworthy – that given by John Smith, *A Sea-man's Grammar* (London, 1627), for example, and, significantly, most range references by sixteenth-century Venetian naval sources[1] are at least within reason – but it seems clear that to the sixteenth-century gunner, long ranges in general and maximum range in particular were a highly theoretical proposition. We should not therefore expect too much accuracy in what he tells us about them.

This is largely a matter of perception: 'maximum range' means some-

---

[1] Olesa Muñido, *La Organización Naval*, vol. 1 (Madrid, 1968), p. 319. Of equal significance, the Venetian values seem to have been maximum *effective* ranges rather than maximum ranges, a far more useful concept which no one else seems to have even attempted to quantify.

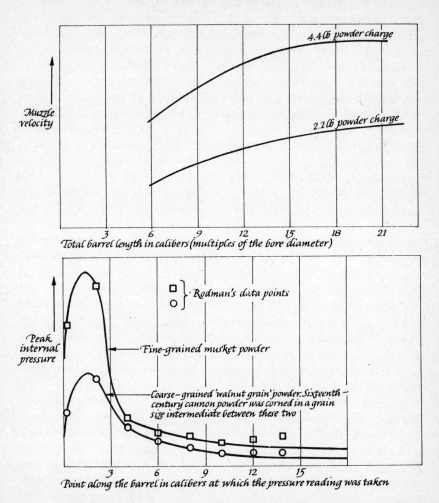

Fig. 16 Changes in muzzle velocity and internal pressure in a cannon as a function of barrel length

NOTE. The data points indicating a slight rise in pressure from 9 to 15 calibers are the result of instrumental error.

Muzzle velocity data, from J. G. Benton, *A Course of Instruction in Ordnance and Gunnery* . . . (New York, 1862), p. 29, relates to an ordinary 12-pound field gun which was progressively cut down to the lengths indicated, one caliber being the bore diameter. The pressure data, cited by Benton, p. 129, is from Rodman and was experimentally derived.

thing quite different to the modern gunner than it did to his sixteenth-century predecessor. Rather than a tactically significant figure which he actually used in battle and strove to determine beforehand through careful measurement, maximum range seems to have represented something of a philosophical ideal to the sixteenth-century gunner. Inasmuch as he could achieve nothing at maximum range except by blind luck, why should it have been otherwise? Most of the so-called range figures which he left us are therefore little more than educated guesses which reflect his prejudices concerning the types of gun which he felt *should* have been able to shoot farthest and which he himself preferred to use when long-range fire was called for.

Our second major point, that 'long' black powder cannon – the culverins – had no intrinsic ballistically based range advantage over the shorter cannons, is a matter of internal ballistics, the behavior of the propellant charge and the projectile within the cannon barrel. Most modern authors, without realizing it, have made the *a priori* assumption that the internal ballistics of black powder cannon are the same as those of modern cannon burning nitrocellulose-based propellants. This assumption is demonstrably false.

While the burning rate of nitrocellulose propellants increases as a direct function of increased pressure and temperature, that of black powder remains essentially constant.[1] The reasons for this phenomenon, bound up in the incredibly complex chemistry of black powder, are not fully understood and are beyond the scope of the present study. The ballistic effects of this difference in burning characteristics, however, are abundantly clear and have been experimentally demonstrated on numerous occasions. These are illustrated in Fig. 16.

Artillery projectiles – cannonballs and modern artillery shells alike – are driven by the pressure on their bases exerted by the gas evolved through explosive decomposition of the propellant charge. The muzzle velocity attained by an artillery projectile is proportionate to the average pressure exerted on the projectile's base multiplied by the time over which it is exerted. In more precise terms, the projectile's muzzle velocity is a function of the area under the time/pressure curve (minus friction losses which are generally negligible insofar as our analysis is concerned). But as the projectile accelerates down the barrel driven by the pressure of the

1 See J. D. Blackwood and F. P. Bowden, 'The Initiation, Burning and Thermal Decomposition of Gunpowder', *Proceedings of the Royal Society*, Series A, CCXIII, No. 1114, 304ff. This article is virtually the only sound, experimentally based, published source of information on the chemistry of black powder. For a general explanation of black powder internal ballistics in relatively non-technical terms see E. D. Lowery, *Internal Ballistics: How a Gun Converts Chemical Energy into Projectile Motion* (New York, 1968).

evolving propellant gases, the volume of gas behind the projectile expands with increasing rapidity. If the projectile is to continue to accelerate, then the burning propellant must continue to evolve gases at a rate sufficient to keep the constantly expanding volume behind the projectile pressurized.

With nitrocellulose-based propellants, the increase in temperature and pressure within the chamber acts to increase the burning rate and hence the rate of evolution of propellant gases as the projectile moves down the barrel. In addition the propellant is generally shaped into grains whose geometry is carefully tailored to produce an increase in the burning surface with time, and hence an increase in the rate of gas evolution as well.

With black powder, however, none of these considerations apply. For reasons connected with the means of propagation of the decomposition reaction in black powder (apparently through a fine spray of molten salts)[1] the burning rate is essentially independent of temperature and, above a quickly reached threshold of about 350 psi., of pressure.[2] Thus the rate of evolution of propellant gases within a black powder cannon is essentially constant. As the cannonball accelerates down the barrel, a point is reached where the projectile is expanding the volume behind it faster than the decomposition of the black powder can keep it pressurized. Extending the length of the barrel beyond this point will result in an actual reduction in the muzzle velocity and range of the cannon.

The point at which this occurs was determined by numerous nineteenth-century experiments and, according to one source, at least roughly by sixteenth-century experimenters as well.[3] Data presented by Captain J. G. Benton, *A Course of Instruction in Ordnance and Gunnery . . .* (New York, 1862), Fig. 31, shows that for a twelve-pound field gun an absolute velocity threshold was reached at a barrel length of about 25 calibers (25 times the bore diameter). Benton's data indicates, moreover, that extending the barrel length beyond 16 calibers resulted in a gain in muzzle

---

[1] Blackwood and Bowden, 'The Initiation, Burning and Thermal Decomposition of Gunpowder', pp. 298–301.

[2] This was determined experimentally in a series of tests conducted under a grant from the Department of History, Princeton University, at the H. P. White Laboratory, Bel Aire, Maryland, on 1 July 1970, by the author and personnel of the H. P. White Laboratory under the direction of Mr William Dickinson, Director, and Mr L. S. Martin, Assistant Director. While the value of this threshold pressure was only approximately determined, there can be no doubt as to its existence, particularly where dry-compounded 'serpentine' powder is concerned.

[3] Benton, *A Course of Instruction . . .*, p. 127, states that a large culverin 58 calibers long was cast for Charles V. On test firing it was found to have a relatively short maximum range. In a series of experiments it was cut down progressively to 43 calibers, gaining about 1,500 yards range in the process. The range is probably exaggerated; but otherwise the story rings true.

velocity of only about $5\frac{1}{4}$ per cent while extending it beyond 12 calibers yielded only about a 12 per cent gain. Due to the effects of aerodynamic drag, which increases as a function of the velocity squared, these increases in muzzle velocity would have resulted in even smaller increases in range. All of these considerations are shown graphically in Figs. 15 and 16.

This data is, of course, not precisely applicable to all sizes and classes of sixteenth-century artillery. The powder charges used in Collado's day were on the whole nearly three times as large as those used in Benton's experiment, a factor which was partly compensated for by greater 'windage' – a greater difference in size between the bore and the ball in the sixteenth century. The time/pressure curve in sixteenth-century cannon would thus have had a slightly different shape and the greater quantity of powder would have physically filled several calibers of the bore's length.[1] T. J. Rodman, *Reports of Experiments on the Properties of Metals for Cannon and the Qualities of Metals for Cannon and the Qualities of Cannon Powder* . . . (Boston, 1861), gives data which indicates that the optimum barrel length for very large black powder cannon was shorter than Benton suggests, apparently because a large mass of powder decomposes more efficiently than a small one. Probably for the same reason, proportionately much longer barrels *do* yield higher muzzle velocities in small arms. This probably applies to some extent to very small artillery pieces as well. Sixteenth-century cannon powder was more coarsely grained than that used in Benton's experiment (though not in Rodman's) and would thus have burned somewhat more slowly. Nevertheless, it is clear that the muzzle velocities of sixteenth-century cannon were not a direct function of barrel length. Indeed, many sixteenth-century cannon – including all of the culverins except perhaps Venetian ones – had barrels considerably longer than the length which would have produced the greatest muzzle velocity. Even if greater muzzle velocities could have been attained, the rapid rise in the coefficient of drag of spherical projectiles which doubles between Mach 0.5 (one half the speed of sound, or about 550 feet per second on a standard day) and Mach 1.5 (about 1,700 feet per second on a standard day), would have acted to level out differences in range.

Instead, as we show in Appendix 3, cannon were cast with long barrels not for ballistic reasons, but for structural ones – to give them added strength and safety.

[1] The larger sixteenth-century powder charges certainly did not result in any significant increase in muzzle velocity. A French experiment with a 36 pound cannon 16 calibers long, cited by Benton, *A Course of Instruction* . . ., p. 130, shows this clearly. When the powder charge was increased from the weight of the ball (the most common sixteenth-century charge) to one and one-sixth times the weight of the ball the muzzle velocity dropped from 1,320 feet per second to 1,170 feet per second.

APPENDIX 3

THE DESIGN AND CONSTRUCTION OF BRONZE CANNON IN THE SIXTEENTH CENTURY

The design of cannon in the sixteenth century was an empirical process, carried on within narrow limits established by the failure which almost invariably rewarded any radical departure from established practice. In the absence of a theory of internal ballistics or a theory relating stress and strain in thick-walled tubing, it could hardly have been otherwise.

In the sixteenth century almost all cannon fell into one of three categories according to design: the culverins, the cannons, and the *pedreros*. These categories cut across national boundaries with the Ottomans and Portuguese proceeding along a specialized and separate line of development in producing very large *pedreros* which do not seem to have been initiated elsewhere. The manufacture of at least the Ottoman *pedreros*, however, apparently differed from that of their western equivalents. More will be said about this later. Hybrid cannon–culverins, usually referred to as bastard cannons or reinforced cannons, were occasionally made; but by and large all bronze cannon cast in the sixteenth century can be placed unequivocally into one of these three categories. These were discussed in chapter 4 and are shown in Fig. 9.

The reason for the concentration of artillery design into three separate and distinct lines of development has to do with the basic developmental technique which prevailed in virtually all areas of technology until recent times: trial and error repeated over and over again with superior forms slowly manifesting themselves and the less efficient solutions slowly being pushed to their logical extremes to wither away and eventually disappear in an almost Darwinian process. Such a process of development, in most cases entirely devoid of any theoretical basis, is customarily looked upon with disdain by modern analysts. It can, however, be highly effective and is, in fact, the only viable system of development where theory is inadequate or entirely lacking.

In areas of technology where the critical variables affecting design are few, a unifying theory is generally worked out which is at least partially successful in defining the problem and suggesting solutions. Improvements are then made systematically as the theory suggests. If things do not work out as they should, the theory is modified and made more sophisticated; but it continues to serve as a touchstone and as a common point of reference. For the historian analyzing technological development this arrangement presents numerous advantages. The development of the theory – usually put down on paper and preserved for his inspection – gives him a built-in thread of continuity to follow in his research. He can document the changes which occurred in technology by reference to published, or at least written, works dealing with theory. Most important, he can generally treat the development of technology, through the development of the theory, in a straightforward chronological fashion.

Where developing technology has followed or paralleled developing theory, such an approach has yielded good results, but all too often historians have attempted to read a backbone of theoretical continuity into a developmental process upon which theory had little or no effect. Even worse, and perhaps more common, is the tendency to assume that because there was no development of theory there was no development of technology.[1] Sometimes this takes the form of conceding that there was development, but assuming that it was more or less accidental and therefore does not deserve closer examination. More frequently, the areas of technology where development has occurred unsupported by a well-articulated theory have simply been ignored, perhaps because of the historians' intellectual bias. A magnificent and almost unique exception can be found in Howard I. Chapelle's work on the development of sailing vessels, particularly *The History of the American Sailing Navy* (New York, 1949). Apart from a handful of works on aviation history, notably Charles H. Gibbs-Smith's superb book, *The Invention of the Aeroplane 1799–1909* (New York, 1966), there have been few attempts to deal with this sort of developmental process in any field. It is worth noting in this context that the history of science is very conscious of its identification as a branch of intellectual history and deals only peripherally with the history of technology, though much of its methodology is directly applicable to areas where theory and practice were in reasonably close harmony.

The design of bronze artillery in the early modern era is clearly a case of developing technology unsupported by a well-articulated theory. This is for a number of excellent reasons: the number and complexity of the critical variables involved in the design of cast-bronze artillery is so great as to defeat any attempt to evolve a coherent theory. Even at the present

[1] A. R. Hall, *Ballistics in the Seventeenth Century* (Cambridge, 1952), for example, is quite correct in holding that the theory of ballistics did not develop appreciably in the sixteenth century, but quite incorrect in assuming that cannon technology therefore remained static.

time, changes in artillery design – and the metallurgy of bronze is, if anything, more complex than that of steel – are empirical, incremental departures from established design practice.

One half of the artillery designer's problem stems from the amount and duration of internal pressure at various points along the inside of the barrel during firing, that is the stress to which his product will be subjected. The sixteenth-century cannon founder had no way of predicting these internal stresses; indeed the whole concept of stress would have meant little to him since he had no way of measuring it.

The other half of the artillery designer's problem lay in his knowledge of the strength which he could impart to his product by varying the thickness and composition of its metal. Even today, knowledge of the metallurgy of bronze is rudimentary and largely empirical.[1] The sixteenth-century cannon founder felt that he was best off using a melt of 80 per cent copper and 20 per cent tin, ignoring the 3 to 5 per cent of impurities of which he was generally aware, but about which he could do little. We have no theoretical basis for believing that he was wrong. First of all, we simply do not know what effect minor variations in the percentages of tin and copper, let alone variations in the quantity of various common impurities, have on the strength and ductility of bronze cannon metal. Secondly, the tin and copper in molten cannon metal partially segregate upon cooling in a complex way which is incompletely understood. Consequently, the composition – and hence the strength and toughness – of the metal varied considerably from one part of the cannon to another.

Beyond the metallurgical problems, there was no theory relating the thickness of thick-walled tubing to the amount of internal stress which they were capable of withstanding.[2] It was recognized that strength did not increase with thickness in a linear fashion, but that was all. Consequently, the sixteenth-century cannon founder had no option but to make incremental adjustments to earlier, successful, designs based upon the rule of thumb and his own empirical judgment. He was sure that care and thoroughness in preparing his moulds and in heating and mixing his metal and ensuring the purity of the alloy would produce better cannon.

[1] I am indebted to Mr H. P. George, who was Acting Director of the Metallurgy Research Laboratory, U.S. Army Frankford Arsenal, Philadelphia, Pennsylvania, when I spoke with him in the summer of 1969 and the early spring of 1970, for having pointed out the fundamental problems of non-ferrous metallurgy to me; and to Captain Wesley S. Crow of the Department of Metallurgy, U.S. Air Force Institute of Technology, Wright Patterson Air Force Base, Ohio, for having pointed out the segregation of tin in a cooling melt of tin and copper.

[2] I am indebted to Professor Robert P. Mark, Department of Civil Engineering, Princeton University, for having spent much of his valuable time and effort in the spring and summer of 1970 in familiarizing me with the basic theory of thick-walled tube stress analysis.

He was right in assuming this. But he did not know exactly why and neither do we.

The composition of the bronze in sixteenth-century cannon varied considerably from cannon to cannon. This statement is made on the basis of some 35 samples of cannon metal extracted from sixteenth-century cannon and analyzed in the mass spectrograph by the personnel of the Basic Materials Evaluation Laboratory, Quality Assurance Directorate, Frankford Arsenal, Pennsylvania, under the direction of Mr Samuel Sitelman, Chief, and a further six samples subjected to chemical analysis by Captain David S. Olson and Captain Joseph J. Delfino of the Department of Chemistry, U.S. Air Force Academy, Colorado.

There was, however, surprisingly little variation in the composition of the metal in cannon made by a given founder. This was revealed by analysis of metal samples extracted from two cannon by the same founder. For example, the pair of *sacres* in the Museo del Ejercito, Madrid, cast by the founder Wolpedacht, showed a variation of less than 0.02 per cent in the amount of silicon in the metal and no measurable variation at all in the percentage of the other minor constituents (nickel, manganese, bismuth, magnesium, zinc, lead, iron, antimony, arsenic and silver).[1] This clearly indicates that sixteenth-century cannon founders, at least the good ones, made a serious and largely successful effort to standardize their production methods. When we consider the primitive conditions under which they worked of necessity and the almost total lack of any direct means of measuring the quality of their product except by destructive testing, either intentional or inadvertent, this level of standardization is nothing short of amazing.

The design of sixteenth-century cannon seems, by and large, to have been governed by the demands of internal pressures and the strength of the metal. This is not, however, intuitively obvious and had to be demonstrated. Within the demands of space and time and the need for a simple and understandable presentation, the only modern analytical technique which showed promise for illuminating the relationship between internal stress and external design in sixteenth-century cannon was photoelastic model analysis.[2]

The results of this analysis, conducted on a scale model of the breech of a Portuguese ten-pound half culverin made by the founder Gregory

---

[1] The samples were extracted from the same location on both cannon (inside the muzzle) to insure consistency.

[2] Professor Robert F. Mark, Department of Civil Engineering, Princeton University, pointed out to me the advantages of photoelastic model analysis and led me through the experiment shown in Fig. 17. I am indebted to him and to Mr Joe Thompson, machinist *par excellence*, who constructed the model on which the experiment was conducted.

Leoffler, probably for the Spanish crown in the 1530s or 1540s, in the collection of the Museu Militar, Lisbon, are shown in Fig. 17. The three-dimensional model was machined from PL-4 resin, carefully selected for its photoelastic properties, principally the fact that relatively small changes in stress produce changes in the way in which light is polarized in passing through the transparent resin.

The model was plugged at the approximate place where a cannonball would have been in a loaded cannon. It was then pressurized internally and subjected to heat for a prolonged period of time, allowing the resin to deform slowly under the strain produced by internal pressure, much as

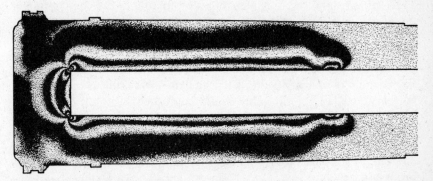

Fig. 17   Internal stress in a sixteenth-century bronze cannon as shown by photoelastic model analysis

the actual cannon would have deformed briefly under the strain of firing. The model was then removed and allowed to cool, 'freezing' into the resin the deformation patterns caused by the internal pressure. A thin slice was then removed from the model along its longitudinal centerline, polished and viewed through a polarizing filter under polarized light. Fig. 17 shows the light patterns which resulted.

The polarization of individual resin molecules within the model is a function of their physical orientation. Their physical orientation is, in turn, a function of the strain to which they were subjected. Had the model been sliced and viewed without any stress patterns being 'frozen' into it, all the resin molecules would have been oriented in the same way and it would have appeared uniformly dark, depending on the polarization of the filter and the light source. As it was, the stress patterns produced by internal strain can be viewed as alternating areas of light and dark called 'fringes'. The light areas near the outer edge of the model represent areas of little or no stress, with each 'fringe' as we progress towards the center representing an increase in stress in the material. Thus the areas near the corners of the chamber, with many 'fringes' concentrated in a small area, represent areas of maximum stress. Significantly, it is precisely here that the cannon was made thickest by the founder. Note also the slight outward bowing of the fringes between the base of the chamber and the location of our hypothetical cannonball. It was in this area that cannon most commonly burst, if surviving examples of burst cannon are at all representative. It would therefore appear that sixteenth-century cannon founders had found a way to overcome the intense local stress concentrations at the corners of the chamber. Although the advantages of a rounded chamber base, which would have eliminated these stress concentrations, were known, few founders seem to have gone to the trouble of casting their cannon with such chambers. This points up the greatest single inaccuracy of photoelastic model analysis of cast-bronze cannon – the assumption that the cannon metal was, like the PL-4 resin in our model, homogeneous throughout. In fact there was considerable variation in the composition of the bronze from one part of a cannon to another, the product of an apparent tendency of tin and copper in a 'melt' of molten bronze to segregate themselves from one another as the molten metal cools, the tin migrating towards the last portions of the metal to solidify. Thus the muzzles of sixteenth-century cannon had a much lower tin content than we might expect, a point confirmed by tests of cannon metal removed from muzzles, with the interior of the breeches being presumably richer in tin. The result might well have been a local increase in the ductility of the metal which permitted the intense local stresses around the edges of the chamber to be transmitted to the portions of the cannon nearer the outside.

It can be seen in general terms that the cannon was made thickest where the strain induced by the internal stress was greatest. These results are only generally indicative since the characteristics of cannon metal vary markedly from one part of the cannon to another and since, at least in theory, the outer 50 per cent or so of the thickness of the cannon barrel made little or no contribution to the cannon's strength. In addition, the cannon shown in Fig. 17 was cast, like all western cannon, muzzle up within a mould of baked clay (see Fig. 18). This had two major results: the metal at the breech, being cast under a greater pressure, was denser and stronger than that at the muzzle, as we have already noted. Secondly, the breech, well underground and hence better insulated than the muzzle, was last to cool. This had the effect of making the metal at the breech richer in tin content than that at the muzzle. As a result, the muzzles of

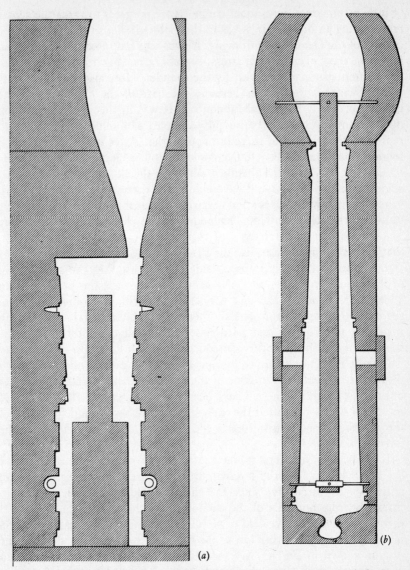

Fig. 18 Ottoman and European sixteenth-century cannon-casting techniques

KEY

(a) Ottoman practice in casting *pedreros*. The gun was cast around a core which was lowered into the casting pit. The main part of the mould was made hollow to fit over it, then lowered over the core.

(b) Western European practice. The gun was cast around a core which was lowered into the main 'sleeve' of the mould and centered by means of an iron 'cross' at the breech, which was cast into the gun. Ottoman cannons and culverins were apparently cast in the same way.

European bronze cannon are very poor in tin (3 to 5 per cent tin and 95 to 97 per cent copper is typical) and hence brittle. This brittleness explains the need for the characteristic flared muzzle which is significantly absent on the large Ottoman *pedreros* which were cast muzzle down.

In both cases the inside of the barrel was last to cool (sixteenth-century cannon were not cast solid and then bored out; they were cast hollow around a clay core). As a result of the tendency of the tin in molten bronze to move ahead of the wave of solidification, this meant that the insides of the barrels were richer in tin than the outsides. It would be reasonable to assume, therefore, that this made the inside of the barrel walls relatively ductile, thus permitting a certain transfer of internal strain to the more brittle but stronger portions of the barrel further from the center. This would presumably have made the entire gun stronger. This is extremely difficult to evaluate, however, without much additional research and testing since modern analytical techniques generally assume a homogeneous material and since the effect of minor variations in the composition of bronze gunmetal on its strength and other characteristics is almost unknown.

APPENDIX 4

COMPUTATION OF THE SPEED OF SIXTEENTH-CENTURY GALLEYS UNDER OARS

From William L. Rodgers, *Greek and Roman Naval Warfare* (Annapolis, Maryland, 1937).

1. *Propulsive horsepower*
$$HP = D_T \cdot V \quad \text{from which} \quad V = HP/D_T$$

2. *Fluid drag resistances*
$$D_T = D_F + D_R$$
$$D_F = S_W \cdot d/ft^2 \cong S_W \cdot \tfrac{1}{3} \text{ lb/ft}^2 \text{ at 7 knots}$$
$$S_W = L \cdot H \cdot 1.7 + V/H$$
$$D_R = C_d H^{\frac{2}{3}} V^4/L$$

Key

HP $=$ Horsepower required to drive hull

V $\;=$ Velocity in knots

D_T $=$ Total drag in pounds

D_F $=$ Frictional drag in pounds

D_R $=$ Residual drag in pounds

S_W $=$ Wetted surface area of the hull in ft^2

d $\;=$ Specific drag force in lb/ft^2, an experimentally derived coefficient

L $\;=$ Length of the hull at the waterline in feet

C_d $=$ Drag coefficient of the hull, a dimensionless coefficient varying from 0.45 for a broad hull to 0.35 for a long narrow hull with clean lines

H $\;=$ Height of the hull below the waterline in feet

APPENDIX 5

THE *OFICIALES*, SOLDIERS AND OARSMEN CARRIED ABOARD SIXTEENTH-CENTURY SPANISH GALLEYS

The lists represent the complement of an ordinary galley of Spain as of the indicated date. The three lists reproduced here were selected as being

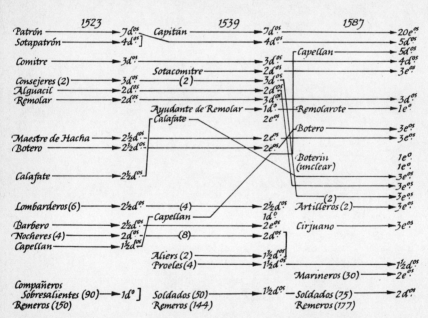

NOTE: The *Patrón* was a sailing master. The *Sotapatrón*, *Comitre* and *Sotacomitre* were roughly equivalent to first, second and third mates. *Consejeres* were skilled mariners who served as pilots. The *Alguacil* controlled the distribution of water and served as sergeant at arms. The *ciurma* was under the command of the *Remolar* and his assistant, the *Ayudante de Remolar* or *Remolarote*. The *Botero* was the cooper and controlled the galley's bottles and barrels. The *Maestre de Hacha* was the ship's carpenter and the *Calafate* (literally 'caulker') the boatswain. The *Lombarderos* were gunners. The *Nocheres* were able seamen, the *Aliers*, *Proeles* and *Marineros* ordinary seamen. The *Barbero* and *Cirjuano* served as medical officers and the *Capellan* was the chaplain.

SOURCES: 1523, *Colección Sanz de Barutell* (Simancas), *Artículo* 5, dto. 2; 1539, *Colección Sanz de Barutell* (Simancas), *Artículo* 5, dto. 17; 1587, *Colección Navarrete*, vol. VIII, dto. 11.

293

representative and retain the order of the original document in each case. The continuity of a given office is indicated by a horizontal arrow; termination of an office is indicated by a bracket to the right of the salary. All salaries are given in ducats (d^{os}) and *escudos* (e^{os}) per man per month as in the original documents. An *escudo* was worth, in theory, between 0.8 and 0.9 ducats.

APPENDIX 6

THE CLASSIFICATION AND ARRANGEMENT OF ORDNANCE ON SIXTEENTH-CENTURY GALLEYS

Though we said a great deal in the text about the quantity and quality of artillery available in the Mediterranean for naval use during the second half of the sixteenth century, we touched only briefly on the early development of artillery armament aboard galleys. Here we will briefly describe the early use of artillery mounted on galleys in order to lay a factual foundation for our treatment in the text of more fundamental issues. We will also give some idea of the rate at which the use of effective ordnance aboard galleys spread. In addition, we will describe in some detail just how the artillery armament on war galleys was mounted. Finally, we will sum up the little that we know about the armament of the smaller oared raiding craft on whose activities so much depended.

Evidence of gunpowder weapons carried on galleys, apparently for use ashore, can be traced back as far as the fourteenth century. It is unlikely, however, that effective heavy ordnance was commonly mounted on galleys for use afloat until after the middle of the fifteenth century. In contrast to the problems which delayed the introduction of effective heavy ordnance aboard broadside sailing ships, this was probably more a matter of economics than of technology. The large and unwieldy removable powder chambers of wrought-iron breech-loading bombards, the first heavy artillery to be used at sea, must have been considerably easier to deal with on the open bow of a galley than in the crowded confines of a gundeck. More important, a single shot from the main centerline bow gun was usually all that was needed and often all that was possible in a galley fight. Heavy wrought-iron ordnance was evidently simply too expensive, too scarce, and too vitally useful in siege warfare to be used to any extent on ordinary galleys until very late in the fifteenth century.

Our evidence for the mounting of effective heavy ordnance on western galleys in the fifteenth and early sixteenth centuries is sparse. The *Real* of Alfonso the Magnanimous of Aragon mounted 'two bombards' in 1481, one of the earliest examples of artillery mounted on a galley of which we are aware.[1] The fact that two bombards are mentioned rather than one or

---

[1] Olesa Muñido, *La Organización Naval*, vol. 1 (Madrid, 1968), p. 280.

three suggests that they were either mounted asymetrically – evidence of a shortage of artillery – or that neither was large enough to require a centerline bow mounting. In 1506 the *Real* of Ferdinand of Aragon mounted 'a large bombard of iron of 43 *quintales* [about 4,360 pounds], two *cerbatanas*, and a *pasavolante*', all of which fired stone shot.[1] Once again, the clearly asymetrical nature of the armament suggests a shortage; still, the weight of metal carried is impressive. The 'large bombard', surely centerline mounted, was some 20 per cent lighter than the full cannons of cast bronze preferred as main centerline bow guns on Spanish galleys some three decades later, but probably fired a considerably larger projectile, perhaps as heavy as 80 pounds. The *cerbatanas* probably weighed in the neighborhood of 2,500 pounds and fired a ball of about 25 pounds, while the *pasavolante* probably weighed around 1,500 pounds at most and fired a ball of no more than 10 or 12 pounds.[2] As we shall see, stone-throwing cannon, with their advantages of light weight and small bulk in proportion to the weight and size of the projectile thrown, were to vanish almost completely from Spanish galleys in the next three decades, almost surely victims of the rising wage–price spiral and the rampant inflation which began to grip Spain at about this time.

Our evidence for the levels of armament aboard eastern galleys during the late fifteenth and early sixteenth centuries is equally sparse, but relates to ordinary galleys and gives us valuable information concerning the methods of mounting. A German woodcut of 1486 giving a panoramic view of the port of Venice clearly shows two war galleys (in the absence of elaborately decorated sterns or distinctive banners they must have been ordinary galleys), each carrying a large wrought-iron bombard mounted rigidly in wooden balks as a centerline bow gun.[3] No additional armament is shown; but this is not necessarily conclusive since the galleys appear to. be laid up for repairs and small swivel pieces would probably have been dismounted and taken ashore. The Venetian woodcut of the battle of Zonchio in 1499 which we referred to in our discussion of broadside sailing ship tactics shows all of the Turkish galleys with a single large swivel piece of wrought iron mounted on a heavy vertical post at the center of the prow.[4] Though the simplified manner of depiction leaves open the likelihood that this piece is representative of several such cannon mounted at the bow, this still suggests that a lighter standard of armament

---

[1] Olesa Muñido, *La Organización Naval*, vol. I, p. 281.
[2] These estimated weights and ball sizes are my own, extrapolated from Olesa Muñido's figures, *La Organización Naval*, vol. I, p. 312.
[3] The woodcut is by Erhardus Reeuwich from Breydenbach, *Opusculum Santarum Peragrinationum* (1486), reproduced in Albert Skira (ed.), *Venice* (New York, 1956), p. 10.
[4] Jacket illustration.

prevailed aboard Turkish galleys than Venetian ones at the very beginning of the sixteenth century.

We can only speculate about the standards of armament aboard ordinary western galleys during the first three decades of the sixteenth century based upon the little that we know about the armament of *reales* and *capitanas*. We have already related the forward firing armament of Antonio Filippino Doria's *Capitana* in 1528: a 'basilisk', two *medios cañones*, two *sacres* and two *falconetes*.[1] These pieces probably corresponded in weight and size of ball to the categorization given in the text with the possible exception of the 'basilisk'. Though the basilisk may have been a long piece of wrought iron, it was more likely a full cannon of cast bronze. In either case it probably threw a cast-iron projectile of about 40 pounds. Interestingly, the *Real* used by Charles V en route to Italy in 1529 is said to have carried 'abundant arquebusiery and musketry'; but the only piece of heavy ordnance mentioned by our source is a single full cannon of bronze, presumably centerline mounted.[2]

Our knowledge of the armament carried by at least Spanish galleys from 1530 on is much more comprehensive. Two dockyard requisitions listing the items required for outfitting 20 ordinary galleys of 24 banks on the stocks of Barcelona in 1530 have survived to give us a fairly comprehensive idea of the standard of armament which was considered desirable and presumably attainable at that date.[3] This included a 'main centerline bow gun' (probably, from what we know of later usage, a full cannon by definition) flanked by a pair of *sacres*. The main centerline gun was certainly on a recoiling mount and the *sacres* were probably mounted on sliding carriages as well (see Fig. 19). These three main deck pieces were interspersed between four heavy vertical posts on which were mounted swivel guns. A pair of *medios cañones* (half cannons) were mounted on the innermost pair of posts. These *medios cañones* were probably (though by no means certainly) bronze muzzleloaders of the type shown in Pieter Breughel the Elder's engraving of the bow of a galley and were probably bored for about a four-pound stone ball, though they ordinarily fired scattershot in battle.[4] On the second pair of vertical posts and on a third, smaller, pair of vertical posts outboard of them (these are also shown in the

---

[1] In a letter from Paulo Giovio to Pope Clement VI in *Diarii Marino Sanuto* (Venice, 1897), vol. XLVI, fol. 666–7.
[2] Olesa Muñido, *La Organización Naval*, vol. I, p. 313.
[3] *Colección Sanz de Barutell (Simancas)*, *Artículo* 3, vol. I, dto. 25, 26, fol. 87–9.
[4] Reproduced by Björn Landström, *The Ship* (New York, 1961), p. 130. Breughel's galley, intended to depict a Portuguese galley of 1565, has no *arrumbada*. It therefore probably represents in fact either an eastern galley, a western galley of an earlier period or, just possibly, a galiot.

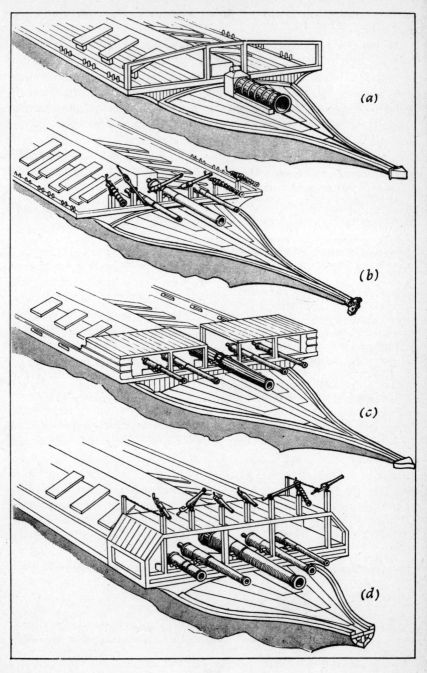

(a)

(b)

(c)

(d)

Appendix 6

Fig. 19   The mounting of the ordnance on sixteenth-century Mediterranean war galleys

Not drawn to scale, but the maximum width of the ordinary galleys depicted here was about 24 feet across the rowing frame.

KEY

(a) Venetian galley, *ca*. 1486. Armed with a single rigidly mounted bombard, probably of cast bronze, though possibly of wrought iron, and a breechloader. Spanish galleys of this period were, in some cases at least, more heavily armed, although the Venetians were probably the first to standardize on the provision of a heavy centerline bow gun for their ordinary galleys. It is probable that galleys of all the Mediterranean nations carried at least some wrought-iron breechloading swivel pieces of the *verso* type by this time; but we cannot be certain where or how they were mounted.

(b) Genoese, Sicilian or Neapolitan galley, *ca*. 1535. A Spanish galley would have been similarly armed at a somewhat earlier date. The deck pieces shown represent a 30–40 pdr full cannon weighing at least 5,500 lb, two 7–10 pdr *sacres* weighing perhaps 1,800 lb each. The addition of one or two 15–18 pdr *pedreros* weighing about 1,200 lb would have made this an unusually heavily armed ordinary galley for 1535 (though assymetrical armament combinations were not uncommon, *pedreros* were relatively rare on the galleys of Spain's possessions by this time).

The swivel pieces shown would have been typical for the galleys of Spain at an earlier date or for those of Sicily, Genoa and Naples in 1535. Working from the centerline out, a pair of half cannons (*medios cañones*), bronze muzzleloaders weighing about 800 lb each, an *esmeril* (starboard) weighing perhaps 200 lb and three *versos*, old wrought-iron breechloaders weighing about 150 lb each.

(c) Venetian galley, *ca*. 1571. Armed with a 52–55 pdr *cannone* weighing some 5,500 lb, two 12 pdr *aspidi* weighing about 1,200 lb and a pair of 5–6 pdr *falconetti* weighing perhaps 900 lb, this would be representative of the Venetian galleys which fought at Lepanto.

A galley of this type would have carried a substantial swivel armament of perhaps eight *bombardelli* (bronze breechloaders similar to Spanish *morteretes*) and eight to ten *Moschetti* (bronze pieces similar to a Spanish *esmeril*, but muzzleloaders); but inasmuch as the way in which they were mounted is unclear, we have omitted them.

Ottoman galleys of the same period would have been similarly armed (though the individual pieces would have weighed a bit more relative to their projectile weight) and would have had a generally similar appearance. In place of the temporary fighting structure shown here (the longitudinal planks were removable), Muslim galleys seem to have had a lower permanent structure which covered a smaller area, leaving the breeches of the cannon exposed.

(d) Spanish galley, *ca*. 1571. Note that the 'spur' has been cut off, as in the case of Don Juan's celebrated order at Lepanto, to allow the main centerline piece to depress fully. The *arrumbada* has not been barricaded with planking and cordage.

The pieces shown represent a 40–50 pdr full cannon weighing about 5,000–6,000 lb, a pair of 7–13 pdr *sacres* weighing 1,500–1,800 lb each and a *pedrero* (starboard) firing an 18–20 lb ball and weighing about 1,200–1,500 lb, plus a half *sacre* (port) weighing around 1,000 lb and firing a 4–5 lb ball. The swivel pieces atop the *arrumbada* are, from left to right, a bronze breechloading *morterete*, a bronze *verso*, two more *morteretes*, a bronze breechloading *esmeril*, another *verso* and another *morterete*. A lantern galley would have had an additional pair of flanking deck pieces, perhaps another *pedrero* and another half *sacre*, or perhaps two more half *sacres*.

Breughel engraving) were mounted *esmeriles*. These were breechloaders, probably of bronze, weighing about 400 pounds and with a bore diameter of about an inch to an inch and a half. At about the twelfth bank back on the starboard side, where a rowing bench was customarily omitted to provide storage space for the skiff, a *medio cañon* was mounted. A similar piece was mounted in the space provided for the cookstove at about the eighteenth bank back on the port side. The poop was armed with eight *esmeriles* and two *morteretes* (short breechloading swivel pieces weighing perhaps 150 pounds and designed exclusively to throw scattershot) on post mounts. Two additional *morteretes* were intended 'for the prow', though just where they were to be mounted is unclear. If ordinary Spanish galleys were provided with an *arrumbada* by 1530 these *morteretes* were probably mounted atop it; but on balance it seems unlikely that this was the case.

By 1536 the actual armament carried by Spanish galleys had surpassed the desired level of 1530 and the armament of the galleys of the Italian client states of Spain had almost exactly equalled it, suggesting a rapid increase in available artillery during this period. This is shown by the inventory of armament of the galleys of Spain, Sicily, Antonio Doria, Monaco and Terranova which we have already cited.[1] In addition, the desired armament of Spanish galleys, as examination of the most heavily armed of the galleys of Spain shows, had expanded to include a pair of half culverins flanking the main centerline bow gun in addition to the pair of *sacres*. This desired standard of armament, however, was far from being fully realized. Of the thirteen galleys of Spain included in the 1536 inventory only eight had both a pair of half culverins and a pair of *sacres*. Two more had their pair of half culverins, but one of these had only a single *sacre* and one had none. An additional galley of Spain had no half culverins, but mounted three *sacres* forward. These examples suggest an inability to achieve a desired standard, indicative of a shortage of ordnance. Even more indicative of this presumed shortage is the fact, already noted in the text, that one of the galleys of Spain mounted only swivel pieces in addition to the main centerline bow gun.

But the strengths shown by the 1536 inventory should be noted as well. Three of the galleys of Spain including Don Álvaro de Bazan's *Capitana* would have rated as lantern galleys twenty or even thirty years later. Each of these had no less than three pairs of deck-mounted cannon flanking the main centerline bow gun: Bazan's *Capitana* had two half culverins, three *sacres* and a *pedrero* (significantly, the only *pedrero* noted), the second

---

[1] See above, p. 230. This is from the *Colección Sanz de Barutell (Simancas), Artículo* 4, vol. I, dto. 42, fol. 121–7.

galley had a pair of half *sacres* in addition to its half culverins and *sacres*, and the third had no less than four half culverins plus the usual pair of *sacres*.

Certain peculiarities in the quantity and apparent location of the secondary armament aboard the galleys of Spain suggest that the *arrumbada*, as shown on the Flemish tapestries depicting Charles V's conquest of Tunis in 1535, was a feature of most, if not all, Spanish galleys by 1536. If this theory is correct, then the *arrumbada* was ideally armed with eight *morteretes* or the equivalent, though four were generally settled for and many galleys had even less. There is no suggestion – and it must be emphasized that our theory rests solely on the fact that the items in the armament inventory were listed in order of their physical placement on the galley – that the galleys of Sicily and of Spain's lesser Italian client states had an *arrumbada* at this time, though they were to acquire one shortly.

Finally, the squadron of twenty-three galleys covered by the Spanish inventory of 1536 appears to have carried a modest siege train of two half culverins and two *sacres*. This stands in sharp contrast to the siege train of 'up to thirty-four pieces of bronze . . . for battery on land and for the breaching of castles' carried by Khaireddin Barbarossa's squadron of 51 galleys two years earlier.[1] This difference would appear to have been an accurate reflection of Spain's essentially defensive strategic preoccupations and the Ottoman Empire's basically offensive strategic posture. Of equal interest, the same source tells us that none of the 51 galleys except Barbarossa's *capitana* carried cannon designed to 'throw iron', but that they carried only *pedreros*. This, even if only an accurate generalization, gives us an indication of the timing of the impact of the wage–price spiral which ultimately undercut the tactical advantages of the *pedrero* throughout the Mediterranean: we know that only 17 *pedreros* were counted among 390 Muslim cannon captured at Lepanto.

Little of a more specific nature can be said about the ordnance carried by Ottoman galleys during the early 1500s. The 'standard' armament of a main centerline bow gun (*baş topu*), four large swivel pieces (*darbezen*) and eight smaller ones (*prangi*) which Haydar Alpagut gives us for a *kadirga* (ordinary galley) must date from the beginning of the century; but we cannot be sure of the date.[2] Cristoforo da Canal, writing around 1540, considered an iron-throwing 52-pound cannon to be a 'typical' main centerline bow gun for an Ottoman galley.[3] The main centerline bow guns

[1] *Colección Sanz de Barutell (Simancas), Artículo* 6, dto. 20, fol. 41–2.
[2] *Denizde Türkiye* (Istanbul, 1937), p. 625.
[3] Cited by Olesa Muñido, *La Organización Naval*, vol. I, p. 318.

of Ottoman galleys appear by this time to have been flanked by two deck pieces (*şayka topu*) which were roughly equivalent to *sacres* in total weight, but probably threw a somewhat larger projectile.

The tendency toward a lighter, but relatively more effective, artillery armament aboard eastern galleys during the first decades of the sixteenth century which our evidence seems to suggest is specifically confirmed for ordinary Venetian galleys by Cristoforo da Canal's proposed 'standard' armament of 1540.[1] In the light of his military experience and political sagacity the armament which he proposed was probably not far from attainable reality. It was centered around a 52-pound culverin for the main centerline bow gun, flanked by two twelve-pound *sacres*. These three cannon would have thrown almost exactly the same combined weight of ball as the full cannon, two half culverins and two *sacres* on one of Bazan's better armed galleys of 1536, but would have weighed much less. The secondary armament was to consist of four three-pound *falconetti*, almost surely swivel mounted on the four heavy vertical posts at the bow, six *bombardelle* (probably similar to Spanish *morteretes*) and eight *moschetti* (similar to the Spanish *esmeriles*).

Our knowledge of the armament of ordinary galleys from the middle of the sixteenth century on is fairly complete and was dealt with in the text. But our knowledge of the armament carried by the smaller raiding craft is deficient because of a lack of sources. This is unfortunate since a number of basic questions relating to the viability of the Mediterranean system of warfare at sea at any given point in time can be answered only through a comparative evaluation of the armament of oared raiding craft – principally galiots and *bergantins* – and that of the merchant craft which were their prey.

We know from the record of Muslim raiding craft captured by forces under the command of Don Álvaro de Bazan that, at least during the 1560s, 70s, and 80s, Muslim galiots of eighteen rowing banks and above carried a centerline cannon large enough to 'count' (probably larger than a *sacre*) and that smaller galiots and *bergantins* did not.[2] This is confirmed by a Spanish report of 1561 concerning the four galiots of the Paşa of Vélez in North Africa.[3] Of the four galiots, the Paşa's *capitana* of 21 banks carried a main centerline bow gun of '38 *quintales*'; the *patrona*, also of 21 banks, carried a centerline piece which was only slightly smaller; the third galiot, of eighteen banks, carried a piece of '25 *quintales*'; and the

---

[1] From da Canal's *Della Milizia Maritima*, cited by Olesa Muñido, *La Organización Naval*, vol. I, p. 322.

[2] *Colección Navarrete*, vol. x, dto. 7, fol. 48.

[3] *Colección Sanz de Barutell* (Simancas), *Artículo* 6, dto. 45, fol. 117–18. This is from a Spaniard who had been captured, served as a galley slave on the Paşa's galiots, and then escaped.

fourth galiot, of seventeen banks, carried no artillery at all. The two largest galiots thus carried a centerline piece equivalent to a small full cannon or a very large half culverin, very respectable armament indeed, while the third carried a piece as large as a half culverin. No flanking pieces or swivel guns are mentioned and, from the nature of the report, there probably were none, the Muslim fighting men relying upon their muskets and bows (which *are* mentioned) for covering fire in the assault.

By contrast, we know that a Spanish galiot of at least nineteen or twenty banks stationed off La Goleta in 1546 carried a *sacre* weighing 2,140 pounds, two half *sacres* of unspecified weight, and four bronze *versos* with two chambers each.[1] Though too much could be made of such scattered data, this suggests that eastern and Muslim galiots, like eastern galleys, carried about the same total weight of artillery as their western equivalents or perhaps a bit less, but carried it in a smaller number of relatively lighter pieces with larger bore diameters.

[1] *Colección Sanz de Barutell (Simancas), Artículo* 4, vol. 1, dto. 138, fol. 421.

SOURCES AND BIBLIOGRAPHY

ARCHIVAL COLLECTIONS

Archivo di Stato Veneziano, Frarii, Venice.
Biblioteca Nacional, Avenida de Calvo Sotelo 20, Madrid.
Museo Naval, Ministerio de Marina, Montalbán 2, Madrid.

UNPUBLISHED SOURCE DOCUMENTS AND COLLECTIONS OF SOURCE
DOCUMENTS

Colección Navarrete, Museo Naval, Madrid (compiled under the direction of Teniente
de Navio Fernandez de Navarrete *ca.* 1789–95; originally in 44 volumes of which
29 survive along with three additional volumes of reconstituted fragments; Index).
Colección Sanz de Barutell (*Simancas*), Museo Naval, Madrid (compiled under the
direction of Teniente de Navio Don Juan Sanz y de Barutell *ca.* 1789–95; 6
Articulos of from one to four volumes each; Index; also *Colección Sanz de Barutell*
(*Barcelona*), Biblioteca de la Academia Nacional, Madrid, dealing with the maritime affairs of the Kingdom of Aragon prior to the union with Castile).
Colección Vargas Ponce, Museo Naval, Madrid (compiled in the same manner and time
frame as the *Colección Navarrete* and the *Colección Sanz de Barutell*; 3 volumes
with self-contained indices).
Documentos de Lepanto, Manuscrito 1693, Museo Naval, Madrid (an extensive collection
of primary source documents, both in the original and in photocopy, dealing with
the battle of Lepanto).
Pereira do Valle, Henrique, an untitled collection relating to early artillery in the
Museu Militar, Lisbon (an extensive collection of data compiled by General
Pereira do Valle containing physical measurements and extensive analytical
comments relating to the characteristics, categorization, origins and historical
significance of cannon in the collection of the Museu Militar).
Venier, Sebastian, *Notice of and Extracts from the Report Presented to the Doge and
Senate of Venice by Sebastian Venier, Captain General of the Fleet of the Republic
at Lepanto, on his Return from Service*, on 29 December, 1572, Rawdon Brown,
trans., *opusculo* 3000, Archivo di Stato Veneziano.

PUBLISHED PRIMARY SOURCES AND COLLECTIONS OF SOURCE DOCUMENTS

Balbi di Correggio, Francisco, *The Siege of Malta, 1565*, Ernle Bradford trans., from
the Barcelona 1568 ed. (London, 1965).
Hakluyt, Richard, *The Principall Navigations Voiages Traffiques and Discoveries of the
English Nation*, 12 vols. (Glasgow, 1903–5).
Marteilhe, Jean de Bergerac, *Galley Slave* (London, 1957).

Rosi, M., *Nuovi Documenti Relativi alla Liberazione dei Principali Prigionieri Turchi Presi a Lepanto* (Rome, 1901).

Schuman, L. O., *Political History of the Yemen at the Beginning of the Sixteenth Century* (Amsterdam, 1961).

Serjeant, R. B., *The Portuguese off the South Arabian Coast: Hadrami Chronicles* (Oxford, 1963).

CONTEMPORARY AND NEAR CONTEMPORARY HISTORIES AND OTHER RELEVANT WORKS

de Barros, Joao, *Da Ásia, Terceira decada* (Lisbon, 1563).

Bastav, Serif, *Ordo Portae, Description Grecque de la Porte et de l'Armée du Sultan Mehmed II* (Budapest, 1947).

Cantemir, Demetrius. *The History of the Growth and Decay of the Othman Empire*, N. Tindal trans. (London, 1734).

Chalcondyle, *Histoire Générale des Turcs* (Paris, 1662).

Garcia de Palacio, Diego, *Instrucción Nautica Para Navegar*, facsimile ed. from the Mexico City edition of 1587 (Madrid, 1944).

Guicciardini, Francesco, *The History of Italy*, Sydney Alexander trans. (New York, 1969).

Katib Chelebi [Haji Kahlifeh], *The History of the Maritime Wars of the Turks*, James Mitchell trans. (London, 1831).

Knolles, Richard and Sir Paul Rycaut, *The Turkish History* (London, 1687).

Kritovolous, *History of Mehmed the Conqueror*, Charles T. Riggs trans. (Princeton, 1954).

de Medina, Pedro, *Regimiento de Navegación* (Seville, 1563), facsimile ed. (Madrid, 1964).

Pantera, Pantero, *L'Armata Navale* (Rome, 1914).

Sanuto, Marino, *I Diarii Marino Sanuto* (Venice, 1897).

CONTEMPORARY WORKS DEALING WITH CANNON FOUNDING, GUNNERY AND BALLISTICS

Biringuccio, Vannoccio, *The Pirotechnia*, Cyril S. Smith and Martha T. Gnudi trans. (New York, 1943).

Collado, Luis, *Pratica Manuale di Arteglieria* (Venice, 1586).
Platica Manual de Artilleria (Milan, 1592).

Tartaglia, Niccolo, *La Nova Scientia de Nicolo Tartaglia* (Venice, 1558).
Three Bookes of Colloquies Concerning the Arte of Shooting in Great and Small Peeces of Artillerie ... Cyprian Lucar trans. (London, 1588).

Vauban, Sebastien Le Prestre, de, *De l'attaque et de la défense des places* (Le Haye, 1737).
A Manual of Siegecraft and Fortification, George A. Rothrock trans. (Ann Arbor, Michigan, 1968).

MODERN WORKS DEALING WITH THE THEORY OF METALLURGY, CANNON FOUNDING, GUNNERY AND BALLISTICS

Army Material Command Pamphlet AMCP 706–150, Engineering Design Handbook, Ballistics Series, *Interior Ballistics of Guns* (February 1965).

Army Material Command Pamphlet AMCP 706–175, Engineering Design Handbook, Explosives Series, *Solid Propellants Part One* (September 1964).

Benton, Capt. J. G., *A Course of Instruction in Ordnance and Gunnery Compiled for the Use of the Cadets of the U.S. Military Academy* (New York, 1862).

Blackwood, J. D. and F. P. Bowden, 'The Initiation, Burning and Thermal Decomposition of Gunpowder', *Proceedings of the Royal Society*, Series A, Mathematical and Physical Sciences, No. 1114, vol. CCXIII (8 July 1952).

Corner, J., *Theory of Interior Ballistics of Guns* (New York, 1950).

Lieske, Robert F. and Mary L. Reiter, *Equations of Motion for a Modified Point Mass Trajectory*, U.S. Army Ballistic Research Laboratory Pamphlet (Aberdeen Proving Ground, Maryland, March 1966).

Lowery, E. D., *Internal Ballistics: How a Gun Converts Chemical Energy into Projectile Motion* (New York, 1968).

Metcalf, Cpt. Henry, *A Course of Instruction in Ordnance and Gunnery*, 3rd ed. (New York, 1894).

Rodman, Capt. Thomas Jefferson, *Reports of Experiments on the Properties of Metals for Cannon and the Qualities of Cannon Powder* ... (Boston, 1861).

Reports of Experiments on the Strength and Other Properties of Metals for Cannon ... (Philadelphia, 1856).

Thornhill, C. K., AGARD Report 550, *A New Special Solution to the Complete Problem of the Internal Ballistics of Guns*, Advisory Group for Aerospace Research and Development (NATO), (Paris, 1966).

MODERN SECONDARY SOURCES

Actes du Quatrième Colloque International d'Histoire Maritime. Les Sources de l'Histoire Maritime en Europe, du Moyen Age au XVIIIe Siècle (Paris, 1962).

Allen, William E. D., *Problems of Turkish Power in the Sixteenth Century* (London, 1963).

Alpagut, Haydar, *Denizde Türkiye* (Istanbul, 1937).

Anderson, Roger Charles, 'Italian Naval Architecture about 1450', *The Mariner's Mirror*, XI (1925).

Naval Wars in the Levant, 1559–1853 (Princeton, 1952).

Oared Fighting Ships (London, 1962).

The Rigging of Ships in the Days of the Spritsail Topmast, 1600–1720 (Salem, Mass., 1927).

Andrews, Kenneth R., *Elizabethan Privateering* (Cambridge, 1964).

Argenti, Philip P., *The Occupation of Chios by the Genoese and Their Administration of the Island 1345–1566* (Cambridge, 1958).

Atiya, Aziz Suryal, *The Crusade in the Later Middle Ages* (London, 1938).

Atti Del 1° Congresso Internazionale Amatore di Armi Antiche Uniformologia Arte e Storia Militare (Turin, 1965).

Ayalon, David, *Gunpowder and Firearms in the Mamluk Kingdom* (London, 1956).

'Barud', *The Encyclopedia of Islam* (new edition), vol. I (London, 1960).

van Bath, B. H. Slicher, *The Agrarian History of Western Europe, AD 500–1850*, Olive Ordish trans. (London, 1963).

Bauer, Landauer, Ignacio, *La Marina Española en el Siglo XVI* (Madrid, 1921).

Blair, Claude, *European Armour circa 1066 to circa 1700* (New York, 1959).

Bouwsma, William J., *Venice and the Defense of Republican Liberty. Renaissance Values in the Age of Counter Reformation* (Berkeley, 1968).

Bowen, H., ''Azab', *The Encyclopedia of Islam* (new edition), vol. I (London, 1960).

Boxer, Charles R., 'M. H. Tromp, 1589–1653', *The Mariner's Mirror*, XL, No. 1 (February 1954).

Sources and bibliography

Brackenbury, Sir Henry, 'Ancient Cannon in Europe', *Proceedings of the Royal Artillery Institution*, IV–V (1865–6).

Bradford, Ernle, *The Great Siege* (London, 1961).

Braudel, Fernand, Pierre Jeannin, Jean Meurret and Ruggiero Romano, 'Le Déclin de Venise au XVIIᵉ Siècle', *Aspetti e Cause della Decadenza Economica Veneziana* (Venice, 1961).

La Méditerranée et le Monde Méditerranéen a l'Époque de Philippe IIᵉ, 2nd ed. (Paris, 1966), 1st ed. (Paris, 1949), and 1st Spanish ed. (Mexico City, 1953), Mario Monteforte Toledo and Wenceslao Roces trans.

Bricker, Charles and R. V. Tooley, *A History of Cartography* (London, 1969).

Brockman, Eric, *The Two Sieges of Rhodes, 1480–1522* (London, 1969).

Carrero Blanco, Luis, *Arte Naval Militar*, vol. II, *El Buque de Guerra* (Madrid, 1952).
La Victoria de Cristo de Lepanto, 2nd ed. (Madrid, 1948).

Carr Laughton, Lionel G., 'Early Tudor Ship-Guns', Michael Lewis ed., *The Mariner's Mirror*, XLVI, No. 4 (November 1960).
'The Square-Tuck Stern and the Gun Deck', *The Mariner's Mirror*, XLVII, No. 2 (May 1961).

Casson, Lionel, *The Ancient Mariners* (New York, 1959).

Catálogo General de Museo de Artilleria, 4 vols. (Madrid, 1914).

Cayetano, Rosell, *Historia de Combate Naval de Lepanto* (Madrid, 1853).

Chapelle, Howard I., *The History of the American Sailing Navy* (New York, 1949).

Chaunu, Pierre and Huguette, *Seville et l'Atlantique 1504–1650*, vols. I–VIII (Paris, 1955–9).

Chuboda, Bohdan, *Spain and the Empire, 1519–1643* (Chicago, 1952).

Cipolla, Carlo M., *Guns, Sails and Empires: Technological Innovation and the Early Phases of European Expansion 1400–1700* (New York, 1965).
Money, Prices and Civilization in the Mediterranean World (London, 1956).

Clephan, R. Coltman, *The Military Handgun of the Sixteenth Century* (London, 1910).
'The Ordnance of the 14th and 15th Centuries', *Archaeological Journal*, LXVIII (1911).
An Outline of the History and Development of Hand Firearms from the Earliest Period to about the End of the Fifteenth Century (London, 1906).

Cockle, Maurice J. D., *A Bibliography of English Military Books up to 1642 and of Contemporary Foreign Works* (London, 1900), 2nd ed. (London, 1957).

Coles, K. Adlard, *Heavy Weather Sailing* (Tuckahoe, New York, 1967).

Corbett, Julian S., *Drake and the Tudor Navy* (London, 1917).

Creasy, Sir Edward S., *History of the Ottoman Turks* (London, 1878).

Davis, Ralph, 'England and the Mediterranean 1570–1670', *Essays in the Economic and Social History of Tudor and Stuart England in Honour of R. H. Tawney*, F. J. Fisher ed. (Cambridge, 1961).

Deroko, Aleksandar, 'Quelques mots sur les plus anciens gros canons turcs', *Armi Antiche, Bollettino dell' Academia di S. Marciano* (No. 1, 1963).

Diccionario Maritimo Español (Madrid, 1831).

Drake, Stillman and J. E. Drabkin, *Mechanics in Sixteenth Century Italy* (Madison, Wisconsin, 1969).

Earle, Edward Mead, *Makers of Modern Strategy* (Princeton, 1943).

Elott, Milan E., 'What's New in Archery? This Expert Contends that Everything Has Been Done Before!', *Bow and Arrow*, VIII, No. 6 (March–April 1971).

Estado Mayor General del Ejercito, Servicio Historico Militar, *Armamento de los Ejercitos de Carlos V en la Guerra de Alemania, 1546–1547* (Madrid, 1947).

Ffoulkes, Charles, *The Armourer and His Craft* (London, 1912).
   The Gun-Founders of England (Cambridge, 1937).
Fischer-Galati, Stephen A., *Ottoman Imperialism and German Protestantism 1521–1555* (Cambridge, Mass., 1959).
Fisher, Sydney Nettleton, *The Foreign Relations of Turkey 1481–1512* (Urbana, Illinois, 1948).
Gibb, Sir Hamilton and Harold Bowen, *Islamic Society and the West* (Oxford, 1950).
Goodrich, L. C., 'Notes on a Few Early Chinese Bombards', *Isis*, XXXV (1944).
Gosse, Philip, 'Piracy', *The Mariner's Mirror*, XXXVI, No. 3 (July 1950).
Guglielmotti, P. Alberto, *Storia della Marina Pontifica nel Medio Evo* (Florence, 1871).
Haggard, J. Villasana, *Handbook for Translators of Spanish Historical Documents* (Austin, 1941).
Hale, J. R., 'Armies, Navies and the Art of War', ch. 16, *The New Cambridge Modern History*, vol. II, *The Reformation* (Cambridge, 1958).
Hall, A. R., *Ballistics in the Seventeenth Century* (Cambridge, 1952).
Hamilton, Earl J., 'Spanish Mercantilism before 1700', *Facts and Factors in Economic History* (Cambridge, Mass., 1932).
von Hammer, Baron Purgstall, *Histoire de l'Empire Ottoman*, J. J. Hellert trans. (Paris, 1835–41).
Hassenstein, Wilhelm, 'Ober die Feuerwaffen in der Seeschlacht von Lepanto', *Leitschrift für Historische Waffen und Kostumkunde*, XVI, No. 1 (1940).
Held, Robert, *The Age of Firearms* (New York, 1957).
Hess, Andrew Christie, 'The Closure of the Ottoman Frontier in North Africa and the Origins of Modern Algeria, 1574–1595', unpublished Harvard dissertation (April 1966).
   'The Evolution of the Ottoman Seaborne Empire in the Age of the Oceanic Discoveries, 1453–1525', *American Historical Review*, LXXV, No. 7 (December 1970).
   'The Moriscos: An Ottoman Fifth Column in Sixteenth Century Spain', *The American Historical Review*, LXXIV, No. 1 (October 1968).
Heyd, Wilhelm von, *Histoire du Commerce du Levant au Moyen-Age*, 2 vols. (Leipzig, 1885).
Hill, Sir George, *A History of Cyprus*, vol. III, *The Frankish Period 1432–1571* (Cambridge, 1948).
Hime, Lt. Col. Henry W. L., *The Origin of Artillery* (London, 1915).
Hough, Richard, *Fighting Ships* (New York, 1969).
Hourani, George F., *Arab Seafaring in the Indian Ocean in Ancient and Early Medieval Times* (Princeton, 1951).
Inalcik, Halil, 'Bursa and the Commerce of the Levant', *Journal of the Economic and Social History of the Orient*, III, Part 2 (1960).
   'Ottoman Methods of Conquest', *Studia Islamica II* (Paris, 1954).
Kahane, Henry and Andreas Tietze, *The Lingua Franca in the Levant, Turkish Nautical Terms of Italian and Greek Origin* (Urbana, Ill., 1958).
Kellenbenz, Hermann, 'Le déclin de Venise et les Relations économiques de Venise avec les Marches au Nord des Alpes'. *Aspetti e Cause della Decadenza Economica Veneziana nel Secolo XVII* (Venice, 1961).
Klopsteg, P. E., *Turkish Archery and the Composite Bow* (Evanston, Ill., 1947).
Koenigsberger, H. G., 'The Empire of Charles V in Europe', *The New Cambridge Modern History*, vol. II, *The Reformation 1520–1559* (Cambridge, 1958).

Koenigsberger, H. G., 'The Statecraft of Philip II', *European Studies Review*, I, No. I (1971).

'Western Europe and the Power of Spain', *The New Cambridge Modern History*, vol. III, *The Counter Reformation and Price Revolution 1559–1610* (Cambridge, 1968).

Kortepeter, Carl M., 'Ottoman Imperial Policy and the Economy of the Black Sea Region in the Sixteenth Century', *Journal of the American Oriental Society*, LXXXVI, No. 2 (1966).

Kuhn, Thomas Samuel, *The Structure of Scientific Revolutions* (Chicago, 1962).

Kurtoğlu, Fevzi, 'Meshur Türk amirali Selman reisin layihasi', *Deniz Mecmuasi*, Cild 47, Sayi 335 (1 ikinjikânun, 1935).

Landström, Björn, *The Ship* (New York, 1961).

Lane, Frederick C., 'Economic Consequences of Organized Violence', *Journal of Economic History*, XVIII (1958).

'The Economic Meaning of the Invention of the Compass', *The American Historical Review*, LXVIII, No. 3 (1963).

'Force and Enterprise in the Creation of Oceanic Commerce', *The Tasks of Economic History*, supplemental issue to *The Journal of Economic History*, X (1950).

'La Marine Marchande et le Trafic Maritime de Venise à travers les Siècles', *Les Sources de l'Histoire Maritime en Europe, du Moyen Age au XVIIIᵉ Siècle* (Paris, 1962).

'The Mediterranean Spice Trade', *The American Historical Review*, XLV, No. 3 (1940).

'Recent Studies on the Economic History of Venice', *Journal of Economic History*, XXIII (1963).

'Venetian Merchant Galleys, 1300–1334, Private and Commercial Operation', *Speculum*, XXXVIII (April 1963).

'Venetian Shipping During the Commercial Revolution', *The American Historical Review*, XXXVIII, No. 1 (1933).

Venetian Ships and Shipbuilders of the Renaissance (Baltimore, 1934).

Latham, J. D. and W. F. Paterson, 'An Analysis of Arrow-Weights in an Islamic Military Manual', *Journal of Semitic Studies*, X, No. 2 (1965).

Lavin, James D., *A History of Spanish Firearms* (New York, 1965).

Learn, C. R., 'The One-Mile Shot', *Bow and Arrow*, VIII, No. 6 (March–April 1971).

Lefebvre des Noettes, Count, *De la Marine Antique à la Marine Moderne, la Révolution du Gouvernail* (Paris, 1935).

Lewis, Archibald R., *Naval Power and Trade in the Mediterranean A.D. 500–1100* (Princeton, 1951).

Lewis, Michael A., *Armada Guns, a Comparative Study of English and Spanish Armaments* (London, 1961).

'The Guns of the *Jesus of Lubeck*', *The Mariner's Mirror*, XXII, No. 3 (July 1936).

Lopez, Robert S. 'Market Expansion: The Case of Genoa', *Journal of Economic History*, XXIV (1964).

Lybyer, A. H., 'The Ottoman Turks and the Routes of Oriental Trade', *English Historical Review*, XXX (1915).

McNeill, William H., *Europe's Steppe Frontier 1500–1800* (Chicago, 1964).

Mahan, Alfred Thayer, *The Influence of Seapower upon History 1660–1783* (Boston, 1890).

Masson, Paul, 'Les Galères de France, 1481–1781', *Annales de la Faculté des Lettres d'Aix*, XX (1937–8).

Mattingly, Garrett, *The Armada* (Boston, 1959).

Manfroni, Camillo, *Storia della Marina Italiana della Caduta di Constantinopoli alla Battaglia de Lepanto* (Rome, 1897).

Marcus, G. J., 'The Mariner's Compass, Its Influence upon Navigation in the Later Middle Ages', *History*, XLI, No. 1 (1956).

Merriman, Roger B., *The Rise of the Spanish Empire*, vol. III, *The Emperor* (New York, 1925).
  Suleiman the Magnificent, 1520–1566 (Cambridge, 1944).

Miller, Barnette, *Beyond the Sublime Porte. The Grand Seraglio of Stambul* (New Haven, Conn., 1931).

Mirkovich, Nicholas, 'Ragusa and the Portuguese Spice Trade', *Slavonic and East European Review*, XXI, No. 56 (1943).

Mollat, Michel, ed., *Le Navire et l'Economie Maritime du Moyen Age au XVIII Siècle Principalement en Méditerranée* (Paris, 1957).

Moncada, Francisco de, *Expedición de los Catalanes y Aragoneses contra Turcos Griegos* (Madrid, 1805).

Monleon, Admiral Rafael, *Construcciones Navales Bajo su Aspecto Artístico* (Madrid, 1948).

Moody, J. D., 'Old Naval Gun-Carriages', *The Mariner's Mirror*, XXXVIII, No. 4 (November 1952).

Olesa Muñido, Francisco-Felipe, *La Organización Naval de les Estados Mediterraneos en Especial de España Durante los Siglos XVI y XVII* (Madrid, 1968).

Oman, Charles W. C., *A History of the Art of War in the Middle Ages* (London, 1924).
  A History of the Art of War in the Sixteenth Century (London, 1937).

Paret, Peter, *Yorck and the Era of Prussian Reform, 1807–1815* (Princeton, 1966).

Parker, Geoffrey, 'Spain, Her Enemies and the Revolt of the Netherlands', *Past and Present*, No. 49 (1970).
  The Army of Flanders and the Spanish Road 1567–1659 (Cambridge, 1972).

Parry, J. H., *The Age of Reconnaissance* (New York, 1964).

Parry, V. J., 'The Ottoman Empire, 1481–1520', *The New Cambridge Modern History*, vol. I, *The Renaissance* (Cambridge, 1957).
  'The Ottoman Empire, 1520–1566', *The New Cambridge Modern History*, vol. II, *The Reformation* (Cambridge, 1958).
  'The Ottoman Empire 1566–1617', *The New Cambridge Modern History*, vol. III, *The Counter Reformation, 1559–1610* (Cambridge, 1968).
  'Warfare', *The Cambridge History of Islam*, vol. II (Cambridge, 1970).
  Past and Present, No. 49 (November 1970).

Paterson, W. P., 'The Archers of Islam', *Journal of the Economic and Social History of the Orient*, IX, Parts I–II (November 1966).

Payne-Gallwey, Sir Ralph, *The Crossbow* (London, 1903).
  A Summary of the History, Construction and Effects in Warfare of the Projectile-Throwing Engines of the Ancients, with a Treatise on the Structure, Power and Management of the Turkish and Other Oriental Bows ... (New York, 1907).

Pereira do Valle, Henrique, *Subsidos para a História de Artilharia Portuguesa* (Lisbon, 1963).

Phelps-Brown, E. H. and Sheila V. Hopkins, 'Builders' Wage-rates, Prices and Population: Some Further Evidence', *Economica*, n.s., XXVI (1959).
  'Wage-rates and Prices: Evidence for Population Pressure in the Sixteenth Century', *Economica*, n.s., XXIV (1957).

Prescott, William H., *History of the Reign of Ferdinand and Isabella*, vols. I–IV (Philadelphia, 1904).

History of the Reign of Philip the Second, Vol. I–IV (Philadelphia, 1904).

Purcell, Mary, *The Great Captain* (New York, 1962).

Rahman, Zaky A., 'Gunpowder and Arab Firearms in the Middle Ages', *Gladius*, vol. VI (Granada, Spain, 1967).

von Ranke, Leopold, *The Turkish and Spanish Empires in the Sixteenth and Beginning of the Seventeenth Centuries* (Philadelphia, 1845).

Rich, E. E. and C. H. Wilson, ed., *The Cambridge Economic History of Europe*, vol. IV, *The Economy of Expanding Europe in the Sixteenth and Seventeenth Centuries* (Cambridge, 1967).

Roberts, Michael, *The Military Revolution 1560–1660* (Belfast, 1959).

Robinson, H. Russell, *Oriental Armour* (London, 1967).

Robinson, Rear Admiral S. S., *A History of Naval Tactics 1530–1930* (Annapolis, Maryland, 1942).

Rodgers, Vice Admiral William L., *Greek and Roman Naval Warfare* (Annapolis, Maryland, 1937).

Naval Warfare under Oars, 4th to 16th Centuries (Annapolis, Maryland, 1939).

Romano, Ruggiero, 'Aspetti Economici degli Armamenti Navali Veneziani nel Secolo XVI', *Revista Storica Italiana*, LXVI (1954).

de Roover, 'The Organization of Trade', *The Cambridge Economic History of Europe*, vol. II, *Economic Organization and Policies in the Middle Ages* (Cambridge, 1963).

Rothenberg, Gunther E., *The Austrian Military Border in Croatia, 1522–1747* (Urbana, Illinois, 1960).

'Christian Insurrections in Turkish Dalmatia 1580–96', *Slavonic and East European Review*, XL, No. 94 (December 1961).

'Venice and the Uskoks of Senj, 1537–1618', *Journal of Modern History*, XXXIII (1961).

Runciman, Steven, *The Fall of Constantinople 1453* (Cambridge, 1963).

Salva, Jaime, *La Orden de Malta y las Acciónes Navales Españoles contra Turcos y Berberiscos en los Siglos XVI y XVII* (Madrid, 1944).

Schubert, H. R., 'The First Cast-Iron Cannon Made in England', *The Journal of the Iron and Steel Institute*, CXLVI (1942).

'The Superiority of English Cast-Iron Cannon at the Close of the Sixteenth Century', *The Journal of the Iron and Steel Institute*, CLXI (1949).

Schwoebel, Robert, *The Shadow of the Crescent – the Renaissance Image of the Turk (1453–1517)* (Nieuwkoop, The Netherlands, 1967).

Servicio Historico Militar, *Armamento de los Ejercitos de Carlos V en la Guerra de Alemania* (Madrid, 1947).

Solver, C. V. and G. J. Marcus, 'Dead Reckoning and the Ocean Voyages of the Past', *The Mariner's Mirror*, XLIV, No. 1 (1958).

Spooner, F. C. 'The Economy of Europe, 1559–1609', *The New Cambridge Modern History*, vol. III, *The Counter Reformation and Price Revolution, 1559–1610* (Cambridge, 1958).

'The European Economy, 1609–50', *The New Cambridge Modern History*, vol. IV, *The Decline of Spain and the Thirty Years War 1609–48/59* (Cambridge, 1959).

'The Habsburg–Valois Struggle', *The New Cambridge Modern History*, vol. III, *The Reformation, 1520–1559* (Cambridge, 1958).

Sprout, Margaret T., 'Mahan, Evangelist of Sea Power', in Edward Mead Earle, *Makers of Modern Strategy* (Princeton, 1943).

Stackpole, Edouard, *Those in Peril on the Sea* (New York, 1962).

Stacton, David, *The World on the Last Day, The Sack of Constantinople by the Turks, May 19, 1453* (London, 1965).

Stoianovich, T., 'The Conquering Balkan Orthodox Merchant', *Journal of Economic History*, xx (1960).

Strachan, Michael, '*Sampson's* Fight with Maltese Galleys, 1628', *The Mariner's Mirror*, LV, No. 3 (August 1969).

Tadic, Joro, 'Le Commerce in Dalmatie et à Raguse et la Décadence Économique de Venise au XVIIᵉ Siècle', *Aspetti e Cause della Decadenza Economica Veneziana nel Secolo XVII* (Rome, 1961).

Taylor, A. H., 'Carrack into Galleon', *The Mariner's Mirror*, xxxvi, No. 2 (April 1950).

Taylor, E. G. R., *The Haven-Finding Art: A History of Navigation from Odysseus to Captain Cook* (London, 1956).

Taylor, Frederick Lewis, *The Art of War in Italy, 1494–1529* (Cambridge, 1921).

Tenenti, Alberto, *Cristoforo da Canal: la Marine Vénitienne avant Lépante* (Paris, 1962).
Naufrages, Corsaires et Assurances Maritimes à Venise 1592–1609 (Paris, 1959).
Piracy and the Decline of Venice 1580–1615 (Berkeley, 1967).

Tout, T. F., 'Firearms in England in the 14th Century', *English Historical Review*, XXII (1911).

Toy, Sydney, *A History of Fortification from 3000 B.C. to A.D. 1700* (London, 1955).

Tucci, Ugo, 'Sur la Pratique Vénitienne de la Navigation au XVIᵉ Siècle', *Annales (Économies, Sociétés, Civilisations)*, XIII (1958).

Usher, Abbott P., *The Early History of Deposit Banking in Mediterranean Europe* (New York, 1967).
'Spanish Ships and Shipping in the Sixteenth and Seventeenth Centuries', *Facts and Factors in Economic History* (Cambridge, Mass., 1932).

Vicens Vives, Jaime, *An Economic History of Spain*, Frances M. Lopez-Morillas trans, (Princeton, 1969).

Vigon, Jorge, *Historia de la Artilleria Española*, vols. I–III (Madrid, 1947).

Villari, Luigi, *The Republic of Ragusa* (London, 1904).

Vollmer, Emil and the Instituto Geografico De Agostini, *Leonardo da Vinci* (New York, 1956).

Wang Ling, 'On the Invention and Use of Gunpowder and Firearms in China', *Isis*, XXXVII (July 1947).

Waters, David W., *The Art of Navigation in England in Elizabethan and Early Stuart Times* (London, 1958).
'The Elizabethan Navy and the Armada Campaign', *The Mariner's Mirror*, xxxv, No. 2 (April 1949).
The Rutters of the Sea (London, 1967).

Weil, Althea, *The Navy of Venice* (London, 1910).

Westrate, J. Lee, *European Military Museums* (Washington, D.C., 1961).

Wijn, J. W., 'Military Forces and Warfare', *The New Cambridge Modern History*, vol. IV, *The Decline of Spain and the Thirty Years War 1609–48/59* (Cambridge, 1959).

Willan, T. S., 'Some Aspects of English Trade with the Levant in the Sixteenth Century', *English Historical Review*, LXX (1955).

Wood, Alfred C., *A History of the Levant Company* (Oxford, 1935).

Woolf, Stuart J., 'Venice and the Terraferma; Problems of the Change from Commercial to Landed Activities', *Bolletino dell'Instituto di Storia della Società e dello Stato Veneziano*, IV (1962).

INDEX

Index